BETHEL PUBLIC LIBRARY

BIO
JOHNSON

Gillette,

Lady Bir[c]

Lady Bird Johnson

An Oral History

Lady Bird Johnson

An Oral History

MICHAEL L. GILLETTE

OXFORD
UNIVERSITY PRESS

BETHEL PUBLIC LIBRARY
189 GREENWOOD AVENUE
BETHEL, CT 06801

OXFORD
UNIVERSITY PRESS

Oxford University Press is a department of the
University of Oxford. It furthers the University's objective
of excellence in research, scholarship, and education
by publishing worldwide.

Oxford   New York
Auckland   Cape Town   Dar es Salaam   Hong Kong   Karachi
Kuala Lumpur   Madrid   Melbourne   Mexico City   Nairobi
New Delhi   Shanghai   Taipei   Toronto

With offices in
Argentina   Austria   Brazil   Chile   Czech Republic   France   Greece
Guatemala   Hungary   Italy   Japan   Poland   Portugal   Singapore
South Korea   Switzerland   Thailand   Turkey   Ukraine   Vietnam

Oxford is a registered trade mark of Oxford University Press
in the UK and certain other countries.

Published in the United States of America by
Oxford University Press
198 Madison Avenue, New York, NY 10016

© Michael L. Gillette 2012

All rights reserved. No part of this publication may be reproduced,
stored in a retrieval system, or transmitted, in any form or by any means,
without the prior permission in writing of Oxford University Press,
or as expressly permitted by law, by license, or under terms agreed with
the appropriate reproduction rights organization. Inquiries concerning
reproduction outside the scope of the above should be sent to the
Rights Department, Oxford University Press, at the address above.

You must not circulate this work in any other form
and you must impose this same condition on any acquirer.

Gillette, Michael L.
Lady Bird Johnson : an oral history / Michael L. Gillette.
p.   cm.
Includes bibliographical references and index.

ISBN 978-0-19-990808-0 (hardback : alk. paper)

1. Johnson, Lady Bird, 1912–2007.   2. Presidents' spouses—United States—Biography.
3. Johnson, Lyndon B. (Lyndon Baines), 1908–1973.   4. United States—Politics and government—
1945–1989.   I. Gillette, Michael L.   II. Title.
E848.J64G55   2012
973.923092—dc23   [B]   2012011580

Frontispiece: "Lady Bird Special," Durham, NC, October 7, 1964. On the platform, from left: William
Brawley, southern coordinator, Democratic National Committee; agent Toby Chandler; Secretary of
Commerce Luther Hodges; Lady Bird Johnson; Rep. Horace Kornegay; Durham mayor Wensell Grabarek;
and Rep. Hale Boggs. *LBJ Library*

1 3 5 7 9 8 6 4 2

Printed in the United States of America
on acid-free paper

For LeAnn, Dave, Kenneth, Rob, and Anna;
And for Lady Bird Johnson's grandchildren: Lucinda, Catherine,
and Jennifer Robb; Lyndon Nugent; Nicole Covert;
Rebekah McIntosh; and Claudia Brod

Contents

Acknowledgments

"Hello, Mike. How would you like to do something zany?" As I began to wonder what Lady Bird Johnson could possibly mean by "zany," she explained: "Would you like to accompany me to my fiftieth high school reunion in Marshall, Texas?" By the time of her phone call in May 1978, we had already recorded the first five sessions of an oral history that would ultimately include forty-seven interviews. She was well aware of my interest in her early life and the fact that I was interviewing some of her classmates from high school and college.

The trip was an extraordinary adventure in time travel. Watching her at the reunion among friends she had known for a half century was fascinating, but three other elements of the trip were equally memorable. We stopped briefly at the small, overgrown Scottsville cemetery where her mother is buried. We made what was for her a rare visit to the Brick House, where she had been born. Finally, we launched jon boats and ventured into Caddo Lake, amid the haunting beauty of Spanish-moss-laden cypress trees. To experience, if only for a day, the world in which Lady Bird Johnson's remarkable odyssey began was singularly exhilarating.

But while the trip was unique, the invitation was so characteristic of Lady Bird Johnson's generosity of spirit. She routinely looked for opportunities to enrich the lives of those around her. In my case, she shared friends and events that she knew would appeal to my interest and advance my work. Not only did she make this volume possible by devoting many, many hours to recording a comprehensive oral history, but she also made each occasion special with her gracious hospitality, her warm friendship, and her unfailing thoughtfulness. To her I owe my greatest debt.

Harry J. Middleton, the LBJ Library's director extraordinaire for three decades, not only nurtured and expanded the Oral History Program; he also conducted the last eight interviews with Mrs. Johnson after my transfer to Washington. The Lyndon Baines Johnson Foundation, under the successive leadership of Frank C. Erwin Jr., W. Thomas Johnson, Larry Temple, and now Elizabeth Christian, funded the enterprise for two decades. The late Joe B. Frantz directed its antecedent project under the auspices of the University of Texas. In addition to Joe, the interviewers included T. Harrison Baker, Stephen Goodell, David McComb, Dorothy Pierce McSweeney, and Paige Mulhollan. Mrs. Johnson's interviews with Sheldon Stern of the John F. Kennedy Library and Nancy Smith, then an LBJ Library archivist, have also contributed to this volume.

My former oral history staff at the library spared me from much of the research, transcribing, and editing the collection of some 1,700 interviews. Over a span of two decades, the staff included Christie Bourgeois, Gary Gallagher, Gina Gianzero, Ted Gittinger, Sibyl Avery Jackson, Donna Cook Jones, Joan Kennedy, Mariella Krause, Jenna McEachern, Lois Martin, Lou Anne Missildine, Jennifer Velez, and Laura White. I owe special gratitude to two, Regina Greenwell and Lesley W. Brunet, whose prodigious research produced the chronologies on which the interviews with Mrs. Johnson relied.

The LBJ Library has a well-deserved reputation for its knowledgeable, researcher-friendly archival staff. It is always a pleasure to work with these dedicated professionals. I am especially grateful to Tina Houston, Claudia Anderson, Barbara Cline, Regina Greenwell, Laura Eggert, Nicole Hadad, Margaret Harman, and Christopher Banks for their assistance with this volume.

I am also grateful to Vice Provost Fred M. Heath, director of libraries at the University of Texas at Austin, for providing access to the region's largest academic library.

My superb Humanities Texas staff's thoughtfulness and spirit of teamwork make my workdays a pleasure. Their diligence enabled me to devote my after-work hours to this volume. Two of the staff even moonlighted to help with the project. Liz James transcribed and edited my two videotaped interviews with Mrs. Johnson on the White House years. Lindsey Elan Wall, upon whom I rely in artistic endeavors, conducted the photo research. My assistant Julia Aguilar helped indirectly by keeping my office running smoothly for these past nine years.

From our very first discussion of the possibility of publishing Lady Bird Johnson's oral history, the vision of Nancy Toff, vice president and executive editor of Oxford University Press, has advanced this project. She steered me through the sequence of channels toward publication, providing wise guidance and encouragement along the way. Associate editor Sonia Tycko thoughtfully kept me on track and on schedule. My appreciation also goes to series editors J. Todd Moye, Kathryn Nasstrom, and Robert Perks for their insights and feedback and to production editor Lora Friedenthal for getting the manuscript between covers. Copy editor Ben Sadock saved me from a number of factual and typographical errors while imposing stylistic discipline.

My wife, LeAnn Gillette, ever fated to share my projects, read the manuscript and offered valuable suggestions and loving encouragement throughout the process. Our three sons, Rob, Kenneth, and Dave, and our daughter-in-law, Anna, have graciously accommodated my extended distraction with forbearance. Kenneth also provided helpful feedback on a number of chapters.

Finally, I am indebted to Bess Abell and the late Liz Carpenter, two friends of many years, who shared with me their incomparable knowledge of Lady Bird Johnson.

Introduction

A young southern girl came of age in a picturesque but isolated and primitive rural setting. She was, in her words, left to her own devices. Motherless before her sixth birthday, she lived with a father whose god was work and whose consuming preoccupation with his business left him little time for his daughter.[1] The maiden aunt who joined the household was so physically and emotionally fragile that the girl eventually became, in effect, her caregiver. With few other young people around, the girl emerged as socially awkward and painfully shy. Yet her solitude fostered a love of reading, a deep appreciation of the natural beauty in her midst, and the inner strengths of self-reliance and discipline. These qualities that her isolation nurtured would shape her transformation into one of most admired and effective first ladies in American history.

Lady Bird Johnson entered the White House under the worst imaginable circumstances: a tragic assassination, which occurred in her home state. The fact that she succeeded the century's most youthful, glamorous, and cultured first lady made unflattering comparisons inevitable. As millions yearned for the elegance of Camelot, her husband performed legislative miracles to enact the sweeping agenda of his Great Society. Yet his progressive domestic agenda angered conservatives, while his escalation of the conflict in Vietnam alienated liberals. Throughout five turbulent years, the first lady provided her husband with an "island of peace."[2]

At the same time, she did so much more. She assembled a professional staff in the East Wing of the White House and mobilized legions of influential, resourceful women and men to beautify and conserve the nation's environment.[3] Focusing initially on Washington, DC, they created a spectacular showcase, where millions of American tourists could see what was possible in their own hometowns. Next she traveled throughout the country to draw attention to its beauty and the threats to the nation's environment. Although the term

---

1. Lady Bird Johnson Oral History Interview (hereafter CTJ OHI; see appendix): 1:14, 17–19; 2:5; 3:5–6.
2. CTJ OHI video interview, 2/4/85.
3. See Lewis L. Gould, *Lady Bird Johnson and the Environment* (Lawrence: University of Kansas Press, 1988); Gould, "Lady Bird Johnson: First Lady Innovator," *History News Network*, 7/16/07.

"beautification" was never satisfactory, she and her allies could not think of a better one. To Lady Bird Johnson, beautification was "just one thread of the whole warp and weave of the tapestry" that consisted of clean air and water, urban parks and green spaces, scenic highways and countryside, cultural heritage tourism, and significant additions to the legacy of national parks.[4] In 1968, when President Johnson presented his wife with some fifty mounted pens he had used to sign conservation and beautification measures, he summarized her contribution with the inscription: "To Lady Bird, who has inspired me and millions of Americans to try to preserve our land and beautify our nation."[5]

Her environmental leadership was only one facet of her work as first lady. She also continued her predecessor's quest for authentic furnishings and important American art for the White House. She recognized the achievements of women with her Women Doers Luncheons. Embracing the Head Start program, she gave it the prominence of a White House launch. She campaigned independently for her husband on a train trip through the South. Finally, she participated gracefully in an endless succession of presidential trips, state dinners, congressional receptions, and other social events, including two White House weddings.

Lady Bird Johnson documented her remarkable experiences with characteristic discipline. During her White House years, she recorded daily events as they unfolded, producing a diary of 1.75 million words. The eight-hundred-page published version, A White House Diary, constituted only a seventh of the complete work.[6] Three years after her husband's death, Mrs. Johnson also began recounting her life in forty-seven oral history interviews over a span of eighteen years. These interviews, released in May 2011, form the narrative of Lady Bird Johnson: An Oral History.

Lady Bird Johnson's odyssey was one of extraordinary personal and intellectual growth, determined political and financial ambitions, and a life shared with a man who was her opposite in many ways. Although her early education in East Texas lacked a "sparkling curriculum," she found intellectual inspiration in her subsequent years at St. Mary's College for women in Dallas and at the University of Texas. At the university, she grew socially as well as intellectually, becoming more outgoing, more aggressive, and more self-assured.

But her formal education was only the beginning of her intellectual growth. Through her husband's career, she entered "the society he thrust me into," a network of brilliant men and women who were changing America. Although Washington was a male-centric society, women gathered in their own circles, convening enlightening seminars in a social atmosphere. For more than a quarter of a century, Lady Bird Johnson, driven by a natural intellectual curiosity,

---

4. CTJ OHI video, 2/4/85, by Michael L. Gillette, LBJ Library.
5. Gould, Lady Bird Johnson, 233.
6. Lady Bird Johnson, A White House Diary (New York: Holt, Rinehart & Winston, 1970).

absorbed a wealth of knowledge and experience from the company of scintillating, accomplished friends and acquaintances.

Lady Bird Johnson's formative experiences influenced her performance as first lady. Her work in LBJ's congressional office in 1942, her management of her Austin radio station, and decades of daily interaction with prominent men and women in public life gave her the confidence to take on a substantive portfolio of activities in the White House. The joy that nature had given her as a youth and her years of automobile travel and campaign trips led her to embrace beautification. Her days as a congressional wife, escorting countless constituents through the National Gallery of Art, and her tours of such extraordinary collections as Winterthur provided an education in art history, one that would her serve her acquisition of American art for the White House. Participation in such organizations as the Congressional Club and the Senate Ladies Club seasoned her for the demanding social life of the White House, while her extensive international travel and enlistment as a stand-in for first lady Jacqueline Kennedy during the vice presidential years prepared her for the role of hostess-in-chief at state dinners.

Her political apprenticeship was also significant. In each of Lyndon Johnson's campaigns she played an increasingly active role, and her zest for politics grew. Excluded from his first congressional race in 1937, she was involved only as a financial contributor and laundress. But in his narrow, controversial 1948 Senate election, it is questionable that he would have even remained in race, let alone won, without his wife's efforts. Although Robert Kennedy exaggerated in crediting Lady Bird with carrying Texas in the 1960 presidential race, she was certainly a factor. Finally, in the 1964 presidential campaign she rode the Lady Bird Special train through the South, becoming the first presidential spouse to campaign independently for her husband.

Would we have ever heard of Claudia Taylor if she had married Dawson Duncan, Victor McCrea,[7] or another of her college beaus? One can easily imagine that she would have led a productive, fulfilling life, but her place in history is inextricably bound to LBJ's political ascent. As she observed, a first lady is elected by only one man. Her star rose along with his, ultimately to the White House. Lyndon Johnson, whom she characterized as "a natural-born Henry Higgins,"[8] also shaped her personally, constantly stretching her with new opportunities and challenges.

Would we have ever heard of Lyndon Johnson had he married Carol Davis[9] or some other early love? Would such men as Sam Rayburn and Richard Russell, who were instrumental in advancing LBJ's career, have spent countless evenings

---

7. Dawson Duncan was an Associated Press reporter; Victor McCrea became a Fort Worth attorney.

8. CTJ OHI, 1/23/87, by Nancy Smith.

9. LBJ dated Carol Davis, the daughter of a prominent San Marcos merchant, in college.

in the Johnson home without the allure of Lady Bird's gracious hospitality and Zephyr Wright's legendary comfort food? Would a marriage to someone else have lasted? Would he have abandoned another wife for someone new? Would another woman have endured the tension and turbulence of marriage to such a volatile, contradictory personality? Could another wife have provided the good judgment and emotional triage necessary for LBJ to remain viable as a politician? Despite her inherent modesty, Lady Bird Johnson's narrative documents how central she was to his political aspirations, gently nudging him forward despite his reluctance or despair, providing sound judgment and unconditional love, while mollifying the friends, staff, and allies whom he had alienated. As biographer Doris Kearns Goodwin has concluded, "Without such devotion and forbearance, without a love steadily given and never withdrawn, the course of Lyndon Johnson's continuing ascent in the world of politics becomes inconceivable."[10]

Could Lady Bird have found a man more completely her opposite? She was conservative, cautious, judicious, and placid; he was liberal, impulsive, audacious, and always in a hurry. Her calm, shy, gracious demeanor contrasted with his expansive, dominating, high-strung temperament. While she was thrifty, he was prone to acts of extravagant generosity. If she was private and fiercely independent, he desperately needed the company of people. She was a studious reader of books; he was at heart a teacher whose text was experience.

Did Lady Bird's judgment lapse when she agreed to marry Lyndon Johnson? Each had experienced enough romantic relationships to sense that this one was different. What was it about him that was so compelling that it overruled her instinctive caution? Many who knew him in the 1930s have emphasized how dynamic and attractive he was, how exciting it was to be around him. "Exciting" is the word she used to summarize their first day together.[11] She was fascinated by his presence.

But there was an additional factor. His raw, honest ambition appealed to her. Like so many others who encountered him, she could sense that he was going places. As she wrote during their courtship, "I *adore* you for being so ambitious and dynamic."[12] Moreover, as Lady Bird Johnson's narrative demonstrates, her ambition equaled her husband's at crucial times. When he was reluctant to run for the Senate in 1948 after having lost the special election in 1941, she had "a certain eagerness" to try again.[13] Their shared ambitions as well as their deep love were the bonds of their alliance.

Their mutual dependence was profound. While he brought exhilaration, purpose, and inspiration to her life, she gave him the love, stability, and thoughtful

---

10. Doris Kearns, *Lyndon Johnson and the American Dream* (New York: Harper & Row, 1976), 84.
11. CTJ OHI 4.
12. CTJ to LBJ, 9/17/34, LBJ Library.
13. CTJ OHI 21.

judgment he desperately needed. In a letter written less than a year after they met, he defined her role throughout their next four decades together. He emphasized how much she contributed to his peace of mind and how she stimulated him to aspire to bigger and better things, he declared: "Never have I been so dependent on anyone," he declared. "Never shall I expect so much of any other individual."[14]

Lady Bird Johnson could have led a very different life, sitting out the campaigns, spending less time in Washington, and focusing more on her children, as many other political wives did. But she chose to adjust her life to his, to become an active participant in his world of politics. If her doing so relegated her to the status of an employee at times, it also made LBJ even more dependent on her. Yet submitting to his challenges and demands, overlooking his faults, and serving as the vital stabilizing force in his life required unwavering discipline. But she was, in the words of longtime friend Elizabeth Rowe, "a woman of great strength" and "the most disciplined person I have ever seen."[15] Consequently, Lady Bird's influence on her husband and his aspirations were as profound as his influence on her. Their lives were so intertwined that it is impossible to assess one without the other.

An old adage describes Washington, DC, as a city of famous men and the women they married when they were young. It was one thing to marry Lyndon Johnson but quite another to remain married to him. Despite the attention of many beautiful and interesting women, LBJ never sought a divorce. Neither did Lady Bird. What held her to him in the face of his verbal abuse and infidelity? Mrs. Johnson did not record in her oral history any discussion of her husband's extramarital affairs. She would have regarded doing so as both embarrassing and disloyal. Off tape, she confided to me her that she tried to improve herself by observing other women whom LBJ found appealing. In her interviews, she occasionally spoke of these women with admiration and even affection. Only once in our informal conversations did she indulge in what I regarded as criticism. While referring to Alice Glass, Mrs. Johnson recited from memory the litany of surnames that Alice had accumulated during the course of her multiple marriages.

As a woman who rarely did anything halfheartedly, Mrs. Johnson intended her oral history to be as comprehensive as she could make it. Our interviews, which began in August 1977, usually took place on weekends at the LBJ Ranch. There, in the yellow sitting room, she could focus on the topic at hand for several hours without the frequent interruptions that were inevitable during her busy weekdays in Austin. A few of the sessions took place while she vacationed with friends in Acapulco and later in Martha's Vineyard. As she explained, her leisure was more pleasurable if she could also accomplish some work each day.

---

14. LBJ to CTJ, 8/17/35, LBJ Library.
15. Elizabeth Rowe Oral History Interview 1, 6/6/75, by Michael L. Gillette, 24.

The interviews proceeded chronologically. While we covered multiple years in our initial sessions, each of her adult years consumed at least one interview session. Particularly significant or eventful years required as many as three sessions.

Preparations for the interviews were similar to those she had used in recording her White House diary. My oral history staff at the LBJ Library compiled a detailed chronology for each year from appointment books, trip schedules, correspondence, and press coverage. Mrs. Johnson reviewed both the chronology and the supporting materials before each session, making notes on items to discuss. She also refreshed her memory by looking through the volumes of photo albums that she kept at the ranch. My questions typically introduced topics and sought elaboration or clarification. To maximize the narrative's flow, the interviewer's questions have been omitted from this book unless they provide necessary context. Unabridged transcripts of the interviews are available on the LBJ Library's website. I have also compressed her reminiscences to eliminate false starts, habitual crutch words, and repetition. When she recounted the same story in two interview sessions, I have drawn from both versions to derive the most complete narrative.

Because the interview sessions spanned almost two decades, it is not surprising that the clarity of her memory varied. At times she was candid, expansive, and revealing. At other times, she was hesitant, vague, and uncertain. The quality of her recollections depended not only on her enthusiasm for the topic but also on whether she had actually participated in the events and how well she remembered them. Her recollections of LBJ's legislative activities, for example, were almost always impressionistic because she was not centrally involved. Nor did she always trust her memory. She occasionally expressed the wish that she had recorded events immediately after they had taken place, when they were "red-hot," as she had done with her White House diary. In some instances, she relied more on the appointment books, letters, and chronologies in front of her than on any independent recollection. This reliance is apparent in passages where she recounted the names of attendees and the dates of dinners occurring thirty or forty years earlier. Some of her recollections are familiar stories that she had told multiple times. Many others are episodes that she had never before discussed in any detail, if at all.

Oral history, of course, is a voluntary enterprise devoid of subpoena power. Interviewees determine whether to participate, what questions they will answer, and how candidly or expansively they will do so. Interviewees also control access to the finished product. If Lady Bird Johnson's participation was motivated by a willingness to enhance the LBJ Library's holdings, one must assume that she also intended to present her husband and his career in the most favorable light. She was his advocate. The more controversial the topic, the more emphatic her advocacy. By contrast, she was inevitably more unsparing in addressing her own shortcomings, such as her neglect of her daughters, than she was in recounting

LBJ's failings. Yet she did offer criticisms of her husband, including the fact that he was sometimes his own worst enemy.

Our interview sessions continued steadily for five years, from 1977 through 1982, when the Lady Bird Johnson Wildflower Center began to occupy a great deal of her time. We recorded only one session in 1983, followed by a break of more than seven years, except for two videotaped interviews that we recorded to accompany an LBJ Library exhibition, *A White House Diary*. Our two final interview sessions, which took us through 1954, occurred in 1991, the year that I moved to Washington to direct the Center for Legislative Archives at the National Archives. Harry Middleton, the LBJ Library's director, then conducted the last eight sessions, which covered Mrs. Johnson's reminiscences through 1960.[16] Her memories of the vice presidential years were recorded by Sheldon Stern for the John F. Kennedy Library Oral History Program.[17] The interviews on the presidential years consist of the two videotaped interviews that I conducted and an interview by LBJ Library archivist Nancy Smith in 1987.[18]

Lady Bird Johnson's oral history, like her voluminous White House diary, represents a unique contribution among the records of first ladies. As both witness and participant, she vividly captures the pulse of life in Texas and Washington through four decades, depicting such varied scenes as small town political rallies before television and the glittering parties of the capital's grand mansions. Her perceptive portraits bring to life the fascinating personalities she came to know through the intimacy of private dinners and the crucible of national politics. The history she witnessed, the lives she shared, and the opportunities she embraced were essential factors in her growth. At the heart of her narrative is the transformation of an extraordinary woman. From the isolation of Caddo Lake to the White House, here is Lady Bird Johnson's story in her own words.

---

16. The tape recording of Interview 39, covering the year 1958, was apparently blank.

17. CTJ OHI, 3/9/79, by Sheldon Stern, John F. Kennedy Presidential Library.

18. CTJ OHI, 1/23/87, by Nancy Smith, LBJ Library.

1

Childhood Memories

Lady Bird Johnson was, to some extent, a product of the Deep South. When her father, Thomas Jefferson Taylor Jr., migrated from Alabama's Autauga County to Texas, he settled in Karnack in the state's northeastern corner. Harrison County bore a much closer resemblance to the Old South than did the state's more western and southern regions. Its feudal society, once sustained by a large enslaved African American population, was now perpetuated by sharecroppers, bound to the land by debt. Although Lady Bird's mother, the former Minnie Lee Pattillo, had more cosmopolitan tastes and views than her husband, she was nevertheless a native of Autauga County and frequently returned there for extended periods. Lady Bird herself spent summers in Alabama with her mother's relatives.[1]

Claudia Alta Taylor was born on December 22, 1912, in the Brick House, an antebellum plantation house built by slaves. The inspirations for her given names were Minnie's brother Claud and her hope that her daughter would grow to be tall. The nickname "Lady Bird," another word for ladybug, attached itself early. Although its origin is attributed to her African American nurse, Alice Tittle, Mrs. Johnson once told me that the nickname had actually come from her two black childhood playmates, who themselves were nicknamed "Stuff" and "Doodlebug." It was later deemed more respectable to assign credit to the nurse and thereby avoid the impression of interracial socialization.

In September 1918 a pregnant Minnie Lee apparently fell on the stairs, suffering what proved to be a fatal injury. Her unmarried sister, Effie, soon joined the Taylor household to look after Lady Bird, but Aunt Effie proved to be a devoted companion instead of a caregiver. Deprived of the company of her parents and siblings, Lady Bird became extraordinarily self-reliant and an adventurous reader. Her early years in this isolated rural setting also fostered a love of the area's rich natural beauty, its lush fields of wildflowers and the enchanting Caddo Lake with its Spanish-moss-covered cypress trees. Nature was both her kingdom and her companion.

---

1. The most detailed account of Lady Bird Johnson's ancestors and childhood is Jan Jarboe Russell, *Lady Bird: A Biography of Mrs. Johnson* (New York: Scribner, 1999), 26–56. Also see Antonio J. Taylor Oral History Interview, 11/23/69, by David McComb, and Dorris Powell Oral History Interview, 4/18/78, by Michael L. Gillette.

MY GRANDMOTHER

I came to know my grandmother Taylor very well, although I never knew her as Grandmother Taylor. Mr. Taylor was her third husband, and after his death she married a Mr. Bishop. So I knew her as Mrs. Bishop. I used to visit her out in the country in Autauga County, Alabama. Cotton was the money crop and the principal crop, some corn, some subsistence farming, many blacks. People were poor, but not that they ever thought of it. My life there was visiting kinfolks in little towns, and going to see Grandmother was always a part of it. She lived in a very simple farmhouse, where actually she lived for more than eighty-five years, having four husbands, thirteen children, and watching twelve of them grow up. That was a matter of great interest to Lyndon. He used to ask me to tell him over and over, "How many husbands did you say she had?" and "How many children did you say she had?" He knew darned well because he had heard it several times.

Her name was Emma Louise Bates, and she married first when she was about sixteen or seventeen. [During] the Civil War, she married a young man who was leaving within a week or a month to join the Confederate Army. He never returned. He didn't die gloriously at Robert E. Lee's side, but he died like so many of them of disease and infection in the army camp. So that marriage terminated very early, and then in a year or so she remarried. He died [of yellow fever], and here she was, twice widowed and still not more than twenty.

Then she married Thomas Jefferson Taylor, and they had four children. She was pregnant with the fifth when it became obvious that [her husband] had a serious disease—I think it was a kidney ailment. The doctor in Selma, Alabama, told them that there was some marvelous new operation that could be performed in Mobile that would cure this disease. So they sold a piece of a farm, got in the buggy, parked all the children with kinfolks and rode in the buggy to Selma, got on the riverboat and went down the [Alabama] River to Mobile, and had the operation. It was apparently successful, and they started home. He began to run a fever, and by the time he got off the boat at Selma it was obvious that he was much more seriously ill. They made it as far as the relatives where they had left the children, and he died.

So here she was, about to have the fifth baby in two or three months and with four other children and a small Alabama farm to run. She named that child after her husband, Thomas Jefferson Taylor Jr. He became my father, and he never even knew his own father. When he was two or three years old, she married a gentleman named Bishop, who had come a-courting in the beginning and between every husband, and she lived to have another eight children.

THOMAS JEFFERSON TAYLOR JR.

So my father, to whom I was quite close and admired very much, grew up with the limited advantages of a small farm and a life of a lot of work. He was an extremely strong physical specimen, and work was his passion and his god. He was determined to get out of there and to do something with his life, although making money or acquiring enough to be comfortable was the form his ambition took.

[My father's move to Texas] was partly [in] the spirit of the times—"Go West, young man." One heard that Texas had great opportunities and lots of land and you could make money. [It was also partly] a very casual encounter. His older brother, Uncle Will, was married to a woman who wrote poetry and published it in small magazines, women's magazines, and in local papers, and perhaps a little wider range. Her poems brought her some fan letters or at least pen pals. One of these was from Marshall, Texas. She turned [that letter] over to her brother-in-law, young Tommy, because this person writing appeared to be a young woman of about his own age, and she said, "You ought to answer this one for me." So he began writing to some young woman in Marshall, Texas. So just a sheer chance was a part of his coming out here, but the real drive was the determination to get to a land of more opportunities.

Also my father was the last child of the Taylor children, and the eight Bishop children began to grow up and fill the house. As the Taylor children began to leave and make their place in the world, he, too, wanted to leave and make his place. Once, for about a year, he went and worked in the coal mines for a dollar a day. He did that long enough to buy himself a horse and saddle for his very own, and that was property in those days which was almost as much of a status symbol and almost as much of a necessity for a young man as a car is now. So he thought he was equipped when he got his horse and saddle. I don't think he had as rich and warm a relationship with his stepfather as one would have liked. All in all, the seeds were ripe for him to leave home when he reached early young manhood.

I sometimes thought that my father, for a man with as much property and as much money as he had, was a little too careful with it. I remember saying that to him. He looked at me, not reproachfully, but, in the tone of voice that one did not ignore or forget, he said, "I remember seeing my mother wanting to make tea cakes for us children, maybe one of us was having a birthday, and she couldn't because there was no sugar in the house and she couldn't afford to buy it." Tea cakes were a delicious but very simple form of cookie. I really never forgot that, because if you have seen somebody you love do without something as simple as two cups of sugar, you know the value of money. He was determined that that not happen to him or his in the future.

He came to Texas. He got off the train practically as soon as he crossed the line. I've often wondered if perhaps my spiritual home were more in central Texas than it was in the land where I was really born and raised, East Texas. I wish perhaps he'd come a little farther, but he was always in a hurry, all of his life. Partly he wanted to get off and meet this young lady he'd been writing to. It turned out to be not a permanent relation at all. I think they liked each other better in the written word than they did when they met. In any case, he looked the area over and decided to buy some land and start a country store. I do not know how he had any money for a nest egg, except I have a vague memory that he said he sold his horse and saddle, and he sold a small parcel of land that he had inherited, that all the Taylor children had inherited from their father. In any case, he was the sort of man who could and would make his way in a raw pioneer land, and he soon did buy some land and set up a small store. He began to go back to Alabama and try to persuade my mother to marry him. For many years, I had in my possession and carried around with me from house to house in a little box letters that he had written her.

He was a large man, wasn't he?
This was an interesting thing, too, which I did not know until I was a mature woman and had been married some time. I said, "Daddy, you have such a fine physique. Have you ever had any real illnesses?" He laughed and he said, "When I married, I was a tall, slim reed." He said, "Your mother sent off and got some dumbbells and some Indian clubs. She'd put a quilt on the floor, and she'd have me doing exercises."

THE PATTILLOS

[Luther Pattillo, my maternal grandfather,] was an extremely eccentric man. I would have loved to have known him. He was what is called a character. I get the impression that he was a bit of a wild young man and a carouser, until it finally dawned on him that he believed he would settle down and get married and make some money. He just planned it all, and it all worked out for him. He was a great reader. He was also a health faddist [and] an ardent believer in Dr. [John Harvey] Kellogg, who had a hospital or a spa in Battle Creek, Michigan.

My grandfather and grandmother Pattillo had four children: two girls, Aunt Effie and my mother, Minnie Lee Pattillo; and two boys, Claud Alfred, who never married, and Harry Gordon. Harry Gordon married relatively early. Uncle Claud was the one who was always left handling the estate, handling the family land, and just taking care of the other members of the family as far as their handling their money affairs went. The Pattillos may have considered themselves, rightly or wrongly, a notch more cultured or successful than my father, although they both certainly came from a very rural southern background. My mother and her sister, Aunt Effie, had gone to girls' schools. They were called, I think, seminary. Mother had had somewhat more advantages and more money than Daddy had, because he was certainly just a fine, fresh young man at the threshold of life with nothing behind him in the way of wealth and expectations to inherit. In any case, he was an ardent courter, and they did get married.

MINNIE LEE PATTILLO

[My mother] was a woman whom apparently many people remembered as distinctive. She was not one who melted into the background and was forgotten. Various kinfolks would say that my mother loved to ride in the woods. She had a horse, and she'd just get out on it, go and take to the woods, freely roaming around, which they thought rather eccentric of a young woman.

I have a vague memory of her having some sort of illness and losing some of her hair, and from then on she did wear turbans a good deal. She did wear white a great deal, and she would walk through the house very swiftly. I was only five years and eight months old when she died, so I do not have many memories of her. I remember that she was ardently interested in some election and went all over the county in a buggy, electioneering for [a candidate] who had been overseas and had fought bravely and whose opponent was what was called a draft dodger then. And, believe me, that was no thing to be if you aspired to a public office. It was considered rather eccentric of her to be so outspoken in politics.

She had more cultural interests than were readily available in Karnack. She was really pretty alien to the scene there, because she was always sending off and getting books, lots and lots and lots of books. Once a year, she would go to New York or Chicago to listen to the opera. She loved grand opera. She had stacks and stacks of Red Seal records by people like [Amelita] Galli-Curci, Madame [Nellie] Melba, [Enrico] Caruso—Caruso was her great favorite—Madame [Ernestine] Schumann-Heink.

She had quite a lot of books and loved historical books. Also, in every decade there are a host of books that tell you how to run your life better, and she had a share of those, too. But she also had a lot of the classics and a lot of historical books and memoirs of characters in the French Revolution and in English court circles.

Would she read to you?
Yes, she did. Nature stories and myths and legends of the Greeks and Germans and all the fairy stories. I just thought it was the most marvelous thing in the world to know how to read. I just loved that. I remember when I first discovered that my daddy could read. My goodness! I never saw him doing it, didn't know he could. He said something to me about, "I'm so sorry you're lonesome and don't have anybody to play with. Do you want me to read to you?" My gosh, it was just like he had suggested something magical. So from then on, he used to read to me. His tastes ran to the Zane Grey books and books about the far north by [James] Oliver Curwood and such as that.

Do you recall any of the books that you had read to you as a little girl having an enduring influence on you?
No. I remember a number of them with affection, but none as having set the course of my life, no. Some of the ones that I remember with affection are no longer read by now, certainly no longer read the way they were written, and

among them is Uncle Remus. Then there was a naturalist named Ernest Thompson Seton, [author of] *Woodland Tales*.

THE BRICK HOUSE

[The Brick House, the house we lived in,] was a beautiful old place. It was built before the Civil War. My daddy bought it for Mother one time when she had gone back to visit her mother and father in Alabama, taking their two little boys with her. It was before my birth, because I was born in the house. I think it had not been inhabited in several years, and it was pretty run down. They had to do a lot to it. In the light of today I wish I had been on hand and knowledgeable and had done it somewhat differently, but it was a great old Greek Revival house with tall white columns and two small porches, main floor and upper floor. On the back side it was an "L" and must have had a Louisiana influence, because it had two long, spacious galleries. It is said that it had been built by someone who had come from Georgia and who tried to build it as much like their old home in Georgia as they could. Colonel [Milt] Andrews was the person who built it back in 1854. The only things that [my father] added were right at the back, a kitchen and a bathroom. The bathroom was put on when I was twelve years old. Up to that time we had just had out-door facilities. You bathed in a big zinc tub and stood close to the stove if it was wintertime. Six rooms had [a fireplace]. In the wintertime, we always had wonderful fires roaring.

That brings me to a character in our life who was an important character to my brother Tony and to me and certainly to my daddy and mother. His name was Goodwin Coleman. As one looks back, he was a sad character, but I never thought of it that way then. He was a man of good family and intelligence who had had a disease or bad fever probably in his early teens [that] had left him mentally—well, he was different. His mind was partially gone, but certainly he was harmless. He lived alone in a rather primitive house on some land that must have belonged to his family. Such work as he did he was likely to do for Daddy. He would show up when he got ready, and that could be five days a week or one day a month. But Daddy could always find something for him to do. He also felt very free and easy about coming to our house. He was always welcome there, and we were always glad to have him. He could build the best fires, and he could tell the most interesting stories to the children. He also could draw lions and tigers and cockatoos and parrots.

He was laughed at by some of the people, but never by my family, particularly by my mother. She always made him very welcome. I remember him saying something rather plaintively once about somebody not speaking to him or not being nice to him, and he said, "And my mother wouldn't have let them ride in her coach," which was one of my first observations on the way society treats somebody who is different.

We never locked the house. If we would hear somebody coming in at night, that was not a matter for any alarm; it was somebody that needed to come in, had business coming in. If they walked up the stairsteps—clump, clump, clump—reciting the names of all the generals of the Confederate Army, that would be old Good. He knew all about the Civil War, and he still got enraged about certain aspects of it. On the other hand, if it was somebody who came in whistling and about ten minutes later we would hear the strains of the Victrola giving forth popular tunes of the day, that would be my brother Tommy returning from a date. And if somebody went upstairs and in about five minutes you heard a loud, stentorious snoring, that would be my Uncle Walter, my father's elder brother, who, after his wife died, became a pretty constant visitor at our home.

I was pretty much left to my own devices, and I did not have many constant companions. Maydelle [Jones] was about the closest, and the period when we were together was several years, but her family finally moved away. I had two little black friends, "Stuff" and "Doodlebug," who were the children of the woman who washed for us. We used to just play house and store and all sorts of things. I would quite naturally explore the woods and climb trees and do all sort of things that you might speak of as tomboy things without thinking of it in that way. My brothers were off at school a great deal during my growing-up years. Tommy was eleven years older than I, and Tony was eight years older. One time they had a couple of boys visiting them, and they were going down to the pond and going swimming, and I wanted to go with them. They didn't want me to go, because I was too little to tag along. They finally just burst out and said, "Lady Bird, we're gonna take off our clothes. You can't go." And I said, "I don't care whether you take off your clothes or not."

I remember that the seasons were a matter of great importance to my life then. The springtime was my very favorite. We had a lot of jonquils in the yard which were naturalized and came up year after year, and a lot of what we called "flags," which are lilies. I would just watch for the blooming of the first one, and I'd pick it and have a little ceremony and crown it the princess. I knew a lot about the woods and where they followed the streams for what seemed to me quite a long way. The bigger streams we'd call "creeks" and the smaller ones "branches." The one that was closest at hand was definitely a branch, but it led through what were then lovely woods. There were lots of violets in the early spring and a good many pine trees, which had the most mournful but distinctive sound when the wind would blow through them.

The Haggerty [property] was always spelled in capitals in my childhood day. When my father began to finally make money, he always wanted to buy more and more land. A piece of land came up for sale, and he bought it. The owners had long since moved away. I remember seeing a piece in the paper, the *Marshall News Messenger*, about the sale of it and how he had come prepared to the sale with all the money in cash.[2] It was quite a large acreage, a large part of it heavily wooded, with a creek running through it and huge old hardwood trees. Then there was a lot of open pasture land. It had obviously belonged to the Haggerty family. The legend was that there had been a great fine house there and a wealthy family. The house had later on burned. There still was an old family cemetery when I was a child. We used to go over there—most often on horseback or in a wagon on very primitive roads, but sometimes walking, because I was a big walker.

There were huge magnolia trees at the site of the house and some crepe myrtles, and underneath them a great expanse in the springtime of daffodils and jonquils and all sorts of bulb flowers, a whole carpet of them. It was a miracle to me. I wish I were enough of a botanist, because I never expected bulbs that were naturalized just to go on for decades. I don't know how long [before] that house had been burned down and those owners had moved away, but those flowers just went on and on and on. We used to go over there with tubs or wheelbarrows and dig up bulbs and bring them home and plant them in the front yard at the Brick House. Flags and daffodils were the two principal ones, jonquils.

EARLY EDUCATION

I recall one rather odd, pathetic thing as a little girl when I was already reading quite easily. I remember climbing up into a finished room above the garage. Mother took that as her place to store a lot of her books, magazines, papers, and things. I remember going up there and looking, and I found a number of catalogs about schools for boys and schools for girls. Indeed, she had already sent my brothers to one or two of the schools that were mentioned there: to Raymond Riordan in [Highland,] New York, and to Los Alamos Ranch School for boys, out from Santa Fe. There were one or two catalogs for girls' schools, though. Here I was only five years old, but she apparently was thinking ahead to the time when it would be time to send me off to school. Gosh, I presume she was thinking of something much younger than high school. There was one in Washington which was still in existence and a very high-class school in 1934 when I got there. It seems like it was named National Park Seminary, and it was in a very wooded section, not in the District of Columbia but [Forest Glen, Maryland]. Lots of the buildings had different sorts of architecture from different countries.

I must have begun school when I was five. It was a one-room school at the top of a hill, about a quarter of a mile, perhaps a half a mile, from the Brick House. The teachers at the Fern School were a parade of sweet, gentle, nice ladies. Each year I was crazy about the teacher. There was one named Grace Nelson. For

---

2. Jan Jarboe Russell provides a more elaborate description of T. J. Taylor's acquisition of and income from the Haggerty property, which had belonged to the county's largest black family. Russell, *Lady Bird*, 48–49.

several years, the latter years, they boarded at my house, simply because they had to stay somewhere that was close and had plenty of room.

There was a big potbellied stove, which in the wintertime it was the job of one of the boys to keep filled and roaring with flame. In the summertime, fall, spring, or any good day, we had recess out of doors and played games like stealing sticks and base and annie over, which involved throwing a ball over the house. The school would consist of eight or ten pupils. They would range in grades from the first grade to the seventh. Even then, the state of Texas furnished the schoolbooks. You were issued your schoolbooks when you first got there in September, and usually they were used year after year so that you turned them in in May. We probably called it primer, which was the first book one had. It began with one-sentence reading lessons: "This is Will. How do you do, Will? This is May. How do you do, May?" It was all very simple, and I loved it. In the fall, we would all rake up the leaves and pile them in great big piles and play jumping in them. Everybody brought his lunch in a paper sack. One would have perhaps a biscuit with a piece of bacon in between and a hard-boiled egg and maybe a little medicine bottle full of syrup, and you could make a hole in your biscuit with your finger and then pour it full of syrup. There was certainly always an apple or an orange or a banana for me; I daresay not for many of the other children, though.

Actually, the school year was arranged so that you didn't begin until up in September, and they would have had a sizeable part of August to pick [cotton], and then in the afternoons when they got home they could pick. There may have been some of the bigger boys that might have been kept home.

Did the teachers attempt to gear the lessons individually to each student according to his age, or was it all just one class?
No, it wasn't one class, because we'd be in different grades. With that few students, I suppose the biggest class would be two or three. Since there was one family, the Jones family, that furnished five of the students, I would daresay that most classes probably just had one person in them.

Always on Friday we had what we called exercises, which was singing patriotic songs. To this day I remember the words to a great many from having sung them at those Friday afternoon exercises, like "America the Beautiful" and "Columbia, the Gem of the Ocean," and even "The Star-Spangled Banner," which was always hard. Then somebody would usually have to say a poem that he or she had memorized, often of a patriotic nature, sometimes a religious nature.

Did you feel at the time, or as soon as you were able to tell, that that primary education served you in good stead when you got to high school, or did you consider yourself disadvantaged?
I certainly didn't consider myself at any disadvantage, certainly not from an education standpoint. By the time I got to [be] twelve or fourteen years old and began to go off to school, I certainly was at a disadvantage socially, because I was

very shy, and I had just not been exposed to many people and certainly not to people that you could consider at all wealthy or socially... whose way of life included parties or elegance. It was very simple.

Did you realize at an early age that you were better off financially than a lot of your neighbors?
Yes, I realized that, but it was not a matter of any importance. I realized that people looked up to my daddy and expected him to solve the hard problems, and considered him the boss. Lots of them had great affection and admiration, and some of them, no doubt, some resentment toward him. I was aware of that, but I just thought that's the way things were.

You spent a good deal of time with Dorris Powell, although she was considerably older.
Dorris was a good deal older, but she was a dear, wonderful friend, and as the years passed, that age variance diminished. She became a kind of a chaperone or big sister by the time I was fifteen or sixteen and beginning to have a few dates. She was always helping plan things and [would] be there as the chief instigator of the fun that went on and the chaperone. I remember she used to come and cut out paper dolls for me and with me even when I was a little girl. But her mother, Mrs. Odom, also was one of those marvelous women who was determined to make the most out of what she had and give her children as good a home as she could manage, and sometimes against odds. There was a period of one or two years when my mother was not at all well. She was in the hospital for a while, and she was staying at home with her mother in Alabama for a while, and Mrs. Odom came out to keep house for Daddy and me and for the boys, for whoever was there from time to time, and of course bringing her own family with her. So she was in the house with us for a while.

Mount Sinai was the black church. I really loved to get taken to the black church by my nurse. I felt very much at home there and liked it. They always had a lot of emotion in their services and a lot of singing, and they enjoyed them. I felt a part of them, and I liked it. Of course, there were a number of them, but Mount Sinai and Peter's Chapel are two that I remember. They would be named after places in the Bible or characters in the Bible. I think there was a Bethel.

There was a summer religious festival close to us, in Scottsville, where they'd have services morning, noon, and night. Families who belonged would usually have a house or at the very least pitch a tent. It was quite the thing to do. Most of the county families had a little house there, and they really would go and stay. There was a marvelous old tabernacle there; it's still there, a very charming old place, one of the prettiest cemeteries I've ever seen. My mother would always go. I do not think she was a member of it, because it was not Methodist. I think my mother was a Methodist. I know we always went to the Methodist church, and my daddy was a mainstay in support of it. Not that he was a very religious man. In my opinion, he thought it was a civilizing influence in the community and kept people from being so rowdy and lawbreaking. So he supported it, I think, as much from community feeling as any religious feeling.

He helped them pay their bills, I understand.
Yes, living and dead he did. He left them something when he died.

Do you remember your mother as being a very religious woman?
No, I don't. That, too, is really quite a loss, not to remember more about her than I do. I remember one thing that's quite pathetic that I didn't know then was pathetic. I remember when she was in the hospital, and I'm reasonably sure she did not recover. It was the last illness. They took me to see her. I had been staying at the house with my daddy and a black nurse and a black cook, and nobody directing them, and Daddy working all the time, except for going to the hospital to see Mother. I walked in and Mother looked at me, and she said, "My poor little girl, so dirty." And she took a napkin off a tray and dipped it in a glass of water and cleaned my face. I can just imagine me walking in there grubby as can be and how disheartening that must have been to a woman who probably knew she wouldn't recover, or knew she might not.

I read that she had had either a nervous breakdown or that she was a very high-strung person, and had—
She was, and, of course, at this late date I really know nothing about it. But I feel sure that if she were in today's society, she would be going to see a psychiatrist and very interested in it and maybe profiting from it and maybe not. But she had psychological problems, of what nature I don't quite know.

Did your father talk much about her after her death? Did he tell you what she was like?
No, and once more I wish to goodness that he had. I do have a memory [that] the preacher came to call. It must have not been long after my mother's death. He was talking about the will of God and being in a better place. My daddy really got furious with him: "How can you tell me that God is good and that God willed that? Look at that little girl. Who's going to take care of her? Who's going to give her all the things her mother would have given her? And I'm a young man. I need her." I had never before seen my daddy mad; and to be mad at a preacher who's so defenseless and in awe of him. I felt sorry for the preacher, and I felt very understanding and very respectful of my father. That was a part of him—that he was needful, too—that I had never known before. I'm glad the thing took place, as much as it must have distressed the preacher.[3] I remember it, and it has stuck in my mind all these years.

---

3. Mrs. Johnson's description of her father's encounter with the preacher also draws from her interview with Charles Guggenheim for the documentary film *A Life: The Story of Lady Bird Johnson* (dir. Charles Guggenheim, Washington, DC: Guggenheim Productions, 1992).

"DEALER IN EVERYTHING"

[My father's] stationery, which had the familiar red fish at the top, [bore the inscription:] "T. J. Taylor, Dealer in Everything." It used to say, "Dealer in General Merchandise." Later on, he put a sign up above the store, "Dealer in Everything," and it would say, "Shipper of Freshwater Fish." There was a lake close to us called Caddo Lake, which became very much a part of my childhood. It was a very scenic, interesting, wild, haunted place, not unlike the Everglades of Florida. There were huge cypress trees with big trunks and gnarled roots and hung with Spanish moss, and still, gray-green water, and some alligators, and lots and lots of turtles and lots and lots of fish, and a few water moccasins, but they never bothered me. Daddy used to have men who worked for him who would catch the fish, ice them down in barrels, and send them on the train to Fulton Fish Market in New York. So that is where that stationery came from with the red fish on the top of the page.

He never passed up an opportunity to see a natural resource or something and try to make some money off of it. He did finance some of the people who had the fishing camps and who were the guides on Caddo Lake, and he did sell a lot of fish out of the lake. He did protest bitterly when the legislature finally stopped them from fishing with nets. He said, "The fish are going to eat each other up. They are cannibals, and if we don't catch them and eat them they're going to catch each other and eat each other." I have no idea which is true. I am sure that we have to have conservation practices, and maybe if he had gone on unhampered he might have caught more fish than [the lake] could stand.

My mother died in September [1918], and that was for my daddy the height of the season for the cash crop of cotton. It is harvested in late August and September and October. The black families that he had been financing all year would bring their crop in, and gin it, and turn over his part to him. They would settle up. They would pay him for everything they had eaten all year and take the balance, if balance there was, praise heaven, and go into debt on the books if there wasn't enough. It was just the most important time of the year. Therefore, it would have been very hard for him to come home every night at six o'clock and sit down at the table with his little girl. So for a couple of months, at least, he did take me to the store a lot.

It was a huge brick building, the business, social, everything center of that small community. He would sit on a high stool in his little office, which was separated from the main part of the store, and work at the books and telephone, and everybody that needed to see him would go back there to see him. I would just wander around among the dry goods and the candy cases, upstairs where they would have things like plows and mattresses and coffins, just the whole business of life. I do remember one night, we must have spent a few nights down there, because we did have a bed upstairs made down for us. I would see those big, long, oblong boxes, and I would ask Daddy what they were. I could hear the slight hesitation in his voice, and he would say, "Dry goods, honey." They were coffins, but he didn't want to scare me unnecessarily by a truth which would have been somewhat frightening to a five-year-old child who associated so much with blacks who were superstitious and who were full of stories about ghosts and "hants" [haunts], as they called them. Indeed, the house we lived in had plenty of "hants," according to local legend.

He was always the boss and always in charge and always put the business first. I think he was sociable enough in terms of being approachable and always ready to have some words with any of the drummers or travelers or local people who came in, but small talk was not his thing very much. He was business first.

Were you afraid of him?
No, but I was probably one of the few people who wasn't, because I knew how much he cared about me and how tender he was toward me. He was a very impressive man, and I am sure a great many people were afraid of him. But I always knew that somehow he cared very especially about me and also that he was softer on the inside than he appeared on the outside.

Could you confide in him?
Not very much. I wasn't the sort who could have in anybody very much, but yet every now and then I would have a most remarkable bit of advice from him. I remember one time when I was about to graduate from college, I was just very casually talking, I wasn't even meaning what I was saying, "I might do this, I might do that, or I might just come back here to Karnack to stay." And my daddy just erupted, "Oh no you won't. You're going to get out of here. There will be better things for you to do." Which astonished me, because I knew how much he liked Karnack. He had spent his life in it. Also, he must have respected it a considerable amount or else he wouldn't have stayed there all his life. But I was very pleased that he could see that there might be a bigger world out there, and that I might be able to fit myself for the bigger world, and that maybe I better have a look at it.

He was the biggest landowner in the county. He did have more blacks working for him than anybody else. He was a man to whom all the politicians came to call and try to get his goodwill and his help, although he never had much interest in politics or much admiration for it.

Do you have any recollections of the Ku Klux Klan in that area?
Oh, yes, some frightening recollections. Not frightening to me personally, but to think that people would behave that badly. I remember one time Daddy got some notes from them, but he paid them no mind. I think they called him a "nigger lover" or something like that. That was something you had better not be if those folks caught up with you.

Why do you think they did that, because he had blacks working for him?
Everybody had blacks working for them, but I do not think my daddy was ever cruel. I think he was about as just as he could be in those times and in that setting with black people. There were some instances of downright cruelty on the part of whites toward blacks, and I have the feeling that the lower the white people were in culture, the more likely they were to be prone to doing it.

[Daddy] never was scared of them or terribly impressed with [the Ku Klux Klan], but Marshall had some bad episodes. In fact, one time when I was on the train going from Austin back to Marshall to visit, one of the few times when I didn't go in my car, I got into conversation with a man. We had some mutual friends, and I asked him if he knew Marshall very well. He gave me a wry smile and said, "I've only been there twice." The first time he went to see a man. He got there, and the man didn't keep the date. Then he read in the papers where the man had been tarred and feathered by the Ku Klux Klan and delivered to Dr. Jack Baldwin's office for treatment. The other time was just as bad, really. There was sort of a war situation there between the Catholics and the Protestants. It was an ugly little time.

Your father's sister wrote at the time of your marriage, "I don't believe I ever saw two people that had a more perfect understanding of each other" than you and your father. Did you feel this way?
I guess I did. I liked him tremendously as well as loving him. He lived a pretty narrowed life, particularly after my mother's death, in terms of having intellectual "grist for the mill" being sparked, having experiences that make you think and grow, and yet I think he was always capable of that. I remember one time we were talking about his youth and his meager education, which was just a high school graduate. He made some very simple, wistful statement, wondering how much more he could have done if he'd had more education. It would be so easy for a completely self-made man to think, by gosh, he did it all, and he didn't have to have any education. Why should the next fellow have to have it? But he was aware that life could have been wider for him.

He did appreciate education—
Oh, you bet he did!

TONY AND TOMMY

Tony, at quite an early age—like eighteen—was sick. He got what was diagnosed as TB. They decided the best thing for him to do was to go to Santa Fe, New Mexico, and he liked that idea. He had been out to Los Alamos to school for one or two years. He was there when my mother died. He went off, and I really didn't see him much. We became very close friends later on, but from the time

I was about ten, I'd only see him when he would come home, perhaps at Christmas, maybe once or twice a year.

Was your brother Tommy much like your father?
In many ways yes, but Tommy was really the nicest one of us. He was such a good person, and he didn't quite have my daddy's toughness. He was physically very much like my father—a great big man, about six feet three, very handsome. I remember one time when I was just a little girl and I was about half asleep and I was lying down on a pallet in the hot summertime. He came in and leaned over and kissed me on the forehead and said something about "my little sister," expressions of tenderness like that. I knew my daddy felt like that, but it would have been hard for him to do it. Tommy had a very tender streak in him. During the Depression, he had a business, which Daddy had helped set up for him in Jefferson, the Jefferson Wholesale Grocery Company. He was the first person that anybody who was collecting for any church or any needy cause would call on, and he was one of the most helpful in the community of Jefferson.

AUNT EFFIE

My daddy, feeling that there had to be some woman in the house to take care of me, looked around among the available women in the family and asked [Aunt Effie Pattillo]. He had always had an affection for her as his wife's sister, but also he thought she was a pretty weak reed. But he thought that she would suffice sweetly and nicely for that job, and he asked her if she would do it. She said yes she would, if he didn't mind me being gone all summer and she could take me back [to Alabama] and we could visit various kinfolks. The ineffably sad thing about her life was that she never did really have a home of her own after her mother and father died. She would just visit around. Now she was very comfortably fixed, in a moderate way, and the people that she visited, mostly she was a big help to them, particularly to her niece, Elaine Fischesser, and also some to other nieces.

Aunt Effie was one of those gentle creatures that were really not meant for this world practically. She was a true eccentric, and her health was never good. I don't know how much of it was psychosomatic and how much of it was real. But she was one of the most loving kinfolks that could possibly be and a great storyteller, and her devotion was so complete. Her love of beauty and nature she certainly helped instill in me. She was a marvelous part of my life, both on the positive side and also on the negative, because I saw what an inhibiting thing her poor health was, and also her absolute dependence on Uncle Claud to take care of her financial affairs, on me and Daddy to furnish her with a need for living, a place where she could perform, where she was needed. So it just made me feel that I didn't want to ever be that dependent or ever in poor health. There were a lot of women like her in the South, spinster ladies who never asserted themselves or ran their own lives.

There was much happiness in her life. In her young days she played the piano; she did a little painting; she loved nature and the outdoors. I always enjoyed being with her. She had lots of good friends as we went through life, which indeed we did from the time I was five until I was twenty-one. Her devotion to me was so intense that I wished it hadn't been quite so much. You don't want to be everything to a person unless you can be it always and always, and it's in the nature of young people to grow up and get married and, to some extent, sever the bonds with those who raised them.

Was she a surrogate mother to you in the sense of telling you what to do?
That is very open to question. She lived in the house and [there was] nothing that she wanted more in the world to do than to take care of me and help me out, but as far as being a disciplinarian or a real adviser, she wasn't, because she was just too weak a character. Which is not to say she didn't have influence, because she did, because I respected and loved her. But she was not the big powerful figure that my daddy was. She wasn't practical. She really didn't know a thing in the world about some of the simple things that a young child needs. My clothes must have been bizarre and inadequate, and certainly she never gave any thought to appropriate companions or the business that so many people think of as putting the "right people" in your path. Never in the world would it have occurred to her.

BATTLE CREEK

My Aunt Effie always made friends at these sanitariums where she went in search of better health. One was the Adams family who lived in Newton, Kansas. We went to visit them two summers, and they took us to Colorado with them. We went to Mount Manitou, close to Colorado Springs. I remember seeing the Broadmoor Hotel and kept thinking what a big, magnificent place it was, although we lived in much simpler fashion. We went to the Garden of the Gods and had a picnic and climbed all over fascinating scenery.

[Aunt Effie took me to the Kellogg Sanitarium] twice. She wanted to go for her own health, so she just took me along. Not that I needed anything; I didn't because I was quite a healthy young child. I think we stayed a whole month one summer.

Dr. [John Harvey] Kellogg was a ruddy-cheeked, white-haired, white-mustached gentleman, quite elderly, but he would bicycle around just like fury about seven o'clock in the morning. Then he would get up and lead us all in calisthenics, the women wearing some kind of rather remarkable bloomers, middy blouses or something, and the men other suitable attire.

Dr. Kellogg began talking about orange juice, vitamins, sunbathing, exercise, before anybody else ever heard of it. He was a great vegetarian and inspired all of his believers in being that. So much that he believed in has since been adopted by the world of medicine and by people in general. You know how much we talk about vitamins [today]. Well, he was talking about vitamins all the time. At that time, everybody just fell out laughing, and they just thought all this [advice] about taking off your clothes and lying in the sun and getting all that exercise was crazy.

There is a hilarious picture of me, age eleven, standing in a field by the side of a biplane in Battle Creek, Michigan. It was a barnstorming thing that would come to a town and land in a cow pasture and take people up for two dollars, or three or four dollars. I did that when I was at Battle Creek, and Aunt Effie either didn't know or thought it was all right. In that instance, there was a grown person with me, a woman who became a friend of Aunt Effie's and took me around.

UNCLE CLAUD

Your Uncle Claud wanted you to go to Harvard Business School.
Yes, and he used to send me business magazines, which I'm afraid I did not profit by. Uncle Claud also was eccentric. He was a dear, wonderful man, but he, too, was not quite of this world, although he was saddled with this world all his life. He could quote Cicero and Plato and a whole lot of Greek and Roman philosophers whose names I barely know. He knew a good deal of the practical side of the farmland that he was supposed to administer and its capability of growing pines and how to market the pines. But his real interests were [in nutrition]. For instance, he kept on preaching to the blacks who lived by dirt farming, just as poor as they could be, to raise a little garden, "Keep yourself some turnip greens, collards, lettuce, green beans," all sorts of green things. They were likely to subsist on a little hog meat and flour biscuits and molasses and just never see a vegetable or certainly not a fruit. So he kept on trying to diversify their diet and encourage them to keep a cow. Well, they would just laugh and laugh because Uncle Claud had the misfortune to have bad health all of his life. I'm afraid that I, too, was one of those guilty of sometimes laughing at Uncle Claud, who did so much preaching but who was not himself a great big, robust, six feet four, tough man like my father. But why should anybody know better than if they had bad health themselves to aspire to better health for themselves and others?

Did he try to persuade you to pursue a business education or become interested in the stock market?
He would talk about it some and give me the opportunities, but no, I guess that I was too young and too unreceptive. And it's too bad. I wish I had availed myself of far more of many opportunities that he made possible for me. He

would do all sorts of nice things [for] the children whom I would be visiting there in Billingsley. I was his niece, and sometimes there would be other nieces, but very frequently they would be just cousins. He would take us on picnics and take us to swim in Mulberry Creek. He was a soft touch in a way. He liked the young folks, and he was kind, and he wanted to help do for them the things that he thought would make childhood and summertime a happy memory.

2

Education, 1924–1934

Lady Bird Johnson's educational experiences in the nearby towns of Jefferson and Marshall freed her from the isolation of Karnack and forced her into broader social settings, but her intellectual growth and inspiration came later—in Dallas and Austin. After attending the University of Alabama during the summer following her graduation from Marshall High School in 1928, a friend encouraged her to attend St. Mary's College for women in Dallas, an expensive Episcopal two-year institution. She was only fifteen when she successfully overcame her father's opposition to her enrollment. In the fall of 1930, she enrolled in the University of Texas, which opened new horizons for her. This time she deferred to her father's judgment, withdrawing from the sorority she had pledged. Yet Lady Bird enjoyed an active social life on the Austin campus. Her narrative documents how much she changed in the four years since high school. After meeting Lyndon Johnson in 1934, T. J. Taylor famously told his daughter: "You've brought a lot of boys home, and this time you've brought a man." Although the second clause is usually emphasized, the first clause, too, is revealing.

JEFFERSON AND MARSHALL

After having finished the Fern School, I had to go somewhere to high school, either Jefferson or Marshall. Jefferson was about fifteen miles away, and Marshall was about thirteen miles away. But by that time, my brother Tommy had married and was living in Jefferson and running the Jefferson Wholesale Grocery. We just thought it would be nice for me to be in a town where he was. Although Aunt Effie would live with me, perhaps he could oversee us in some way. I did see a good bit of my brother Tommy, who was very kind to me and always solicitous and did everything he could for me.

I remember Jefferson as a romantic old town and quite a patrician town. But it was dying on the vine. The revival which the women brought about had not begun then; it was still in the grip of the depression. Jefferson is a remarkable little community. There had been a time, in the 1870s, when Jefferson was the second biggest town in Texas because of the shipping that came up the bayou.

Dozens of ships that came up from New Orleans would dock there. It was an agricultural town with many beautiful old homes. It was one of those towns that after the period of vitality, success, and growth dried up around the turn of the century when the railroad really got going.[1]

So I went to school in Jefferson for two years and began the business of meeting dozens of people my own age, whereas before there had only been an occasional one here and there. I was very young and also very young for my age. I started there in September of 1924, [when] I was eleven, and left there in May or June of 1926, at which time I was only thirteen. So I didn't have any dates, but I went to parties at which both boys and girls were. I remember watching the bigger girls do the Charleston. I never learned how. I may have tried, but I'm sure I was pretty inept.

Nevertheless, I soon had a few friends. We'd spend the night at their house, or they would come to the country with me, because I went home every weekend. Games like Parcheesi and all sorts of very juvenile games were very much a part of the life of young folks; I daresay we probably still played Old Maid. We did some ridiculous things like going into some of the kinfolks' closets and finding old-fashioned clothes and dressing up in feather boas and long skirts and parading around. One time Nellie Ford and various others and I dressed up in all these costumes that we found and took a lot of pictures. I remember once when I went out to see Nellie, I made my one and only attempt at riding bicycles. Growing up in the country at Karnack there were no highways, there were no paved roads even, so I never had met up with a bicycle. Around Jefferson there were some sidewalks, and certainly there were streets, and lots of the youngsters did have bicycles. So I managed to stay on, but I discovered myself going downhill and I didn't know how to stop, much less slow up. I finally headed straight for a mailbox on the side of the road and did indeed stop with a loud crescendo and got tossed over the bars and into the ditch. Not much damage except a little bruised and scratched.

Aunt Effie and I boarded at Miss Bernice Emmert's home. That was one of the first times that I was exposed to extremely intelligent people. These two maiden ladies, Miss Bernice Emmert and her sister, Miss Alice, were real scholars.[2] They had been teachers, and Miss Alice, I think, still was. Their lives had been very much constricted by having to take care of elderly parents. They had never married, but they had good educations and had read just about everything that had been written, and they spoke beautiful English.

---

1. For an analysis of the economic impact of the removal of the Red River raft and the construction of the railroad, see Fred Tarpley, *Jefferson: Riverport to the Southwest* (Austin, TX: Eakin, 1983), 151–82.

2. The Texas Historical Marker on the Emmert House states that Alice Emmert was one of the first women in the state to be elected to public office. She served as Marion County superintendent of education from 1908 to 1920.

Finally they were reduced to the status of having to keep a few boarders. We had the good fortune to be boarders as well as roomers. I don't remember eating anywhere else. They were great friends of Aunt Effie's, and they were very kind to her. I'll always remember with happiness that time that she had them for friends.

Why did you decide, or perhaps your father decided, that you would finish high school in Marshall?
I don't know really. As I look back on it I'm really not quite sure why. When I was thirteen, my daddy started sending me into Marshall. Of course it meant him detaching somebody to drive me to school. It might be a clerk, a book-keeper, a butcher, or a black man who drove the truck. Then, because it would have been about a six-hour wait, they went on about their business and came back and made a second trip in to get me later in the day. That was very time consuming, and my daddy got the idea he had better buy me a car. I was so relieved when he did, for sometimes Daddy sent me off in a pickup truck carrying cow hides. I had absolutely nothing against the pickup, but I didn't like the cow hides one bit. They smelled to high heaven. I would get out a couple of blocks from school, walking the rest of the way and hoping nobody had seen me.[3] I learned to drive at thirteen. Jack Moore taught me, as I recall.

How did Marshall differ from Jefferson at this time?
It was bigger and a good deal more frightening in terms of meeting a lot of strangers. As a town it really didn't have the charm that Jefferson did. It had a football team, and I soon started wearing a red and white skirt and jacket and getting out there and hollering for the team and being interested in a lot of things that there were.

One story concerns your desire not to be valedictorian at Marshall High.
Yes, by that time I was fifteen years old. The horror of that would have been that I would have had to stand up and make a speech. Also, I knew that my very good friend Emma Boehringer wanted it very, very much and was a good student and did indeed deserve it. My recollection is that she got it and that someone named Maurine Kranson got second and that I got about half a point below Maurine, which was an entirely satisfactory state of affairs.

There's another story about the glamorous boy that went to Marshall High School that was always trying to speak to you, but you were too shy to answer him.
[*Laughter.*] Yes. I don't know where that came from, but I do remember there was a very nice young man who was captain of the football team and therefore

---

3. CTJ's description of the pickup truck with the cow hides is taken from her remarks for the 50th reunion of the Marshall High School class of 1928, May 27, 1978, LBJ Library.

a big person in the class. He was just a country boy, every bit as country as any of us, but he would come in and sit down by me and ask me about our assignment and this, that, and the other. I would make some excuse to leave or go out and get a drink of water simply because I couldn't think of what to say next.

Shyness is a fairly common phenomenon, particularly when you get to be about thirteen or fourteen. But if you've been raised way out in the country and not associated with a variety of people, it can be pretty excruciating, and in my case it was. I imagined that everybody knew more about how to behave and dressed better than I did. I probably went on wearing socks long after all the other girls were getting into silk stockings. I was very slow to adapt to the standard behavior of my peers.

Do you think your shyness may have been partially because you spent more time with adults than you did with peers?
Yes, I'm sure that it was. Except for my trips to Alabama in which I associated constantly with my peers, it was a pretty secluded life. Even in Alabama all of those were my kinfolks and a few of their friends, and they were people I knew very well. There was no such thing as a class of thirty children. That was not a part of my experience.

Jack Staples was a very handsome boy that all the girls thought was so attractive. Clayton Fields was just a big, tall, gangling, agreeable fellow as I remember. They were from Marshall. They were in a world apart as far as I was concerned. I would go with a crowd down to Caddo Lake with Dorris as our chaperone. We would all do things together like go swimming along with lots of turtles and a few snakes and maybe an occasional alligator, and have picnics. I suppose we explored every slough and bayou around there.

I decided I would like to be on the school newspaper, which was called the *Parrot*. I did write some articles which appeared in it. I think they had bylines.

Did you have any contact with either of the two black colleges there in Marshall, Wiley and Bishop?
There was a time when the president of Wiley College was the only resident of Marshall who had a PhD. I remember a vice president of the bank saying, "When he comes into the bank, I just call him Dr. So-and-so." As strange as this may seem today, there was a little problem then. One found it difficult to call blacks Mr. or Mrs. Smith or Jones. You had no hesitance at all if they were old and respected and longtime friends of your family in calling them Uncle Sam or Aunt Sarah or something like that, but you couldn't quite bring yourself to call them Mr. Jones or Mrs. Jones, which is laughable now, but a little sad. But this person was explaining that she always called him Dr. whatever it was; indeed he was a doctor.

ST. MARY'S

My lifelong friends began by the time I was about fifteen, approaching sixteen, and began to go off to St. Mary's. Emma Boehringer was a good friend of mine.[4] She had an older sister, Gene, who had gone out into the world and done exciting things. She'd come down to Austin and had a year, I think, at the University, and had gone to work in the Capitol for the then-chairman of the Railroad Commission, Mr. C. V. Terrell. They had a brother named Karl, who was one of my first dates, if you could call it that. We all paired up and went off and did silly things, going fishing and exploring what a taste of homemade beer or "white lightning" was like. That was in the days of Prohibition. I met Helen Bird at Marshall.

Let me ask you about your decision to go to St. Mary's.
Well, it was purely by chance. Helen Bird, as the daughter of an Episcopal minister, could, I'm sure, get a very favorable rate there. The tuition, however, was fairly high. It was a school that was at one time the rival of, and comparable to, a very well-known and splendid school, Hockaday. However, for some reason, St. Mary's was already descending when I got there and came to an end a year after I left—closed its doors. I left there in 1930, so the Depression may have been having an effect.

In any case, I did decide to go. My daddy made one of his rather unusual explorations to see what he thought of my decision. He drove up there and drove around the campus and stopped and talked to the headmistress and some of the people, as I recall, and came back and delivered a very negative view and said he just thought I would do a lot better to go to the university or someplace else, which only sealed my determination to go. He said, "All right, you absolutely can do what you want to." It was really one of the few times that he made an effort to discover what I was doing, and also one of the few times he gave a positive advice against doing it, and I didn't take it. Usually he was very much hands-off. In this case, having expressed himself, he then was hands-off.

Why was he opposed to it?
I think he sensed the fact that it was a dying institution and maybe it was also one of these excessively full-of-rules-and-regulations institutions. I expect that girls' schools everywhere were pretty rule ridden. You had to be chaperoned whenever you went anywhere, even shopping downtown. You could go across the street to the drugstore; they called that "our privilege." You were required to go to chapel every morning unless you were sick. They made no effort to make you become an Episcopalian, but it was a pretty hidebound school.

---

4. Also see Emma Boehringer Tooley Oral History Interview, 6/2/78, by Michael L. Gillette.

On the other hand, there were many good things that I got there. I got to see many other sides of life. One lived in a dormitory. I had as a roommate Helen Bird. Many of the girls there were the girls of wealth, whose families had had social standing throughout the state. There were a lot of debutantes. When they'd finish with St. Mary's, they'd make their debut. All of that had never been a part of my life at all, and I can't say that it made me yearn for it to be. But anyhow, I observed it; I saw that side of life.

The first real mental stimulus that I can remember was at St. Mary's, the first exciting times of learning. Of course, just learning how to read was the most marvelous key from the very beginning. But as far as getting excited by a teacher and having real philosophical explorations and arguments, that didn't happen until I got to St. Mary's. I found myself exposed to several good teachers. There were two ladies named Boyce, Little Miss [Helen A.] Boyce, who taught Latin, and Big Miss [Ethel] Boyce, which was a sort of a misnomer because Big Miss Boyce was quite thin. But she had a great presence; you knew at once that she was somebody. From her I learned a love of the English language and the right words.[5] She had a beautiful command of the English language and intense passion about the use of it and about training people to use words in the most effective way. She was always having us write themes.

Was it this English class or the several classes at St. Mary's that taught you to write well or to express yourself?
I think it certainly was a help; I'll always be grateful for being exposed to it. It also shows me what kind of a ripple effect a really talented teacher can have. I was there only two years, but I have remembered it ever since. Perhaps it was Miss Boyce, perhaps it was a later course in the university, but I remember in talking about the use of language, this teacher said, "Don't just say a man is cruel; walk him onto the stage and have him do a cruel thing. And be very sparse in the use of the verb 'to be.' Instead of saying, 'It was stormy,' saying, 'Thunder rolled across the heavens and crashed through the mountains,'" or anyhow, some much more colorful language than the constant use of the verb "to be."

I did take some domestic science and cooking and sewing. I liked cooking all right and came to the conclusion that anybody who could read could learn to cook. I didn't like sewing at all, never knew what I was sewing on. They finally just gave up and just said, "Sew from here to here." [*Laughter.*] I didn't know or care whether it was the hem or the sleeve, and I always wanted to find somebody

5. When asked by the Associated Press in 1968 to name the teacher who had influenced her the most, CTJ wrote that Ethel Boyce "more than any other teacher, made us want to capture the vivid world around us with words." CTJ to N. J. Wing, 10/8/68, White House Social Files, LBJ Library. Boyce, who held degrees from the University of Iowa and Bryn Mawr College, left St. Mary's after the 1928-29 school year. *Dallas Morning News*, 9/21/24 and 7/21/29.

else who could do it. After that course was over and out in the big world outside, I was going to find somebody else to do that for me.

You took French, too, there?
Yes, I did. I think a foreign language was required and that, too, is a good thing.

I discovered drama, and that, too, was a great addition to my life. We had some plays, and everybody pretty much had to be in them. I found myself playing the part of Falstaff, a jovial, fat, philosophic character in a Shakespearean play. I liked it because I was in costume and nobody knew who I was, so I could be completely somebody else. I was in several plays and liked it fine and just thought maybe sometimes I would try to go on and be in some more.

Your shyness didn't bother you here?
No, because you didn't have to be yourself. You were immediately somebody else, and often you had on makeup and certainly you had on a costume. I remember being in at least one other play, whose name I can't think of. But I discovered the theater in another way, too. The Dallas Little Theater has a long history of excellence, and the school would take us in a group to see some plays. I sometimes puzzle over their choices, but I remember seeing [Ferenc Molnár's *Liliom*]. It was later revived as *Carousel*. I saw at least a half a dozen plays a year. It whetted my appetite for them, and it has been a great resource for pleasure ever since.

One of the interesting experiences I had there with teachers was of different viewpoints. The world wasn't black and white with absolute truths and absolute rules, and oddly enough I came across that in Bible class. You were supposed to take Bible, but the teacher was an interesting woman who taught it from a rather unexpected vantage point in a church school, perhaps. I thought it was good because you emerged with just as much reverence and devotion for the Lord, but you also had a different viewpoint.

For instance, she described the people in the Old Testament as being a nomadic agricultural tribe in search of the reasons for life and death and the things that happened to them. You got the idea that God was their invention, their way to figure out why sometimes it was famine and sometimes prosperity. It was a different approach from the fundamental Baptist teachings that I discovered in Alabama where everything that it said in the Bible was absolutely pat. Incidentally, that fundamental Baptist teaching was on the side of my father's family and not on the side of my mother's family, who were much more exploratory and willing to look at religion in many forms.

Did you accept these new ideas readily?
Well, I found them interesting, and yes, I was glad to make them a part of my life. I wasn't sure what I thought. I was shopping around. But I certainly wasn't appalled or offended. I was interested.

I became an Episcopalian for the very good reason that if you are exposed to something repeatedly at a young age, it's likely to take. At St. Mary's we had to go to chapel every morning for thirty minutes. We came there as Methodist, Baptist, Episcopalians—I do not think there was a Catholic there. I think there were one or two Jews. I don't think [the school officials] proselytized among us to join. They did mention it, talk about the church, invite you, but they never pushed. I remember going to the University of Texas in September after getting out of Saint Mary's in June, and I missed something. There was some kind of a vacant spot, a vacuum, and I finally decided it really was that [experience of] going to chapel. So I started going to St. David's [Episcopal Church in Austin]. I don't know whether this was in 1931, or whether it took until 1932 for me to find out where the vacuum was. So I went down to St. David's and it suited me fine.

Did you feel like St. Mary's was a big step in your life? Here you were really away from home.
Yes, it was a big step, because it was so much more into the outside world. But it was just the same a walled world; very, very lonesome and very little contact with boys or men. You were eternally grateful to those few friends who would come and take you out to dinner. And, believe me, they had to come highly recommended by your family and with a letter or at least a phone call from your parent or guardian authorizing it. Gene Boehringer's sister Marie had married a big, jovial, kind man whom we called "Johnny" Johnson. They took us out to dinner a few times. Then, delightfully enough, Emily Crow became a friend of mine. She was a day student, and she lived about two blocks from the school in a big, rambling old house with a sister and two brothers, an absolutely pixie, delightful family. The house was full of books and old family possessions, and it was just the sort of family you could write a play about. They had a rich intellectual life, but their sense of values was just different from lots of folks. The household would be a little higgledy-piggledy, but interesting things would be going on in it.[6] One of the nicest things about them, they were so generous, so free and easy, about having us boarding students over for dinner or to spend the night or just for anything. The school thought that was fine because they were quite respectable Episcopalians.

Aunt Effie lived there in a nursing home?
She came up for a fairly lengthy period and stayed in a hospital there. She felt the need to go to a hospital somewhere, and then she probably chose that one because it would enable us to see each other several times a week.

---

6. Emily Crow's recollections of St. Mary's are found in Emily Crow Selden Oral History Interview, 1/10/80, by Michael L. Gillette.

Did you see much of Dallas?
A little bit, yes. With a teacher as a chaperone, we'd go down and shop, but I had absolutely no sense about clothes. I guess it's fortunate that we wore uniforms, because you couldn't vary from that. You did have a few clothes to come and go in, and maybe if you went out to dinner, you didn't have to wear a uniform then.

AUSTIN

I did have an interesting door open to me in April of my last year. I decided to go take a look at the University [of Texas], and I decided I would ride a plane down there. Commercial planes were pretty much in their infancy then. Nevertheless, I got on one in early April and went down to Austin. I was going to be met by and visit my friend Gene Boehringer. I rode down to Austin on this plane and arrived so nauseated I could hardly get off the plane. It was an experience, alas, that was oft repeated through the years. Airsickness is not uncommon, but it's awful. One eventually gets over it, but it took me many years.

But there opened up one of the most delightful weekends in my life. April is a divine month. The countryside was at its best, and Gene took me around to lots of places. I was seventeen, and the world was just beginning to open up to me. She got me a date with a newspaperman, Dawson Duncan. He was really very good-looking and filled a lot of the pictures of the romantic newspaperman. He was an excellent letter writer. I don't know whether I ever kept his letters or not. We did ride around and see the bluebonnets, and I am reasonably sure we must have gone on some picnics. I made up my mind right then I wanted to come to the university to school and never changed it.

Then we made plans for them to come back to Dallas and see me. "Them" consisted of Gene and Dawson, whom we called "Dunc," and another man. I don't know whether we had anyone else along; I think there were three of them. So they did [come to Dallas], having a misadventure of hitting a mule on the way. Anyhow, they finally made it. Then, by some rules certainly not approved by the school, I got out and did go and join them for dinner. [*Laughter.*] I'm sure I must have said I was visiting somebody else.

[The University of Alabama] may indeed have been my Aunt Effie's preference, because she was always fearful of me getting completely away from us sharing our life. All the time, of course, I was heading more and more in that direction. Although in the University of Texas, some of her Jefferson friends had a sister there. Aunt Effie went down and stayed with her for a month or so, and I would be in their home a great deal.

You stayed at Mrs. [Felix S.] Matthews' boardinghouse.
Yes. How I found it I do not recall, but there were a number of boardinghouses. At this time dormitories were few. There was Scottish Rite Dormitory; there was Grace Hall for Episcopal girls. By that time I had had my fill of anything that

sounded like a girls' school. The boardinghouses would have a limited number of girls, say from eight to twenty, depending on the space they had. Miss Matthews' was one of the very smallest. It was a big old white frame house at 301 West Twenty-First, which I later was told had been the home of the [Swante] Palm family, one of the early Austin residents of considerable prominence. Mrs. Matthews and her husband were doing it to help make their living during the Depression.

Roommates were absolutely a matter of chance, and by great good fortune I soon became crazy about my roommate; Nell Colgin was her name.[7] I think Nell was my first roommate, and there was a Florence Bammet from Port Arthur. Cecille Harrison became my second or third roommate. I was just crazy about every roommate I had.

Were these people that you roomed with and that lived there at Mrs. Matthews' also the people that you ran around with?
Yes. Pleasantly enough, it turned out that way. I somehow or another felt it was better just to take a chance than to make arrangements to try to get so-and-so to come live with me. If a good friend rooms with you, it would be very hard to attempt to change and get another roommate somewhere along the way, whereas if [you room with] an absolute stranger [when] you start out, within a short while you would have no difficulty in trying to shift your plans. But as it turned out, I never needed to shift mine because I liked them all.

Did your dad ever come up to Austin while you were there and visit?
I don't recall that he ever did, but he was a pretty good correspondent. He wrote me just about every week, and I would go home at least once a month. I did have a car, and I soon had that road memorized. My feeling is that I would have a new car, and it would more likely be a Chevrolet, a Ford, or some small car. Aunt Effie once in her lifetime did own a car, and it was a Buick. She never learned to drive it; I drove it. She did make some attempts and plans to, but it just turned out to be more than she could manage, really. I did indeed drive her car, and I'm sure it was bought new and did become old, because I daresay she would have kept it a good long while.

You pledged Alpha Phi sorority?
Yes, but only briefly. It was a chapter I don't really like to remember very well, because I wasn't really much of a joiner. I did get asked [to parties] by a number of [sororities]. When you first get there, you get asked. If any of [the sororities] think they might like you, you get asked. I went to several parties—Chi Omega,

---

7. Nell Colgin recounts sharing a room with CTJ in Nell Colgin Miller Oral History Interview, 10/4/78, by Michael L. Gillette.

Alpha Phi, Tri Delt, maybe a few Kappa. There comes a time when, if they decide that they want you, they all begin to congregate and give you the hotbox technique. They were very nice girls and very studious and all had good records, and perhaps that's one reason why they wanted me, because my high school records were good. As I recall, this didn't begin until after you'd been there four and a half months or your second term.

I did pledge it, but when I told my daddy about it, he said, "You mean it costs three hundred dollars?" or whatever it was, and this was the depths of the Depression. He said, "I think it's the biggest fool thing I ever heard of. Are you sure you want to?" I said, "Well, not if you think not," or something. There's a period in which you are a pledge, and then you get initiated. I decided this was one time there was no need in telling him yes, that was one of the things I was going to do.

The Alpha Phis doubtlessly regret it to this day.
Well, I feel bad about it. I should never have done it unless I was willing to stick to my [decision] with determination. He would have given in, but he thought it was foolish.

Were most of your friends independents, as opposed to sorority?
No, I had a lots of sorority friends. I soon discovered that although it was undoubtedly a help, you could have just as much fun as you wanted without it. Nell Colgin was a Pi Phi, and Nell was possibly my best friend for that first year. One of the other girls there at Miss Matthews' was a Chi Omega, and she did make an earnest attempt to get me into that later. But I knew if I had said no to the Alpha Phis, it wouldn't make any sense to bring up the issue again, so I didn't. Another one was a Tri Delt, and she was very nice to me, too, but once that bridge was crossed there's no need in going back over it.

I majored in history and minored in philosophy, of all things. I was very fortunate in both courses to have some extremely good professors. One was Dr. [Charles Wilson] Hackett, and he was a passionate teacher. He loved his subject, principally the history of South America and Mexico. He used to just really get mad that the histories of the United States were written as though they all began at Plymouth Rock and up there and the Anglo-Saxons coming to this country, when indeed Spaniards were here very early in Mexico and in St. Augustine, Florida. We had a lot of folks besides Anglo-Saxons on the rock-bound coast of New England and Virginia.

Were most of your other history courses British history or European history as opposed to American?
I had American history and British history over and over from high school to St. Mary's through the University of Texas. Oddly enough, the continent of Asia hardly existed after you got past the period way back there in ancient

history of civilization being born between the Tigris and the Euphrates. I studied Greece and Egypt and Persia a little bit, but from then on, Asia dropped out of existence in the school curriculum. I don't know why. And Africa, with the exception of Egypt, never made it in. That kind of ignorance is vast and very bad. It was only by chance that I stumbled into taking History of Mexico and South America. I was just looking through the catalog, and they were well presented and sounded enticing. And after all, Mexico was our neighbor, and this was our part of the world, so I just decided I'd specialize in that.

I did hear a great deal about Dr. Bob Montgomery,[8] because he was one of the wonderful, controversial, exciting, stimulating people on the campus that you just had to hear about. I went to at least one of his lectures, although I never had classes with him.

Did you take any other languages while you were at the university?
No. I persevered in French, but I can't say it was very fruitful, because it never was conversational, and it just has to be that way. The least fruitful course I ever took was chemistry. That seems a shame, too, because there's got to be something about chemistry that touches our daily lives and that is important to a homemaker or just somebody who's going to eat always. Chemistry must be more important than it ever was made to seem to me. It was the hardest course. It was the only thing in which I ever made a D. I did not flunk, because I don't think that was a permanent term grade. It may have been, but if so, I'd gotten a C+ one other time, and so I squeaked through. I did have two friends, a boy and a girl, who were terribly good at it, and they would help me.

Were there any other teachers or professors that you remember as being particularly inspiring or important to you?
Certainly DeWitt Reddick, who had great enthusiasm for his subject and for young people, made you want to write about the things around your hometown, the things that were a part of your life. I feel sure that suggestions [for stories to write about] must have come from him. I did write about or explore Captain [Roy Wilkinson] Aldrich, [J. H.] "Daddy" Walsh, Saengerrunde Hall, and Hamilton Pool.[9]

---

8. Robert H. Montgomery was a professor of economics.

9. DeWitt Reddick was a member of the journalism faculty for more than forty years, beginning in 1927. He later became the first dean of the School of Communication. Saegerrunde Hall was built by a singing group of German immigrants in the late nineteenth century. J. H. "Daddy" Walsh was a retired Southern Pacific Railroad official who became involved in Austin civic and philanthropic activities. Roy Wilkinson Aldrich was a Texas Ranger. Hamilton Pool is a natural pool west of Austin.

What about your experiences writing for the Daily Texan? *Did you do this when you were in the journalism school?*
Yes, and it was in Old B [Brackenridge] Hall, which was a great big old gothic, bat-ridden building, full of legends, much remembered by all the old news hands around the state. Old B Hall was torn down after I left, but I know it was in existence when I was first there.

When I first got there, the old Main Building was still standing. I think geology was taught there, and there was a museum of geological items, artifacts. There were a lot of classes taught there, but it was ancient, somewhat crumbling, and it really did have bats in it. It was torn down while I was there. A number of the old buildings were torn down, and they were soon engaged in this huge building program. In wintertime, the campus became a sea of mud with plank walks across it. There were lots of open spaces where there were wildflowers in the spring. It was much more open than it has become. Buildings have sprouted up on practically every available square foot, but there were lots of open spaces then.

What kind of stories did you do for the Daily Texan?
Feature stories. I did all sorts of assignments, but I preferred the feature stories because I would get to go and meet interesting characters.

I made a decision, having graduated with a major in history and a minor in philosophy in June of 1933 to continue on for another year, because I didn't have anything pressing that I needed to go home and do, and because I just loved the university and had a lot of fun there.

Was the decision to return to the university for a following year to pursue a journalism degree a difficult decision?
Not at all. It was a very relaxed approach to life. I was at a very happy time in my life, enjoying it, and I wasn't pressed financially. I was not pursued by ambition. I knew I was going to buckle down to some kind of way of making a living, although I always eventually just assumed I'd get married. But I rather liked the idea of doing something for a living for a brief time, five years or so. Through Gene Lasseter principally and through Dawson Duncan, and then in various ways, I met a lot of newspaper people. I found that they were plunged into the happenings of the day. They met the actors of the day. They really saw what was going on, and I liked the opportunities. I just thought I would like to sample that.

Did you enjoy the journalism curriculum?
Yes, I did. I don't remember too much about it except Dewitt Reddick and the who, when, where, why, what. I do remember Dr. Paul J[ennings]. Thompson, and I liked him. It seems to me I had several courses in advertising from him. I even remember one of the ads that I wrote. It went something like this: "Behind every product, a man," and I had Mr. Buick who was making Buick automobiles, and I wrote a lot of fine fiction about him. [*Laughter.*]

Were you torn between the inclination to study and the inclination to pursue other activities? Did you feel pressed?

No, not really pressed, because I always liked what I was studying, with the exception of chemistry and maybe of one or two things. So I really did them because I liked them.

Did you study quite a bit?

Yes. I was certainly not brilliant, but I found it easy to master most of the things I was working on. I made cum laude most terms, and one term I made magna cum laude.

"PICNICS WITHOUT FOOD"

For the first time in my life, I began to get a more balanced life of sparkling, entertaining things and dates, and a wide variety of friends, and all sorts of funny little moments. Somebody calls you up and asks you for a blind date. He's a friend of your good friend so-and-so. You say quickly to your roommate over your shoulder, "Get out the *Cactus* [yearbook] and look his picture up." She comes back and she says, "He looks like he's about five feet high and kind of fat," or maybe she comes back and says, "He's real good-looking, and he's into everything." You would just talk along until you could get a little input from whether you better say "yes" or "no" to a blind date. Sometimes they were very funny and sometimes very, very nice.

Did your friends study as much as you did?

Not necessarily. Nell studied just as much as she had to to get along; that was all. She was an absolutely delightful girl and very zany. For instance, we were talking about our fathers one time, and I mentioned that my father was a very strong man and that one time he had lifted a bale of cotton. She looked at me with her big round eyes and said, "Oh, but cotton is so light." [*Laughter.*] But a bale is five hundred pounds no matter what way you look at it. Cecille, too, was quite a zany character. For instance, her mother would send her a check, and she would say, "I'm sure you need some clothes. Go down and get what you need." Cecille went down and got a riding jacket, some boots, a derby, and quite a nice fancy ring, none of which things did she need terribly much.

We had lots of just good fun. There was a place called Dillingham's Pasture that all the young people used to go to on picnics. One of my first discoveries when I got here was that if three boys and three girls went off for a picnic in Dillingham's, there wasn't necessarily anything to eat, which was a great disappointment to me. It was likely to be a tub full of beer iced down, or there might, at most, be some cheese and crackers. But my idea of a picnic was more like fried chicken and sandwiches.

You would rent horses at Steiner's and go horseback riding quite a bit.
Yes, for several years during our life there that was something we did a great deal and enjoyed. It was the only time in my life I was really proficient in riding a horse, and I enjoyed it and got a lot of pleasure from it. I can remember watching the spring change to summer, and the cornfields that we'd go by come out of the ground and grow up tall. Gene Lasseter had a wide acquaintance in the Texas legislature and among the lobbyists as well. One of her friends, Mr. Hiram King, was a lobbyist for Sinclair Oil. He used to take her to dinner, and he got into the habit of taking her young school friends. He was a nice man, and he liked to ride. Sometimes he'd rent horses and ask us young folks if we'd like to go with him, which we just about always did.

I had some zany friends, too, who were young men: F. D. Brown and Gordon Abney. I wouldn't say I had dates with them, because they were quite companionable, more like brothers. They were the people you would call if your car was broken down and you wanted to go out to Anderson's Mill and look for bluebonnets or see if you could find an old log cabin or just explore. I really did have quite a range of friends. Each spring there would be some new young man that I would see a lot of and be terribly interested in, but they really never amounted to much. Dawson Duncan didn't last very long in my life. I guess he was really probably more sophisticated than I was. I suppose he soon decided that I was too young and childish for his interests. My cousin Winston Taylor would always have me over to his ATO fraternity house for Sunday dinner once or twice a year.

I went to a lot of the [dance parties] and sometimes had a real good time. Sometimes I was horrified to look around the room and not see anybody I knew and be gripped in this feeling of, "Will anybody ever break?" and "Am I going to have to dance all night with this one young man?" and "What will he think?" I can't say that I was ever an extraordinarily popular girl; I wasn't. But I had lots of friends and lots of fun.

Did your discussions and activities with friends supplement what you learned in the classroom?
Oh, I think it did! I think it did, and particularly in experience. Also, my love of adventure in the outdoors was pretty much a part of my life there. This is beautiful country around here, and then it was a great deal more so. Out on Bull Creek Road and walking up Barton Springs Creek and out to Anderson's Mill there were wonderful things to explore, and Hamilton Pool was such fun. We went to all those places. If it was springtime, there were wildflowers around. Just about every weekend we'd find some new clear stream with the chalky cliffs and take off our shoes and go wading. This could be just three or four girls or it could be dates or it could be these two boys who were just like fellow adventurers in the world.

I used to have dates with an odd young man named Wayne Livergood,[10] a darling boy, blonde and also zany. He reminded me of one of the Marx Brothers.

---

10. Wayne Livergood was killed in the Pacific during World War II.

But he was a gentle, sweet person. Nobody you could be serious about, but just one of those characters that you'll always remember. He had a bright red touring car. He didn't seem to have much definite family, but he always seemed to have plenty of money. He was very generous with it, and he would help out all sorts of people. One night I went out with him and some more people to Dillingham's Pasture, and something got the matter with his car. It apparently wasn't going to run, or we weren't going to be able to get back. So we looked and looked all over Dillingham's big old pasture and found another bunch of young people who had a car, but there were about six of them in it. They said, "Okay, we'll take the girls back. We'll crowd up, but we just can't carry more than eight or nine." We were all sitting on each other's laps and laughing fit to kill, and so we said, "Good-bye, you all. Spend the night." So Wayne and one or two other boys spent the night.

The next day, in the afternoon, Wayne came around to see me and said, "Okay, come on. We're going back out to Dillingham's." I said, "What happened to you last night?" And he said, "Well, we woke up the next morning. We just lay down in the car and went to sleep. When we woke up the next morning, we were hungry as bears, and we just didn't have a thing to eat. So we started walking and came to what was a tumbledown shack, where a bunch of people [had] just moved onto Mr. Dillingham's property." They were just living there, squatters. They had a few mangy chickens, and they caught one and killed and cooked it and provided those boys some breakfast. So Wayne just loaded the car up with all sorts of groceries. I remember oatmeal and a side of bacon, which was fitting enough. I also remember snuff. He had noted that they used snuff, so he was taking them some of what they wanted.

Did the university help you overcome some of your shyness?
It certainly did, and it made me much more outgoing. I can't say that it completely rid me of it, but it certainly made me more assured, more aggressive in tackling the world and trying to find out just what my thing is, just what can I do.

Do you think you felt more confident after you went there?
Oh, yes, lots more, lots more. I had lots of interesting trips, too, particularly Gene and I did, and Wayne. We were always doing something, making a wacky trip of some sort. There would always be a group of people. We'd go down to the border and spend the night and walk the streets of Nuevo Laredo and of Laredo.

One time Gene Lasseter and I went to Longhorn Cavern. I'm not even sure it was named at that time. It was certainly not open to the public. It was just at a point of being explored by the Parks Department of the state of Texas. Through Gene and with some of her friends, we went to Burnet and out to the cavern and went through it, sometimes on our hands and knees and sometimes standing up. It's quite a big cavern and has its store of legends about bandits hiding out in it or being a place where Indians used to live there, or retreat there in warfare. There were several men with us. Somebody with a lantern would be in front, because there was no such thing as steps or electric lights. We did take a picture, and it appeared later on in the brochures of the park service as "Burnet High School Girls Exploring Cavern." Gene and I got a big laugh out of that.

When we finished with the cave, we went to a road gang, of all places. A "chain gang" is what the old expression used to be. I don't think they had on chains. They were convicts who were working on the roads of Texas at that time. I really think somebody connected with Texas highways must have taken us through on this adventure. We went and had dinner with all the convicts and the one or two men who had taken us on this trip. It was all very cheerful and convivial. We'd all line up right along with them and get our plates. Everybody was laughing.

Captain Aldrich was a very interesting man and another one of the unorthodox adventures in my life. Gene knew him as she knew all sorts of diverse people, politicians, business people, and journalists. He was an old man, but he was a character. He'd been a Texas Ranger. He was not married. He had been married; I expect probably it was a divorce. I don't know; it was long in the past. He had a big old rambling house and enough animals that it amounted to a zoo. It was not a huge zoo by any means, but a couple of dozen, among them some wolves. I wonder now whether they were Texas wolves, which, as a matter of fact, have almost disappeared from the scene. He also had some of the prettiest countryside—rolling hills with lots of bluebonnets on them, huge live oaks, a stream. It was great walking country and exploring country. He had a library full of books [shelved in] stacks almost like in a regular library. There were history books, and a lot of Texana, and a whole shelf full of erotica. I remember getting one of these books out and looking through it with my eyes out on stems. He came around the corner, and he took the book out of my hand and smiled and closed it up and said, "That one's not for you."

PLACES, POLITICS, AND ISSUES

I would go down and watch the legislature a lot with Gene. I became very much a frequenter of that beautiful old Capitol building and very interested in it. She had friends who stayed at a marvelous old house which looked like a castle. It was the property of the Austin Women's Club, but they took in business and professional women and gave them a room there. I don't think they boarded, but they had rooms there. She had an occasional friend who stayed there, and maybe Gene herself may have had a room there for some time. I was there as a visitor a good many times, and it is a very romantic old house.

Do you recall being actively involved in any political issue on behalf of any candidate during this period?
No, not really. One of the young men that I went with and had liked very much was studying premed. He was a younger brother of Senator [Earle B.] Mayfield.[11] His name was Jack Mayfield. I used to hear him talk about it a good deal. I became mildly interested therefore. This was the Depression, when farms and ranches all over the country were being taken over by banks. People were being expelled from property that they had worked on for years because they couldn't continue their payments. It was a pretty frightening period. The state of Minnesota passed a mortgage moratorium [that] said you couldn't foreclose anymore. You had to just stand still for six months, even if they weren't paying you. I presume this was addressed to banks that held the mortgages. In some class we were assigned to write how we felt about it one way or the other. I remember taking the side that I thought it was a good thing. I just felt that the unrest and anger and bitterness might well up into something that would be serious business for all the rest of us, no matter whether we had a mortgage on our place or not, and also because it was cruel hard on a lot of those folks.

I really became aware of [the Depression]. It didn't come home to me in a frightening fashion, but I remember when the banks closed. I remember a phone call from my daddy, most unusual, and I remember getting a letter from him with a dollar bill enclosed, which was really fantastic. He just said, "The banks are closed. I don't know how long it's going to last. I think everything is going to be all right, but I just hope you have some money." He always made a habit of putting everything in the bank, practically day by day, and keeping a very small amount of money in the store. Everybody there was in the same boat. I remember the Paramount Theatre did a very wise thing; they just said, "We're going to show the movies, and it's free. Everybody come." We all just felt so good toward them. It just happened that I had bought myself a meal ticket just a day or two before at Wukasch's, so at least I could eat for about fourteen more dinners. My recollection is that I got breakfast at Mrs. Matthews'.

What did you plan to do with your life at this stage?
I had given it considerable thought with no positive, definitive answers. I had had enough dates with newspaper people, enough contact with them, to find them interesting and to think that they were always where something was happening and that conversation around them was lively and changing. It intrigued me. I thought I might get a job in the newspaper world somewhere.

---

11. Earle B. Mayfield served in the United States Senate from 1923 through 1928.

I understand that you were interested in becoming a drama critic for a New York news-paper. Does that ring a bell?
No, but it would have suited me admirably, because I was just really quite crazy about the theater and I'd like to write. As for what I expected to do with my future as a way of making a living, I began to think seriously about it about my third year there.

Too, I had taken enough courses in education where I could get my foot in the door as a teacher. It was what was called a second-grade certificate. I did not really have any drive to become a teacher, but I thought it might be very interesting to get a job teaching in some romantic place like Hawaii or Alaska. I did not want to teach in Karnack or Lee, next door. But the idea of the travel was intriguing enough to make me think I might do that. I'd even gone so far as to find out the name of the delegate [from Alaska Territory, Anthony J.] Dimond. I had written him a letter to inquire about the possibility, but I never really wrote and applied for a job.

I took a course in typing and shorthand, which I had a moderate capability in. I was never really good. But I must say that the shorthand has served me well throughout life, because I could at least make a brief résumé of a telephone conversation or a happening and tell Lyndon about it later on when it became useful, or make that kind of notes in my own date book for myself. Particularly when I was doing my White House diary and I'd have some fascinating encounters at a state dinner and I was too tired to talk into my machine for forty-five minutes or an hour, I could at least jot down in my date book three interesting things that happened.

Could you see yourself as a journalist? Is this what you intended to do after you got out?
Among those three things, teaching or being a secretary or being a journalist, I just in a dilatory fashion thought I would make a choice and see where fate led me. I was not dedicated to anything or driven by anything. I did always intend to get married sometime. That was just what happened to people. I also intended to spend most of a year at home working on our old house, for which I had a great deal of respect and affection, in trying to establish a somewhat more comfortable and orderly home life for my daddy.

You're quoted as saying that "all the doors of the world were suddenly swung open to me" at the university.
I was very grateful to it and for the chance of going there. It did indeed enlarge my life in every way—the variety of people and the regular feast of knowledge [that] was open to me. I can't say that I profited from it all as much as I should. I enjoyed my courses in philosophy. I learned something there that has since entirely deserted me, I'm afraid, and that is the kind of discipline that will keep you reading and concentrating on a purely intellectual subject. Now my mind just wanders if it is not an exciting whodunit, and that's bad.

3

A Whirlwind Courtship

Lady Bird left Austin armed with degrees in history and journalism, a teaching certifi-cate, and secretarial skills, but her plan to spend a year in Karnack remodeling the Brick House allowed her forestall a career decision. Her father's graduation present of a cruise to New York and Washington, DC, gave her a glimpse of the city that would be her home for most of the next thirty-four years. Although her friend Gene Lasseter encour-aged her to introduce herself to Lyndon Johnson while she was in Washington, another young man occupied her attention at the time. But her first encounter with her future husband would come only three months later in Austin.

A TRIP TO NEW YORK AND WASHINGTON

My daddy gave a trip to New York as a graduation present. He was a dear about giving me things and doing things for me that were rather expensive in those years and in my milieu, but I think maybe the idea did come from me. Cecille Harrison, my roommate in college, was all for the idea.[1] She's one of those excitable, amusing, capricious, thoroughly delightful young women—and also sometimes maddening. Cecille and I thought that to travel on a boat would be the most glamorous way in all the world to take this trip. In those days there was a tour boat that went from Galveston to New York. It took six days. The pictures of the state rooms looked lordly and sumptuous, and the whole thing just sounded so romantic. This was the depths of the Depression; the prices were so cheap.

Why did you pick New York and Washington?
New York was the most fascinating town in the whole world, and also I knew a young man in Washington, Victor McCrea. He had gone to work up there. I think his uncle, who was an assistant postmaster general and a man of

---

1. Cecille Harrison's account of the trip is in her oral history. Cecille Harrison Marshall Oral History Interview, 2/19/76, by Michael L. Gillette.

considerable substance, had gotten him a job. He was writing me back about the city, and he said he'd be my guide when I came.

Gene [Boehringer Lasseter] had a fondness for getting people together. She liked Lyndon very much. They had some dates, but mostly in just camaraderie of mutual interest. She had been a good friend of his father's. She told me I ought to meet this young man, and she was going to write him that I was coming to Washington. She wrote down his name and address on a slip of paper, and I think perhaps his telephone number too, and put it in my purse and said, "Now you take that out and you call him when you get there. He's going to be expecting you." I never did take it out the whole time and did not intend to, because I hadn't met him and I had plenty else to do.

We drove my car to Galveston. A big storm came up on the way, just rain, rain, lashing rain. We wondered if we were going to get there. We put the car in a parking garage, and my recollection is we went up on the roof of the Rice Hotel and had dinner and lived it up, felt so grown-up and sophisticated. I think the boat sailed the next morning. I remember how high the waves were lashing up on the sides of the boat when we got on board. I was kind of scared.

When we got to our room, it was tiny! We had to take a choice of either putting all Cecille's luggage in there or of keeping the one chair that was in there. So we got rid of the chair. Cecille traveled with more luggage than anybody conceivably needed. She was scatterbrained, but delightful, and we just had a marvelous time.

There were some friends on board. M. D. Bryant from San Angelo and his wife were along, and they had the best suite on the boat and shared it with us a number of times. "Come down and have a drink and let's all go to dinner together," or "We're going to have a party and invite some more people." There was a middle-aged widow from Pampa who had a daughter about our age. We quickly made friends, and we just did all sorts of lively things together. I feel sure Cecille fell in love going up and in love with somebody else coming back. I don't remember that I did. Going up, Cecille must have stayed up all night and I nearly all night, because I think we reached New York and docked shortly after sunrise. We wanted to see the sunrise over the city.

When we got to New York we stayed at the Taft Hotel on this marvelous tour rate. Some of my East Texas friends would have said it was a "wagon yard." It was right downtown where all the big lights came on all around. It's just about at Broadway in the theater district. We considered ourselves perfectly safe and we were.

Mr. Hiram King had written some of his friends up there to take these two young girls out. They asked us to come to a party. This time we were a little concerned. We didn't know whether we wanted to meet two perfectly strange men or not. When we looked at the address and saw it was Park Avenue, we decided we had to go. So we went. It was glamorous and lived up to our expectations. Another friend of mine, Emily Crow, had asked her uncle to ask some of his friends to have us out. That time we really got into quite a lively political argument, because this man had an absolutely bitter opinion of President Roosevelt. He was a wealthy man. I think we may have left in a huff. I learned something about the extremes of political life.

This tour also included going to a nightclub. Our eyes were out on stems; we had a great time. We were not the least bit apprehensive about going to a nightclub. There was a person there named Nils T. Granlund, who was quite the toast of that day.[2] I think the word one used then was *soigné*. We went up on top of the Empire State [Building]; we went to several shows. For the first and only time ever in my life, I went to an aquarium. We took two marvelous bus trips, uptown and downtown. The bus going uptown was the double-decker, and we rode up top. There was a man who called out the places that you were seeing. Many great houses along an elegant downtown part of the city were still standing in 1934. There were fabulous houses that belonged to such people as the Rockefellers and the Astors. [The tour guide] would have exciting stories about each one and often exaggerated stories that he'd throw in about a few movie stars here and there and where they lived and some tales of their love affairs.

Then we went down in the dreadful part, the really skid row part of town. We'd see people huddled on the sidewalk, clutching a bottle or asleep or raggedy. Of course, this was June and it wasn't as miserable as it probably was in January, but it was an eye-opener.

Had you seen that kind of poverty before?
Never, never. Not like that. We kept on seeing signs up in a window that said "Loft to let," and I wondered, "Why on earth all these lofts?" and "Who wants to rent a loft anyway?" and "What would you do with a loft?" I was later told that that is where people did sewing. You would get a very small sum for a garment, and some entrepreneur would rent a loft and get ten or twelve women or children of age enough, let us hope. The garment making was terribly low-paid labor, doing a tedious, repetitive job. That was an eye-opener to me too.

We went through Wall Street, and I remember how impressed I was. I always loved, loved waterfronts and harbors, and we went up and down the streets where the big boats came and docked. That was one of the most fascinating things that I did.

Did you have an urge to live in New York?
None whatsoever. But my eyes were out on stems, and I was very excited, took it all in.

---

2. Nils Theodore Granlund was a producer who operated a series of nightclubs.

IN WASHINGTON, DC

My friend, Victor McCrea, had suggested that we take rooms in a hotel named the Chastleton on Sixteenth Street. Once more the rooms were relatively inexpensive, but the hotel was impressive and big. Victor took me [to lunch] in the garden of the Carlton Hotel. I believe the little area is still there, but I don't think lunch is served there anymore. It was elegant then, and it's elegant now. It's one of my favorite places. He took me to a place called the Cotton Club. It was sort of Dixieland music.

One of the young men that Vic lived with had a sister. His somewhat older sister had come [to Washington] and gotten an apartment. Vic had moved in and invited a couple of roommates, and this young woman had quite a household over which she presided. All these young people were there together. They invited me over, and I think I spent a night there. I had a meal or two with them. It was a way of life that's [gone].

I remember very distinctly going through the Supreme Court building. It had just been finished. There it stood in white splendor, just a majesty of a building. It was [in a state of] slight confusion of winding up a job before anybody has moved in. Cecille never believed in signs that said "no entrance" or anything like that. There may not have even been such a sign. We found ourselves walking around in the interior of that building with nobody to stop us. We went through the judges' chambers, and she sat in the seats and so did I! We noticed that several of the chairs were different heights, because each of the "nine old men" that was going to move in very soon had a favorite chair more or less suited to his comfort. They had been men of considerable tenure at that point, as I recall, and different statures and sizes. Nearly all of those chairs were different.

I remember going through the Library of Congress, which was the most ornate building I had ever seen and is still one of the most ornate Italian Renaissance architecture on the inside. We drove by all the embassies. I was very much impressed by them. I thought it was a glittering life.

My father had a woman friend from his very rural beginnings in Autauga County. She was perhaps somebody he dated in his youth who had married a man who achieved a certain eminence. They lived in Washington in an apartment on Connecticut Avenue. They asked me to come to a cocktail party, and there I met a congressman. I remember writing my father a postcard about it. I really thought, "Gee, this is exciting." I immediately liked it. I thought it was intriguing. It never occurred to me that I would return, but I liked it.

Cecille and I went back to New York the day before the boat was going to sail. It was going to sail at some very early hour. They cautioned us to be sure and get there not later than nine o'clock. It took a long time to get down there to the dock. So I packed all my things, and just saying over my shoulder, "All right, Cecille, hurry, hurry, hurry. We've got to leave at such and such a time!" She wasn't ready. She had innumerable amounts of clothes. I patted my foot. I waited awhile. She wasn't ready. I was mad as I could be, and I said, "Cecille, I hope you miss the boat. I'm going!" So I got in a taxi with my luggage and went on out and got on the boat. A lot of the people were there, but not nearly all of them. Gradually all began to come on. About an hour and a half after the time they were supposed to sail, here came Cecille blithely up the [ramp]. A few minutes later they left. It never occurred to her, though, that it was real and that she should have been there at the regular time. Once more, we had a delightful trip back. I really loved that trip.

"SOMETHING ELECTRIC"

Did you have any idea of where you would be at the end of the summer?
I always had thought I should stay at home one year—that was the limit I gave it in my mind—and work on the Brick House and make it more comfortable and habitable and hopefully more gracious. I wanted to see if I could get a servant who was better trained and who would give my daddy more of a variety of meals and take care of him a little better. I just wanted to be at home for one year for him and also to teach myself how to do some of those things with the house.

Was this something that he had expressed an interest in having you do?
Not at all, not at all. In fact, I'm not even sure how welcome it was at first, because he was a very independent man and he was so used to being alone. I'm sure he had his own lady friends, but they were not a part of his domestic life.

Was the remodeling your idea?
Entirely. But once more, he let me do it and was glad to pay for it. He probably had less ambitious ideas than I had. If I had stayed there that whole year, I would have learned a lot, and I would have done a vastly better job. As it was, after I got back in July, I began to look around for an architect. I think we must have started probably in September. I didn't do enough study. I was not educated enough in it. I had a great old house at my disposal. If I had persuaded my father, and if I had learned more about it and raised our sights as far as the amount of money to be spent, quite great things could have been done with the house. Instead, I'm afraid we did at least some wrong ones.

It was red brick. We painted it a buff color with a white trim around the windows. That was often done to an old colonial house, particularly in Virginia, I'm told. The architect, whom I got in Shreveport, convinced me that it was a good thing to do. I really think we should have probably left it red brick and put on the proper size and scale of white shutters, because the windows were too narrow. Dorris [Powell] tells me that when my father bought it, it had great big sixteen-light windows. That means sixteen panes, big windows, but that they did not have the weights in the side. They were the early construction where you just had to raise them up by dint of considerable muscle power. So as an improvement, it was considered then, my daddy had put in weights where you could really raise them very easily, and to do that required narrowing them. And then, oh dear, I don't know whether it was I that did the sacrilegious thing of covering up those wide floorboards, with the very primitive nails in them, with hardwood or not. We did a nice job of painting it. We did many good things and some bad ones.

I learned a good deal about buying and comparative values and shopping around. My father, having several stores, could get things wholesale. I pretty much always had to come back to the places where he could get them wholesale, which were limited, but yet good ones. I did [have] a definite sense of satisfaction. I do think I improved the menus and the service. Daddy noticed it and liked it and was just amazed. He didn't know anybody was ever going to try to take care of him like that. My mind soon got so absorbed in Lyndon that I didn't do enough. I didn't set my sights high enough. I didn't follow through enough.

Hugo Kuehne, the [Austin] architect I went to see, was a good friend who had an office in the Littlefield Building. He must have advised me to get one closer to home and probably even recommended this one in Shreveport, which was just about forty miles from our house. Gene and I would always get together as often as we could think up a good reason. She was Mr. C. V. Terrell's very trusted secretary and had been for some years. I think I just went into Mr. Terrell's office. That was one of the great old offices in the Capitol, an impressive office with high ceilings. And Lyndon walked in. So she went on a lot about "Here I've been trying to get y'all introduced all this time," and "I'm so glad," and told each one of us a lot about the other one. I'm not sure whether [Dorothy Muckleroy] was in the office or not.[3] Lyndon had already made a date with her. My memory is that he asked Gene and me, and possibly Dottie was along with us, to go and have a drink. And we did. We had a pleasant little hour, but he already had a date with Dorothy. So he asked me to have breakfast with him the next morning.

In front of the others?
I don't remember that, but I know he did. I wasn't quite sure I wanted to.

Do you remember his initial conversation with you after you were introduced?
No, I don't remember anything precise. I know there was something electric going, that he did ask me to have breakfast with him the next morning, and that I was unsure whether I wanted to or not and didn't call to make it firm. I started by to see Hugo Kuehne, whose office was next door to the Driskill

---

3. Dorothy Johnson Muckleroy was a young widow whose husband had been killed in a gas explosion in Monahans, Texas. Gene Lasseter's recollections of this encounter appear in Eugenia Boehringer Lasseter Oral History Interview, 3/10/81, by Michael L. Gillette.

[Hotel], and there was Lyndon, sitting in the dining room on the other side of this big plateglass window where I was just walking past. He looked up and flagged me down. He was there waiting for me. I don't know whether psychologically all the time I meant to go or not. It was a near miss. I'm not sure whether I said I'd be back in ten minutes and went up to see the architect or whether I then had breakfast and went up to see the architect, but one or the other. It's really a bit vague.

After breakfast and after the architect, we did get in his car and ride and ride and ride. He did a great deal of talking of a surprising sort of nature for me. He told me all sorts of things about himself, and not the least bit in a bragging way but just factual things about the jobs he'd had, just a brief history of his life. He was explicit about how hard it had been to get through school and how it was a struggle for his parents to try to get the rest of the children through school. [He told] what his job was, and he was really burning up with excitement about his job. He said he was planning on getting into law school. I believe he told me then that he was at night school at [Georgetown].

How was he different from the other young men that you knew at this point? Was there anything distinctive about him that struck you right off?
Well, he came on strong, and he was very direct and dynamic. I didn't know quite what to make of him.

Did you sense that magnetism?
I did, quite clearly. I do believe before the day was over he did ask me to marry him, and I thought he was just out of his mind. I'm a slow, considered sort of person generally and certainly not given to quick conclusions or much rash behavior.

Were you still riding around in the car when he proposed?
We were. We rode around all day long. I knew Austin much better than he did. The Capitol was just about the main thing he knew or was interested in. We did drive around to some of my favorite haunts, which were the lovely little country roads around Austin where there were these clear streams running over the white rocks and the chalky limestone outcroppings. I think we went out Anderson Mill Road. It was exciting. It was intensely exciting. Also a little bit frightening because I was far from sure I wanted to know him any better.

He proposed on that first day?
I do believe it was. It sounds absolutely too outrageous, but he has said so many times himself, and I think he was correct.

I've read that when he proposed you didn't say yes and you didn't say no.
No, I didn't. I just sat there with my mouth open, kind of. [*Laughter.*]

Did he seem more serious in general?

Yes, he seemed more serious about his job, about his plans for the future, about his life, about me. He had a lot of exuberance, but it certainly was not the exuberance of a youngster.

Was he fun to be with that first day?

I wouldn't call it fun. I would call it exciting. Also, I think he was trying to be very fair, too, because I remember at one time he said something like this: "I want you to know you're seeing the best side of me, just the best side of me." I think that was when he was getting serious and wanting to warn me that—[*Laughter*].

Did he also inquire at great length about you?

Oh, a great deal! All about my father and my life and when my mother died—because he knew a little bit about me from Gene—what I liked, what I wanted to do.

Did he seem surprised that your plans for your own future were not more definite?

Not exactly surprised, but I gathered that he thought I just better start taking them in hand. The schoolteacher aspect of him was very often in evidence in his life.

He asked me to go and meet his mother and father and drive on down to meet his boss. I, feeling like the moth in the flame and not at all sure I wanted to be a part of any of that, did go, and very uncertainly. That night I told Gene I didn't know whether I would go or not. I think she was both anxious for me to go and a little concerned about me going, too.

She was promoting this?

She was promoting it up to a point, but I think it was going a little faster than she had anticipated and perhaps a little more seriously than she had anticipated. [*Laughter.*]

Did you start the next morning for San Marcos?

Yes, he came by and picked me up. I was hesitant and unsure, but I knew that I didn't want to say no and walk out of his life. We went to see his mother and father. They lived in quite a modest house. I think we met Lucia, Birge, and Josefa. I think Rebekah was already at a job in Washington.[4]

Were the parents expecting you?

I think he had called them, but he had probably given them all of an hour's notice. His mother seemed a little apprehensive. She and I were in some ways

---

4. Rebekah, Josefa, and Lucia were Lyndon Johnson's sisters. Birge Alexander was Lucia's husband.

somewhat alike, because she was afraid her first born, her chief dependent, her dearest loved one, was getting taken in by somebody. I don't know what he told her, really, but I think she sensed that he might be in a serious frame of mind about somebody she didn't know enough about.

What were your first impressions of her?
That she was very much a gentlewoman who had had trials and a lot of work and that she was intelligent and gracious. Life had not made her way as comfortable and easy as might have been expected.

What was his father like?
Mr. Johnson was much older than his years. He had really taken a beating from the Depression and from an earlier depression, too, in 1922. Probably the last twelve years of his life he had been under severe economic pressure, whereas he had enjoyed much more affluent years before that.

Did he seem closer to either parent than the other?
Yes, I think he was actually closer to his mother, although he was more like his father.

But he had some of his mother in him. He had a strong filial quality for both of them, both his obligation to take care of them and to respect them and to love them and just a very real liking [for] them as people, separate and apart from filial regard.

We did stay an hour or more. I remember, too, noticing at least one of his sisters, Josefa, regarded me with an interested eye, like, "What are you doing here, young lady? What are your ideas about my brother?" I remember thinking, "Oh, I just wish I could reassure you, dear lady. I have no idea of taking your [brother] away from you. Be calm!" But I didn't, because I wouldn't be that presumptuous.

Did you feel that his mother also had some concern here?
Yes, I did.

Did she quiz you?
Oh, good heavens, no. She was always the most perfect lady. She was never the least bit pushy in expressing either affection or annoyance. She was a very civilized person and really an elegant person.

Did you travel around San Marcos and see the campus?
Oh, yes. He told me a lot about the campus. We didn't travel around it much, but he just began filling me with stories about San Marcos and his life there from the first time I laid eyes on him.

We went on down to Corpus Christi and stayed at a hotel. I might as well say there was a certain apprehension on my part when I went up to my hotel room, and Lyndon was very long in saying good-bye. But I got the door shut all right. [*Laughter.*] I think, really, he was relieved.

He took me out to see his boss the next day and his boss's mother [Alice Gertrudis King Kleberg]. The King Ranch was one of the most impressive places I had ever seen. I have never seen it since, and I hope I will some day. It was a great house, impressive, rather overpowering, and so was Mrs. Kleberg. I was a bit in awe of her, not exceedingly—I was at ease enough—but she was a bit awe inspiring. She was really the aging duchess. But she was very crazy about Lyndon. This was her son's secretary, but he was more than that. He did a lot of things for her son. He handled the finances. My impression was that Mr. Bob [Robert Justus Kleberg Jr.], who ran the ranch and made the money and handled the money, gave his brother his portion of it carefully. It was up to Lyndon to pay the bills and do the bookkeeping and see that it didn't get all squandered, which got him into a certain amount of disfavor from time to time with Mr. Kleberg's wife and children. It was not easy to handle. In return for the confidence and respect and affection that Mrs. Kleberg had for him, she would do nice things for him. He told me once that she sent him a suit every Christmas, a nicer suit than he had ever had. In fact, that was the beginning of his taste for good clothes, I expect. [*Laughter.*]

She was very affable. She seemed to like me a lot. When somebody took me around to show me some more of the house, I noticed she and Lyndon were having an earnest conversation. Lyndon told me afterwards and told innumerable people that she had told him that this was the one he ought to marry. I think she had told him this before he told her that this was the young woman that he was going to marry.

Did you meet Congressman [Richard] Kleberg?
I did, and he was one of the most delightful people I have ever met. I came to know him as exactly the other side of his brother Bob. Bob was tough and strong and just work, work, work was his thing, running the ranch and making the money. Mr. [Richard] Kleberg told the most wonderful stories. He was a great raconteur. He liked to play the guitar. He spoke Spanish as well as any native. He liked to sit out on the front porch with the ranch hands as the sun came up and drink coffee and trade tales with them. He was perfectly content to let Lyndon handle a lot of his congressional work and take a great deal of the initiative and also cover the district and do a lot of his politicking for him. He enjoyed that, but not a steady day-after-day diet. He liked to play golf, and he would give Lyndon a rather extraordinary amount of running room in the office.

People have said that LBJ was the congressman for all intents and purposes.
It became my observation, yes, which was a wonderful learning experience for Lyndon. It did not detract from the charm and interest of this man, but grinding work was not his thing. He was more of a poet and a philosopher. I guess you

would have called him a playboy. I don't know that that word was around then. Lyndon was just crazy about him, and he was, I think, about Lyndon. He wasn't terribly serious, in my opinion. Of course he was always the boss, and Lyndon knew that and respected that but used every bit of opportunity to learn and expand and act. Loyalty, from the very beginning of his life, and this is something his father taught him, was spelled in capital letters and was the keystone of any job you handled. He certainly always had it for everybody he worked with.

The next afternoon we started driving back. I think we might have gone back by Austin. Lyndon was just about to start back to Washington because he was going to register in night law school. Although I don't know whether Congress was in session or not, the office was open and doing business. Somebody had to be there. I asked him to come by the Brick House and meet my daddy. We did several of those trips by car together. I don't know whether I went on home ahead and waited for him or whether we actually did come together. I have a recollection of him gathering up his secretary, Gene Latimer,[5] and also Malcolm Bardwell, who was secretary to Maury Maverick, and them coming along behind us in another car and me being in the car. Maybe he rode with me in my car. We all went to the Brick House.

Lyndon took to [Daddy] at once. Daddy, as has been quoted a number of times, said later to me, "You've brought a lot of boys home, and this time you've brought a man." I began to talk to my daddy about [the fact] that he'd asked me to marry him and I didn't know what to do. The only thing I knew I didn't want to do was to say good-bye to him and put him out of my life. That much I was sure of. I really wanted to think about it for about six months. That was what I thought was the sanest approach. My daddy said, "Huh. Some of the best trades I ever made have been on short notice."

Did he give you the advice you were looking for, or do you think he was too blasé about it?
No. Somewhere I had a letter from him later [in which he wrote]: "I'm the one who cared the most of all, and I'm the one who said the least to you about it." No, he just let me talk, and then he said that about the short notice. Later on, he did say with very considerable vehemence that if I waited until Aunt Effie was willing for me to marry, I would wait forever. I thought that was a cruel thing to say, but it may have been an accurate thing. Not that she would have done it with any desire in the world to hurt me or my future or to prevent me from happiness, because that's what she wanted most in the world. But she would inevitably have seen it through her own eyes, and it would have been hard for her ever to agree. Also, it's hardly good sense to marry somebody you've only known as short a while as we did. Actually, it took us about two and a half months, but

---

5. Gene Latimer, one of LBJ's former high school debaters, was by that time a congressional staff member.

even that is very short notice. I really can't say how quickly Lyndon thought we might get married. In his opinion, two and a half months was a long time; in mine, it was a preposterously short time.

A LONG-DISTANCE COURTSHIP

Lyndon may have stayed two days and nights, but he went on to Washington quickly, because he did all things quickly.

Had you reached an understanding at the time he left?
No. Just that we would write and talk and visit as much as we could. So then began that series of letters and also phone calls, which were funny over a country telephone where probably a lot of folks were listening in and there was a lot of cracking and popping and noise. I began to go into Austin to one or several friends' homes, especially one, a lovely redheaded girl named Shirley Scales, to use their telephone to get a better line.[6] Lyndon began sending me a barrage of letters, and also some books, among them a congressional cookbook.

Had you decided that you would marry him? Was it just a question of wanting to wait awhile?
I don't know if that would have worked. Because I was perfectly willing to say, "Let's be almost sure we'll get married in a year." But he was saying, "No, if you wait that long, if you don't love me enough to marry me now, you won't a year from now. It will do nothing but keep me in a turmoil and make life unbearable for a long time, and then we'll slip away somehow or another." I think he, too, was fearful about Aunt Effie, who was not, dear heavens, a person to be afraid of. She was a person to have a loving sympathy and kindness for. But the silver cord could have throttled us if he and Daddy both hadn't been so positive.

Did you get any idea then of what you were marrying in terms of his career?
Oh, yes indeed. I did not at that time really think in terms of Congress, but I did think in terms of Washington and activity and expanding horizons and ambition and drive and excitement. What was going to happen I didn't know, but I knew it was going to be something important.

There is the quotation from one of your letters wondering "what the deal is," and saying, "I hope it's not politics, because I would hate for you to go into politics." Why were you against it?
I grew up in a milieu in which politics was not what you would want your son or your husband to go into, really. I remember in deep East Texas there was a

---

6. Shirley Scales was a friend from Marshall who also attended the University of Texas. CTJ may have intended to say that she drove to Marshall, not Austin, to use Scales's telephone.

general expression that "He ought to have the job; he's got eight children," or "He ought to get elected to that; he hasn't got but one leg." [Politics] just wasn't regarded as one of the top professions in the life I had lived. I came very soon to change that opinion, but at that time I thought it was too hazardous, uncertain, not the life that I would like to be a part of.

At this point was he thinking about becoming a lawyer?
He was seriously thinking about becoming a lawyer. It was obvious that he was very serious about it. In retrospect, I'll probably get very big black marks as putting an end to it. Although his letters were loaded with the number of hours he went to school and the number of hours he studied, he just couldn't conduct that courtship, hold down his job as congressman['s assistant], go through law school, and then, especially, couldn't have a brand new wife to whom he didn't give any time at all. Because those two other activities were consuming about sixteen hours a day, and really, I'm sure he just must have known it wouldn't work.

He dropped out of law school [after you married]?
Yes. It was really too bad. I did not really know what I was doing then in depriving him of the assurance of the future. But who knows what way fate would have taken us? But he couldn't do all of those things, and he loved being a congressman's top assistant.

He was always sending me something in that brief while, candy or books. His letters had been growing more and more determined to reach a conclusion. I felt that wisdom and caution and all sorts of things said, "Wait until you know this person better. He should want to wait until he knows you better. You might not really suit him." So I was in a desperate state of uncertainty as to what to do. The only sure thing was I didn't want him to drop out of my life. That I was sure about. But how to keep him a part of my life and not marry him was the hard problem, because he was convinced that, if we did not go on and get married, that either my Aunt Effie's need of me [or the] request that we wait would separate us. He was an impatient person all his life. When he wanted something, he put out every effort to get it, tried with all his might, and then if he couldn't, he did indeed turn away and begin something else. I saw that a number of times, in the Senate race of 1941 and in an attempt to become a member of the [House] Committee on Appropriations.

I remember one of the things I did when I was unsure, I just got out the Episcopal wedding service and read it through from beginning to end. When I got to that line, "forever and ever till death do you part," that was when I really got so unsure. That was the big hang-up in the few weeks before. Because even at twenty-one years old, I had seen many changes in myself, and I was not the same person that I was at sixteen. I didn't know how much more I might change in the next five or ten years or, indeed, how much he might change.

He came down to Texas about Halloween. He left Washington, and I counted the number of days—three—that I thought it would take him to make the trip, driving at a sensible pace. Instead, he drove night and day. He had, I think, Gene Latimer with him, and they did not stop except for gasoline or a hamburger. They didn't stop to sleep or to sit down at a restaurant and have a decent meal. They just got pick-up food, and one would drive for four or five hours and the other would take over and drive. To my great consternation, he drove into Karnack about two days, or certainly a day and a half, before I was expecting him. He did call me when he was within an hour or two's drive of home. Oh, it really threw me into a great fluster, because I had not gone to the beauty parlor, as any normal woman would want to do. So I lit out for Marshall to the beauty parlor, flinging orders over my shoulders to our somewhat casual help to finish what you would make for having company.

I vaguely think that by the time I got to Marshall, got my hair done, and got back home, he had already arrived. I walked in the house, and someone told me that he had already arrived, and I said, "Where is Lyndon?" I remember the black woman who helped us said, "He's gone." And, oh, my heart went down in my boots. He had gone down to the store to see my daddy, a very sensible thing to do when he didn't find me at home. But for a breathless moment I was really filled with consternation.

Had he talked to your father at this point about marrying you?
I think he had. He certainly did on this visit. I think he had talked to my daddy [before] and given him the definite impression that he was very interested. I'm not sure he had been quite as clear as "I want to marry your daughter." But he did talk quite clearly to Daddy and to me about it this time, convincing me to my great dismay that he absolutely was determined to marry me or else to make his departure. His argument went something like this: "If you don't love me enough now, you never will. If we let something stand in our way now, something will separate us."

He spent one or two nights at the Brick House. Then we drove on down to Austin. I stayed a day or two with Gene. In that interlude there, we had proceeded as far as becoming engaged and getting an engagement ring. We had gone in Carl Mayer's jewelry store in Austin and selected an engagement ring, a very small, dainty, pretty engagement ring which had a matching wedding band.

"MORE CONFUSED THAN EVER"

Then he said he had to go to Corpus Christi to handle some of his boss's business, and I went to Alabama. There are moments that stand out as vividly with the sharpest clarity, emotions and scenes, but there are also just whole passages that I don't recall exactly the sequence of. But I think it went something like this:

I said I just had to go to Alabama to see Aunt Effie and talk it over with her and try to win her understanding and sympathy, if not her wholehearted approval.

I've read that you took a picture of him to show your aunt.
Oh, without a doubt, I certainly did. I remember my cousin Elaine looked at it and said, "Oh, he's a regular [Harrison] Fisher Boy" or something like that. There was an artist at that time who drew pictures of handsome young [wo] men, and they appeared in all the magazine illustrations. It was just as well known as a Gibson Girl in another period. It was an extremely handsome picture. I have it and still love it.[7]

It was a very sad, bleak trip to Alabama because Aunt Effie was so unutterably dependent and vulnerable and lost without me. It was just like deliberately hurting a small child. Yet I was much too young and vital and reasonable to be content to give up my whole life to taking care of her. I had to admit she had a lot of good sense on her side. To marry someone you have known two months is a risky business. To marry anybody, anytime, is a risky business. She kept holding out the idea that maybe I might find somebody just a little later on that was everything I wanted and needed, and that [there was] no telling what bright horizons might open up because I was only twenty-one. As a matter of fact, I was going to be twenty-two in a few months, so I was not all that young.

Did you conclude your conversation by saying that you were going to marry him?
No, I couldn't tell her definitely that I had, because I hadn't really [decided]. She must have felt that the chances were I would marry him, because I just couldn't bear the thought of him suddenly dropping out of my life, and by that time, I was convinced that he would.

So I went back to Texas feeling very dejected and more confused than ever. There ensued one of the funniest twenty-four hours that anybody ever lived through. Once more he arrived at the Brick House. This time he just spent one night. I had a suitcase full of clothes that had just traveled this journey to Alabama, and for some reason which I can't quite understand there was a pair of riding boots and a whole lot of ridiculous gear like that in them. He said, "There's no reason in the world why we just don't go on and get married tomorrow." I said, "Well, we said that we were going to have Welly Hopkins[8] for best man, and I am going to think about who I would like to have in my attendance. We just don't have time. We haven't gotten out any invitations. We just couldn't. I don't have a dress." He said, "We'll stop in Marshall and you can get something." It was really hilarious.

---

7. Elaine Fischesser's recollections of the visit and the photograph are in her oral history interview. Elaine Fischesser and Ellen Taylor Oral History Interview, 12/9/67, by Douglass Cater.

8. Welly K. Hopkins, an early political ally of LBJ, was a state senator.

I had bought exactly two new fall dresses, one of which was a little gray plaid dress and jacket, as I recall, with a little stripe of yellow in it, which I thought was quite smart and perky. The other was a violet-colored dress, silk, with a bunch of artificial flowers at the waist or the shoulder. It was what was called in those days an afternoon dress. So I packed those together with what was already in my suitcase, which was a ridiculous assemblage. We stopped in Marshall, and while Lyndon was perhaps going to the doctor to get a blood test, I went into a shop and bought a beautiful negligee.

It was an all-day trip practically, because it's about three hundred or perhaps three hundred and fifty miles. Although Lyndon was a very fast driver, cars in those days were not as powerful as they are now.

I had not at this time firmly made up my mind. We were heading for Austin or San Antonio. I would either get off at Austin, visit Gene, just say good-bye forever, or I would go on to San Antonio. We talked as we drove down the road. He was saying, "But you would have Cecille in your wedding anyway. She lives in San Antonio. That would just be fine. I have lots of good friends there. If you want to get married in the church, why, that's what we'll do. I'll phone up Dan Quill and arrange to get the license."[9]

So that is what he did to get the license and also a ring. He said when we got to Austin, "I'll stop and get the matching wedding ring." But somehow or another I couldn't bear to stop in Austin. Austin was my past. Austin was all of my life before then. I practically had to close my eyes as we went through.

Were you afraid that you'd change your mind?
Yes, I guess that was it.

Why didn't you get married in Marshall or closer to your home?
That does seem strange, doesn't it? I suppose, actually, it was my inconclusiveness as to whether I was going to get married at all or not. That was one reason. Frankly, I can't answer it very well except that I had thought of having Cecille in my wedding all along. San Antonio, old St. Mark's, all of those things appealed to me. There was a certain romantic quality about San Antonio. I had gone there on a lot of happy weekends.

In the back of your minds there was also a planned wedding?
I probably thought when it was going to be a planned wedding with proper invitations and all that it would naturally be either in my home or close by. But I really had no closeness to a church in Marshall. I did have a closeness to St. David's in Austin, but the whole city of Austin encompassed all my past. This was such a break with my past that for some strange reason I didn't want to be married there.

---

9. Dan Quill was the postmaster in San Antonio.

THE WEDDING AND HONEYMOON

So on this ridiculous ride Lyndon stopped a few times to make phone calls to Dan Quill about the ring and the Episcopal church and the Episcopal minister, with whom incidentally they seemed to have had quite a time convincing him that we weren't a couple of people out of our minds, getting married on such short notice. He was not quite convinced that he wanted to be a party to it, but in the end he was. He was an extremely delightful man, Reverend [Arthur] McKinstry. Sometime I must have made a call to Cecille, because she showed up down at the hotel shortly after I arrived. I was getting dressed and talking a mile a minute, still uncertain whether it would be wisest to jump out the window or go on and get married.[10]

Did she encourage you to marry him?
Oh, she was very excited about it. She thought it was a great lark. Yes, I would say she did encourage me.

I've heard that you made up your mind while walking up the steps of the church.
No, no, no. I don't think that's quite so. By that time, it all seemed inevitable. I can't imagine myself fleeing from the church door. I think that I committed myself that far; that that was it. We went over to St. Mark's. By the time the ceremony started, I was quite calm. It was Lyndon who was holding on tight to—I think he was nervous and uncertain at the very moment of the ceremony.

I remember walking back across that lovely little park from St. Mark's after the ceremony. Several of Lyndon's friends were there. Maury [Maverick]'s secretary, Malcolm Bardwell, must have been there; Dan Quill, of course, was, and there was a lawyer who was a great friend of Lyndon's, Henry Hirshberg. I believe it was Henry Hirshberg who had a pleasant little supper for us on the roof of the St. Anthony or whatever the pleasant dining place in the St. Anthony was in 1934. The conversation was very much centering on Maury Maverick, not on us. [*Laughter.*] Maury at that moment was being operated [on] at Mayo's for some very severe troubles.[11] They were all great friends of Maury's, and they had lots of concern for him. They had all helped him in his campaigns, and they didn't want their hero to go down. They wanted to see him come back strong, and this

---

10. Most of those present at the ceremony have recorded their recollections in interviews: Cecille Harrison Marshall Oral History Interview, 2/19/76, by Michael L. Gillette; Daniel Quill Oral History Interview, 5/10/65, by Eric F. Goldman; Malcolm Bardwell Oral History Interview, 10/17/68, by Dorothy Pierce; Henry A. Hirshberg Oral History Interview, 10/17/68, by Dorothy Pierce.

11. Maury Maverick, a pro–New Deal member of Congress from San Antonio, had been seriously wounded in the Argonne Forest during World War I. He underwent major back surgery at the Mayo Clinic in November 1934. Richard B. Henderson, *Maury Maverick: A Political Biography* (Austin: University of Texas Press, 1970), 24, 62.

was a serious operation. So they were getting bulletins on the phone once or twice during the evening on how he was doing.

We sent my daddy a wire and Lyndon's mother a wire the next morning. I don't think we told anybody, not even Gene, before the wedding. I think we must have sent Gene a wire, too, because she had been so much a party to it.

Whose idea was it to go to Mexico?
It was his, and I immediately jumped at the idea.

Was this part of his persuasion to get married?
Yes, I think it was. It certainly didn't weigh heavily in the scale, but it was a very enticing thought.

So we went on to Mexico on our honeymoon, which lasted as long as our money lasted. As I recall, it was about ten days. We went in Lyndon's car to Saltillo, and I remember the hotel there. It was so charming and very picturesque and had a corner fireplace. We certainly stopped one night in the city that makes all the glass, and also steel and beer. It's now the industrial city of Mexico. Monterrey is not the most romantic of cities of Mexico, but it has a lovely old hotel called the Ancira. I remember looking out the window at a perfect view of the cathedral. I think of my frequently expressed taste for the picturesque and the scenic. Well, Lyndon certainly got a dose of it in those ten days. But he was very anxious to show me everything that was picturesque and scenic. It was a long time before he did that much sightseeing again.

But that doesn't sound at all characteristic of him to take off for ten days and just [sightsee], even on a honeymoon.
No. No. I really think that all of his friends were just shocked. They thought he'd be back in about three. It may have been only a week. He told me when he left how much money he had, and we just had enough to get home comfortably. We stayed in lots of lovely hotels. We did a lot of sightseeing. We even went to see the pyramid excavations in Mexico City.

Did that interest him?
I don't think it interested him, but it interested him to make me happy and to have me receive from him something that I thought was wonderful. He always loved giving people gifts that they wouldn't get otherwise or that pleased them greatly. We went to the gardens of Xochimilco, which I do not know whether they are still there or not. He bought me loads of flowers, just arms full. We rode around in those ridiculous little low boats, and we had some pictures made that are horrible to look at. We are both grinning broadly. I should have thrown away the negatives.

Did you have any regrets at that point, or did you feel that you'd made the right decision?
Well, it's a chancy thing. That's a day-to-day business. But, no, I don't think I did.

Did those first weeks together seem to confirm the decision?
My sense of excitement mounted and certainly didn't decline. I just found it more interesting as we went along. I suppose it takes a longer time to confirm a judgment that's supposed to last a lifetime.

This was the period when Congress is out of session, and we went to Corpus Christi. By that time it was about December 1. It seems to me we did go to either Lyndon's house or mine for Thanksgiving, and then we went to Corpus Christi.

Was his mother upset by the marriage?
Yes, she was, and who wouldn't be? She was indeed, but she wrote him a lovely letter. To her, marriage really was eternal, and she thought, "Now what I must do is to make the best of it and win this young woman and try to help her make the happiest life possible for my beloved son." So from then on, there was no backward looking for her. We soon became just the greatest friends. The girls were not all that big on the idea. They were looking at me from a distance. Mr. Johnson, Lyndon's father, was just terribly sweet and nice about it. I was fond of him, as I was of Mrs. Johnson, although I was much more understanding, sympathetic, and like Mrs. Johnson than Mr. Johnson.

Where did you live in Corpus?
We lived in the [Nixon] Hotel, thinking that when we would come back for a longer stay we would do something else, but that was only going to be three or four weeks. We went to a few nightclubs, and we went out with Lyndon's friends there. He made me better acquainted with the Fourteenth District. That was when he began to try to teach me all these leading figures in each community.

We went back to the Brick House for Christmas. There we met Aunt Effie, and that was a straining time. She was aloof and withdrawn and so sad. Vulnerable is the very best word for her. Lyndon really put himself out to win her. He really went all out. My father was sort of impatient. He didn't think that she had a right to dominate my life. He wasn't as understanding of her as he might have been. Of course, it was exciting to show Dorris [Powell] my new husband. In fact, Dorris had been tremendously helpful to us all along. She had sent out the wedding announcements, had them made and addressed them. I would be on the phone, of course, giving her the list.

Somewhere along the way, Lyndon and I, on a trip through San Antonio, stopped at a great big, handsome jewelry store that's still right there in downtown San Antonio. We went in and selected silver. Once more, that was one of those rush-rush things which seemed to fill up my life from the moment I met him. I would no doubt have taken several weeks to select my silver and would have researched it and looked through all sorts of magazines and asked all my friends. He said, "Let's run in here and choose some silver, because Mr. Sam Fore says he wants to give me X number of spoons or forks or knives or whatever.[12] So-and-so wants to give you some, and so and so wants to give you some. Go in there and select it." He thought I could do it in about five minutes. I was appalled at the idea, but I did go in. I finally wound up by eventually selecting some, although I really didn't think that was the way to go about it.

Were there any wedding presents that were particularly memorable?
There were quite a number of them for such a hurried wedding. We did send out the proper announcements, so presents began to come in. There was a set of after-dinner coffee cups from a boy, just a real friend, not a beau. I used them and used them throughout the years until finally there was just one left that wasn't broken. So I put it away. The same with some handsome crystal glasses that one of my real beaus gave me. When there was just one of those left, I put it away. Mrs. Johnson gave us a silver tray that in their circumstances was a gift they could hardly afford. It is lovely, and I still have it.

[Dr. Cecil Evans was] the first complete stranger that ever wrote me a letter.[13] He wrote me right after our marriage. Here I get this letter from somebody I never had met. He introduced himself as the president of this school where Lyndon had gone. He was telling me the sort of young man I had married. Lyndon then immediately began to tell me all about him. It was a beautiful letter.

---

12. Sam Fore was a prominent newspaper publisher in Floresville, Texas.
13. As president of Southwest Texas State Teachers College at San Marcos, Cecil E. Evans had given LBJ a part-time job.

4

1935–1937, A Future in Politics?

After spending the Christmas holidays at the Brick House, the newlyweds traveled to Washington, DC, before the Seventy-Fourth Congress convened. Lady Bird's many automobile and train trips between Texas and Washington would deepen her love of the nation's natural beauty. They rented a small one-bedroom apartment in a complex near Rock Creek Park.

LIFE IN WASHINGTON

[We moved into] the most ridiculous little apartment at 1910 Kalorama Road. One side of Kalorama is a very elegant place; it's where the French Embassy and lots of the great old homes of Washington are. The other side is quite a different story. It was perfectly respectable but very middle class. I'm sure we were surrounded by secretaries and civil servants and people of moderate means. The apartment had a living room with a couch that made down into a bed, a tiny screened porch, then a wee little kitchen, and a comfortably sized bedroom.

Lyndon would come home rather late for dinner even then, but earlier than in the succeeding years. I'd be getting dinner ready and looking out the one little window in that kitchen. All of a sudden I'd see his car come into the back parking lot which was provided for a few of the tenants. He would park right underneath the window and get out and wave at me, just a few feet apart, right out that window. That was always an exciting moment. Things picked up from then on.

It was my first exposure to lots of snow, because snow in East Texas was always just a big event and you got the camera and ran out. But in Washington it would stay on the ground for weeks and weeks, and all of the trees would be heavy-laden with it. When it was fresh, it was just absolutely fascinating to me to get out and walk all over that part of town. I would do it just for fun, just to see how all the homes and how every bush and tree in Rock Creek Park looked in their mantles of snow. There was a song at that time that was very popular called "Walking in a Winter Wonderland." To this day, if I hear that song, it evokes that feeling that I am about twenty-two again and walking in a winter wonderland.

I did all the cooking and cleaning. It was two or three years before I began to have help. But I learned to cook. I was never a talented cook, but I put fairly good meals on the table and really took pleasure in doing it, although I never for a moment thought I was going to make a life's career out of that. I was just doing it until we had a more expansive household and more means.

Did you have financial worries at this point?
No, I don't remember ever worrying financially, really. I knew Daddy would come to my rescue if I needed him to. Also, I very early got the feeling that somehow or another Lyndon would manage. He was very determined that I should learn all about his finances. In fact, he was an extremely open person, far more open than I was. He would say, "We've got—" I believe he got a raise to $325.00. He said, "I think we ought to buy a bond every month." So we did. We began probably the month after we got married, and we bought a bond every month. It was just a twenty-five dollar bond that cost us $18.50. But nevertheless, that was a 5 percent chunk out of that.

He always had insurance, and he always told me just what his insurance was and who it was made out to. I told him that he didn't need to get any more for me. He had it made out to his mother. I told him that was just the way it ought to be and that was fine and he didn't need to get any for me. I don't know whether he did insist on getting some made out to me or not.

Did you keep the budget or did he?
I certainly did. Those who knew me now would be surprised at how very knowledgeable and organized I was about where every penny I spent went. I had a very clear picture of how much for groceries and utilities and rent. Clothes were something that I always handled myself out of little bits of income, at least my own clothes. If I wanted something, I always felt that I could manage that. I had a car. I never had been without one since I was thirteen. I just said [to my father that] I'd like to take it up to Washington.

It [was] like a Marx Brothers comedy to remember the number of people we sometimes had staying with us in that apartment, because Lyndon, I early learned, was very close to staff, family, and lots of friends. He just thought nothing of inviting them to come and stay with us, and the same had always been true of me. I immediately began to write Aunt Effie and my various Alabama kinfolks that they must come see us in Washington and see some of the great sights. I remember one unbelievable time when Aunt Effie was there and Lyndon's uncle George [Johnson] was there at the same time. We moved out of the bedroom and gave that to Aunt Effie. Then one of my Alabama cousins whom I had invited up to see the sights arrived. There were twin beds in the one bedroom, so that was fine; she could have the other one. Lyndon and I slept on that roll-down sofa bed, and I'm sure Uncle George must have slept on [a daybed in] the little screened porch. It was quite a chummy household, and there was just one bath.

My cousin probably didn't stay more than a week. Uncle George stayed several weeks, and Aunt Effie stayed probably a couple of months. In the summertime I early formed the habit of going back home to see Daddy for two or three weeks. If we thought Congress was going to adjourn on X date, I would go down a little bit early, driving the car. Lyndon would either drive his [car] the day Congress adjourned or turn it over to a secretary and fly, as he later began doing. In this particular year, Uncle George and Aunt Effie and I and Poofy, a pretty little white fluffy cat, all set forth for Texas in the car. Uncle George was a teacher of American history in the public schools of Houston since time began and a true southern gentleman, as it says on his tombstone, and a lover of history, especially Civil War history. We read every Civil War monument through the states of Virginia, Tennessee, Arkansas, right down to Texas, and believe me, there were plenty. We'd barely get started before we'd stop and read another one. My Aunt Effie sat there beaming from ear to ear and just soaking it all up, because she loved a good conversation. The Civil War was right back where her ancestors had played a part, and she was very familiar with the names of all the generals and all the battles. Poofy was an expensive gift from Lyndon to me and a well-loved pet, but a most obnoxious traveling companion. Its sole ambition was to get out of that car. The cat was scratching and jumping from front seat to back and trying to get out. It was a bit hard on the nerves, but yet very funny.

[Bill White's home was] the very first house that I went to.[1] At that time he was married to a beautiful woman named Irene, and they lived in a picturesque house in Alexandria, Virginia. It seemed to me that we went there on New Year's Eve. From that night sprang a longtime family joke. I was the butt of the joke, but I didn't really get mad at it. Newspaper people were fairly heavy drinkers, and at this New Year's Eve party there was quite a lot of drinking going on, and it was cheap whiskey. I had several drinks of it and it really made me sick, so that I began my career in Washington the next day not in the best of condition. Lyndon just teased me and laughed about it for years and years and years, and he also teased Bill. He was a natural-born tease.

Terrell Maverick [Maury's wife] decided it would be a nice idea to gather up the young wives of secretaries or young Texas girls whom she knew were in Washington. I think she had about half a dozen of us. It was spring. We had a tour of the Capitol, and I think we had lunch in the House dining room. I remember distinctly that we all had our picture made under the cherry blossoms out on the grounds of the Capitol. It may even have made the paper. We all sent pictures home. At least I did, to my daddy, and I bet others did. It was a

---

1. William S. White was a reporter for the *New York Times*.

big deal for me to be in the company of a congressman's wife and to be that close to that great big Capitol. I felt like I was on the stage.

Lyndon introduced me to one of his old girlfriends that he had told me a lot about. He did tell me all sorts of things about his own past: the people he'd gone with, the achievements he'd made, the failures, the embarrassments, the losses, every last thing about his financial life. This young woman was the daughter of a Supreme Court judge in New York. She had apparently taught him a lot, and they had been real intellectual—she sharpened him up. Not that it was a purely platonic relationship; I think they were both quite fond of each other. He always had a very reasonable gratitude for people who helped educate him, and there were a number along the way.

What were his ambitions during that first year you were married? Were they political or related to business?
It was to be the best secretary that a congressman ever had and to really take care of that Fourteenth District. He loved that Fourteenth District and Corpus and all those counties. One of the first things he asked me to do was to memorize the names of the counties, the county seats in each one, and two or three of the *jefes*, the *alcaldes*, the important men in each community. As we would drive around, from one community to another, he would say, "Now do you remember who we met down there at Beeville?" or Alice, or whatever the name of the town was.

It's generally conceded that he was more liberal on New Deal legislation than Congressman Kleberg was.
I think that is quite the case. Congressman Kleberg was a kind man and a nice man. But, although he had lived close to the Mexicans all his life and talked their language and loved telling stories with them, the fact is he hadn't been intimately exposed to hunger and deprivation himself. His general philosophy was that he didn't know how hard it was. Lyndon really was a very sympathetic person. He knew a good bit of it firsthand, but he was even more keenly attuned to it, even if he hadn't experienced it, than a lot of people.

He told often how he felt when he saw a ragged army of veterans, as he would describe it, in the Capitol. They made a march on the Capitol asking for the bonus. It was a time of really desperate need. President [Herbert] Hoover was still in office and he called out the army. It was [Douglas] MacArthur himself who dispersed them in a very curt military manner. Lyndon was deeply incensed and concerned what might happen next. He thought they got a raw deal in that kind of exercise of power. It just might lead to explosive anger then or in the future that would just be bad for the government and the country and the society.

Mamie [Mrs. Richard] Kleberg was beautiful, statuesque. She, too, was very, very fond of Lyndon, in the beginning, but the relationship [became] a disruptive, abrasive situation for Lyndon. He regretted it so much because he had begun feeling so much admiration and affection for Mrs. Kleberg as well as for the congressman. He never lost it for the congressman, but Mrs. Kleberg really did come to have a feeling that Lyndon was a part of leading her husband astray, helping him in having affairs with other women, which I expect were nonexistent. She had an exceeding jealousy of her husband in which Lyndon played some kind of a part. It was quite trying, and it made him sad because it was frustrating. He didn't think he deserved to have her think that of him, and he couldn't change it.

Also, Lyndon had the unhappy job of having to pay the bills for the family. The money was dispensed by Mr. Bob [Kleberg], who always ran the family business with a pretty iron hand. The bills would stack up and stack up and stack up. Lyndon would call or write Mr. Bob and say, "We've just got to pay these, Mr. Bob." He'd say, "But I just sent X dollars three months ago. What's happened to that?" He would try to hold them down. Lyndon would do his best to appease the members of the family, all of whom had expensive tastes. He would write the checks and dole them out as well as he could. He did get tired of being the man in the middle.

THE NATIONAL YOUTH ADMINISTRATION

Sometime in July [1935], I went home and spent two weeks with Daddy. While I was there, I got this call from Lyndon. I could tell by the decibels in his voice that something exciting was happening. The firecrackers were shooting off. He said, "How would you like to live in Austin?" which was just like asking, "How would you like to go to heaven?" I said, "I'd love it." He said, "I've been offered a job as [Texas] head of the National Youth Administration." Then he went on to describe all about it. I could tell that he was excited about it and wanted to take it. He just thought that what he could learn and do and achieve in Mr. Kleberg's office had already been done. He had gotten all out of that job that he could.

I can certainly remember the thrill in his voice and the triumph like he was bringing me a diamond the size of an egg when he said over the phone, "How would you like to live in Austin?" That was just sheer heaven and an utter surprise because he knew I loved Austin. When he was offered this job and the fact that it was going to be in Austin, he knew that would just have me beside myself with pleasure. I just practically jumped up and down.

What did he say on the phone about the NYA [National Youth Administration] job?
I guess he described what they would do to keep young men and women in college by giving them small jobs, or those that were not destined to go to college by giving them some training that would enable them to get a job, whether it was mechanics or painting or cooking.

Did he indicate how he had been selected?
He said that Maury Maverick had talked either to President Roosevelt himself or to Harry Hopkins[2] and recommended Lyndon. I think several other people had also been recommended by others. It was a little uncertain at first who would get it.

Dr. [Bob] Montgomery and his wife were delightful, way-out people. He wore long hair and red shirts at a time when nobody else did and, of course, got himself roundly criticized at the university, especially by regents. But he was terrifically popular with the students. He could make the subject of economics sound like the most fascinating thing in the world. People flocked to his classes.

He had been called to Washington in one of those many temporary jobs [for which] the New Deal gathered professors from all over the country. It was just a great pouring in of talent and expertise in the New Deal days. He went up there for a year, maybe longer. His house was going to be available to rent. He met Lyndon. They had plenty of opportunities and could have rented it to somebody else for more, but they decided they wanted to rent it to us.

2808 San Pedro hung out over the edge of a cliff, and it had at least two levels of gardens. It had a great big vine of queen's wreath that grew up all over the house. There was a little sundeck off the upstairs bedroom and an iron balcony and railings and stair steps that went down into the garden. I felt that it was a thoroughly romantic house, and I was utterly charmed by it. I'd be almost afraid to go back and see it now for fear it had shrunk, as things do when you remember them through the lens of the years.

I remember [Dr. Montgomery] saying that he wanted to think it would be a happy house, with nice things going on. Well, it was certainly a full house, because we promptly began to take in all the staff. As Lyndon would hire them, he would just say, "You can stay here at the house until you find a place." So the house sometimes was bursting at the seams with people who did move out in anywhere from three or four days to two or three weeks. But it was sort of a stopping depot.

I suppose it was a scene of many late night NYA meetings.
Yes, many, many late ones. Most of them were 100 percent business, but every now and then they would get off on a talking, laughing, or card-playing spree. I remember one Saturday night after dinner when they were playing poker. Finally, about twelve o'clock, I went to bed. The next morning, I woke up rather early, and Lyndon wasn't there. I went downstairs, and there they were just breaking up the game! [*Laughter.*] I was furious at them for no good reason. I should have been delighted that they could let off that much steam and occasionally enjoy themselves that much.

---

2. Harry Hopkins was head of the Works Progress Administration in 1935.

Many [NYA staff] figured all through our life later on. Charlie Henderson and his brother [Herbert Henderson] were very important in our early congressional years. Kay Alexander was the brother of Lyndon's brother-in-law, Birge Alexander; Ray Roberts, who's now a congressman, but a lifelong friend; Bill Deason, the closest of the close; C. P. Little and Fenner Roth; A. W. Brisbin; Tony Ziegler. All of them have remained a part of our lives.

I remember distinctly when I first met Jesse and Louise [Kellam]; they hadn't been married long. Louise had been one of the Bluebonnet Belles at the University of Texas. She was almost timid, but very pretty, delicate, and gentle and every inch a lady. Jesse was a handsome young man. Talk about the work ethic, he was practically vaccinated with it when he was born. He was a mighty hardworking man. Jesse had been a schoolteacher and a football coach in Lufkin. Lyndon had known him at San Marcos at college, although he was older than Lyndon. He was a leader, and they had been opposed to each other in the [rival Black Stars and White Stars, secret fraternal organizations,]

I remember the urgency, the need of speed, the feeling that it all had to get done yesterday. Their office was in the Littlefield Building. I remember what late hours they kept and how much they traveled. I remember how some of the young men were just breathless and wondering, "What the heck do you think we are?" But they all soon became imbued with the spirit. If they didn't, [there] must have been a few of them [who] left. One at least got on a high horse about how much was demanded of them. But he was, and is, one of our best friends forever and ever, and that's Bill Deason. At one point, though, Lyndon said he wanted to send him out to El Paso to be the director out there. Bill clearly felt that he was being sent to Siberia, because he had said that they were working too hard and too fast and that they'd do better if they worked a little slower.

Ray Roberts described the NYA as a crusade rather than an organization.
Yes, it was. It produced a feeling that comes from working on a significant project and pouring out everything you can. That's a sort of a comradeship that was very special and lasted all their lives.

[It was a challenge] to get the message to the young people, because, oddly enough, they didn't come swarming to the door. You had to find them. A lot of them were locked in the hills and hollows. You really had to go to them and get the message to them. Lyndon traveled to a lot of the schools and colleges to explain the programs. It was a double-faceted thing. One was to teach skills: auto mechanic work, iron work, painting, carpentry, all sorts of work, to young boys; cooking, sewing to young women. That is, to the sort of people who, at the best, would get out of high school and never have any further education. Then the other side of it was to give small jobs to young men and women in universities, colleges, who couldn't otherwise stay, helping in the library, or as janitors, or as just anything, clerical work of any type. He went around to a lot of the schools to explain the program to the college presidents and administrators and win their aggressive assistance.

He especially thought that he did well at Prairie View [Normal and Industrial College, a historically black institution]. He enlisted [President W. R.] Banks; he was easy to get. That was a man that he really wanted to serve his constituency. He and Lyndon worked hand in glove. Prairie View was a very special place to Lyndon, [who] felt that [Prairie View] had a good program. He really felt that they struggled to keep their young people in school, and also to teach them a saleable, marketable skill.

Do you know how this idea of roadside parks originated?
I don't really, but I know Lyndon has always been very proud of it. He liked and respected the highway department because he thought they were an efficient organization and knew how to spend their monies well and get their money's worth. He liked anything that could give boys a skill and keep them working hard out of doors. I daresay it sprang from the fact that he himself had worked on the road, not building parks but just doing hard manual labor for a year or a year and a half, before he made up his mind to go back to school. I daresay that lingered in his mind, and the chrysalis of it may have been right then. He was interested in youth. I don't think it's too much to say he was interested in the beauty of Texas and proud of it. He thought the roadside parks would just be a nice addition to the highways.

I have a picture that the highway department gave to me at one of these highway maintenance foremen's awards. It's an artist's rendition of this picture of the first highway park, a nice sentimental thing to have. I'm so glad it was [presented to me] while Lyndon was still alive. Another thing that I have that was done by the NYA that has great nostalgic value to me is a little copper coffee service, a pot and several mugs, and a little tray, handcrafted by NYA boys in San Antonio on the banks of the river in La Villita.

It's a wonder he didn't press you into service.
It is. I often wonder how I escaped. I guess maybe I was being useful putting some dinner on the table for them. Or maybe it hadn't occurred to Lyndon that I could do anything.

Did you feel that you didn't have enough time together during this? It seems like he must have been working all the time.
We certainly didn't have much time together! But then, fortunately, I was always fairly independent, and I did not feel deprived or mad at the job or mad at him. I always felt that each job we were in was a significant job. [Austin] Mayor Tom Miller used to have a saying, something like, "Each of us is in search of the significant." It was satisfying, and it was significant. I wanted it to succeed. I liked being part of it, although I had a mighty small role. If I had it

to do over again, I think I would have learned more about it and tried to be more a part of it.

I just played a very supporting, minor role in the NYA and with all those young men. They became my friends as well as Lyndon's: Bill Deason, Ray Roberts, just a lot of them, Jesse Kellam of course. All of them were dear to me and very much a part of my life. I was crazy about the house we lived in. I did have a bridge club, which I enjoyed once a week or more. I went to St. David's Church, and, at a distance, I saw something of the university. I went swimming at Barton Springs.

[The NYA] was almost like a maturing process for Lyndon. He had a lot of self-confidence, but he also had a very practical knowledge of his own short-comings. Pretty soon he thought this was a job he could handle, and he was on top of it. In fact, they were some of the best years of our lives, and they were not really two years even. It was just from August of 1935 till February of 1937. The ambiance of the whole period [was one] of youth, vitality, high hopes, and determination. Just about everybody there would remember it as one of the best years of their lives. He often referred to the NYA all out of proportion of the one and a half years of chronological time. He learned a lot from it. It was a big part of a lifetime of experience.

A FUTURE IN POLITICS

When did you realize that he was going into politics?
Oddly enough, it was perhaps something that L. E. Jones said to me.[3] Lyndon was in the NYA. L. E. and I were driving down the street in Austin, and he said, "In a few years, he'll be in Congress." I just practically ran the car off the road and said, "What do you mean?" He said, "Well, don't you know? Don't you think he's always heading in that direction?" I had not, which was probably quite stupid of me, but from then on I somehow knew that it was going to happen.

> *On February 22, 1937, James P. Buchanan, the veteran congressman who had represented the Tenth Congressional District of Texas for twenty-four years, died suddenly. Lyndon Johnson now had a rare opportunity to return to Washington, not as a secretary but as a member of Congress. He would need only a plurality to win the special election.*

When did he first discuss [running for Congress] with you?
From the very beginning, I would think. It was right after Buchanan's death, within, say, a few hours. I'm sure that a lot of his staff and friends and fellow

---

3. L. E. Jones, formerly one of LBJ's star high school debaters, subsequently worked in Kleberg's congressional office.

workers converged upon him and talked to him about it. Uncle George was very quickly in the picture suggesting that he run for Congress, which showed an extraordinary boldness on Uncle George's part, because this was a very young David setting out after some very large-sized Goliaths. Uncle George put at his disposal practically his entire savings. I feel sure we paid him back, I hope to heavens—I believe we did. Bill Deason said, "Well, I don't have any money, but I have a new car, and I'll just turn it over to you." And he did. We practically used it up, drove it so far and so fast.

There was some thought that Buchanan's widow might run.
There was, and we debated long and hard as to whether we ought to wait and see if she did. Everybody knew her to be the quietest and most retiring of little women, certainly not given to the combat of active political life. But we also felt that we just couldn't wait and wait and wait until she made up her mind. So Lyndon did go on and announce.

Lyndon went charging into [Governor] Jimmie Allred's[4] office and told him he was going to run for the Congress; what did he think of that? Jimmie Allred said something to him half joking and half sincere, "You never will get elected in that city-boy hat. Here, take my hat." It was a typical western Stetson, light-colored. Lyndon put it on; he [wore] that type of hat forever since then.

As far back as I can remember, Senator Alvin Wirtz was our friend, adviser, and mentor; our brain trust.[5] I generally think of him as a conservative; he was a corporation lawyer. On the other hand, he had a strong populist streak. Lyndon had the greatest respect for his sound common sense and his ability to see through a tangled web where you might not be able to tell what was right from what was wrong or everything was hazy and gray. Senator Wirtz was a sort of a godfather in that he cared greatly for Lyndon and guided him and gave him sage advice. Whenever we were weighing something, all big problems were likely to be run by Senator Wirtz. There would be meetings at night at his house. I remember the back porch of his house and sitting there with just him and Lyndon and Kitty Mae, his wife, and having a drink and talking until late. I remember meetings with a bunch of men over there, sometimes over dinner, sometimes just late-night meetings, some of which I went [to] and mostly not. Less frequently he would come to our place, 4 Happy Hollow Lane, the simplest little frame duplex, a dull little place that we rented for five years.

I asked Senator Wirtz to talk to me for a while, and we went walking. I said, "Do you think he's got a chance?" Senator Wirtz was never one to tell it big. He would tell it exactly like he saw it. He said, "Well, actually, he has a chance, and that's about all he's got, because it's not going to be easy and he may not make it. But this may be the best chance he'll ever have. It's a big gamble."

---

4. James V Allred was elected governor of Texas in 1934.
5. Former state senator Alvin J. Wirtz was an Austin attorney in 1937.

He made me feel that it was possible. I just thought if Lyndon wanted this as much as he seemed to and was as determined as he was, that I'd just love to borrow some money from my own estate, which Daddy was handling for me. My mother by that time had been dead about eighteen years or so. I called up Daddy and said, "Daddy, I think it's time I want to get some of the money Mother left me. We'll say it's a loan, and we'll pay it back when and as we can pay it back into the estate for our own later use." He asked, "How much you want?" I said, "We need ten thousand." He said, "Hmm? Sure you can't get by on five?" Lyndon was standing by me, telling me he had to have ten.[6] So I said, "No, we have to have ten." He said, "All right." And I said, "Can you have it in the bank for me in the morning?" This was eight or nine o'clock at night, not very late, because you couldn't have gotten my daddy out of bed after, say, nine o'clock. In a slightly exasperated voice he said, "No, I can't." I just gulped. Then he went right on and said, "Tomorrow's Sunday. I'll have it there Monday morning at nine o'clock."

Was your father enthusiastic about the congressional race?
Oh no, far from it, because his opinion of politics was rather dim. On the other hand, he had a high opinion of Lyndon. He thought if this was, peculiarly enough, the career that he wanted to follow, that he would probably do very well in it, and he'd be glad to back him. If I wanted it, if Lyndon wanted it, yes, he'd be for it. But he would have been far more glad to see him enter some field of business.

How about his own parents?
I'm sure he talked at length with his father, because his father was enthusiastic from the very beginning and marvelously helpful within the limits of his physical strength at that time. I believe Lyndon's mother's father [Joseph Wilson Baines] had run for that [congressional seat] and had not made it. There was a little sentimental background of that nature.

What were some of the other considerations making that decision [to run]?
First and foremost was the size and caliber of his opponents. He was quick to gauge them and to know that they had a broader network of friends, in business particularly, and more experience. Then his very youth at that time was decidedly not in his favor.

How well-known in the Tenth District was he?
Hardly at all, and it was enormously presumptuous of him. As he himself expressed it, he was born in the smallest populated county of the ten counties.

---

6. Robert A. Caro cites Ed Clark's estimate that LBJ's campaign spent between $75,000 and $100,000. Caro, *The Years of Lyndon Johnson*, vol. 1, *The Path to Power* (New York: Alfred A. Knopf, 1982), 408–9.

He was the youngest of the [nine] candidates. There was one candidate named C. N. Avery, who had been a close friend and confidante of Buchanan and had been a Washington lobbyist and working, I think, for the building material that the Capitol was made out of, the granite quarries and all sort of building material, native stone, who certainly knew his way around in Washington very well. Then there was a judge named [Sam V.] Stone from Georgetown. There was a marvelous criminal lawyer named Polk Shelton, who was politically savvy and kin to everybody in Austin. He was an enormously likeable and politically astute man, possibly ten years older than Lyndon. Then there was a state senator named Houghton Brownlee, of a respected old Austin family, who had a wide range of supporters.

There was a sizeable field of really important candidates, and they must not have taken Lyndon very seriously at first. It really was presumptuous of him, as I look back on it. But he had enormous interest and zest. If anybody asked me what [our] political machine was, I would have to say in this campaign and certainly in later campaigns for him, it was the people that he went to school with at San Marcos, the people that he worked with in the National Youth Administration, and a goodly sprinkling of his father's friends, and his inheritance from working in the Fourteenth District. He had friends from the Fourteenth District who could really get out the message.

Much of his help with the press was an inheritance from his years with Mr. Kleberg. Lyndon became such a dear friend of Mr. Sam Fore, who was at one time president of the Texas Press Association, all of the Texas weeklies and small town papers. Mr. Fore called upon every editor in the Tenth District personally, and, I daresay, he would have written them on that old Oliver typewriter several times thereafter. I think that there were others in the [Fourteenth] District who might have been in the wholesale grocery, or mill and elevator, or grain businesses, in various other walks of life, who got in touch with the people in the Tenth District that they had known in their own business connection. So his Fourteenth District connections bore marvelous fruit in his Tenth District effort.

I became well acquainted with the names of all the ten counties, the county seats and some of the people in each one. Austin was the hardest nut for us to crack. Lyndon was somewhat buffaloed by the big town in his district. [His opponents said he was] a newcomer to the district. As a matter of fact he had been born and raised in Blanco County, which was in the district all right, but it was way over in the corner of the district. It was the smallest county in the district and certainly a very small town. But believe me, it was very strong for its native son. There was a considerable rivalry, a really bitter rivalry between the two major towns in Blanco County, Johnson City and Blanco. It was a very old but still smoldering feud. It was an old fight over who was going to get the courthouse. It had been in Blanco at one time. The county vote had wrested it loose and established a new one in Johnson City around the turn of the century. But Lyndon managed to get the votes from both communities because, as he laughingly and very happily said, "They voted for me in Blanco" because he was Miss Rebekah's son, and they voted for him in Johnson City because he was old Sam's boy. His mother's friends and his father's friends—very especially his father's—were mighty helpful to him all his life. In fact, he used to have a saying that the richest inheritance of any son is his father's friends.

This was the first time I really encountered the fact that we, the United States, Texas very especially, is made up of diverse ethnic groups. I came from a part of Texas which was either Anglo-Saxon or black. People were all English, Scotch-Irish ancestry or black. In this district where we were there was a very heavy strain of Germans down in Washington County around Brenham, of Czechs and Poles in both Washington and Lee counties and around La Grange [in Fayette County]. I made the discovery that they were likely to vote pretty much in blocs. If the leaders were impressed by somebody, they were somewhat more able to pass on that influence than we individual Anglo-Saxons were.

He felt secure in San Marcos. He knew a lot of people there. A lot of them thought he was a comer, thought he was congressional material. That was a strong place for him. I believe he made his first speech in San Marcos in the gym for sentimental reasons, because San Marcos was a town where he could claim some following. I think the gym was decorated in part by Mrs. Ed Cape[7] and some of her teacher friends. Every member of the White Stars had been alerted to it. That was the fraternity of debaters and writers that he had belonged to when he was in school. I'm sure that Bill Deason and Dr. Evans and everybody who was a part of his life were around.

Saturdays, of course, were the big day. The courthouse square was the scene on Saturdays. Everybody came to town to "trade." Lyndon would have as many set up meetings as he could. Mostly you'd just have to get your own crowd by starting speaking in a courthouse square and hope people would stop and listen. There were strong figures in each community, of course, just as there had been in the Fourteenth. The barber was somebody you sure wanted to know because he was a communicator. The blacksmiths' shops were a center where people came and went. That's something that's passed so totally from the scene now, it sounds like you're antediluvian. Posters were a part of the scene. You'd get little boys to go out and tack them up on trees. The county agent saw a lot of people. You hoped that you could become friends with the communicators—the ministers, the county agents, possibly the school superintendent, and, yes indeed, the barber—and imbue them with a sense of wanting to help you. It was a much more personal thing than it is now. Lyndon would hit the courthouse square and just go from store to store and go in, stick out his hand, and say, "I'm Lyndon Johnson, and I want very much to be your congressman. I hope you will listen to me and decide you like me," or something like that.

---

7. Edward M. Cape was a prominent San Marcos banker.

Unfortunately, and I'll always be sorry about this, I did not go along with him on any of these. At that time, it would have been an unusual thing and probably not a well-accepted thing if I had. At a formal meeting the wives did indeed go and sit on the platform with folded hands and look interested and howdy and shake afterwards. But that was the extent of their activity, except of course I'm sure even in those days we did a bunch of licking stamps and folding envelopes.

We happened to have a manager, Claude Wild, who was very good, but he didn't believe in women messing in campaigns. He made that clear in a joking but positive manner. That suited me fine because I was retiring, and I guess shy is actually an accurate word. I certainly didn't yearn to do it, but, believe me, I was not pushed to do it. I was not aggressive enough. I was a fairly newly married young person and didn't know anything really about politics, so it was easy to get me to stay home. My part in it was trying to give Lyndon a good square meal whenever I could catch him, which wasn't often enough, because he would leave very early. He would often eat something like sardines and crackers and Vienna sausage and cheese and Coke in some country store. I'm sure that it was a concerted six weeks of that which caused him to wind up with appendicitis. At least that and fatigue must have played a part in it. Then I tried to make sure that he had clean shirts readily available, because I became aware that when he worked terribly hard—made speeches which were likely to be emotional and a lot of hand waving, long hours, tenseness, striving every moment—that he could sweat down three or four shirts a day. The main thing I could do about it was try to keep him in plenty of clean shirts.

Then I answered the phone a lot and gave him a lot of messages. I was a conduit for many messages to him. I spoke to all the people who crossed my path, like the postman and the laundryman and the grocery fellow and the dry cleaner, and my bridge club ladies. I'm sure I must have written notes to my rather limited number of acquaintances.

THE ELECTION

To some extent, Lyndon preempted the field as the aggressive young liberal, as being the most [pro-]Roosevelt of the candidates. He did it both deliberately as a choice and because he really felt that way, because Texas was not a forerunner in any liberal sense. He came out for the Roosevelt proposal to "unpack" the Supreme Court, or "pack" it, whichever way you want to say it. His friends said it one way and his enemies another. The "nine old men" on the Supreme Court, as Roosevelt described them, who kept thwarting all of the legislation that got passed. [FDR] had some kind of scheme to increase the number on the court. Of course, it did not pass, but Lyndon came out in favor of it. He said that he was the only man that was ever elected on that, and I'm sure that's entirely true.

Do you think that's why he won?
I don't know. I have the feeling that he probably won because he covered more miles, shook more hands, spent more time, impressed some strategic people, perhaps who were the country editors, the educators. He really started from way out back as far as knowing the businessmen, but he always had respect and interest and determination to get to know them.

On the Thursday before the election, he was stricken with this appendicitis attack. Was he standing in a receiving line?
Yes. This was a very important, crucial meeting right at the end of the campaign. We had hoped that it would be one of the biggest ones we'd have. It was in some public building in Austin, and what comes to my mind is the courthouse. He was in the receiving line, and people were coming by. You always hope that there are lots and lots of people, and indeed there were. I looked down the line two or three people and saw a familiar couple, Mr. and Mrs. Felix Matthews. I had roomed at their house for three and a half years when I was in the University of Texas and was quite fond of them.

You always hope that the candidate, be he your friend or indeed your husband, is in fine fettle when he meets people that you've been talking to about him, trying to tell them what a very special, wonderful person he is. Well, just as the Matthews were about to get up there, I saw his face cloud up and a dreadful, pained look come on him, a stricken look. I thought, "Oh, my Lord, what is the matter? I hope he can hold out." Which is a terribly selfish thing to think, just hoping that somebody will stand there and look good for your purposes. But I'm sure it's something that everybody who is helping the campaign has thought. Well, he leaned over in just a second or two and whispered to me, "I've got to get out of this." And my heart sank. He hurriedly shook the hands of a few people, and then he sort of stumbled out of the line. I don't think we finished the whole receiving line. I think somebody quickly took over for him. We left to go where he could lie down and where we could get a doctor.

I do not remember exactly how quickly we got to Seton Hospital, but indeed we did. We called one or two doctors. As soon as it was diagnosed as an appendix that ought to be operated on right then, Lyndon was insistent on getting the opinions of at least two doctors. One, he just hated to have to stop. He thought it might even lose him the election to be out of it for the last thirty-six hours. And then, two, it may have been in the back of his mind, I know that it was voiced by some people, that really this was just a play for sympathy. In any case, he was insistent on having a couple of opinions.

This could have spelled defeat for him, couldn't it?
It was very much in his mind that it could have. But there was absolutely nothing else to be done. He could not hold up his head. He could not put one foot in front of the other.

It was excruciating. I do not know whether it ruptured, but it was certainly on the point of rupture. By the time we got to the hospital, it was something like nine o'clock at night. All the diagnoses were made during the nighttime, and I believe it was very early the next morning, six or seven o'clock, when he was operated on. He was just coming out of the effects of it on the afternoon of the last day [of the campaign].

Was he eager to learn more and more about the campaign?
When he began to come to, yes, indeed. I'm sure he was one of the worst patients they ever had. If the election had been a few days later, he probably wouldn't have carried that hospital, because he was impatient and hurting and letting it be known that he was hurt. He was just wanting everything to be different.

By Saturday morning when the polls opened, he was recuperating. He was out from under the operation. It had been a success; the crisis was over. I got on the phone and took to the polls group after group of old ladies, friends that didn't have cars, people that asked me to get them to the polls. A sizable job connected with campaigns then and always was getting your friends who needed transportation to the polls, and also reminding people. It's not the most important thing in the lives of people who are quite strongly for you, after all. They just might get busy and not go. It's a good idea to remind them all day long.

I worked doing that until the polls closed about seven thirty in the evening. Then I was at the hospital for a while. Then Senator Wirtz and Kitty Mae and one or two other people picked me up, and we went out to a friend's lodge house out on the hills, out of Austin, and had some drinks and some refreshments, just cheese and crackers, peanuts and things like that. I found myself just eating vast quantities of it. It suddenly dawned on me that I hadn't had lunch and I hadn't had dinner, and so I came to and realized I was hungry. That should have given me more understanding of Lyndon and his campaigning habits.

My recollection is that we were feeling awfully good by ten o'clock that [Saturday] night about what was coming in. My feeling is that when we were sitting at these people's house—and we stayed there and listened to reports quite a long time—I remember a general feeling of optimism, even elation.

The fact that he was unable to vote must have been a source of frustration.
Later on, of course, a source of laughter, but it was certainly a source of frustration at the time. It caused me to go to all sorts of lengths to vote absentee in later campaigns, that and another event or two. I've done an awful lot of absentee voting.

He stayed in the hospital a good while, maybe ten days.
It was certainly longer than the usual stay because he was completely exhausted. I don't know whether the appendix had ruptured or not, but anyhow, it was just on the point of it. He was a very sick young man.

I do remember something that I was later to learn was typical of politics. He was barely out from under the ether before he began to get requests from people to do things that a congressman was connected with. I was standing guard to try to ward off any visitors, and a man came to the door. I didn't know him. He said it was just so important that he see Mr. Johnson. He just had to see Mr. Johnson. You have to use your judgment in cases like that, and I didn't have much judgment. I was pretty new at that sort of thing. So I decided to let him in. It turned out Lyndon didn't know him at all, and the man wanted to get a job as a cook at a CCC [Civilian Conservation Corps] camp. So, poor soul, needless to say, he didn't get the job and left in rather a hurry. I didn't like that, and yet since then I have learned how one's own needs can be so pressing and you cannot think too much about the other person. That happens in politics on both sides. You ask when you shouldn't when you're the candidate, and you ask when you shouldn't when you're the constituent.

He did indeed have a lot of visitors that fired him up and that he learned from. I remember Governor Jimmie Allred came to see him. Jimmie Allred was an extraordinary man, young, handsome, pretty liberal for that day or for any day. He and Lyndon were natural friends, and Lyndon was later helpful in getting him onto the federal bench. Then Mr. C. N. Avery very graciously came to see him. I think he had a wire or a visit from just about every one of his [eight] opponents. That was a lifelong pattern. I was to learn that he always set out to win his opponents over after a race, or after an argument was over, sometimes to the annoyance of some of his close friends who had carried his banner. C. N. Avery's family threaded through our lives from then on. His daughter, Helen, and son-in-law, Bob Phinney, became lifelong friends and actually headed a later campaign for us.

Did you enjoy this first run at elective office yourself even though you stayed in the background?
I was a highly interested observer. I wasn't really an active helper, except to back it financially and to thank and to be on the other end of the phone line. It was a learning experience. I was curious, and I was excited. I can't say that I really enjoyed it, because I wasn't enough of a participant.

Lyndon became the congressman instead of the congressman's secretary. He became the one whose obligation it was to vote and to learn how to vote and to get the job done for the people of his district, rather than just for the boss who was the congressman. It was an exhilarating thing, something to be proud about, something also to be humble about.

We went to Karnack. I believe Bill Deason and Carroll Keach[8] went with us. That's another one of those funny things; Lyndon always took his staff and his

---

8. Carroll Keach, another one of LBJ's former high school students, had worked for him in Kleberg's office.

close friends with him wherever he went if he could get them to go. Somewhat to my dismay, I must say, there was not always enough time for just the two of us. But he didn't realize that. We stayed about ten days at Daddy's great big Brick House. We went walking a lot. He actually ate well and gained quite a lot of weight.

Then, the important thing of that time was him going to meet President Roosevelt in Galveston. I do not know just where Lyndon went with President Roosevelt on the train, perhaps to Houston and College Station, and then on to Fort Worth, and then catching a plane to Washington, where he was sworn in. I remember him saying that he wanted Sam Rayburn to walk down the aisle with him when he was sworn in, because Sam Rayburn was his father's old friend. They had been desk mates back when Mr. Sam Johnson and Sam Rayburn were in the Texas House of Representatives.

I drove to Washington with Delle Birdwell. Lyndon had asked her husband, Sherman Birdwell, to be his secretary.[9] So Delle and I set forth on this great adventure by car. We drove by Alabama to see my Aunt Effie, who was ill. All through the southern states we ate ham. We just couldn't get enough of that marvelous spicy ham, whether you call it North Carolina ham or Virginia ham. Going through the mountains and all along the winding roads, there would be little stands where arts and crafts were for sale, baskets, chairs made out of slats, quilts. Beautiful country! Ah, how many times I've traveled that road, and I've always loved it.

---

9. Sherman Birdwell had been a member of LBJ's NYA staff.

5

In Congress, 1937–1940

New political and social opportunities greeted the Johnsons upon LBJ's return to Washington as a congressman. Lady Bird quickly became acquainted with the wives of other legislators and New Deal officials. The couple rented an apartment in the art deco high-rise Kennedy-Warren apartment building next to the National Zoo on Connecticut Avenue.

We arrived in Washington and went to an apartment which Lyndon had already obtained for us. It was at the Kennedy-Warren, number 1127, I think. It belonged to Dr. M. W. Splawn, who had been a president of the University of Texas. Roosevelt had appointed him to the Interstate Commerce Commission. The apartment was spacious and comfortable and much more attractively furnished than most of those that I lived in for some time thereafter in Washington. And true to Lyndon's habits, the Birdwells moved right in with us. Sam Houston [Johnson][1] was also living with us.

The office was made up of Sherman Birdwell and little Gene Latimer. Carroll Keach came up for a while to help set up the office, and we borrowed L. E. Jones from another government agency.[2] They went to work in the Old House Office Building. Sherman said when he first opened the door, he fell over twelve full sacks of mail. A good little while had elapsed since Lyndon was elected on the tenth of April and then his stay in the hospital and then his recuperation at Daddy's and then getting up there. Much of that mail was concerned with "getting a job for me." Lyndon would get lots of letters from his daddy, who was so proud of his son being in Congress, and nearly all of them dealt with "Can't you help get a pension for poor old so-and-so?" They were all expressing some human need for somebody. The desperate shadow of the Depression was still hanging

---

1. LBJ's younger brother.
2. Gene Latimer, Carroll Keach, and L. E. Jones, LBJ's former high school students, had worked for him in Kleberg's office. Sherman Birdwell had been a member of LBJ's NYA staff. Carroll Keach Oral History Interview, 4/1/65, by Eric F. Goldman.

over the land. I can't say, though, that I really understood the tragedy of that then. I was terribly excited about being there in Washington. I looked out of the windows of that apartment down onto Connecticut Avenue. I thought what a fascinating new step this was. Lyndon was put on [the] Naval Affairs [Committee]. I've always had it in the back of my mind that it was an interest of President Roosevelt's and that President Roosevelt encouraged him to ask to get put on it.[3] For years and years, [the] Appropriations [Committee] was what [Lyndon] always had his eye on, never successfully. But Naval Affairs turned out to be a wonderful source of interest. Many of the people on it became lifelong friends and great influences, particularly the chairman, Carl Vinson of Georgia, one of those rock-like figures in the Congress who practically lived forever and taught whole generations of younger men. Then there was Warren Magnuson, who later became a fellow senator and always a good friend. Then on the other side of the political line there was Sterling Cole of New York.[4] So Lyndon made many friends, and we saw a good deal of the members of the Naval Affairs Committee. It was a big part of his life. Lyndon would talk about the members of the [Texas] delegation. It was a very strong, cohesive delegation. Every Wednesday they would get together for lunch in the Speaker's dining room.[5] They would talk about their problems. Sometimes they had a closed meeting; sometimes they brought guests. Always the head man to him was Sam Rayburn, a great influence in our lives and someone who Lyndon loved and who loved him. From my own district there was Wright Patman, who interests me enormously, because he was a country man from a country region and never lost that touch. Yet he learned how to deal with the great big outside world. He was a low-interest man; he became the scourge of bankers. He could stand face-to-face and do battle with some of the biggest people in the country. And yet when he'd get back home to Karnack and Jefferson, he would be the most simple of country people.

There was Lyndon's old boss, Dick Kleberg. There was Bob Poage; agriculture was his love and his forte the whole way through. George Mahon early got on the Appropriations Committee and grew with the years, really a great figure. Lindley Beckworth was the youngster of the crowd. Cousin Nat Patton called everybody in the whole wide world his cousin. He was from deep East Texas and a professional East Texan. There was our neighbor, Charlie South. We had both a South and a West in the delegation at that time: Milton West from [south] Texas, and Albert Thomas of Houston, the most formidable opponent in debate anybody could ever have. It was mighty hard to outdo that man. And Ewing

3. For a description of Roosevelt encouraging LBJ to seek assignment to the Naval Affairs Committee, see Lyndon B. Johnson Oral History Interview, 4/16/70, by Michael L. Gillette.

4. Carl Vinson (D-GA) served in Congress for fifty years. Carl Vinson Oral History Interview, 5/24/70, by Frank Deaver; Warren Magnuson (D-WA) Oral History Interview, 3/14/78, by Michael L. Gillette.

5. Sam Rayburn was first elected Speaker on September 16, 1940.

Thomason was one of those wise counselors to whom Lyndon always looked. Lyndon's father used to tell him, "Son, if you ever are uncertain about what to do, just notice what Ewing Thomason does, and just follow right along behind him." He said the same about Judge Marvin Jones. Judge Jones had been replaced [in 1941] by a young, handsome, affable congressman named Gene Worley. He and his wife, Ann, became some of our closest friends. Then there was Hatton Sumners from Dallas, quite a character, one of the most conservative humans I've ever known.

Our two senators were for so many years Tom Connally, a towering figure, arrogant, aristocratic, enormously able man, very intelligent, and then gentle, sweet Senator Morris Sheppard, whose wife was a lovely woman. It was a marvelous delegation. They had a great esprit de corps among them.

THE LIFE OF A CONGRESSIONAL WIFE

My social life was constituents and the Seventy-Fifth Club and the Texas delegation and the Congressional Club. I soon learned that "constituents" was a word spelled in capital letters and mighty important to a congressman and to his wife. One thing I could do to help Lyndon was to take those constituents out when they came to Washington. Even in those days when nearly all the travel was by train, there were quite a few people coming, on business and on vacations. Washington was a great big lodestone for everybody's summer vacation. So, beginning that first summer, I would take constituents out to Mount Vernon and through the Capitol.

The Texas delegation women as well as men were very closely knit and cohesive. The women of the delegation all got together once a month and had a luncheon. You could invite a limited number of your constituents, and you chose very carefully. I loved being able to help Lyndon in that way. I really felt like it amounted to something, and the people at home in the Tenth District remembered it too. One lady would be in charge and would choose the place to go. Maybe we would go to a lovely place out in the country called Normandy Farms, or maybe we'd go out to a huge old colonial house on the banks of the Potomac called Collingwood. It was a big event. At some of those meetings we would make little talks, such as Mrs. [Morris] Sheppard would tell us about how she had chaperoned a bunch of South American girls to the Mardi Gras. As for me, I would be just full of tremors and just wouldn't have dared, but I recognized it as something that I was going to have to tackle sometime.

Another big event for me was the Congressional Club. Every Friday afternoon we would have a tea where someone would speak to us. Occasionally, we would have even somebody from the cabinet or we might have an ambassador or we might have someone give us a lecture on interior decoration. They were very interesting times and well planned. Like a great many congressional wives, I was always in search of soaking up what there was to be had in Washington to learn from.

Also, soon I learned about the existence of clubs named after the [number of the Congress] in which one's husband came to Congress. Ours was the Seventy-Fifth Club. The wives of the men who were elected then would get together once a month, and we would have a program. We were hungry to learn about the city and our husbands' jobs, but we were very much on the periphery. Women's participation in politics in those days was nothing like as vigorous and equal as it later became.

There were also thrilling things like being invited out to the [Harold] Ickeses' for lunch.[6] Lyndon and I had been out there to lunch a number of times, always on Sundays. Then I was invited out to a luncheon in honor of Mrs. Roosevelt. There were cabinet wives there, even including the wife of the secretary of state, Dean Acheson, and Mrs. [Henry] Morgenthau and Mrs. [Felix] Frankfurter, and an old friend, Helen Gahagan Douglas. I remember as we sat around the lunch table, Mrs. [Jane] Ickes, who was really a very bright hostess, wanted to liven things up and make it really a more memorable party by going around the table and asking everyone, very briefly in a couple of sentences, to say what her role was, what Washington was to her. She was the wife of a cabinet member and she did so-and-so, or whatever. I remember how I trembled as it got closer and closer to me. Somehow or another I managed to get through it, though, because I left in a glow.

It was the custom of that day that a new congressman's wife called on all those who preceded her, especially all the members of her own delegation. You called on the wife of the chairman of your husband's committee, and you called on the wives of the cabinet and the Supreme Court. It was also expected that all the new wives called on the embassies. Each group had its day. I think Tuesday was the House, and Thursday the Senate, and Friday the embassies. Monday may have been the Court, and Wednesday the cabinet.

Those poor cabinet wives, for instance, were really expected to be at home from four to six and have some tea and cookies and all sorts of goodies laid out for Lord knows who might call on them. You certainly called on the White House, but it was not expected that Mrs. Roosevelt would be at home. You simply went up there and handed your cards to the butler. At other places, you would knock on the door. Usually a bunch of us would get in the car and carpool it, each of us taking our cards and wearing our white gloves and big smiles. Somebody would drive, and we would go up to the Senate wives or whoever we were going to call on that day and leave our cards. You left your husband's and your card, "Mr. and Mrs. Lyndon B. Johnson." Women did not call on men. Women called on the women. If they had daughters of an age above eighteen, you would leave a card on them. It was quite a complicated and funny little

---

6. Harold Ickes was Secretary of the Interior; Henry Morgenthau was Secretary of the Treasury; Felix Frankfurter, a Supreme Court justice; and Helen Gahagan Douglas was an actress who was elected to Congress in 1940.

thing, and it came to an end with the war. It killed it off as it did so much of protocol. But in those days you did it, and then people returned your calls.

I met a lot of interesting people that way. For instance, I dared to drive up that imposing driveway to Tregaron, where the wife of Senator Millard Tydings of Maryland was living. That was my first sight of that magnificent house. I remember meeting Mrs. Bill Douglas[7] that way. I went to Mrs. Hugo Black's[8] to call on the regular Monday that one went to see the wives of the members of the Supreme Court. She was a beautiful and gracious southern lady, quite different from her sister, Virginia [Durr], but just as marvelous in her way. That's how I met Mrs. Clark Foreman [Mairi]. She was at home. She said, "Come right in." We had a very interesting time. She was more interested in intellectual pursuits than most of the women that I knew, and bright. Clark was one of the exceedingly liberal members of the New Deal group.[9]

Lyndon was a nonpartygoer. I was an ardent partygoer, to the limited places where one could go without one's husband. As the wife of a congressman of not many years' seniority, I didn't get invited to all that many places. But I duly made my calls, [including calling on] the diplomatic corps, and [I] soon began to go to all of the national days. The national day for England was the most outstanding one. Lyndon and I did not go out a great deal to things that were unrelated to business, but everything was related to business. Sometime the Speaker and Wright Patman and Lyndon and I would go out. Lyndon was always taking me places where the other wives didn't necessarily go. I liked it very much. I had little to say but much to listen to. We would go to a seafood place named Hall's down close to the river, where they had absolutely marvelous lobster and beer in pitchers. I wish that I had been a recording machine for all the interesting stories that I heard. It's the men that I remember and their conversations. Except in a few brilliant cases, the conversation among the women was not nearly as fascinating, and I was always glad to stick around with the men.

The women with whom I spent some time were and still remain my good friends: Virginia Durr, Elizabeth Rowe, Jean Kintner, Anita [Mrs. Aubrey] Williams, and of course, always Kitty Mae Wirtz.[10] We would get together for lunch either at my little apartment or one of their houses. Without the men the conversation was less sparkling, but it always had warmth and breadth to it.

---

7. William O. Douglas was appointed chairman of the Securities and Exchange Commission in 1937 and associate justice of the Supreme Court in 1939.

8. Josephine Foster Black was married to Alabama senator Hugo Black. He was appointed to the Supreme Court in 1937.

9. Clark Foreman was director of the Department of the Interior's Division of Public Power.

10. Alabama liberal Virginia [Mrs. Clifford] Durr was the sister of Josephine Black. Jean Kintner's husband, Robert, was a reporter for the *New York Herald Tribune* and later a broadcasting executive. Aubrey Williams was director of the National Youth Administration in Washington.

REPRESENTING THE TENTH DISTRICT

There were two important facets of Lyndon's office in those years of 1937 to 1940. One was that he began sending out early what I would call the "State of the District" letter. The Department of Agriculture issued a lot of little bulletins [with] all sorts of useful information: how to cure your hogs of cholera and how to put up jelly. Then there was one that always made us break up in laughter: what to do about mountain lions if they were catching your stock.

There was a poll tax list in those days. Everybody had to pay a poll tax to vote. So we would take the poll tax list from each of the ten counties of the Tenth District, and we would address an envelope to each one of these and insert one of these folders from the Department of Agriculture, on the back of which Lyndon would have written a letter explaining what all had gone on in his district that year, what he had achieved, what he had worked for but hadn't been able to put over, the general tenor of the country and especially of the district, and asking them if they wouldn't like to send in and get some of this information furnished by the Department of Agriculture. To do that vast job Lyndon would enlist all of the free help he could get, the wives of his secretaries and me, of course, and anybody else that would work for free. They worked such late hours at night that we wives often found ourselves up there addressing envelopes. I'd bring a great big plate of cookies; somebody would put on a coffee pot, or maybe we would come up and work an hour or two before dinner. Then we'd all go out to some cafe and we'd return and work two or three more hours.

He'd get a list of all the graduates from every high school in his district and write them a letter congratulating them on completing their education and what a lot he thought that ought to mean to them. Then he would ask if there was anything he could do to help them out, and to be sure and write him if he could. To this day, I always encounter somebody in a big crowd who tells me that they received such a letter long, long ago.

Did this reflect his high regard for education?
Oh, yes, always. I am looking at it in retrospect now from 1979 when maybe some of the bloom is off the rose, but America had a huge commitment to education from America's inception, and Lyndon was a real believer.

All through the first two and a half years of our lives in Congress until the Depression turned us loose and the war grabbed us, I remember dams, dams, dams; the series of dams along the lower Colorado River, which were built to furnish cheap power for that section of the country. That was the biggest thing that Lyndon was just in love with. [Building the dams to provide] soil conservation, the cheap power, the saving of property and even lives when those floods would strike, was a goal that he was just totally committed to. Senator Wirtz was very much a part of it because he had dreamed it back in the days when it was going to be done by the [Samuel] Insull power, this great big organization from the East which had fallen apart and never got it done. So the government had come on the scene and entered the project. The series of dams was underway when Lyndon came [to Congress]. There was Buchanan Dam, and then Mansfield [Dam]. And then Inks Dam, which was the lovely scenic, smaller dam. Every step in the progress of those dams was something that would cause Lyndon to come home with a great big smile and a sense of euphoria.

It was always Alvin Wirtz and [Austin] Mayor Tom Miller, a rare man, and George and Herman Brown, who were building the dams.[11] I remember both of them well and long and with admiration and love. Both of them were just marvelously optimistic. They were period pieces out of what we imagine the American scene to be. They could get the job done. I know Lyndon always rejoiced in the fact that their contracts were done on time or sooner.

But Herman came on so strong. He was extremely masculine, extremely volatile, very strong. George was soft and gentle and persuasive and always highly imaginative. He was as full of ideas as a pomegranate is of seed. Lyndon had the highest respect, and it came to be affection, for George and Herman, after having begun in a very cool way back in 1937. I think they actually had worked for our opponent. When I would be out of town staying with my daddy in East Texas especially, if George were in town, he and Lyndon would see a lot of each other. They were close as brothers as the years went on. Lyndon and George would have knock-down, drag-out arguments, which neither ever won and neither ever gave in and each affected the other in my opinion.

I guess the biggest thing that happened to Lyndon in [1938] was [securing an appropriation to raise] the height of the Marshall Ford Dam. I began to get acquainted with his way of touching all the bases, a thorough preparation and in-depth homework; first, selling the idea to Secretary Ickes, and then winning the director of the budget's approval. Always foremost with him was checking in with the president and getting his approval. Then he talked to every member of the Texas delegation about it, and as many of his other colleagues as he could. Once having achieved it—and that was the heady wine of success—the next thing to do was to let the folks back home know just what it was going to do for them in terms of more jobs for more men. He made sure the newspapers got that word through his good friends [at the *Austin American Statesman*], Gordon Fulcher, Charlie Green, Buck Hood probably, and Raymond Brooks, how many jobs there would be, how much the power bill would be reduced.

In describing what this would do for the area, Lyndon said it would turn the benefits of one of our great natural resources back to the people, instead of sending thousands upon thousands of dollars in profits from power consumption each year to the money centers of the North and East. A lot of congressmen

---

11. George and Herman Brown were partners in the engineering and contracting firm Brown and Root.

in those days looked upon our part of the country as a stepchild, with a great deal of justification. We were glad every time we could make a stride in bringing ourselves somewhat more even with the East. "Wall Street banker" was a bad word that appeared in a lot of congressional speeches.

Do you recall his going to President Roosevelt to talk to him about getting funds for the dam?
He would go to him and explain it with so much enthusiasm and zest and belief in his own project. He could paint a mental picture of all those women out there, old before their time, bending over the washpot, and all those men getting up before day on a cold winter morning to milk those cows, when there could have been electric washing machines and milking machines. Then there was a whole lot of good soil rolling down the Colorado into the ocean that could have been saved if there were dams and soil conservation measures. The utility of the dams was multifaceted. So he was a persuasive advocate, and Roosevelt came to like him. One time he was invited for an appointment at eleven or twelve o'clock, and the president said, "Stay and have some lunch." Lyndon described how they just set up a bridge table in the president's office and brought it in and Roosevelt's wheelchair was wheeled up, and he sat there with him.

In November 1939, LBJ unveiled a program for recreational parks on the lower Colorado River.
That is more interesting in retrospect than it was then, because the dams, as we all thought of them in those days, were for flood control and soil conservation and cheap power. Actually, recreation did have its genesis right then on just a small amount of money. Five thousand dollars was going to be for park facilities around Inks Dam. Lyndon made high-flown statements that "Austin is destined to become the greatest recreational center in America." All of that might have happened much earlier if it hadn't been throttled by the war, because we were so soon propelled into concentration on war effort, both in all our available money, our thoughts, our concerns, and our interests. So recreation along the series of lakes in the Colorado had to wait awhile for its bloom.

Tom Miller was a marvelous man, portly, well-dressed, quoted Shakespeare at the drop of a hat, in love with the city of Austin, a marvelous storyteller, talked at great length on the telephone. If you got him on the phone late at night, you were liable to go to your next day's work pretty bleary-eyed. The mayor spoke of himself as a man of an evening nature, and indeed he was. He stayed up late at night. He was eccentric. He just didn't fit the mold of most people. He was intensely practical on the one hand in being a politician and knowing how to get the votes of different segments of the society. And he had the touchiest feelings; he was easily hurt. He was out of the ordinary. He was a great benefactor and boon for the city of Austin, of which he was mayor off and on for about twenty years.

He and Lyndon became good friends early. They would spend a lot of time together. They would go down to the newspaper together at night. They'd always stop on the way home and have a great big double dip of ice cream, because they outdid each other in liking ice cream. Not that he and Lyndon didn't have their deep conflicts, one of which became the fact that Lyndon wanted that cheap power, and when Austin bought a piece of the Rural Electrification Administration, he wanted it to be known that the power was going to be cheaper. My recollection is that it didn't get cheaper, that since the city owned the plant, the mayor somehow or another managed to divert the funds saved into other perfectly worthy, perfectly desirable city endeavors, such as parks, swimming pools, and recreation.

Lyndon soon met a great many people in the administration. I learned early that secretaries could be very helpful; Lyndon had known that since his own time as being one. He made friends with Grace Tully, who was a private secretary to FDR, and he became a friend of Jim Rowe.[12] A little bit later we met Abe and Carol Fortas.[13] So we early became a friend and of increasing intimacy with some of the young people in the New Deal, some of those who kept the lights burning all night to remake America. It was a time of high excitement.

Our life became peopled even more with some of the fascinating characters of the New Deal: Interior Secretary Harold Ickes; the new justice Bill Douglas was early a friend of ours; Jerome Frank, who took his place as chairman of the Securities and Exchange Commission; Leon Henderson, an economist; and by now our old friends Tom Corcoran and Ben Cohen and John Carmody,[14] with whom Lyndon had had so much to do in building the dams; Lowell Mellett, with whom he'd worked on the southern report.[15] Others who peopled our life were Tex and [Elizabeth] Wicky Goldschmidt,[16] for whom I had a great fondness. One of the first Georgetown houses that I became acquainted with was theirs, with those narrow little staircases and the straight-up-and-down houses and the aura of age. That was before Georgetown really became fashionable as it later was. It emerged sometime in the Roosevelt years, but it didn't put on that patina of elegance for quite some while. It wasn't all painted up and pretty.

12. James H. Rowe Jr., a legal advisor in the Reconstruction Finance Corporation, would become an administrative assistant to President Roosevelt in 1939.

13. Abe Fortas was the Public Works Administration's general counsel.

14. Leon Henderson was with the Works Progress Administration; Thomas G. Corcoran was special counsel at the Reconstruction Finance Corporation; Benjamin V. Cohen was with the Department of the Interior's National Power Committee; John Carmody was head of the Rural Electrification Administration.

15. National Emergency Council, *Report on Economic Conditions of the South* (Washington, DC: GPO, 1938).

16. Arthur E. Goldschmidt worked in the Department of the Interior's Public Power Division; his wife, Elizabeth Wickenden, was Aubrey Williams's assistant.

DEATH OF A "THOROUGHBRED"

Then his father, who had heart trouble, began to have a series of attacks. At one point Lyndon was down in the district on business, and he called me and he said, "I wish you would come. My father is very ill. I'd like for you to come." I got on a plane and left Washington. It was the only time I ever rode on a sleeper plane. I remember distinctly there was a berth. The airport in Washington was very small indeed. The one in Austin, of course, was just quite primitive.

From late summer until his death in late October, Lyndon's father had a series of recurring attacks. Part of the time he was in Scott & White [Hospital] in Temple. The family always had great faith and confidence and affection in Scott & White and the doctors there. Sometime he was in the hospital in Austin, but where he wanted to be always was in his own home back there in Johnson City.

One of the stories that Lyndon used to love to tell was when he went to see his father in the hospital, his father said, "Son, bring me my britches." Lyndon said, "What do you want with your britches, Daddy?" "I'm going to put them on. You're going to take me home." And Lyndon said, "Daddy, we can't get you any oxygen at home, and you won't have the sort of nurses you have here. They can do things for you here. You ought to stay here." And Mr. Johnson said, "No, son. Bring me my britches. I want to go home where they know when you're sick and they care when you die." And he did go home to Johnson City, at least for a while. I remember being there visiting him, and I remember all the people that would just come and go and make it a part of the routine of their day to call on Mr. Sam. There's a very beautiful little mental picture in my mind of Mr. Johnson lying in his own bed in his own home in Johnson City, very sick. They were talking about some good friend of long ago, and Mr. Johnson said, "He was a thoroughbred." Mrs. Johnson went up and put her hand on his brow and said, "You are too, Sam."

Lyndon had learned an awful lot from his father. He had the greatest respect for his philosophy and for his very real caring about people. He was a populist. It was bone of his bone and heart of his heart. He was a genuine populist. He really cared about all those people he had represented in the legislature and all those people that lived in Johnson City and that were a part of his life and that he'd ever helped. He was also a philosopher. He was also very quick of wit and mind and movement until the years and the troubles ate on him so long. Mrs. Johnson often would say sadly about how graceful he had been as a young man and how swiftly he moved. I'm afraid I could see that, too, in Lyndon's last year or two. When he no longer walked swiftly down the hall, it was sad to see.

His father actually died a few days after his sixtieth birthday. That was something that Lyndon—in his later years—always remembered and often quoted. He had an uncle, too, who died of heart trouble at about that age. Lyndon always felt that that was something that ran in the family. I used to remind him with considerable asperity that he also had Aunt Frank [Martin], who lived to be eighty or so, and Aunt Jessie [Hatcher], who lived to be up in her eighties.

When Lyndon's father died, we were in 4 Happy Hollow Lane. Mrs. Johnson was there with us. My first act was to bring her a cup of hot tea, a small foolish thing to do, but tea was always her small little bit of help. She used to say, "The [cup] that cheers yet not inebriates," quoting some poet. She never had a drink of liquor in her life. No crisis could have compelled her to have a drink. Nor did she like others to.

I remember distinctly what Lyndon did and that was so much in character. He got on the phone and began to make all the calls to the undertaker, the close relatives, to other people. In between making a call, he would sob. Then he would get back on the phone and he would make another call. Then he would catch his breath and let out a sob.

He was totally business, but he was doing it at the same time he was deeply grieved. The rest of us were sitting around, and he was handling everything.

Did his father leave behind debts that had to be taken care of?
Yes, he left behind quite a lot of debts. They were debts that were accumulated only because he was a real victim of the earlier depression of 1922, from which he did not recover. They had five children to raise and put through college. He worked like a beaver and did the best he could. One of those depressions [had come] when cotton was selling for about forty cents a pound. Everybody thought, "I'll just plant all the cotton I can, and I'll make a killing." He borrowed a lot of money, bought tractors, rented land—mostly from his brothers and sisters—land that had belonged to his father. His father had left him some, too. He hired Mexican families and "stood for them" at the store, as the expression was. Whatever they got from the store to eat and live on during the year he promised to pay for. Then cotton dropped that fall to some hideously low price, five cents a pound, from forty cents to five cents. He took such a licking and was so much in debt he just spent the rest of his life bailing out of that. He paid just as much of it as he could with great sweat of his brow and great honesty. But from then on, it was hard sledding. Mrs. Johnson borrowed from her relatives. All of the children who could work did work in varying degrees. For about ten years or so, they'd been hard going.

So his father did leave debts. And one of Lyndon's first actions was to make a list of them, see how much he felt he really was honor bound to pay, and he paid and he paid and he paid. But he didn't pay them all, because some of them were too shadowy, too vague.

Now that his father was gone, did he have to do even more of this? Was he sort of a surrogate father?
Yes, he was, for several reasons: one, he was the oldest; two, he was a naturally strong person that people turned to for help, advice, and management; and three, because of his mother, whom he loved dearly and who did load him up with a lot

of that. She was one of the dearest and most marvelous people I was ever to know, and never wanted anything for herself. We really just had to work at buying her a pretty outfit when we could afford it, or taking her on a pleasure trip, because she only wanted things for her other children, not for herself. She really did turn to Lyndon very often to secure jobs, loans, help of any and every sort for them all. Naturally, that's not the best of climates. It made them resentful. They didn't want him to boss them, and yet there was a close feeling. They needed each other. But it taught me the value of independence. It's something I sought and cherished. Although Lyndon practically always did it, he sometimes resented having to do it.

MOTHER-IN-LAW

We drove back to Washington, taking Mrs. Sam Johnson with us. We wanted to give her a change of scene and relief from the surrounding sadness. She had a great curiosity and interest all of her life. So Lyndon, Mrs. Johnson, and I set out in the car, stopping the first night at Daddy's. Then we usually made it a three-day trip. Lyndon was always impatient, hurrying, striving to get there to get things lined up before Congress began. I always wanted to stop and see all the sights. I particularly wanted to show them to Mrs. Johnson. I lost; we hurried. I think we did stop at the Natural Bridge of Virginia for maybe a meal.

We arrived to the apartment that we had rented on Columbia Road, right out beyond where Eighteenth and Columbia intersect, close to where the Mormon temple now is. It was a pleasant apartment, roomy, comfortable, several bedrooms, and had a shabby elegance and warmth to it. It had a long living room with ever so many windows that opened out to look down toward Rock Creek Park, down into a lot of greenery. Rock Creek Park early established a place in my heart and in my mind in connection with Washington.

The annual congressional reception given by the president and Mrs. Roosevelt took place early in the year. They always invited all the members of Congress, the House and the Senate and their spouses, in one big evening affair. Women wore their very best long dresses, and the men went out and rented white tie and tails and top hats. Some of them probably had their own. It's my recollection Lyndon didn't ever get that until he went to the Senate. But the high point of that reception was that they included Mrs. Johnson in the invitation. We were so proud and happy to take her. I remember standing in line and approaching the president. It was always surprising to see that he was leaning on somebody, even a little. He was so vigorous and forceful. Mrs. Roosevelt had splendid posture. She really looked quite regal.

What did President Roosevelt say to you?
He said just, "How do you do?" or something, nothing memorable. His eyes lit up and he clapped Lyndon on the shoulder or made some gesture more than just a hello.

We'd take Mrs. Johnson to just as many of the events as we could. It was hard to do anything for her, because if you gave her any money, there would always be a need greater than her own, she felt, with one of the other four children. So it became a habit of ours that I would take her downtown and we would find just the prettiest outfit we could.

One particular year I took her down shopping with me, and we found a particularly lovely lavender tweed suit and a lavender hat loaded with flowers, just the perfect color for her, although it was not Lyndon's favorite color by a long shot. With her white hair, she looked beautiful in them. The only trouble was it was already early May and getting late in the year for tweed. But I decided that we'll just throw our hats over the windmill and get this one. It was an expensive suit on sale. It turned out to be a very chilly spring, so she wore the suit over and over, and everybody just exclaimed about how beautiful she looked.

She had a lively intelligence and idleness was not for her. She had finished the big jobs of her life, taking care of her husband and raising her children, and they were all out in the world. What she liked to do was to read, to meet interesting people. Ancestor hunting just became a hobby. We'd go down to the county courthouse and look in the deed records and the marriage and wills. We'd go to the cemetery. I had no interest whatsoever in ancestors, but I did in scenery, and I became interested just because it gave her so much pleasure.

She also loved antiques, early American pressed glass or antique furniture for her apartment. It had to be a very great bargain, but in those days they were to be had.

I remember one absolutely hysterically funny time when we went antique hunting in Maryland on a beautiful sunny afternoon. We bought a sizeable chest of drawers, a sizeable mirror with gilt frame, a number of other objects, and I kept on saying, "But Mrs. Johnson, how are you going to get these things to Texas?" Well, she had the idea that the Lord would provide, and sure enough, he did. Lyndon had a number of secretaries who traveled in their cars, and he would just portion out a piece to each one of them or to friends. I have in the ranch house now a mirror she and I bought on one of our trips that she later left me in her will and a chest of drawers that is upstairs in the purple bedroom. We had a lot of fun times together. We delighted in each other's companionship.

On one of her very first trips to Washington, a man from a well-known Texas family who had courted her in her youth asked if he might come over and take her to a Sunday afternoon musical concert. So he did, and I am quite sure that he asked her for other times, too, but she refused. She didn't like to be teased by her children, who promptly began to tease her about having a date with so-and-so. She said, "If I had ever wanted to further my romance with whatever-his-name-was, I would have done it back before I married your father." We just thought, my gosh, why not have a little second romance?

CHARLES MARSH AND ALICE

An influence that was to permeate our lives for many years started the summer of 1937. That was Lyndon getting to know Charles Marsh.[17] I used to know Alice Maffett Glass in Austin when I was in the university and she worked at the Texas legislature. She was a tall, statuesque, beautiful, highly intelligent young woman, a little bit older than I, and with very intellectual interests. She dropped out of my life. We heard that she had married a man named Manners[18] who was a diplomat and spent most of his life traveling, and that she had a beautiful home where he had ensconced her in Virginia, out from Culpeper. Then that summer of 1937, I believe it was, she called me and said, "Come down and have lunch with me at the Mayflower Hotel," and I did. It was just so pleasant. She was even more beautiful than ever and many interesting things had happened to her. She said she wanted to meet my husband, and she wanted us to come out and spend the weekend at her place in Virginia sometime soon, but that she was leaving very soon to go to the music festival in Salzburg, Austria. She did call us later. I don't know whether it would have been later that summer of 1937. Knowing Lyndon, he would have taken his own steps to meet the man who owned a number of important newspapers in his district. Nevertheless, that is how we met Charles Marsh, at Alice Maffett's house, where he was every time we went.[19]

[He was] one of the most interesting men I was ever to know. He had a head like a Roman emperor ought to look. He was exceedingly intelligent with wide-ranging interests. He was pretty domineering. His lifestyle was on purpose different from other people, and I think he did it in a way, perhaps, to irritate some people. He was a very picturesque character, had a lot of staunch men friends, in particular George Brown and Herman Brown were among them. He no doubt also had a lot of women who were in love with him in the course of his life. He had quite a lot of newspapers and a great facility for making money, and yet money was never to him the end. He had a certain amount of contempt for it, too.

This house was a lovely house called Longlea, beautifully furnished, great view of the Virginia countryside. It was a new way of life to me. They had gardens and a tennis court and a swimming pool. They had a real salon, which would include people from politics or business, or particularly the world of art, in which he was very interested, and Alice was also very interested. It was there that Lyndon and I met Erich Leinsdorf and many people who wrote.[20]

---

17. Charles Edward Marsh owned a number of newspapers, including the Austin *American* and *Statesman*.

18. Manners was a product of Alice Glass's imagination. Caro, *Path to Power*, 480.

19. The most extensive discussion of LBJ's relationship with Charles Marsh and Alice Glass is in Caro, *Path to Power*, 476–92.

20. Erich Leinsdorf was an Austrian orchestra conductor of New York's Metropolitan Opera. LBJ, at the initiative of Alice and Charles Marsh, assisted him in remaining in the United States after the Anschluss in 1938. Erich Leinsdorf Oral History Interview, 3/18/69, by Joe B. Frantz.

[Marsh] affected Lyndon's life in many ways. He formed a very strong attachment for him, and it certainly went both ways. He introduced us to a world of elegance, which neither one of us was acquainted with, not only that home, but also he would take us several times down to the Greenbrier in White Sulphur Springs, a lovely resort in West Virginia that's been there forever. Sheer heaven!

During the summer [of 1939] I went home and spent a while with Daddy, as was my custom. Then, in late August, while I was at my Daddy's, I got a call from Lyndon saying that he was going to the Greenbrier Hotel with Alice and Charles Marsh, and for me to get right on the train and come right on up, because it was going to be such fun. I was filled with dismay, because I had gone home to see my daddy, taking only my tennis shoes and mostly country clothes. I knew I wasn't ready for anything as elegant as the Greenbrier. But Lyndon was very persuasive and just said, "Well, you can buy some more clothes."

I got on the train and went up there. I was a country mouse come to town. Alice was elegant. Everybody there was. Charles always—he knew all about clothes, although he didn't care greatly about them for himself. He must have taught Lyndon a good deal about them, and Lyndon was an apt learner and enjoyed them. I remember feeling very much forlorn and sort of left out. I did manage to go and buy a thing or two. But it's the most glorious part of the world, so green and beautiful.

There was one little respite down to White Sulphur Springs with Charles and Alice during a summer. I believe that was the time when Charles talked to Lyndon about selling him some of his oil properties in which he was involved with Sid Richardson at a very moderate price. It was a big block of property. It was lots more money than we had to buy anything with. It was just no way we could buy it. Charles was determined to sell it to us at a price that amounted to so much of a gift that it was just no way that we could accept it. My feeling about that was that Charles just felt like a doge of Venice or a great manipulator. He saw a person that he considered a terrifically bright young man who might or might not dedicate his long life to politics, who was extremely fitted to be in politics, and who would go far. But Charles thought he had to have a living, and it was pretty apparent you couldn't live very comfortably on the ten thousand dollars a year that we got. So Charles just presumed to think that he could make it possible for him to do that. He had a sort of a kingly attitude.

I do not think he wanted to manipulate Lyndon or have his vote in his pocket or give him any directions on how to expend whatever power came his way. Mr. Marsh was an eccentric man, and he was entirely capable of doing it on just that basis. But Lyndon was an extremely practical man, and he just knew there was no way he could do that. He finally got mad. He and Charles were arguing about this in pretty heated words, and finally Lyndon told me to pack our suitcase; we were leaving. By that time it was getting dark, and that was the most winding, mountainous road you ever set foot to between White Sulphur Springs and Washington. We had come in our car, a convertible. Well, we did; we loaded our suitcases in that convertible and said good-bye to Charles and Alice. Alice, of course, was trying to placate everybody, and so indeed was I. It really was a hilarious scene. I remember Lyndon and Charles leaning over the hood of the car, just talking, one still determined to do it and the other determined not to do it. We got in and drove home, and we got in at some preposterous hour like 2:00 a.m.

Did the two men stay mad at each other for any length of time?
Oh, no. I don't remember the next meeting, but Lyndon had made his point, and made it stick. So far as I know, Charles never mentioned it again. No, they were not mad.
Lyndon just had to turn away quick and firm and make Charles know that he couldn't and wouldn't.

Lyndon might have had a niggling doubt in the back of his mind, "Is this man trying to buy me?" But I think he had too much confidence and affection in Charles to really believe that. I think he thought Charles was indeed trying to make him financially independent. But he also thought that the public wouldn't buy that.
The newspapers wouldn't buy that. Everything becomes known. Nobody would believe it, and he would be trapped into a very hazardous political situation.

In a much more substantive and important way, Charles affected Lyndon in opening up to him the vast world outside the United States, intellectually speaking. Lyndon's interests had been greatly centered in the Tenth District of Texas and in the state of Texas and in the United States. But he had not cared intensely or studied much about the global world. Charles could range through civilizations and centuries and countries in a very exciting fashion. He was the first person that ever made me realize what a threat Nazism could be to our country, and what a fearsome thing it could be to Europe, to that whole continent, and also to us, and to the whole world. I was happily provincial; Lyndon was too. But Charles sure did pull back the curtains to me and to some extent to Lyndon on a wider world, fascinating, dangerous and bound to affect us, whether we liked it or not. Perhaps Charles Marsh and the Naval Affairs Committee together opened Lyndon's eyes for what was going to be the next stage of his development, and that was his interest in the war.

ALVIN WIRTZ'S INFLUENCE

One [legislative proposal] I think of as Lyndon's first almost misstep. A bill came up sponsored by a congressman from some very interior state that said that you had to have a public referendum before you could declare war.[21] Lyndon thought about all the young people that would go to fight the war and thought it was only fair they have a chance to vote on whether it ought to be declared or not. He made some statements to that effect and was about to get interested on the side in favor of a referendum. And Senator Wirtz called us. I forget how they got together, but he just drenched Lyndon in all the reasons why that wouldn't work. Senator Wirtz was one of the most effective persuaders I have ever known. He never beat the table. He never made you do anything. He just laid out the alternatives. Somehow or another when you walked out of that room, you knew which alternative you wanted to lay your bet and lay your life on. Lyndon did a complete change and was scared at how close he had come to committing himself to what would have been a totally pandemonium-producing thing.

There was a near tragic, but really funny, episode in our lives. Maury Maverick, running for mayor [of San Antonio], had earned the enmity of a good number of people who got him indicted for buying poll taxes for people who would vote for him. For once, Maury was scared. He called Lyndon and said, "Lyndon, you've got to get Alvin Wirtz to represent me on this." Lyndon called Senator Wirtz, who was leaving the country to take his wife on a vacation cruise. Oh, the senator just hated to face his wife, and yet he just couldn't say no to Lyndon and Maury. So he undertook the case.

As he delved into it, it began to look darker and darker. The accusation was that some [northern-based] labor unions had sent a good deal of money down to Texas to help in this campaign. Senator Wirtz must have looked at the evidence with a certain amount of dismay and fading heart, but the course he took was just really hilarious. He decided that all that was left open to him was the following: he got a very well-chosen jury and then he got up and said, "For years, those northerners have been coming down to the South and taking our money and going back up to the North with it. Here comes somebody who goes up there and gets some money up there and brings it down here to be used by people who certainly needed it."[22] He won it on that hilarious basis, and they almost laughed it out of court. It was a close call, a very frightening thing. But there was a lot of relief among some of us when Maury was acquitted of it.

IN THE DISTRICT

Lyndon spent a very busy fall covering the district. I was to learn that was the pattern of our lives for many years. One covered the district whenever Congress was not in session. The minute Congress adjourned, you started packing and went home. I used to say dark didn't catch us in Washington on the day that Congress adjourned. His goal was to visit every post office and

---

21. The crucial vote to discharge the Louis Ludlow Amendment from the House Judiciary Committee came on January 10, 1938. Cordell Hull, *The Memoirs of Cordell Hull* (New York: Macmillan, 1948), 563; also see 83 Cong. Rec., part 1, 282–83 (1938).

22. I have deposited in the LBJ Library a text of Alvin Wirtz's statement to the jury.

almost every country store. That is, any community that was big enough to have a post office he would make at least a call there, let the people know he was coming, through whatever services they had, a local paper or through his always-friend the postmaster. Anybody that wanted to [could] come and talk to him or listen to him, maybe he'd have a set-up speech, or maybe he would just walk around the square and speak to the merchants and everybody he met. He was not one to spend the time between sessions in Washington, or, to my great dismay, to take any of those wonderful trips that so many congressmen seemed to be taking.

Lyndon's campaign for the Austin Public Housing Project has got to be one of the big interesting accomplishments. The subject of government housing had come up and he was trying to get it for Austin. We were home for Christmas in 1937. On Christmas morning, he got up before sunup and made a walk all over East Austin, where a lot of poor people lived, and he counted the outdoor toilets. [He] just walked around, up and down the streets and into people's yards. If anybody saw him, I guess they thought he was touched. He saw that there were many houses where there were outdoor water taps, faucets, and people could go out there and get themselves a bucket of water and take it inside for washing the dishes or bathing, but no inside plumbing facilities whatever, and toilets out behind each house, just as one had in the country, the old-fashioned privy. He spent several hours doing that and just came back all fueled up and ready to do battle for a better type of housing in Austin.

He enlisted immediately some of the good businessmen, the real establishment. How he got them is really remarkable, but he got Mr. E. H. Perry, who was one of the most respected and successful businessmen in the town, to be the chairman of the [Austin Housing Authority].[23] He got several businessmen whose reputations standing behind it would appeal to the citizens and make them think this had to be a responsible, worthy going concern. He began to take measures to get it for Austin and predictably encountered a good deal of opposition. Businessmen said that they didn't want to go into competition with the government. They believed it would take Austin fifteen years to grow to adjust itself to the two hundred fifty house vacancies that would be caused by building two hundred fifty units of housing. Lyndon went on the radio and made a speech about conditions in Austin that Austin people themselves wouldn't know because one doesn't look for that. He called his speech "The Sorrows of the Violet Crown." I think that was an O. Henry description of [Austin] years ago. He said he was going to take his listeners on a tour of the Austin slums. People were a little mad because they didn't want to admit they had slums. But he had really taken out some marvelous insurance by having persuaded Mr. E. H. Perry to be chairman of the Housing Authority.

---

23. E. H. Perry was a prominent cotton broker.

I remember Lyndon being very proud of the finished product. I can see in my mind's eye a picture of him and Mr. E. H. Perry and Nathan Straus, who was Washington head of the [Federal Housing Authority], standing in front of a plaque pointing it out, and Lyndon beaming from ear to ear that this was certainly one of the first finished public housing units in the country. There was an optimistic strain in him that made him think that the government could be better and the government could take a hand in making it better. The housing project did furnish jobs for a lot of people in desperate need of them.

In 1939, we also made a complete change in office staff. Dorothy Jackson was the first one who came aboard, as I remember. She was a tall, thin, redheaded, freckle-faced, eager young girl from Cotulla, a place that had made a big impression on Lyndon's life.[24] He knew a lot of her background and family. She was fast and bright. John Connally entered our lives. I think he formally started working for us in mid-October, but we were together in discussing it earlier. He was from Floresville, one of Mr. Sam Fore's boys. That's a mighty high recommendation to Lyndon. Senator Wirtz had already interviewed him and given him high marks. He had been president of the student body at the University of Texas. He was in law school at that time. It seemed to me he either graduated or just had maybe one course [to complete]. It was obvious from the beginning that he was top caliber and he was someone who could handle a big load and leave Lyndon free to operate. Then Walter Jenkins came with us a little bit later. Walter had been chief assistant to one of the deans at the University of Texas. Herbert Henderson was still with us, writing speeches. So that was a foursome.

We had lots of fun during those first congressional years. One of the most fun times we had and one of the first real recreational activities I can remember us doing was going up to Buchanan Dam. There was a great big administration building that had some meeting rooms and some bedrooms, dormitory-like space, lots of cots, and a big kitchen. People with a connection with the Lower Colorado River Authority could reserve it. We did that a number of weekends. We would go riding on the lake. The more adventurous of us would swim. We would play cards. We'd sit out on the front porch and watch the sunset and put our feet up on the rail and tell stories. We were all very young and life was good. It was a happy time.

That was one of my first long, continuing battles with the telephone. We would all get around the breakfast table. Everybody would come when he got ready, and the wives would usually just prepare the breakfast for their own husbands, or maybe three or four of us would join together and do it. Lyndon wanted fried eggs, and I brought him a couple and put them down in front of him. About that time, the phone rang for him, and he went to get it, and talked and talked and talked. By the time he got off the phone and started back to the

---

24. Dorothy J. Nichols Oral History Interview, 9/24/68, by Joe B. Frantz.

table, I knew those eggs weren't going to be fit to eat, so I quickly prepared another couple, set 'em down in front of him. Same thing happened all over again. [*Laughter.*] That happened three times before I finally got him to sit still and eat.

"GATHERING CLOUDS"

The two things that I remember best about [1939 and] 1940 were the gathering clouds of war in Europe and the continuing question, "Is Roosevelt going to run for a third term? Nobody's ever done it. Is he going to? And if he runs, can he win?" It's easy now to think of his time as a long, continuing honeymoon. It wasn't. There were rising tides of dissension and anger from a lot of groups, from the doctors, the conservatives, the people bent on peace, and the people bent on involvement in the war.

How did you feel about the third term?
I guess I'm naturally pretty much of a conservative, and I was concerned about doing something that never had been done before. But on the other hand, I have an overweening admiration and attachment to [FDR], and I never considered myself wise, particularly politically. So since Lyndon was very much in favor of it, I was too. It was quite a thing to work out that Texas situation where John Nance Garner[25] really aspired to the presidency. It was always Lyndon's desire to effect a compromise and not a fight. He used to say to newspapermen, "You all want to stir up a fight. I want to stop one." It finally was worked out, at least where there was no ugly confrontation, and Texas did vote at least once for Garner as its favorite son and then was committed to Roosevelt from there on.

Much of the talk was about what was happening in Germany and in Poland and in all the surrounding countries, and what would England do, and what would France do. On our weekends down at Longlea, I remember getting chills down my spine when Charles Marsh would describe Hitler's charismatic hold on those people and the fact that he had done things to make them proud of themselves and to make them a cohesive nation. Whereas before, they had been not only weak, they apparently had not had national pride in that interim before he came to power in Germany. Charles made it all seem very vivid and very frightening and very close, and close was what we didn't want it to be. All the people of this country, it seemed to me, just seemed to be pulling the curtains around us and trying to ignore it. I just remember it as an aura in a heavy cloud. I don't know why it wasn't more of a blockbuster of a period to me, since the explosive beginning of the world war happened soon thereafter.

---

25. John Nance Garner of Texas was vice president from 1933 to 1941.

6

1941, "A Learning Experience"

Lady Bird Johnson's vivid account of a single year, 1941, reveals her enthusiasm for the political life into which she was increasingly drawn. She documented that eventful year with shorthand diary entries in her datebook and with her newly acquired movie camera.

THE WORLD'S WORST PATIENT

1941 was a watershed year for us as it was for so many people. But it began in the way all those years after we went to Congress began. I drove the car. Lyndon had gone on ahead in the plane. I left Marshall on a gray, rainy January 1, taking Ray Roberts, who'd been asked to come up and go to work for the Speaker. The road was full of us going to Washington in those days. The next day we met up with Walter Jenkins and went as far as Roanoke, where we spent the night in a tourist home. There were lots of rather nice-looking old homes, usually Victorian with white gingerbread and verandas and a sign out front, "Overnight Tourists."

We got to Washington the next day around noon and went first to the House Office Building. The very first person I ran into after walking into the hall was Cousin Nat Patton, who said that Lyndon was in the hospital. He had pneumonia, and they had taken him to Doctors' Hospital the day before with fever of 104. Of course, I went right over there. Dr. Adams was in charge; he had given him a sulfa drug, which had brought the temperature down. He was much, much better, but he was still a very sick man; he'd been out of his head. He'd already fired one nurse.

Lyndon was one of the world's worst patients. Mr. Marsh and Alice were the only people who were being admitted. I'm sure the hospital rued that day that they first let them in. Mr. Marsh was as hard to live with in the hospital as Lyndon. The day after I got there, Mr. Marsh was in Lyndon's room when a young intern came in and mistook Mr. Marsh for Dr. Adams. Mr. Marsh caught on immediately, didn't deny it at all but began giving instructions about how

Lyndon was to be treated, which the intern was taking right down onto his chart. Oh, later on the hospital was so furious!

The next day, Sunday, I felt secure enough about Lyndon to go to Virginia Durr's for lunch, which was always a marvelous treat for me. The intellectual fare was rich and made up for whatever might have been lacking in the precision of the way the household was run. One of her houseguests, who truly came for dinner and wound up staying probably a year, was Decca [Mitford] Romilly. She was one of the sisters of a famous British family. [They were] as colorful a family as ever lived, three or four sisters, all very different and all personalities that walked across the stage for several decades. This one, Decca, was very liberal, pro-Communist, very much interested in the civil war in Spain. There was much heated talk of [Ernest] Bevin[1] in England and of the expansion of plants for defense contracts and how democracy was going to be saved. There was always lots of philosophical and political talk around Virginia and Cliff Durr's table.[2]

That night, I went to one of the most glittering things that I had experienced in Washington up to that time. It was a big dinner given in honor of the Speaker and Miss Lou [Rayburn's sister] at the home of a hostess with a capital H, a Mrs. Denegre, who had a house on Massachusetts Avenue, one of those great old homes of stone with ceilings about twenty feet high and a ballroom on the third floor, something that belonged to another day. We passed about six liveried footmen and butlers before we got to the drawing room, where our hostess greeted us. There were flowers and mirrors everywhere and exquisite furniture and about forty guests, including Justice [William O.] Douglas, the attorney general, Mr. [Robert] Jackson, charming Senator [Alben] Barkley, a governor or two with their wives, and then, of course, the Speaker and Miss Lou. I remember Alben Barkley sitting next to me. We were talking about a well-known Washington couple and their marriage relation. I [asked]: "Are they getting a divorce?" He said, "Well, I would say their relation is tenuous." I liked his choices of words.

The arrival of Miss Lou was always a clarion call to the Texas delegation to the height of the social season, because the Speaker, for all his folksiness and his simplicity, had a marvelous family feeling, a great love and respect for his sisters and brothers, and especially for Miss Lou, who was the duchess of the clan. She spent about two or three weeks with him every January or February. She was a tall, erect, patrician woman. Her hair was rather salt-and-pepper and full, and she had a very fine profile. You would have known this was an aristocrat wherever you had met her, however simple her manners were. The Speaker always was proud that he took her in on his arm to dinner at the White House and to

---

1. British Labour Party official.
2. Clifford Durr was appointed to the Federal Communications Commission by FDR.

all these elegant places. It was a sparkling event in her life, of course, coming from the quiet life on the farm at home.

Monday, January 6, was the day of the president's State of the Union to Congress. All of those were great days, year after year. Almost always, I would occupy my seat and practically lean over the rail and listen to every word. Sometimes if there was a constituent big enough in town that I felt that I should give my seat to, I would. Then at the last minute, somebody sweet would always find me another seat, even if it was sitting in the aisle, on the steps, which happened a good many times.

This time the Republicans were silent as stones, because, by January of 1941, Roosevelt was talking about lend-lease. He was nibbling at the edges of help to Britain. As a nation we were not scared, and we were not sold on it. He was trying to take us as far as we would go, but he had to have the Congress and the people behind him. I remember I felt it was rather anticlimactic after his Fireside Chat a few nights before.[3]

At this time, Lyndon was still in the hospital. He didn't get out until two or three days afterwards. As soon as he got over the really serious, frightening part of an illness such as this, his hospital room became a revolving door. Everybody came to see him. He was being deluged with gifts from Charles and Alice. They gave him a red velvet smoking jacket and lots of books and magazines during that siege in the hospital. The diet kitchen was just getting absolutely furious with Lyndon. Tray after tray would go back untouched because the Marshes were bringing him in everything he ate.

From time to time, my date book became almost a diary, because I would write in shorthand in it. Thursday, January 9, [contains] a description of what our life was like so much of the time:

Today has been a mad endurance contest. When I arrived at the hospital, in turn the following came in such rapid succession: Wright Patman, Roy Miller, Perry Bass, Mr. Shirley, Mr. Marsh and Alice.[4] Then came John [Connally] and the ambulance man, and we carried Lyndon home. The nurse failed to come, so we left without her. She called later in a huff.

At home, business picked up as it always did when Lyndon was there. There was a constant stream of people: Ray [Roberts], Sam Houston [Johnson], Tex Goldschmidt, Bruce Catton of the Newspaper Enterprise Association with John. I served everybody drinks and roasted pecans.

Our house was just like a Marx Brothers movie in those days, with the doorbell and the telephone and the maid and everybody talking at the same time, guests coming and going, and me trying to cope with getting them something to eat

---

3. Fireside Chat, December 29, 1940.
4. Roy Miller was a prominent Texas lobbyist; Perry Bass was the nephew of Texas oilman Sid Richardson.

and hanging up their coats and all like that. Lyndon flourished on it; rarely did he get tired. It was amazing. In spite of his serious illnesses, he had the great capacity to bounce back, to put in long hours, and so did I. I really didn't know what it was like to be tired, and that was the way with all of us when we were young.

Albert Thomas called. [I wrote:] "It looks like a pitched contest." That was the important line of the day, because it was beginning one of the big battles of Lyndon's life which he roundly lost. He wanted very much to be on the Appropriations Committee. So did Albert Thomas of Houston. Albert had about five months more seniority than Lyndon. He had been sworn in in January of 1937. Lyndon had been sworn in in May of 1937. Also, Albert was one of the most able and determined politicians that ever lived. I wouldn't want to pitch a battle with him on anything. But Lyndon did so want to be on the Appropriations Committee. He worked to the last day to make it. The delegation voted to endorse Albert Thomas for the Appropriations Committee. The vote was ten to eight. Lyndon took it with very good grace and thanked all his lieutenants with a gay little speech in which he said, "There will be other times and other fights." But he was deeply disappointed to the bottom of his heart.

SOCIAL EVENTS

We watched the inauguration of FDR in January. [Lyndon had given me] that movie camera for Christmas. I always hated machinery; I never liked anything with more than one button that said "off" and "on," but I was determined to learn how to use that dad-gum thing. I mastered it and took a lot of movies. I was told, however, that I couldn't take my camera to the inauguration. Afterwards it looked like everybody there had theirs, and I was so mad.

One of the delicious moments of this winter of 1941 was going to lunch at Mrs. James Forrestal's.[5] It was a beautiful house. She was a glamorous woman, worldly, quite outside my range of acquaintance. I was fascinated. There were real Marie Laurencin paintings in her bedroom. The whole thing was so far beyond what I had experienced in sophistication and elegance. I felt very small but very eager.

February of 1941 was a rich and varied social life and intellectual life. One night we went to dinner at the home of Evalyn Walsh McLean, a very famous hostess of those days. This was a one and only time for a young congressional couple like us. First thing, Lyndon didn't like to go to parties and kept on turning things down that I was wild to go to. Second, we were really pretty small-fry to be invited there. But this time there were a hundred and six people, so my little diary says, and I remember course after course of rich, jellied, elegantly made-up,

---

5. Josephine Ogden Forrestal.

beautifully presented things passed. Afterwards we saw a movie. But what lingers in my mind is the sheer opulence of the evening. Walking through room after room of collections of various kinds of china, objects of art, a whole room full of china dogs.

Sometimes I did things that at least served to sharpen my mind and teach me something. I went to the Lend-Lease hearings with Elizabeth Rowe, and we listened to James Bryant Conant, the president of Harvard, and to the bouncy little mayor of New York, Fiorello La Guardia. I remember Wendell Willkie[6] passed me in the hall, one of the most vital, vivid men I've ever seen. He didn't look to right or left; he was moving just as fast as he could and preceded and followed by an equally determined coterie of men.

Of course, the stellar event of that February was going to dinner at the White House. I wondered if it was going to be my first and last dinner there. This one was for the duchess of Luxembourg, who was the president's house guest. I sat next to Senator Sherman Minton[7] on one side and on the other Representative Joe Casey from Massachusetts. I remember how handsome he was, and his wife was equally good-looking. They were Roman Catholics. They had a whole houseful of children, and I was so impressed and a little bit envious that, looking so young, they had so many.

Everything was managed just with watchmaker's precision, and that stuck in my mind, too. After dinner, the gentlemen stayed at the table and Mrs. [Eleanor] Roosevelt moved us into another room, and she would pass from group to group and chat with us.

Then finally we went upstairs and saw a movie, *The Philadelphia Story*. Long, long afterwards, I got to know the wife of the author, Mr. [Philip] Barry. Another of the high spots of this winter was going to lunch at the [Harold] Ickes' home. We went several times. It was always on a Sunday, out to their farm in Olney [Maryland]. This particular time there was only the Speaker and the Wirtzes and us. I was always impressed by what a gracious, smooth hostess Mrs. Ickes was. She was very redheaded. She talked well and vigorously. Of course the secretary took the lead, but she was able to hold up her end of it.

That very night, too, we had a Mexican supper at our house. Mexican supper for the Texans was a signal to "let's be us," and every now and then you just had an impulse that you just had to do it. Not that we wouldn't invite outsiders, too, because we did have the Jim Rowes and the Corcorans to this one, but principally it was the Speaker and the Wirtzes and the John Connallys and us. Tom brought his accordion and played "Tim Doolin." The Speaker gave an introduction to the last song, "I Am a Dirty Rebel," and what a funny thing for this southerner to be hearing from an eastern man. I got it all down on a record.

---

6. Republican presidential nominee in 1940.

7. Senator Sherman Minton of Indiana was defeated for reelection in 1940. He was appointed to the United States Supreme Court in 1949.

Besides my movie camera, I also had a [Presto cellulose-coated disc] recorder. That record went around with us for years and years. I remember unearthing it at various moves, and finally one time it was just in ripples from having been stored in too hot a place.

But one invitation that I perhaps savored most and always was to go to the Speaker's upstairs apartment at the Anchorage[8] and have dinner. One, I did because Lyndon was always willing to go and eager to go, and I didn't feel like I was imposing on his time and strength. And two, always there were interesting people, and the Speaker was a natural host. He wanted to put you at your ease and make you have a good time. His bachelor apartment was about the third floor up, and one ascended in a tiny elevator or walked. It was very simple, somewhat Spartan. He would have a meal sent over from across the street where there was an excellent cafe. They took pleasure in giving him their best and taking care of him.

We had so many good evenings there, and the talk would flow. I remember a particular time [when] the Tom Corcorans were there, the Felix Frankfurters, and, surprisingly enough, the Dick Klebergs and the Ewing Thomasons, [who were] were always, of course, good friends of his. Ben Cohen was there. It was [an] across-the-board sort of a gathering, all of whom loved the Speaker, all of whom profited from their association with him, from a give and take, from learning and sharing. The best of all times were when he would reminisce about the whole broad stretch of his life in Congress. He was a remarkable catalyst in the House and indeed in the whole government field for a long, long time. He came [to Washington] during the [first] days of Woodrow Wilson's [presidency].

Did he have friends that were not in politics who would attend these evenings?
The whole town was politics. That's what the press was all about. No doubt there were people who lived there that we were inclined to call "the cave dwellers," who just owned businesses and were no part of us and may even, for all I know, have looked down on us. We didn't know them, and they didn't know us, hardly.

Another of the things I liked best was on the way to some dinner I'd be picked up by the Speaker in his great big long black car. I never had such a feeling of elegance and being taken care of. His chauffeur, George [Donovan] had lived in Washington for many, many years, had served other speakers or majority leaders, knew where everybody's house was, who all the hostesses of the decades had been, and could tell the most wonderful stories, if you happened to get picked up first in the rounds and could talk to him. The Speaker very kindly took care of picking up the wives of several of his friends when the men would all go together from the floor of the House and join us at the dinners.

---

8. The Anchorage is a small apartment building at 1555 Connecticut Avenue NW, near Dupont Circle.

Women's luncheons were very much the order of the day. What was it about those times that was different from these? Women seemed to have a lot more leisure time in the middle of the day. I guess the simple fact was that we all had help in those days, and so we would get together and go to lunch at places with names like Tally-Ho, or Iron Gate, or the Parrot, Collingwood and talk.

Our Seventy-Fifth Club had its luncheon in honor of Mrs. Roosevelt. I was on the committee that helped make the arrangements. I remember feeling very important and hoping that it would get me over my sense of shyness by participating in club activities and making some of the decisions. One of the things I wanted to do was to take some movies of Mrs. Roosevelt at the luncheon, so I wrote her secretary and got an answer back that, yes, it would be all right. We decided to have it at the Kennedy-Warren. I invited Mary Rather, Nellie [Mrs. John] Connally, and Juanita Roberts.[9] On the dollar seventy-five that we were paying for our tickets we made a profit! The profit that we made went to buy a wheelchair for a cripple that Mrs. Roosevelt had taken an interest in. Some of us—it certainly wasn't me—had gone to her and asked her what charity or what good purpose would she like us to put the money to, and she told us. That incident and actually that individual, because we learned a lot about him, have stuck in our minds; how she could turn her attention to one person as just a beginning on a good cause.

I saw [Eleanor Roosevelt] a number of times, always in large parties. She was always very purposeful, very serious, and very earnest. I suppose the most remarkable thing I remember about her [was] walking through slums of Washington with her. She invited a number of congressional wives to walk with her. Here she just strode forth with long steps and a relatively smallish number of us following her. It was a learning experience, and it was interesting to see that she dared do it, one, because it certainly wasn't a cup of tea and roses-and-lace sort of thing to do; two, that she cared. And it was a learning experience just to see how dirty and grubby and, in a way, frightening and foreboding the area was.

Then a big personal thing that happened to me in the spring of 1941 was to move to the Woodley Park Towers. For a good many years, I had been thinking rather wistfully about a house and about getting settled and having something permanent in my life to look forward to instead of just another campaign. I've always loved houses and had a sentimental attraction for one's home seat. The Woodley Park Towers was the next best thing to having a house, because the apartments were big and roomy and it hung out over the edge of Rock Creek Park. We did make that move in midspring into a spacious living room and a raised area at the end of it with bay windows all around where you looked down into the park, and two bedrooms—we always managed to keep the other one full—and a pleasant and capable enough, although rather old, kitchen.

---

9. Juanita Roberts was married to Ray Roberts; she later became LBJ's secretary.

Lyndon always went to work on Sundays. He didn't quit going to work on Sundays until well along into his career. I cannot remember exactly when, but it was a big change in our life when he did. He called me from the office one Sunday and said that he was talking to all the LCRA [Lower Colorado River Authority] crowd and he would like to bring them all home to dinner. There were about thirteen of them. Happily, it didn't matter, because I always had a smoked turkey if it was anywhere within six months past Christmas, because we usually received several for Christmas, and I had a half a ham in the icebox. So, Nellie and I pitched in together, and we put together a good buffet supper for them. Of course, the Connallys and the Wirtzes were there. I had that very feminine feeling of having put on a good party and being real proud of myself. It was one of Lyndon's delightful characteristics that he always noticed when I had tried very hard on something and the result had been good, and he would just praise me afterwards and tell me how fine it had been, and I'd just beam. It was obvious though that he was carrying the problems of the co-op on his shoulders, he and the Senator both, and were unhappy and frustrated about them.

A SUDDEN SENATE VACANCY

It was April, the ninth, when Senator Morris Sheppard, that venerable figure in Texas political life, died. In the custom of the day, I went over to Mrs. Sheppard's. All the wives of the delegation would go and try to help out whenever a family was stricken by death or misfortune of any kind. On occasions like that you would take something for all the family to eat, because at the center of the tragedy the people just seemed to be in a state of paralysis. So their neighbors did things like bring food, answer the telephone, open the door, and meet the guests, and receive the condolences, just anything you could to help. After we had been there quite some while, it was beginning to get dark and time to go home and see about dinner. Some of us said, "Oh, but Mrs. Sheppard, several of us are going to stay here with you. We don't want to leave you by yourself." Her children, it appeared, had just not reached the house yet; they were en route. I remember she said, "No, no. You must go on and go back to your husbands while you have them."

Mrs. [Lucille] Sheppard was handsome all of those years: in the thirties, forties, fifties, and sixties. She was married successively to two United States senators.[10] One of the most interesting luncheons that I went to was when we prevailed upon her to tell us about her twenty-five years in Washington. It was the occasion of her twenty-fifth anniversary of coming to town. She had come as a young student at one of the elegant girls' colleges there. Her family had told their then congressman, "Watch out for their daughter," and he did. He paid her

---

10. Lucille Sheppard married Tom Connally after Morris Sheppard's death.

a visit. He was some years her senior, and I expect that Senator Sheppard was all of his life a very quiet, gentle, judicious man. She was, I'm sure, quite lively as a girl. That soon turned into romance and marriage and the beginning of her long life in Washington.

Of course, the death of Senator Sheppard pushed to center stage a big question in Lyndon's life. Should he take the leap? Should he try to make the next step? Did he have enough nerve to run for the Senate? I do not recall his ever having talked over with me the pros and cons of such a race and any clear-cut decision. It just passed between us like osmosis. I knew what he was thinking. I had had many talks over the four Washington years with the Speaker about Lyndon's future. The Speaker advised a cautious waiting game and told me about how long it had taken him to advance from this to this. He also said in a few years he was going back to Bonham and raise prize cattle. He probably even mentioned the number of years, and he missed it by a long shot. For much longer than that, I had had talks with Senator Wirtz about Lyndon's future. I'm sure Lyndon had long discussions with the Speaker, and with Senator Wirtz, and I expect with Charles [Marsh], and possibly Alice. I'm sure that when he came close to it, he would have [spoken] with John Connally and with others in his staff. He was a good listener, when he wanted to be.

He did go to Texas to make a speech to the Texas House of Representatives, and I have an absolutely wonderful picture of that which lives in my mind. The day was April 21, San Jacinto Day, dear to the heart of all Texans, and the subject was Texas independence and the future of world freedom. [In] the picture you see Coke Stevenson's dour face, with his pipe gripped in his teeth. He's listening intently to Lyndon. He was the lieutenant governor. The governor was [W. Lee] "Pass the Biscuits, Pappy" O'Daniel.

[Lyndon] flew straight home from Austin to Washington and went right to the White House. He had a conversation with the president and came out and made his announcement on the White House steps. I knew it was in the making, but the timing came upon us very suddenly, as far as I was concerned. It was evident from the moment he made the announcement on the White House steps that he had ardent backing from FDR, and that was carried out through advice and help from Jim Rowe and other friends in the administration.

He called me immediately afterwards to tell me. I was having a tea at home for an old friend of ours, Nan Wood Honeyman, who had been a member of Congress from Oregon. [Lyndon] told me that he was going to hit the cold water. He had announced for Sheppard's seat. It was not many hours afterwards that he flew back to Texas to get geared up and going. I drove down. Juanita Roberts came with me, and we stopped and did some sightseeing along the way. I clearly remember going through Andrew Jackson's home more leisurely than I ever had with Lyndon.

I think we were actually the first [to enter the race]. "Pass the Biscuits, Pappy," the sitting governor, announced just a few weeks later, and also the terrifically well-known, very popular chairman of the [House] Un-American Activities Committee, Martin Dies. He was a national figure, far better known than we were. [Another candidate, Gerald Mann,] was a fine young man who had been a star football player and attorney general. His nickname was "The Little Red Arrow." He also had strong connections with the Bible Belt. Each one of them had their formidable constituencies.

It was really brash of a young congressman of four years' standing in the House and not quite thirty-two to imagine that he could win in a field like that. Yet I remember 1941 as just about my favorite campaign. I don't know exactly why I should say that. Mainly it was still the rich wine of youth was running in our veins very strongly. We hadn't gone through a lot of searing experiences as we did in the next few years. It was a summer of enormous effort.

Was there a campaign strategy?
Backing FDR all the way, strong national defense, reliance on what he had done with REA [Rural Electrification Administration], the whole complex of dams along the river which had brought hopefully cheap electric power to a big section of the state and flood control and soil conservation. That was the main theme. There was a backdrop that followed us everywhere, and it was the picture of Lyndon shaking hands with FDR.

There was much in 1941 that was so similar to 1937. We opened in San Marcos; we closed at his boyhood home in Johnson City. The same factors were strong helpers—the people he had gone to school with at San Marcos, the people he had worked with in the NYA. And this being a statewide campaign, there was a very strong element of support from the old Fourteenth District, Mr. Kleberg's district, where Lyndon had served as secretary for four years. There were caravans of cars that would set out across the state to accompany him as he was going to show up here and there and yonder. Once more, as it had been in 1937, the people would talk to their counterparts. Mr. [Sam] Fore would talk to the newspapermen, and some rancher friends from the Fourteenth District would talk to other rancher friends, and businessmen to their fellow businessmen.

And so began a blitzkrieg summer of two months until June 28. Lyndon wore seersucker suits, which would be frightfully rumpled by the end of the day, and shirts that after about the second speech would get wet with sweat. I used to call days a "three-shirt day" or a "four-shirt day" or whatever. One of my principal contributions was to follow him around, packing bags and unpacking them and getting the laundry done. He often rode on small planes, scary to look at, landing in just little fields. Sound trucks with advertising of Lyndon Johnson all over them were the trademark of the campaign. The scene was very likely to be the courthouse square. That's the way it was in the thirties and forties until television took over in the middle or late fifties. It was the politics that I knew and liked.

Sometimes he would make as many as twenty speeches a day, but that would not mean major speeches. There would usually be a big rally at night and then maybe a meeting with a chamber of commerce group or a service club, a breakfast meeting, a lunch meeting, a lot of stops in between. The state is a big place. It was not nearly as simple as it had been in running in the Tenth District. You couldn't just stop in Taylor and Georgetown and walk around up and down the two or three main streets and go in every store and speak to every merchant and every customer. You had hopefully enough friends to set up an organized gathering. It was up to your advance men, your best friends, to get the people to it.

He traveled mostly by automobile. Carroll Keach was his driver to everywhere. One time somebody looked at Carroll and said, commiserating, "Carroll, that sure must be a hard job." He said something like this: "Well, every one of us can do something for him," just as though it was just his pleasure to do that. It was up to the fellow who was driving to remind him, "Now, Mr. Johnson, this next town you're going to meet Mr. John Jones, and you remember John Jones used to be with you at so-and-so and so on." So then you could bounce out of the car with some assurance and some names and memories on the tip of your tongue.

The courthouse square was the scene of confrontation, and the courthouse square was duplicated 254 times across Texas. It was where the man came to present his case and where the folks came to hear him. There were certain days that were better. Saturday was the choice day.

Everyone made an effort to have some kind of entertainment to entice the voters to come and listen or to keep them interested until the candidate got there. At the least you had a sound truck playing loud, cheerful music, lots of patriotic songs. It would go around and around the square and announce that you were going to speak at such a time and such a place and everybody come. When you really were trying and when you could manage it, you had a band, an entertainer, the familiar picture in the background of FDR and Lyndon, flags waving. You usually tried to have some of the outstanding people of the community on the platform with you, or to introduce you, or at least highly visible in front of the crowd. Harfield Weedin located a singer called "the Kate Smith of the South"; Sophie [Parker] was her name. She must have weighed about three hundred pounds. She really could belt out "God Bless America," which she always closed with.

This campaign was very heavily recorded by my little instrument, that camera that Lyndon had given me in the Christmas of 1940. I used it myself lots, and when I couldn't, I'd turn it over to somebody; Juanita Roberts did some of them. We have pictures of W. Lee O'Daniel on the courthouse square in Marshall. It's fascinating to study the faces of the voters. They're all so intense and they're sizing you up. You can just see them there like a Greek chorus, just figuring you out. There was a good deal of blue shirts and overalls and western hats with sweat on the hat band. There was usually in the crowd an old Confederate veteran, all aged and dried up but in his uniform full of medals. Somebody else that was always in the crowd was the old trail driver. The farther west you went, the more you got, because naturally their habitat was where they had been trail drivers. They were always Lyndon's friend, and the [Trail Drivers Association] was strongly his friend.

At W. Lee O'Daniels's rally, his pretty daughter Molly was going through the crowd with a little wooden barrel with a sign on it, "Drop in your quarters," or your dollars, because they made quite a thing out of their contributions really coming from the folks. We also have Gerald Mann standing on those same courthouse steps.

I traveled quite a lot. The funny thing, I must have worn the same beige gabardine suit every day with a different blouse, thank heavens, and a great big beige hat and a big leather purse with a huge brass ornament, which, incidentally, Lynda still has, and [it] will last forever. This appears time after time in those movies. If any of the folks were traveling with us they must have gotten the idea that we were a thrifty set.

"YOUNG AND ALL TOGETHER"

In Austin we had headquarters at the Stephen F. Austin Hotel on the second floor, opening out onto that balcony. There was a whole marvelous, wonderful coterie of young women typing away and lots and lots of volunteers. Senator Wirtz resigned his job as under secretary of the interior and came down to be the mastermind. I remember so many evenings late at night sitting out on that back porch of his and talking about what to do for the next day. Somewhere in the vast recesses of the hotel, John Connally was holed up and working night and day. John was the tremendously able and effective director of the campaign. Everett Looney[11] was a confidante and planner and helper. Harold Young was too, and we were always getting messages from Charles Marsh. Roy Hofheinz,[12] who had a great sense of showmanship and as much vitality as Lyndon, was a star figure. It was a wonder to watch him [introduce Lyndon]. When he would get going real good, a lock of that straight black hair would fall down across his face. Ernest Thompson—"Bogger Red" was his nickname—who had been on the Texas Railroad Commission forever, was a strong supporter of ours, and Beauford Jester, who was later to become governor. There was a women's division. Marietta Brooks headed it. Betty Long had a big part in it; I'm sure she had an office.

We had county men and district men. Every county had a county man. My brother, T. J. Taylor Jr., was his county man in Jefferson, from Marion County. Cameron McElroy was county man for Harrison County in East Texas. At the end of every election Lyndon always looked first for the votes of Blanco County and I for Harrison County, and then both of us intently for the Tenth District.

---

11. Everett Looney was a prominent Austin attorney.

12. Harold H. Young Roy was a liberal Texas protégé of Henry Wallace. Hofheinz was county judge of Harris County (where Houston is) in 1941.

An odd thing about the Tenth District, I don't believe he ever changed much, either to win or lose, from 1937 on to the end of his career. Almost all the time it would be between 64 and 67 percent. That's plenty good.

Bumper stickers on cars and posters that you put up in store windows or tacked on trees told your story. Often one of my jobs was to take [posters] around and a hammer and a bunch of nails in the car and tack them up on trees and highly visible places or ask a merchant if I could leave one in his store window. My jobs were hardly very demanding cerebrally, but I did get tapped at least to make small speeches when Lyndon couldn't get to a place, and especially if it were in the Tenth District, which we considered our personal fiefdom. Our attachment to that never wavered in all the years in office. So I didn't mind standing up in Brenham, for instance, and telling the people of Washington County how much they meant to Lyndon and how much he needed them, and making a very small speech. That and packing bags and the unending effort to get him to eat fairly balanced meals at somewhat sensible hours. And also to thank, thank, thank. If I had to say what the job of a political wife is, that would have to be in capital letters first and last. There are so many people who give so much over and beyond anything you could pay them for, and often some of the hardest workers didn't get anything. They just did it for love. I could come along and thank them and express our gratitude with a great big pitcher of lemonade and cookies for the volunteers in headquarters or just telling them or writing them.

One of the outstanding and never-to-be-repeated facts of this campaign was that we had a great press. So much of the press was with us. The *Fort Worth Star-Telegram*—Amon Carter—came out for us. All of the Harte-Hanks papers came out for us and were strong supporters. All of the Marsh-Fentress papers were for us. One of my favorite stories about Charles Marsh and about the campaign in general is Charles Marsh dictating a long wire to Gordon Fulcher over the phone telling his papers what to say in endorsement of Lyndon. [He] finally got it finished and he said, "Now, Gordon, send that to every one of our papers. By the way, I think it would be a good idea if you also sent a copy to all of the weeklies and all of the dailies in Texas and suggest that they might want to look into him and perhaps they might want to endorse him, too." Gordon was saying, "But Mr. Marsh, but Mr. Marsh," and Charles was just going right on over him like a steamroller. Finally Gordon got to say, "But, Mr. Marsh, that wire you dictated, it would cost thousands of dollars to send that to every paper in Texas, every little weekly." And Mr. Marsh said, "Gordon, when are you going to learn not to bother me with details?" I don't know where the money came from, and I don't know whether the wire in fact ever got sent to every one of them, but I rather bet it did. Lyndon has often said that he's run a campaign when the press was for him and when the press was against him, and it sure was a lot easier when the press was for him.

Lyndon was chain-smoking in those days, always hot, always walking fast and going fast. I'd just trot along behind him when we were walking someplace.

But the signature of the campaign was always this incessant, fast handshaking at the end. That must have been an exhausting thing. It was a lot of exercise. You did your best to remember names, faces, an appropriate word, a pat on the back, a kiss for women that you were close to. And down the line they went. Sometimes I used to say to Lyndon, "Don't do it so fast. You're going to make a bad impression. You're going to make people think [you're] trying to get on with them," which he was, of course.

What did he say when you told him that?
I'm afraid he paid me no mind.

Lyndon, after a vast spurt of energy and exertion in the month of May, went to Scott & White Hospital with his throat. He could hardly whisper. All of his life he had trouble with his voice. If he had ever taken off and studied voice control consistently under an expert teacher I'm sure it would have served him well. There never seemed to be those gaps of time.

We wound up the last days of the campaign approaching Johnson City. I remember he stopped in a blacksmith's shop, of all things. The last rally was on the front porch of his boyhood home. Tom Martin was the master of ceremonies. When I look on those old pictures I can see Uncle Tom Johnson in the crowd and Cousin Oreole and Corky Cox as a little boy. I think that was where Dr. C. E. Evans and Ernest Thompson were on the front porch. We voted in Johnson City after the speech from the front porch of his parents' home, necessarily a very sentimental speech. Lyndon was naturally a very sentimental person. His home town and the height of his dreams and the end of this long and arduous campaign just put you on a peak of emotion. Then we went to the hotel in Austin to wait out the returns.

CLIFF HANGER

It seems like we literally lived in the Stephen F. Austin Hotel from Saturday night until the following Wednesday. We had this setup with a great many phones and a blackboard. Walter Jenkins was the chief manager of the telephone squad and the one who would write down the votes on the blackboard as they were announced by the Texas Election Bureau. We'd get constant calls from this county, that county, this part of the state, that district manager. Lyndon would be grabbing up first one receiver and then another. John was on one, Senator Wirtz in another room on another, calling in figures. Pandemonium and high hopes and drinks and food grabbed at odd hours and staying up all night. Those are the hallmarks of after an election.

The Texas Election Bureau announced that Lyndon was elected with a five-thousand-vote lead at some point. The *Dallas Morning News* on Monday morning had a whole half page of pictures of Lyndon, from six months [of age] to as he was now as a member of Congress; a whole page about him and then a great big spread on the front page.

The votes slipped away in the last final days; do you recall the events?

I suppose it would be impossible to erase from memory the feeling, if not the precision, of the facts, as they marched one, two, three. We stayed in a hotel room, having meals sent up. At first there was this buoyant exhilaration, this five thousand lead over O'Daniel, and the paper saying only a miracle could keep FDR's anointed out. Gerald Mann was entirely out of the race, but he was running third, and Martin Dies was a poor fourth. But the votes were still trickling in. On Sunday we were getting swamped with congratulatory wires. I remember the figure three thousand. Lyndon was talking about [Senate] staff, making plans on who to put in what slot.

Then we began to get this report: the votes from the forks of the creek in deep East Texas began to come in with this very disquieting reversal in areas— Martin Dies's home district. There were several counties where the late votes coming in did not follow the trend set, which had been naturally in favor of Martin Dies, the hometown man who got large segments of the votes. O'Daniel and Lyndon pretty much divided the rest, Mann some. But Dies didn't get hardly [any]. In the last bit he dropped off mightily, and O'Daniel picked up mightily. And Lyndon's fairly substantial little amount trickled to nothing. So this continued throughout Monday and Tuesday with Senator [Wirtz] getting more and more worried and concerned. I have pictures of him on the phone and pictures of John lying down spread out all over the sofa, Lyndon lying on the bed. Utter weariness in every line of them, but also this foreboding of impending disaster written on their faces. Darling pictures of Mary Rather listening to the returns and then holding her nose and waving her hand in the air with distaste.

By Wednesday morning, W. Lee O' Daniel was declared winner by the thin margin of 1,311 votes. So we had a meeting on what to do next. There was a lot of talk about "Shall we contest?" Lyndon was not for it. He just couldn't remember having heard of any contest where one either won or won with a feeling of satisfaction in the end. They were just messy things. So he said, "There will be another ball game," and he called this one quits. He left very soon after the governor was declared elected. I know that Lyndon made an effort to thank everybody, and so did I. I stayed behind to do more of that while they were dismantling the headquarters.

I'll never forget the picture of him leaving, which has to remain only in my mind's eye now because, although I took it with that little camera, the film is gone. He was wearing a rumpled seersucker suit and he was marching out to get on the plane. He looked so jaunty, and I knew that he had had to pull that up from the very depths of his resources and spirit to appear jaunty for me and for all of his campaign workers. He turned around and he waved at us and he got on that plane and off he flew, still the congressman from the Tenth District but defeated for the race for the Senate. I felt so proud of him and never more so than when he said good-bye.

I remember the letter that I wrote Lyndon after it was all over, in which I was telling him how much I had loved it and that I wouldn't take a million dollars for the experience. I characterized it as having had the thrill of living among people who were working at the very top of their capacity. I bet that's the feeling that people had in wartime. It was strong exhilaration. You were sure that what you were fighting for was right.[13]

How did you take that defeat yourself? Was that hard for you?
Oh, no, no, no, I really and truly couldn't. I didn't ever regard it as a defeat but as a learning experience. It happened early in our years. Lyndon was only thirty-two and still in a job with a great place of usefulness, having gone into a race with three strong men with statewide friends, acceptance, power. For a very small David to take on all those Goliaths and come out as well as he did was a mighty good show. I'm glad to say that Lyndon walked out of it, to the best of my belief, without bitterness and with a lot of learning.

As a matter of fact, within not much more than a month, there was something so poignant I almost felt eerie about it. Lyndon as congressman went back to resume his duties on the floor. Speaker Rayburn asked him to be one of his lieutenants in trying to get Roosevelt's extension of the draft passed. Here we were in August, four months away from Pearl Harbor, and we were about to run out of the draft. There wasn't enough support for it to be at all sure you were going to get it passed. Speaker Rayburn was just trying with Herculean efforts to get everybody to vote for it and to make sure that anybody who was going to vote for it didn't get sick or have an important appointment someplace else, [and] that they showed up on the floor if they could barely walk. Lyndon was a chief lieutenant. It passed by one vote. Always since, it's almost made my hair stand on end to think how close that was for us all.

Six months later or thereabouts, former governor Jim Ferguson's daughter, Ouida Ferguson Nalle, came to see me and brought me a beautiful piece of needlepoint that she herself had done. She said something about like this, "You know, our family had always been your husband's friend and his father's friend. We thought he made a good congressman and he probably would have made a good senator. We just want you to know we think of ourselves as still your friends." To explain this, a lot of speculation had gone on in those days between Saturday night and Wednesday, when the vote began to change and when the vote from the forks of the creek came in, that it was the old-time Ferguson vote, and that it was the master hand of Pa Ferguson that was being felt over there in an area where he had always been particularly strong. I have no knowledge, but that was a feeling among a lot of old timers. I've always particularly cherished that piece of needlework.

---

13. CTJ to LBJ, circa 7/41, "Love Letters," LBJ Library.

"NOW WE KNOW WHERE WE STAND"

About Thanksgiving 1941, my Uncle Claud in Alabama died suddenly in his sleep. He had managed my mother's estate and, after her death, my share and my brothers' share of her property. He had no wife or children, so it was always generally understood that we, the Taylor children, would be among his heirs. Uncle Claud had managed my Aunt Effie's property all of her life, and we expected that I would eventually inherit from her. He died without a will, although he was a very careful, conservative, intelligent man. So the estate was really in a very considerable muddle. His remaining sibling, his brother, Uncle Harry Pattillo of Selma, became administrator. There were others involved, too, because my grandfather, Luke Pattillo, had married a widow who had two daughters, and these daughters had numerous daughters. My dear cousin Elaine, with whom I was always very close, was the daughter of one of these daughters of my grandmother Pattillo. It was evident there was going to be quite a lot of dissension about how everything was divided up.

We were all going over the books and trying to count the property. I must have gone down to Montgomery in early December and stayed at my cousin Elaine Fischesser's. It was an opportunity to do two things: be with Aunt Effie at Elaine's and work on Uncle Claud's estate. I had gone out to Billingsley on the morning of December 7 and spent the morning looking at his books in the huge old frame store, two stories high and vaulting, that topped a hill in Billingsley where I had spent so many childhood hours climbing around all over the roof with my cousins and dragging toy wagons up and down the porch areas. Billingsley marked my childhood and was very dear and familiar to me. I was going back over these books and observing timber sales on the Alabama lands, the earlier ones written in my grandfather's hand, and from 1912 to 1941 in Uncle Claud's hand, in recording the sales of cotton production on these rolling, green hills of Autauga County and farmlands of Chilton County. Most of it was in tenant farms, and some of it, the most productive crop really, was in pine trees.

All of a sudden, into Uncle Claud's office there burst a man whom I can only describe—this sounds cruel—but he was thought of as the village idiot. He was a perfectly nice person but of low IQ. He was good natured and very affable and mighty talkative. In fact, he just went around talking all the time. But he said, "Lady Bird, the Japanese have bombed Pearl Harbor! We're going to war!" I thought, "My goodness, he's just really gone too far this time. That can't be true." I simply didn't believe it. However, it shook me up, enough that I pretty soon packed up all my records and went back in to Montgomery, and sure enough, it was true.

How did you find out there?
I certainly knew it the moment I walked into Elaine's house, because all of Elaine's family, all the other cousins and relatives, were just well-informed,

bright as could be, just jumping at the news of the day. There was my cousin Edwina [Mitchell], a lawyer, a very able woman, who was head of the pardons and parole board, and my cousin Elaine and Aunt Effie and various people. They were all just chattering away and listening to the radio and excited and scared and uncertain and confused, as we all were. In fact, we had had long discussions about the situation with Japan the night before and that morning at breakfast before I drove to Billingsley. I remember with appropriate dismay how I had said [a Japanese attack] was absolutely unthinkable: "Just look up on the map. How could that little old bitty bunch of islands fragmented over there, sitting in the middle of the ocean, possibly attack us thousands of miles away?" But so much for that kind of assurance.

I began to try at once to reach Lyndon on the phone. I must have tried for hours. Understandably enough, all the phone lines were terrifically in use, but I eventually got him before the day was over. I remember the excitement in his voice and the anger in his voice, and just the flat statement that they have destroyed our navy at Pearl Harbor. It wasn't quite that bad, but Lord knows it was terrific enough.

I am not sure what he said right then about his plans. I think he said he was going down the next morning and ask for active duty, because he had said during the campaign repeatedly, "If I vote to send your son to war, I'm going with him." I believe he said that on the phone to me. I know he lost no time in going down to report for active duty with the navy. He had been in the reserve for some years. He told me to come on back to Washington, which I, of course, was going to do anyhow, because everybody wanted to be at their home base to await whatever was going to happen.

But the next morning I did go back out to Billingsley for one windup time. It was in front of the old courthouse in Prattville in the shadow of the Confederate monument that I and ever so many of the assembled townspeople of Prattville heard FDR's voice make that speech about this day "[which] will live in infamy."[14] There was a loud speaker hitched onto the outside of the courthouse, because I daresay in that poor rural section of Alabama not nearly everybody had a radio. In fact, they might have been pretty scarce.

Do you recall your reaction to the speech and the reaction of those [around you]?
Oh, sure. Tense, excited, and yet a kind of exhilaration. "Well, here we are. Now we know where we stand."

I gather it was a unifying experience.
Oh, indeed it was, absolutely. God prevent, but if ever again we're in a war, may it begin with something like Pearl Harbor or the Alamo, or else we'll go through that same eroding effect that took place in the Vietnam War.

---

14. Franklin D. Roosevelt, Speech to a Joint Session of Congress, December 8, 1941.

So I went back to Washington. Lyndon got put on active duty with the navy. We began to make plans for the office, which he was just going to leave open and functioning. John Connally had already left or left right soon. It was obvious he wasn't going to be there because he was going to have active duty with the navy. Although Walter Jenkins would be there maybe a little bit longer, it was obvious that the strength of our office was going to be greatly reduced. There was one young man in the office, O. J. Weber, who had such a bad eye problem, wore real thick glasses, that he could not get in right away. He began to drink carrot juice practically by the case in an effort to get his eyes jacked up to the point where he could go to officer training school. There must be something to it, or maybe their standards got lowered, because within a few months he passed the test, and he was poised to leave us. In fact, before the summer was too far along we were really in a bind for labor. Jake Pickle came in and helped us out for a while. He was having a problem with his teeth, poor man, and in order to get into [the service] he had an awful lot of dental work done which later on proved unnecessary, but which Jake, with his marvelous sense of humor, was able to laugh at. In spite of the gravity of the situation, it was a pretty much upbeat time. You knew you faced something new and demanding and exciting that would just enlist every ounce of ability you had, and you didn't find that thought too hard to take.

Christmas of 1941 was one of those odd little islands of stillness in the midst of a great turmoil. A watershed of history was happening to us, and yet we knew for just a brief while we would be still and visit with our family. We arrived in Austin at Christmas and were there with Mrs. Johnson. I remember Lyndon in his uniform, and he really was resplendent. It was so becoming. That cap and that huge heavy overcoat stayed with us all through the years. I remember that he was heading for the West Coast before New Year's. I was going with him, which was one of the best things that ever happened to me, because it opened up a lot of new worlds to me. I remember Mrs. Johnson's little house on Harris Boulevard and all the children there. Rebekah and Josefa and Sam Houston and Lucia and Lyndon. Aunt Lucy and Uncle Sterling were there with us. I remember Mrs. Johnson presiding over us all and just so proud to have us there. She had a Christmas tree in the living room close to the window that faced on the street. We always had fruitcake and coffee and never, never one touch of anything alcoholic.

The main thing that brought us there was Mrs. Johnson, because every last one of them loved her, although there was not always harmony between every one of them. It was a dramatic time because we didn't know what would be happening next and when we would all meet again. I knew it was a particularly straining time for Mrs. Johnson to see her eldest leave in uniform for God knows where. As for me, with the optimism of youth, I just felt completely sure that he would return, safe and sound and with some achievements. Lyndon had already made arrangements, and he was joined, I think, specifically by Josefa in helping arrange to get that house for Mrs. Johnson. He had already put in her name a modest amount of income and an insurance policy. Our means were not great at that time, but he had thought about it and done something about it to the extent that he could.

Lyndon started for the West Coast right after Christmas. I went with him, and I do believe that Bill Deason was along with us. We went on a Pullman [car] and had a drawing room or a stateroom, pleasant smallish quarters. I remember having a little portable typewriter and my shorthand book, and the resolve that I was going to learn to be a good secretary. I did take some notes as he talked on the train going out. I always loved train travel. I think it was somewhere along the way that Bill Deason came up with the idea that as soon as we had said all of the good-byes out on the coast and he was shipped off to Lord knows where, that I ought to go back and work in his office. I do not know really when that decision was made, but I rather think it might have been on that train trip, and I do remember Bill Deason as the father of the plan.

7

1942, Managing the
Congressional Office

World War II gave millions of American women an opportunity to leave the domestic sphere and join a workforce that was being rapidly depleted by enlistments. LBJ, determined to have a role in the war without relinquishing his congressional seat, left his Washington office in the hands of Lady Bird, while he was on active duty in the Navy. Her year in the congressional office taught her about the workings of the federal government and the many demands on a member of Congress. The experience also strengthened her confidence, preparing her for an even more demanding assignment the following year.

MIRED IN RED TAPE

The first few weeks of 1942 were a strange, detached life, living in hotels on the West Coast and Lyndon going out each day to navy yards and training programs. This was a part of James Forrestal's program.[1] It must have been increasingly frustrating to Lyndon. He was used to working fast with a purpose, [where] he was the boss and he knew what the aim was and he could do it. He probably found himself mired in a lot of agencies and red tape and indecisive situations.

What he was supposed to do was help launch a training program to bring a lot more workers into shipyards and later into aircraft factories with some kind of on-the-job training or a training school from which they would go into the job. It was to try to meld the work of the NYA with the new war effort. The idea seemed to be a good one, and his being put there to help crank it up a good idea. It was only partially successful. He would spend long days going out to places like Burbank and Wilmington and San Diego and back to Los Angeles at night.

---

1. Forrestal was under Secretary of the Navy; he later became Secretary of the Navy and the first Secretary of Defense.

I would be in the hotel and would amuse myself delightfully, no trouble there. One time when we were close enough to San Marino, I went to see the Huntington Library, which is a great colossal place in a vast green garden. I was just filled with enchantment, although many of the paintings had been taken out and put up because of the war.

There was a fear that the West Coast might be the next point of attack.
There was indeed. Every morning I would go down to the newsstand to get the newspapers. I could see the big black headlines about two inches high about a half a city block before I could get to them and read them. I would practically break into a run thinking that the Japs had landed on the coast. What else would produce such a huge headline? I soon got accustomed to them. They could make a big headline out of just about anything. But there was a very real feeling that we might look up some morning and out there would be a bunch of Japanese submarines firing at us or planes overhead.

It was a queer, offbeat sort of existence, much more fun for me than for Lyndon, I'm sure. One evening we went to the Tom Clarks' and had dinner. That was the first time I remember seeing them. This was in Los Angeles. It took us forever to get there. I vowed I would never live in a town like that, ever, ever. Mary and Tom Clark[2] were so soft-spoken and gentle and sweet. I thought, "I want to be friends with these people," and indeed they did become some of my closest friends from then on all through life. They were already Lyndon's friends.

I loved San Francisco and those steep, steep streets. I had some good moments of sightseeing there. I kept on telling Lyndon that I wanted to go shopping and buy something. Finally, we were leaving, and I just put in my bid, "Let's stop." So Lyndon told the taxi, "Stop right here," [and he said to me,] "Now you get in and go in there and buy yourself something real quick." I went panting into a shop, one of the numerous Japanese shops that I presume were destined to soon close up, and bought some prints, which I believe to be Chinese, which I love. These delicate prints with peonies and flowers and butterflies and the colors of coral and orange and yellow and green which have fitted into all of my houses— they made the round trip with us to the White House. Indeed, now they're in my little apartment in Austin where one gets off of the elevator in the vestibule before you go in the living room. I always pass them with a smile, thinking of how young we were and what an adventure it was, in spite of the overhanging gravity and anger and determination.

I remember well the trip from Seattle across this continent, particularly the first part of it going through the great woods, those huge trees of the far north-

---

2. Texan Tom C. Clark was a special assistant to the U.S. attorney general and was involved with the relocation of Japanese Americans during World War II. President Truman appointed him attorney general in 1949 and associate justice of the Supreme Court in 1949.

west. It was magnificent country. I love train trips, and there was no better way to see it. You were just filled with a sense of respect and love for the country as you went clackety-clack across it and saw the changing scene out the train window. All I remember about Chicago was how desperately cold and windy it was. Lyndon went to some more naval training stations there and worked on the plan of trying to further the training of young men to make them ready for service and what was going to have to be one of the biggest outpourings of war matériel ever. Then toward the twentieth of the month, or thereabout, we were back in Washington, and it was time to put into practice this idea of me going to work in the office.

Lyndon quickly announced that he was not going to be taking his pay as a member of Congress, and so that reduced us. It seems to me that we went from something like $850 a month as a congressman to $275 as a lieutenant commander. It affected our standard of living. It took some doing, and the first bit of doing we did was to move out of our nice apartment in the Woodley Park Towers and rent it furnished, which not only paid the rent there but [also provided] a nice little cushion above it. Apartments were much in demand, especially furnished ones, because people didn't know how long they were going to be where, and the town was filling up with dollar-a-year men and all sorts of specialists and businessmen. I think [our renters] came from some suburb of Detroit and were terribly nice. In fact, I never had any trouble renting houses and never any really bad experiences.

A NEW LIFE

I have a memory of John [Connally] and Lyndon leaving on a plane together and of Nellie and Speaker Sam Rayburn and me going with them down to the depot and seeing them off. I think that was toward the end of January. Nellie and I were feeling forlorn, and as we turned away from the last good-bye, I remember how loneliness began to descend upon us. The Speaker said in his brisk voice, "Now we're going out to dinner. I'm going to take you young ladies, and we're going to get you the best meal in town." As I remember, we went to a seafood place and it was a jolly evening. He was a rare, thoughtful man and always knew when to make his friendship evident. There were others who would take us out. When Everett Looney came to town, he'd take us to a big hotel or seafood cafe or some excellent place for dinner. So would Senator Wirtz. That was always cause for celebration when he would come.

As soon as John and Lyndon left, I went to live with Nellie Connally out in Buckingham Apartments on George Mason Drive in Arlington. She was a delight to live with, giggling all the time. We had such fun. We would go home, bone weary, and cook dinner and have some constituents over, because our social life was not at an end even if our husbands were off at war and our days were tremendously long and hard. Roy Hofheinz came over one night. Oh, such fun we had.

Then staff people like the Philip Nichols[3] would come over, and we would show them our home movies. We had dinner number one and dinner number two—the things that we cooked best and the quickest to prepare. I'd say to Nellie, "What shall we have tonight? Number one or number two?" She'd go to the grocery store, and I'd go home and get started on what there was there. We would divide the work.

We began to have the first blackouts while I was there. It lasted from eight o'clock at night until six o'clock in the morning. I remember a blackout when we had gone to dinner in Georgetown. We emerged from the dinner party. All the lights were out everywhere in the city. Our car was quite a ways away, and we walked in those dark streets. It was an eerie feeling, and we paused in the doorway of a church and all giggled quietly to each other about how strange this was.

Early February of 1942 found me settled in Washington, Lyndon gone, and a new life beginning. It was roughly divided between business school, which took up about five or six hours of the day, and the office. I went to a very ordinary sort of loft place and took typing and shorthand for about three hours and then studied for a couple of hours. Then I was taking exercises. That's gone on and on throughout my life with very mediocre results, but I had the instinct to make the best out of my physical self and to get fit and to lose pounds and inches. Then, the third part of the day, the real thing, was getting to the office. I probably got there around anywhere from four to five o'clock in the afternoon, but it was not unusual to leave at ten thirty at night. It's marvelous looking back on that period to wonder at the amount of energy one has when one is young.

Gradually, the work in the office became so all-encompassing—and I felt like I could really make a contribution there—that it was out of balance with the time spent in business school. So I decided to dispense with business school. Maybe sometime I would get back to it later. I'd gotten fairly proficient on the typewriter and moderately capable in taking shorthand. It was about the last week in February that I quit business school and began to go to the office full-time.

The first thing that we decided was that I was going to work without pay. Lyndon was strongly of the opinion that I should say in every letter that I wrote: "I am working without pay in the office." But that seemed an awful bald and ugly statement to me, so I cooked up something much gentler, like: "I'm contributing my time while Lyndon is away on active duty, doing what I can to help out in the office while Lyndon is gone." Sitting at Lyndon's desk, I read all the mail and signed it, "Claudia Johnson." I had a little typewriter moved in there, and I would type a lot of the personal letters myself.

In the office, there was O. J. Weber, who handled all the departmental work, and Mary Rather, who knew all of our friends throughout our past and dealt

---

3. Philip Nichols was married to Dorothy J. Nichols, one of LBJ's secretaries and a friend from Cotulla.

with an enormous amount of constituent mail. Nellie Connally soon moved in, first as a volunteer and then somewhere along the way as a paid worker. One of the first things that I did was to compose a letter to each of the old sturdy friends in each of the towns of the tenth District, the *jefes*, as we would think of them. I would get a little help from Malcolm Bardwell on that. When Senator Wirtz would come to town, I'd get help from him, both as to the list of friends and to the content of the letter. Every day I would send Lyndon a summary of what I was doing. One of our friends also suggested that we watch the newspapers for births and deaths and golden wedding anniversaries and write the letters of congratulations or condolence. That first became Mary's job and then was transferred to Nellie as she joined the office.

Gradually, it began to develop that somebody in the office had to be named the secretary. I thought it ought to be O. J., because he knew the most and did the most. Lyndon decided that it should be me and addressed letters to me in that way. So I progressed quickly in about a month; however, there was never any lack of knowledge on my part as to where the real wisdom and experience lay, and that was in O. J. and Mary.

My place in the office had to emerge by doing because there was no job description for it. I couldn't vote, nor could I serve on the committees, but a congressman's office is largely a service organization. He deals with his three hundred thousand or so constituents and tries to lead them by the hand through the vast labyrinth of red tape that is the federal government. He tries to answer their questions. He tries to serve them, keep them current with what's going on in the district. Then secondly, we didn't want to let those people out there forget Lyndon, because here he was gone in active duty with the navy, but here was an election coming up that summer. We wanted to keep the lines open between us and all our constituents so that his place would be there whenever he returned from active duty. That was a question mark, as the whole world was a question mark right then.

Although O. J. Weber was infinitely more knowledgeable than I was, there were some substantive things that I could do. It might be possible for a cabinet officer or a fairly high official to talk to me on the phone, to let me, as the wife of the congressman, put my foot in the door, when it wouldn't be for them to see a secretary whom they had never met. Lyndon knew a great network of people in the departments, and simply having his name and, in some cases, the fact that they were his friends would get me in the door.

One of the benefits that emerged during these months in the office was much more understanding and consideration for Lyndon. I had to change the gears of my mind so often during the day from a problem of one constituent on the telephone to the letter that was next up on my desk when I finished. It was straining. By the time we finally left the office, which might be eight thirty, nine, nine thirty, to go out to dinner, I wanted somebody else to choose the place. I wanted it to be good, and if it wasn't good, I was likely to be mad at them when that was absolutely no fault of theirs. So I could much more understand Lyndon's late hours and sometimes irascible nature at the end of a long day. It was very useful to me.

Those weeks emerged as a watershed time in my life. I grew to have a sense of knowing how to do something and being capable of making my living if I had to. The first seven years of our marriage, although they had been highly exciting and my zest for life has always been at a high pitch and Washington a vastly interesting place, still we did not have a home; we did not have children. There was a sound base missing for me, whereas Lyndon had a very sound base, his work. I learned that I could do something useful, and it has stood me in good stead ever since.

One of the things I had already known that I reinforced in this brief time in the office was that to be in Congress you ought to have a heart. If you didn't have a lot of sympathy for each individual case, you were in the wrong job. On the other hand, you sure did get some characters, freeloaders, who were wanting something done that they were not entitled to get done, that did not have merit on their side. But there were so many more constituents who just deserved a helping hand in guiding them through the red tape of bureaucratic Washington.

Lyndon had a policy to be sure to answer a letter before it's twenty-four hours old. If you had to call departments and get help, just write them and say you're going to call the necessary agency or department and get right back to them. My work boiled down to dictating some mail, reading all of it, signing it, meeting with constituents, taking telephone calls galore. Lordy mercy, there would be at least one a day from Mayor Tom Miller of Austin, and that would be a long one. I would meet with constituents who would come to Washington. Washington quickly became a magnet to which all sorts of business people came, wanting to get some extra materials so they could build that terribly necessary plant of theirs, because quickly all materials were put under restrictions. [Some other constituents wanted] to get into the Officer Candidate School instead of being called up as a private. I remember one particularly, who was just determined to get in and go overseas and fight as soon as he could, and that was Colonel Willard White, to whom [Lyndon's sister] Josefa was married. About all we could do for them was put them in touch with the proper agency. We could cut some of the red tape and sort of guide them by the hand.

Certainly the most awesome visit that I had was to a man who has awed far more people than me, and that was the secretary of the interior, Mr. Ickes. This was about one of the Civilian Conservation Corps parks in our district, which was a beautiful park and had a manager who was a good friend of ours and we thought a very good public servant. He was in danger of losing his job. I had to go and make an appeal for him. I think it turned out all right. Secretary Ickes was very nice to me. I had the very firm opinion that he wouldn't let that man stay there thirty minutes just because Lyndon wanted him to stay, but I did gather that he would really look into it and see what his record was and whether he was worth keeping his federal job. I believe it turned out that he did stay.

The office was busy. We had a host of visitors. Roy Hofheinz was in and out working on his [radio] station in Houston. He wanted to get [a] license from the FCC even though being able to get the material to build it was very doubtful. Roy did get to see Cliff [Durr], and he must have told his story so convincingly that Cliff believed in its justice. I think very soon that he would get his permit.[4] I saw a good bit of Roy. He and George Brown were trying to think up some ideas of starting a morale-building program to step up production in George's shipbuilding and other defense plants in Houston, like letters from a Houston boy in Java telling in pitiful terms about how badly they needed the guns or the ships, or giving medals to the workers who drive the most rivets, and pep talks to the workmen in the plants from an admiral or a general or a movie star. One of my favorite pictures of those years is George and Herman Brown and their aged mother and Lyndon and Secretary [Frank] Knox of the navy and quite a few of them all lined up there. The satisfaction on their faces was so visible, and the Brown shipbuilding yards were receiving an "E" for efficiency from the navy. Lyndon was about as glad about it as if it had been part his.

Lots of the mayors of the little towns [visited] wanting some installation to make their city a part of the war effort. One of the things we hoped for the most was to get some unit of the armed forces stationed in Austin, because it would build the city then and later. What we seemed to have a chance for was an army air support command. It is what later developed into Bergstrom Field. All during those early months of 1942, the plans for that were being made and pushed and urged. One of the things I did was to go to see Assistant Secretary of War for Air [Robert] Lovett on Lyndon's behalf to talk with him about this and what we wanted. He knew all of the reasons why; they had been told him by the mayor and delegations from that city in far more emphatic and substantive manner than I could. But with that being done, my request to him was to let the congressman's office know a few hours ahead of time when they reached their decision, very especially if their decision was yes, so that we could notify the papers. [If the announcement] would emanate from the congressman's office, people would know that he was on the job, his deputy was on the job, still working for them. The number of telephone calls I had with Mayor Tom Miller about this would stretch from here to—a great number in any case.

Bergstrom Field did come about, but it was almost a snafu, because the news leaked just at the last moment. We just got in under the line, thanks to the real devotion of the mayor. The mayor got a wire from somebody who wasn't supposed to wire him. He held onto the wire and didn't issue it to the press, but called our office. It was a weekend and difficult to get people. We couldn't get Lovett; we would even have gone to Lovett. We just called and called and called until we finally found someone in the War Department who had said that that

---

4. Clifford Durr's assistance to Hofheinz is described in W. Ervin James Oral History Interview, 2/17/78, by Michael L. Gillette, 10–13.

wire was not from the top and wasn't supposed to have been sent. They would get off the real one right away that they were approving the site for the military installation in Austin. The mayor did put it in the paper that the news had come from the congressman's office. So we just slipped through, and it was high excitement. I was very thrilled to be a part of it and got a lot of credit, which I didn't deserve, from our kindly mayor, Tom Miller.

LBJ'S LETTERS

There was a constant daily flow of letters between Lyndon and me.[5] It's also marvelous to remember how quickly they came and went from Texas first and then California and all up and down the West Coast. Lyndon's letters were full of advice to me about things to do. First and foremost, keep up with the Texas delegation, pay calls on them, ask their advice, and at the head of the list, always in capital letters, the Speaker, Mr. Sam Rayburn. This I did with great pleasure every now and then, but I didn't want to overdraw my bank account with him. Lyndon told me that he thought it would be a very good idea if I would invite some of the women I knew up to a lunch at the House restaurant, for instance Libby Rowe or Mrs. [Josephine] Forrestal or Mrs. [Vanetta] Gingrich, Admiral [John] Gingrich's wife, and he thought it wouldn't be too expensive for me to spend as much as thirty dollars a month on that sort of thing.

Lyndon told me to start leaving wide margins on my letters, and he would write something in the margins, his opinions or suggestions. He asked me to do the same with all the staff every day, to get them to have a one-page memo about what they'd done that day and what they thought about the office. He also gave me a lot of advice, like for me to approve or disapprove everything that requires a decision from the head. Don't hesitate to do one or the other, even if you're wrong. I can't say I was very aggressive. But he also said, "You can do more good by contacting people in an hour than you can by staying in the office three hours." So he was anxious for me to keep up with all connections with friends, and this meant on the Hill with the Texas delegation, among his friends in the departments, and first and foremost and always, the constituents back home in the Tenth District. One of his expressions was "Don't let those fires go out."

He also asked me to keep a close tab on all the office expenditures. Oh, golly, how some of the folks must have resented that. They knew so much and I knew so little. But it's good to know that somebody is observing. There's nobody that cares quite as much about your business as yourself, and next to yourself, your wife or husband very likely, although we were always blessed with great staff. He

---

5. For an example of the correspondence between LBJ and CTJ, see CTJ to LBJ, 3/7/42 (with marginal notations by LBJ), LBJ Library.

did expect me to fill that role and keep a tight hold on the reins of how much was spent for everything from stationery to pencils to telephone calls.

His letters were also full of earnest imploring of me to continue with my exercises. When I read some of my measurements that he required me to send him, I can see why. I was just about as heavy as I am now. It was just deplorable. Thank heavens, there came a time in the middle years when I was fairly nice and slim. He would tell me to "remember exercises and wave sets and smart clothes." He was always telling me that I wouldn't sell for what I was worth if I didn't pay attention to looks. Regrettably, I rather stubbornly dug my heels in and refused to admit that the way one looked was as important as he said. He was right, and I was dull not to spend more time on it. I had an odd feeling that it was frivolous and a waste of energy and effort, that you ought to spend your life working on higher things. That was dumb. Higher things there are indeed, but you can just look your best with a small enough effort.

Almost every letter from Lyndon would tell me about some present that he had bought me, a purse, a blouse, some china. I think it was some gray china, a breakfast set that I used for years and years. It has finally disappeared from the household. One of the delicious things that happened to me at Valentine's was a gift from Lyndon from Gump's in San Francisco, a fantastic red velvet hostess gown with a lot of oriental design embroidery on it. Oh, it was so beautiful. He just loved to get me pretty clothes and extremely elegant, fancy clothes, far more than my life made necessary. But it gave him pleasure, and it gave me pleasure for many years. At one time I wrote him and said if he just would use that money and pay off a debt to Mr. So-and-so, that [as] much as I loved him thinking about me, wouldn't it be good if we could feel free from obligations and absolutely without debts? Then we could feel that we are unencumbered and have no little drags on our mind. That is a feeling that has continued with me all my life.

The real meat and bread of that whole period when Lyndon was gone were the letters from him, and, I hope and believe, my letters to him. I do know it was a time that strengthened me and that brought us closer together. We valued each other more and we understood each other more because of this time. Reading the letters from Lyndon and mine to him, they are now so evocative I can almost taste and feel the way it was in those times. I spoke of Saturday, that luscious day when I would sleep until eight and then get up and go to the office and work all day. It was your day to do with what you wanted. One time I wrote Lyndon that I went out to the Rowes' for dinner, long dress and everything, and it turned out in the next letter that I had had two dates, Tom Corcoran and a Mr. Howland, and a corsage. I was highly pleased to report that for him.

We continued to send Lyndon word about people in the district who were having a baby or getting a promotion or somebody in the family had died, so that he could send them a postcard. He did a lot of that in his spare time out there. I daresay he had more spare time than he was ever used to having, because as the tone of his letters sank more and more into a state of depression, you could see that initiative and hard driving just could not be done in the anomalous job in which he found himself then.

Letters at first from Lyndon were high-spirited and full of the work he was doing and with enough of a sense of achievement to be satisfying to him. I think he got some training programs going reasonably successfully in Houston and Corpus [Christi] and San Diego, and then gradually they began to come apart. Either the NYA Washington office couldn't approve them, or the navy wouldn't accept them, or the industry with which he was working, like Lockheed, would have some restrictions that made it impossible. It was a period of frustration for him and sometimes a sense of just aimlessness and lack of cohesion in all the forces all around him that went against the grain very much.

All through March, the tone of the difficulty of accomplishing what he wished to do in the work of training more young men grew more and more doubtful that he could be useful in it. He said, "I should be doing more. I should be producing and driving and working my damn head off." But it didn't seem to be possible where he was. He said, "I'm degenerating fast at this." In one of his letters he used the expression that it gave him the feeling of "stale beer after champagne." He was also wondering what would happen to him and whether he would be reelected to his seat. He just said it would be anybody's guess, but he would rather suppose an O'Daniel stooge will take us on soon.

Along into March, I myself was getting disheartened. In a letter to Lyndon, I talked about the Washington picture being very distressing to me.

> I wish we had several dozen of you. I think if there was some place the President could put you where you could make things move, ships or tanks or planes or supplies, I would say for you to get out of your present status, which the people back home interpret to be one of combat or preparation for combat, and get behind a desk where you could make lots of people function and just let politics take care of itself.

We geared up awfully fast, as you look at it in hindsight, but in the days as you live them there was a lot of jealousy and sloth and ineptness and just backing and filling.

ALABAMA PROPERTY

The Alabama property was still in a very chaotic state. Uncle Harry Pattillo was trying to find his way among the vast labyrinth of books as to who owned what. Senator Wirtz said he would try to go back by way of Alabama, and I would go with him, maybe sometime around the middle of February, and if there was an inventory of the property prepared at that time, we would try to reach a settlement. We made several trips to Alabama, Senator Wirtz at one time, and John [Connally] with him. We stayed in a hotel in Montgomery.

I remember distinctly a funny little incident. Everybody in the coffee shop where we were having our breakfast began to run to the windows and look out the windows and chatter, chatter, chatter. Only our waitress remained faithful and brought our food and put it down in front of us. We said, "What's that going on over there?" She said, "Oh, Clark Gable is stationed out here at Mitchell Field, and they see him driving up out there." Then she looked at John and said, "But you never mind to go. You're just as good-looking as he is."

A good thing that happened in the search for untangling the Alabama estate was that Aunt Effie's friend in Jefferson, Miss Bernice Emmert, found among all Aunt Effie's things there a letter and a telegram, an exchange between Aunt Effie and Uncle Claud where she had told him she wanted to make her will and how much did she have approximately, and was it all in absolutely good legal order. Uncle Claud responded to both questions, giving her the amount and that everything was in good order. So that was helpful. Senator Wirtz was getting ready to go to Alabama and meet with the administrator, Uncle Harry, and all the heirs, and so we felt a little more armed for the visit.

I got word from the Senator that he would be ready to meet with us in Alabama about the twenty-first of the month and made my plans to go, notified Edwina and Uncle Harry and Tommy and Tony, and of course, Lyndon, and got all my plans and arguments in mind, and all my papers as well as I could. I had a whole suitcase full of them. When we finally got there on March 21, and I got off the train in Montgomery and was going to go to Selma in a taxi, I got out and left the suitcase! In terror I discovered it a little while later, went back, found the taxi, found the man, and recovered my suitcase absolutely intact. There were just so many nice people in Alabama just willing to give you a helping hand.

When we finally had our meeting in Alabama, it was really a pleasure to watch Senator Wirtz operate: always tactful and slow but had his facts all lined up and very forceful and knew right when to move in. Aunt Effie had complete confidence in him.

Uncle Harry was wary. [He] was slow to be convinced about the rights of heirs. It all went with reasonable amiability, but inconclusive. But we felt that we were making strides. Senator Wirtz was unraveling the whole mixed-up ball of twine.

It was about this time, when it looked like we might be able to settle the Alabama property and come into some ready cash, that I began to really look at houses in earnest.

It was my Sunday afternoon vice. I would get the paper, and I would write down the places that I wanted to see, and I would drive and drive and look and yearn. I described to Lyndon one that I'd found, a whitewashed brick with a huge living room and a lovely fireplace, a master bedroom with four closets, and a private bath and three exposures, and two other nice bedrooms. Well, two interesting things about it: it cost $15,750, and the other is we didn't get it. I kept on writing Lyndon about it, and telling him one of the main reasons I wanted him to have it was so we could have a place where we could eat at least and he could be free to work as hard as he wanted to, using all his talents, and not have to worry about whether we'd have a roof or whether we'd lose out at the polls, because that would constitute a kind of freedom. For somebody in political life, oh, golly, that's the greatest bulwark you can have.

If you had found one that you wanted to buy, would you have bought it, or would you have waited for him to get back?
No, I would not have been that aggressive. One, I would have waited until the money was in the bank from the Alabama settlement, and two, until he at least had had a chance to see it. Or, if he'd told me that he wanted me to, I guess I would have. But I wouldn't have tried to force the issue with him thousands of miles away. I was already thinking about what to do with the backyard and how we'd put a barbecue pit in it so he could fix some steaks for company. And maybe at least we could raise, as I said in one letter, "one crop of roses before the Japs and Germans get us, and one is better than none," which is something I've never changed.

"WIDOW HAVEN"

Meantime, we were considering moving back into my apartment. We told the [renters] that we would like to have it back April the first. I planned to ask Mary Rather to move in with me. It had been marvelous living with Nellie Connally, but it was possible that John was going to be back in Washington for a few weeks or a few months, and I did love my apartment. When we moved there, I, who had so long pushed and longed for a home, told Lyndon that I would just love to live in that apartment practically forever. The windows looked out onto Rock Creek Park, always one of the joys of my life.

I had asked Aunt Effie to arrive April the first, and Mary was going to move in with us, and then Nellie, until she knew what was going to happen to John. At least it was going to be in readiness for her to move in with us. We called our apartment "Widow Haven."

When Aunt Effie came, I always wanted to give her some of my time, to share some of the sparkle and the activity and the youth that went with my life. This was an extremely busy time, and I'm afraid she got a small share. But whenever there was enough time, and, as the war progressed, it depended on the gasoline, but whenever I could, I took her driving. She loved to drive around in spring-time Washington, particularly in Rock Creek Park.

In April or May, we had one of those fun little events. We put on a play [in the apartment]. We had a recording machine, and we also had my movie camera. This play involved a silly little melodrama called "My Mother Was a Lady."

Nellie was the director; she also got all the props. I played the heroine, of all things, a young girl who had just gone to town to make her living in the big, wicked city. Mary was my mother. One of the young men played the part of the villain. This was a hilarious play. We still have it recorded in a movie. I had it, complete with lights, performed in one end of our living room at Woodley Park Towers.[6] We had a lot of fun with that machine, both the movie [camera] and the sound. There was another play, "Twas a Dark and Stormy Night When Little Nellie Went Away."

The mood of the day among the general populace was a mixture. For one thing, it was just a gung ho patriotism. Propaganda for buying defense bonds was just going at high speed. I myself got a very deep thrill out of taking some money that came to me from something that Aunt Effie had sent me for Christmas and a little bit of dividend from some investment I had and bought a defense bond in the name of Lyndon Baines Johnson and Claudia Taylor Johnson. "I trust it will purchase one small and ardent gun" was the way I expressed it to Lyndon in a letter. But that was the way everybody felt, determined to get in their little piece of the answer. There was just a general atmosphere of scuttling a whole lot of the achievements of the New Deal, and yet you could sure see the reasons why. The very people that it had helped were fueling the fires for returning us to earlier days, days that had been oppressive for them.

About the middle of March, we began to get an appalling number of letters in angry language denouncing the action of labor. Labor was stalling; labor was talking about striking. Labor didn't want to work overtime apparently. The situation was getting ugly, and Congress itself was increasingly the object of criticism and distrust. With Lyndon away in the navy, just about all the Texas delegation came out for suspending the forty-hour week as long as the emergency lasted.

One day I went to visit the Speaker in his office in the Capitol behind Statuary Hall. He began by saying, "You can call on me anytime for anything that you want me to help you with. I've got a lot of folks around here, and I could help you in lots of ways." Then he said, "I want you to tell me something. Do you think it would hurt anything if those boys were to be ordered back here about the last of spring?" I said, "Yes, sir, I think it would. Why? Do you have any idea of ordering them back?" It was obvious it was on his mind, and he was getting a lot of other congressmen [who] were having to weigh whether or not they should go. He was thinking that he'd really like to have them all come back. I guess that was the first time that it entered my mind that Lyndon might return home, all of the congressmen who had gone into active duty might return home, at a fairly soon date and not just the big question mark, the end of the war.

---

6. This film is preserved in the LBJ Library. For Mary Rather's description of the production, see Mary Rather Oral History Interview 4, 6/10/82, by Michael L. Gillette, 6–7.

One night I went to a party at Mrs. [Frank] Gray Bane's that I described as being a "gathering of the clan" to which we used to belong: the Aubrey Williams and the Maury Mavericks. [I described] getting Aubrey Williams off in a corner and him saying that he really thought Lyndon ought to be back and working in a more productive capacity, and that [Aubrey] was going to start talking to Harry Hopkins about it. He'd like to see him back here and [would] put him in Harry's outfit.[7]

I went on to say to Lyndon that I wanted to go back to see Mr. Rayburn and tell him that my ideas had changed. Early in February, Sam had told me that he wanted to consider asking the boys back, and what did I think about it? I had said no, I hoped he would not. [Now] I was asking Lyndon if he would mind if I would talk to Mr. Rayburn about the possibility of Lyndon coming back [and being] assigned to something more useful. Of course, what Mr. Rayburn wanted him back for was to be right back at his job on the Hill and helping him corral some of the congressmen. But I was restive, and I surely would like to start talking to Mr. Rayburn or to Jim [Rowe] or Ickes or Aubrey or somebody about a more vigorous place for him. I'm surprised at myself for being that aggressive.

The angry letters about labor increased in number and in emotion. I went to see Speaker Sam Rayburn and showed him the sort of letter we were writing in reply. He said it was a fine letter. It seemed to me weak and inconclusive. I never was quite satisfied when we couldn't just come out firmly one way or the other. The Speaker said that he never had seen the country in such a state, which is something I'm sure that he would have said many, many times. We've gone through so many waves of emotion. I took this occasion to talk to him about my earlier visit, and I told him I wanted to take back what I had said about Lyndon staying quietly in the service. I saw on every side so many jobs that needed doing and so much red tape that needed slashing and so much that I thought that Lyndon would be a good man to do. I wish he were in the middle of the maelstrom fighting like hell.

What was the Speaker's reaction?
He said, "I wish to God I thought that was the way Lyndon felt about it. I'd go to the president and get him to order the whole bunch back here Monday morning."

Didn't the Speaker really want him back to help corral the other congressmen and line up votes, and, more important, to help Democrats get reelected?
That's exactly what he wanted. He was talking about all the things he had to do, and he said, "Now, see, if Lyndon were here he could do that for me. I figure he has the heart and the head of a legislator, and a man with one-third the ability

---

7. Aubrey Williams had been director of the National Youth Administration when LBJ was state director; Harry Hopkins headed the Works Progress Administration.

he has could be doing what he is doing in the navy." The last thing he said to me was, "Tell Lyndon I need him and need him like hell." So at least now the Speaker knew how I felt and how Lyndon felt.

LBJ'S REELECTION

[A petition campaign] was getting organized. I'm sure Senator Wirtz was a key man behind it. Mayor Miller [served] as chairman of the movement. The grass-roots heroes were Bess Beaman and Jake Pickle. Ed Clark was frequently in the picture, transmitting the numbers of signatures that had been received. Everett Looney would have been helping, and all of Lyndon's old, strong folks from the NYA and the San Marcos school were getting organized for a campaign to sign petitions for him to run again, thinking that if they showed up with great huge petitions early in the spring, that would head off anybody running against him. By April 8, news came that five thousand folks in Austin had signed the petition, that Burnet was going great, Blanco, of course, going great, and that there were a total of twelve thousand signatures over all the district.

Also, there was a fight for Lyndon's future brewing between two giants in our life: the long and steady giant of Senator Wirtz and then the meteoric catalyst that made things happen, Charles Marsh. Charles was firmly of the opinion that Lyndon ought to run for the Senate, and he was going to make it happen. Senator Wirtz, on the other hand, just firmly believed that he should not. He thought people would think he was trading on his uniform and that would ruin his future political career. Also, he thought Lyndon had an obligation to Jimmie Allred, and a man must perform his obligations.

Sometime in the middle of May Senator Wirtz filed the document that made Lyndon a candidate for reelection to his seat in Congress. In writing to me he says he hoped I approved the action taken by him, and he said, I guess rather wryly, "I suppose this makes me a lifelong enemy of Charlie Marsh." That die was cast long before, it seemed to me, the decision as to which office Lyndon would run for.[8]

I was looking at the Allred possibility of election. I did not feel in the least sad about our lost chances. I was also sure, as I wrote Lyndon, that "I know the day will come," and I meant when we would be in the Senate, if we wanted to. I was, however, unhappy about the present mood and state of affairs, and Lyndon's lack of participation. I told him that everywhere I turned there was confusion and distrust between congressmen and the bureaus and a running around from one agency to another trying to find out whose job it is to do what.

---

8. John Connally recalled that he and CTJ made the decision after consulting with Wirtz. For his account of this disagreement with Marsh, see John B. Connally Oral History Interview, 10/1/69, by Joe B. Frantz.

Confusion was the name of the game for a while, because there were lots of rules and regulations, and whose job it was to enforce what was uncertain. I began to wish more and more that Lyndon were back in charge of some agency or body that could speed up production and get people moving and with a core of young can-do men.

LBJ'S TRIP TO THE SOUTH PACIFIC

Toward the end of [April], Lyndon came back. He had nearly two weeks at home and then left early in May. It was a hectic fortnight with so many people to see and so many decisions to be made, but a joyous time nevertheless. It was about the last of that month that he received orders to go to the South Pacific with four other officers on a trip to look over our armed forces out there and come back and report sometime. An example of how really methodical he was underneath all of what people sometimes thought were his rash and exuberant and quick decisions: he sat down and made a will. And it's a very sensible thing for somebody to be going overseas to do. The office force witnessed it. It was handwritten. Then on that very day—that was May the first—he left, going by Austin, where he did get to tell his mother good-bye, and then on out to [the West Coast], looking once more at those training bases he had tried to help get established in Portland and San Francisco, and then actually leaving from San Francisco early in May.

When Lyndon came back [from the South Pacific], he told me about what those three weeks in May were like, going from Hawaii across the wide expanse of the Pacific, stopping at Suva and Nouméa and several small islands, finally getting to Auckland about the twenty-first of May, and then on to Sydney, Australia, which became a kind of a base for him, on the twenty-third. Everywhere he landed, when he had time, he looked up the servicemen, particularly the enlisted ones. If he ever found any from Texas, if he had any frame of reference to them, he'd say, "If I get back before you do, I'll phone your family."

When he got home, many events had left a mark on him, a real deep wound in his thinking about our ability to run our country. That was one of them, because he felt that the quality of the planes was poor, and that we were sending men out to fight in inferior machines. He felt always that the people we sent out were top-notch, just great. Some of them were not trained enough; we were sending out mighty young, raw sailors and soldiers and airmen compared to the Japanese. That was the trip that he told me about when he came back, that he spoke of as the "all-out raid," everything that the United States could muster in the southwest Pacific at that time, and it was a grand total of about five planes. That, too, filled him with anger that this giant had no more than that, so quiescent had we been for years and years, no buildup.

He wound up with high fever in the hospital in the Fijis with a lot of strange doctors and customs. He never felt so lost and helpless in his life. He practically got up and walked out of the hospital. However, he was so sick that he was taken back to a hospital somewhere. At that point, he looked up into the face of somebody whose first words were so southern that he knew he was in the hands of somebody from his part of the world. This was a Dr. Harris from Birmingham, Alabama, whom he just felt was his savior, and indeed, he did get him through some bad times, because Lyndon was subject to chest troubles and respiratory troubles and pneumonia all his life. He had pneumonia somewhere along this way. He also had dengue fever. In the course of the rather brief while, he lost about thirty-five pounds.

But this is not to say that the whole thing was awful. There were some moments that he remembered with gratitude and even happiness that took place mostly in Sydney or Melbourne. The people of Australia were very hospitable to American soldiers. He liked the Australians, and it was a liking that remained and colored his feelings all the rest of his life. As often happens in wartime, a lot of good-hearted people would have the soldiers to their homes for dinner or entertainment. There was one such lady, Mabel Brookes, who later on was made a dame by the queen. She and her husband had an elegant home and a very cultured, fine way of life. They really opened their home to young American servicemen and were particularly kind to Lyndon.[9] All the pretty young girls in town would come to parties to laugh and chat and give them a little respite from the dirt and danger of the war. There's a nice picture among these movies of Lyndon walking in a park with such a young lady.

I just remember my astonishment at how haggard Lyndon was and how much weight he'd lost and feeling protective toward him. But he didn't want rest and coddling at home; he wanted to go right back to work and he asked very soon if he could have an appointment with the president. He went right on into his office and all the work at hand on all cylinders. He's bound to have told the president about the inadequacies in some of our matériel, how good the Jap Zeros were, the slowness with which things reached our men, and the ineptness of some of the top brass—indecisive, selfish, incompetent and bickering among themselves and among the services. That, I am sure, he must have talked about. What I remember later on from time to time is changes that were made out there in that theater of operation that he would hear about, see in the paper or hear about, and he would express satisfaction and relief about, thinking maybe that he had been somewhat useful in carrying a message.

The main thing I can recall about that period is that he was different: remote, bitter, scarred, shaken, because he had really thought this country was the most undefeatable nation the Lord ever created, and he was shaken. [He was] determined, but he could see the dangers. He was so concerned and distressed and almost angry at the incompetence he thought he had seen on many levels in

9. As president, LBJ renewed his acquaintance with the Brookes when he visited Australia and when he entertained them at the White House in July 1965.

high management of the war and in the slowness in getting supplies and maté-riel to the men. He never had anything to say but great praise of the men themselves.

Toward the end of the month there occurred one of those occasions that Lyndon was at his best in and that he loved. He went to San Marcos to deliver the commencement address. It was to be the last time that Dr. [Cecil] Evans would preside as president, ending his thirty-one years there as president. And Lyndon gave it all he had. He was very sentimental and talked about the old gentleman. He said, "I had not been in Dr. Evans's vicinity long before I began to learn that the supreme essential in life is service, making the world a better place to live in, bringing help, enlightenment and advances to all our people, helping to make the democratic way of living the universal way."

He talked about how Dr. Evans would take those young farm boys, those rural Texans of meager background, and turn them into the kind of people who were going to be able to go out and match wits with the toughest that the Fascists and the Nazis had to give and were going to be able to defeat it. He talked from his own experience when he would say that sometimes Dr. Evans would scrape up a loan of ten or fifteen dollars for tuition to help them through school. He was the one who had given Lyndon the job of [doing] janitorial work and dig-ging out campus rocks and working on the grounds, the very first job that had enabled him to start going to school.

It was an occasion that Lyndon relished right down to his bones. It was also an absolutely prime setting to talk at length about the war, about all the things that we weren't doing that we must do, and to deliver a blast at both the smug people who said the danger was not all that intense and at those who were tak-ing it easy and making money off the war and at those that were just letting red tape get in the way of getting something done. I'm sure there wasn't anybody who left those speeches complacent. Everybody was fired up, determined to do more himself and get his neighbor to do more. That's what Lyndon felt the home front had got to do. He was always a strong defense man, but seeing how weak we were face-to-face with the danger shook him, and it was an experience he would never forget.

8

Nesting and Investing, 1942–1943

Since Lady Bird Johnson's uncle Claud Pattillo had managed Effie's assets as well as his own, the eventual resolution of his estate meant that Lady Bird would have access to two substantial sums: her inheritance from her uncle as well as Aunt Effie's infusion of capital.

The Pattillo wealth enabled the Johnsons to make a significant business investment, the purchase of the radio station KTBC in Austin. Lady Bird's months in the congressional office had given her not only management experience but also the confidence that she could transform the struggling station into a profitable enterprise. LBJ's increasing reliance on her judgment, however, did not deter him from issuing directives and setting goals. Their extensive network of allies in the Roosevelt administration meant few regulatory hurdles, while friends in the communications industry helped the station prosper. KTBC not only gave Lady Bird Johnson a stake in her beloved Austin; it also became the cornerstone of the Johnsons' wealth.

"YOU BETTER BUY THAT HOUSE"

If 1942 was a watershed year because I learned to work by my months in Lyndon's office and acquired a new sense of self-worth and a new facet to life, it was indeed a watershed year for several other important reasons. We bought a home. My memory is that it was on a Sunday sometime in September. I haunted the real estate portion of the newspaper, and Sunday afternoon was the time to look at the possibilities.

Lyndon and John Connally and I were riding around to see one that had been advertised right off of Connecticut Avenue in Ellicott Hills at 4921 Thirtieth Place NW. It was a red brick colonial, center-hall residence, with thousands of them in every city all across the United States, absolutely nothing distinctive about it. I had always held out for charm and something unusual. Yet this place was in delightful surroundings. It might as well have been on a dead-end street, because at the far end of the street there was the big Peruvian Embassy with huge grounds. It was quiet, very little traffic. Right behind it there were woods. It had a nice long living room, or so to my eyes it seemed then, with a fireplace, a great essential, and it opened onto a big screened porch, which is what sold Lyndon on it. The screened porch looked down into a small but pleasant backyard with a huge tree and flower beds. The ad described it as [having] ample closet facilities; alas, that one changes with the years; it looked good to me in September of 1942. There was a rather small dining room and an adequate kitchen, and upstairs four bedrooms and two baths, none of which was large. On the third floor there was a large unfinished room, but it was insulated, and it would be suitable for a playroom. I envisioned all sorts of things we could do with it. And there was a double-car garage downstairs.

I wanted to buy it immediately, partly as the result of having waited so long, and partly because I thought by the time I finished doing what I wanted to with it, it would acquire charm, and it had so many basics. It was $19,500, and they didn't want to give occupancy until November, as I recall. I walked out of the house thinking that we had really agreed to buy it. As we drove down the street I said, "Lyndon, when are you going to give him a check?" And Lyndon said, "Well, we're not going to buy it!" And I burst into tears, which were very angry tears, something I practically never did. And I said, "All I've got to look forward to is one more damn campaign!" And I really let him know what I thought of the fourteen or so moves we had made in the eight years of marriage. So he looked shocked. John looked at him and kind of grinned and said, "I think you better go back and buy that house."[1]

I was upset by my own outburst and went on back to Woodley Park Towers, where I got out and Lyndon and John went on away. I wasn't quite sure what for. What Lyndon did was to go back to the place and tell them, "Well, we'd been thinking it over, but we really did need a place before the first of November, and it would be pretty inconvenient for us to wait that long, and 19,500 was a lot of money." The gist of it was that the people offered to let him have it by October 1 for nineteen thousand. So, before the day was over, he gave them a thousand-dollar down payment. We agreed to buy the house. Aunt Effie and I worked out a wonderful plan by which she would give me, as she knew she would at some time in the future in her will, $12,000, which would reduce the amount we owed to about a $6,000 note, which we could carry, and which we did complete the next day. So I was replete with satisfaction and looking forward very much to the moving in. The ad described the house as promising that it would provide many hours of pleasure and contentment, and that's just what it did.

---

1. John Connally's account of this episode appears in his memoir, *In History's Shadow: An American Odyssey* (New York: Hyperion, 1993), 71.

Was LBJ as happy about having purchased the house as you were?

Quite soon he became so, and you would have thought it had been his idea all along. He began to recommend it to all other young congressmen, whereas his opposition to buying a house had been partly based on the fact that he felt the people of his district would consider him as having sort of deserted them, become a Washingtonian, planted his feet in Washington. It was his philosophy and desire to leave home the very day Congress adjourned and to start heading on down to his district to tell them what he had been doing and why. Even at that youthful age, he had seen a good many people succumb to the Washington lure and not go home so often, and then they were finally beaten to retire to living in Washington or to take up some other occupation, perhaps being a lawyer or a lobbyist. He had a scorn for—home was really always Texas. We were just sojourning in Washington because of a job we had and loved.

At about the same time, several things coalesced and not in the order in which they should have. Just before we bought the house, John Connally had been looking in the paper ads and had seen under "furniture for sale" what sounded like a delightful opportunity. Two elderly sisters were breaking up housekeeping after having lived in the same house for over fifty years, and everything was for sale. He went out, looked at the things, bought an item or two, and came back to us with the news that there really were some good things out there, and they were inexpensive, and we ought to go and look at it.

Well, I went. We were, at this time, living in the Woodley Park Towers, and the place was very adequately furnished. We had not at this point found that house on 4921 Thirtieth Place. I knew we wanted to be homeowners, which would require more furniture, but it was in the future. It was a dream only. I got out there, and she had some rather delightful antiques. I looked longingly at some of them and finally bought one pretty divided dish, which looks like hand-painted china. I still use and love it for serving hors d'oeuvres. [I purchased] a few more things, probably not more than twenty dollars worth of small items. I think the dish was four dollars. I went home beaming to myself.

Then the next day I decided I would go back and look again and maybe get one or two more small items. I went out there, and one of these two ladies greeted me brightly and said, "Your husband has already been out here, and he's bought the living room set, and the dining room set, and the bedroom set." I sort of staggered backwards, and I said, "You mean John Connally, the other gentleman who told us about you all?" And the lady said, "No, isn't your husband's name Lyndon Johnson?" And I said, "Yes." It turned out that he had indeed been out there, decided they were a bargain, and bought them, with us having no place in the world to put three extra sets of furniture.

I was just rocked by his audacity. We had no place in the world to put the furniture, and the old ladies wanted to move out right away to a smaller place.

But Lyndon talked to the owner of the Woodley Park Towers. He gave us temporary storage in the basement, and we hauled the furniture there. It was not more than a week later that we found the house, so that problem all coalesced very well together.

What was your reaction to his having bought a whole house full of furniture?
Mad, because I hadn't had the say-so in doing it. I, a cautious and conservative person, [was] horrified: What were you going to do with three sets of furniture when you don't have any place to put them? He knew I liked it because I had just been chattering about it the night before and describing to him everything, and the price was incredibly cheap, like the sofa and the two chairs were seventy-five dollars, and I think that included a china cabinet, too. We have ever since referred to all of that furniture as "the old ladies' furniture."

The bedroom set was a tall brass bed, very good-looking as today's styles would have it, at that time not sought after by anybody. Then in the living room she had a short, tufted loveseat with claw feet of a high Victorian vintage and two matching slipper chairs. They're still in my life. The loveseat in a different bright plaid is in my granddaughter Lucinda's bedroom in McLean, Virginia.

That brass bed is not the one in the purple room, is it?
It is the one in the purple room. It has been with me in many houses.

Our next-door neighbor on one side was a Dr. O. E. Reed and his lovely, gentle wife. He worked in the Department of Agriculture in an important capacity. He knew so much about gardening and trees and grass and vegetables and flowers, and he helped me. Every day I would see Dr. Reed and ask him something. They were marvelous neighbors. Their children were grown and gone, but as was the way in those days, the war brought some of their children back home. A husband would go away to the war and the wife would come home, bringing one or two small children. So by the time our own came along, there were often little ones right next door.

Another neighbor we knew only at a distance, because his way with the whole world was to remain at a distance. It was good since he was who he was: J. Edgar Hoover. But he and Lyndon always had great respect for each other.

I did get to know my neighbors, because, as the years went on, I found myself collecting for the Red Cross in three or four blocks surrounding me and got to know everybody by name and by the amounts they gave. It was a very interesting experience. Some people were so gracious and so generous, and some were not. It frequently followed that they had had an experience with the Red Cross, that it had helped some of their family. Their eyes would light up, and they would invite me in and talk about it and give me whatever they could afford. I did that about five or six years in a row, all the war years.

ZEPHYR WRIGHT

Another very good thing that happened to us that fall of 1942 was hiring Zephyr Wright, who was a part of our lives for twenty-five years. I went to Texas in the last of August, and sometime early that fall while visiting Daddy at Karnack, I drove in to Marshall to see Dr. [Matthew] Dogan at Wiley College [the president of the college]. He was a very sensible, practical, capable man. I liked him. He and Lyndon had worked together in the NYA, and so I already had an introduction to him. The fact that I was T. J. Taylor's daughter was another introduction.

I went to see him to ask if he had any graduates that he might recommend for going to Washington to cook for me. He told me about two or three, and I went to see them. As soon as anybody asked, "Do you have six o'clock dinner?" that was a sign off for me, because we had dinner whenever Lyndon came home, and I don't remember that he ever got home by six o'clock, and I just must adjust my life to his, whether I was the cook or I could hire somebody to put up with it. Then Dr. Dogan recommended a woman named Zephyr Black, whom I went to see and liked, although she was pretty hesitant about whether or not she wanted to venture to a faraway place [as] Washington. I called her reference, and her reference said she was a wonderful cook and that she was sorry to see her go. But she had left her about a month ago, so I didn't have the feeling that I was taking anybody. I asked Zephyr what's the most people she'd ever cooked for in a party, and she said, "About a hundred." And knowing the family for whom she'd worked, I knew that they would have been giving some very handsome parties. I was very realistic in telling Zephyr what sort of family we were and how my husband's job was so important that I had to adjust my hours and therefore the staff's hours to his. That didn't faze her a bit. She just felt like she was ready to do and dare. So I hired Zephyr, and she returned to Washington with me. I am almost sure that we went together in the car.[2]

We moved into the house about November first. There was a room in the basement for Zephyr. As I look back on it, it was not a tenth as nice as she deserved, but at that time both she and I thought it was an all right room. I fixed it up with bright spreads and plenty of lamps and pictures.

Did you stop cooking regularly after Zephyr came to work?
Oh, you bet I did! If I could get somebody to do it for me, I was not going to keep on cooking. Obviously, I had found such a person in Zephyr, and she remained a very valued and wonderful part of our lives for over twenty-five years. We early got into a habit in that house of having lots of company, very

---

2. Zephyr Wright indicated that she was enthusiastic about the opportunity to go to Washington. Her description of the interview and the trip with CTJ appears in Zephyr Wright Oral History Interview, 12/5/74, by Michael L. Gillette, 4–6.

casual company, but it soon was a center of good friends getting together to plan, work, and sometimes just to relax and have fun. We discovered that Zephyr was a top-notch cook, and we would invite the Speaker out for country suppers with cornbread and fried chicken—I can't remember whether he was a black-eyed peas and greens man—but all the things that he had and loved, the things that reminded him of home.

Lyndon and Zephyr became very good friends. I remember one time she had a special party, a birthday or something, and he got some champagne and put it in the icebox and got it good and cold and then opened it up himself and poured it into champagne glasses and walked down the steps and took it to the guests.

"WE'RE ALL IN THIS TOGETHER"

Mary Rather in the office was our great keeper and mother superior and one we always turned to with all sorts of questions. One day I was out of town, and Zephyr called up Mary and said, "Miss Mary, we ain't got no more coffee stamps, and I got to get Mr. Johnson some coffee. We're out of coffee." And Mary said, "Well, I gave you all I had last week. Any of the extras in the office we've been saving them for y'all. I don't think there's a one left around here. You'll just have to tell him, Zephyr, there's a war on! And he can't have any more coffee." Zephyr said, "Yes'm, I know. But I don't want to be the one to have to tell him!"

A year or so later when things were tighter and scarier, I was standing in a line at the local Safeway buying our groceries. The woman behind me was really bitch-ing about how she didn't have any more sugar stamps. And I was saying, "Well, I don't mind." She looked at me real angrily and said something. I replied, just as angrily—and I don't very often get angry—"I'll tell you why I don't mind: because the 36th Division from Texas landed in Italy yesterday, and they're slugging it out and a lot of them dying. You hear it on the radio and in the papers, and they don't have any sugar!" That was the way most of the country felt. Most absorbed food rationing with a grin and a lot of good stories, and it was universal.

In addition to rationing, how did the war change your day-to-day life?
I rode the bus more than I ever had and rode it rather a lot. I'd walk or perhaps drive my car just two and a half blocks up from our dear home on Thirtieth Place to Connecticut Avenue, where the bus went. It went by real regular and stayed real full; frequently you had to stand up. I also picked up strangers in my car when I had gas, thought nothing of it, nothing bad ever happened, always got a nice smile and a nice "thank you." When you were riding in a taxi, you didn't mind a bit if they stopped and loaded it until you were practically sitting on each other's laps. You rather expected it. There was a sizeable amount of goodwill and camaraderie, and "we're all in this together." If you had gas, they understood. If your menus were limited, [dinner guests] might bring you a stick

of butter and many other similar things. I remember a wife of a Supreme Court justice arriving at dinner one day, bringing me a stick of butter.

The annual parties of many organizations came to an end during those war years, and the annual entertainments at the White House for the House and Senate, for the judiciary, for the Speaker, those set-up things that had gone on year in, year out, stopped as a patriotic gesture. They consumed time, that most valuable thing, and they certainly consumed money and gas. It was well accepted. Nobody thought ill of the Roosevelts for stopping them; they applauded it. The general mass of us plain folks saw less of them. Of course, Mrs. Roosevelt was just everywhere. You saw her.

KTBC

The fall of 1942 had still one more important event for us of a business nature. Lyndon was greatly attracted by the communications industry. He would have liked most in the world to own a newspaper. We soon found that they cost more than we could ever hope to put together. We even considered buying the little *Jefferson Jimplecute*. It was close to home. We certainly could have managed to buy it, but it's just as fortunate that we didn't. Lyndon made some inquiries. I don't think he got very far down that trail though, because he had lots of vision about what was going to grow and prosper and expand. Perhaps he could foresee that Jefferson, with all the charm that it did have, was not going to be a rapid-growth place.

We heard about a little radio station, KTBC, in Austin that was going to be for sale. It was part-time, low-capitalized, only nine employees, in debt to everybody in town, went off the air at sunset, had everything against it. It had three absentee owners who paid little attention to the station. One of them was Bob Anderson of Vernon, our old friend who goes back as far as the NYA days when he had been on Lyndon's advisory board.

The station was within our price range. There were several people interested in buying it. We presented our proposal quicker than [the others]. When we heard about it, we got in there real quick with all the best backup of reasons why. We bought it for a very modest consideration; seventeen thousand is the figure that sticks in my mind as something my daddy wanted to pay me right away from Mother's estate. Daddy wanted us to relieve him of the responsibility of continuing to manage her estate. All we had to do was to persuade the owners and to persuade the FCC that we would be competent holders of the license.[3]

What considerations does the FCC make in agreeing to a purchase like this?
Whether the person who wants to purchase it has the financial capability of running it, the moral standing of doing a good job—to send out over the airwaves

---

3. For CTJ's conversation with FCC commissioner Clifford Durr, see Clifford and Virginia Durr Oral History Interview, 3/1/75, by Michael L. Gillette, 25–26.

that belonged to the whole country something that would be beneficial and not harmful.

Is there a political dimension?
A separate body like the FCC would guard its political detachment very warily and sternly. Yet it's composed of human beings, and there will always be some in there with philosophies and opinions one way or another. I think they would always try to be judicious and sometimes maybe they're not. But I do think their intentions are always to base it on what's better for the community and the general public.[4]

Wesley West[5] had lent the owners some money and held a sizeable note against it. And so he would be a party to the decision. It led to us getting acquainted with Wesley, who had been an ardent critic of Lyndon in his elections. A very conservative man, a conservative family. Jim [West] was somewhat more unapproachable and eccentric. It was at first a hostile meeting with either or both. It mellowed, and soon we became dear, lifelong friends, especially with Wesley. I believe it was that fall that he began going out to Wesley's place out in Blanco County. It may have been later. Anyhow, they have a hilarious tale about how they went out there, about four men, before Mrs. West, Neva, had finished furnishing the house. She did not have it stocked with blankets. It was fall; a cold norther came sweeping down. The house got cold as ice. They got up and took all the curtains down and wrapped themselves up in the curtains.

Were you both enthusiastic about buying the station originally, or did one have to persuade the other?
Lyndon was always the more adventurous, daring, visionary in the sense of looking down the road. I guess the better word to use is having vision of what something may become. I was completely willing, because I trusted his judgment, and I wanted and always have wanted, and always will want, a foothold in the city of Austin, a piece in the life of Austin. It was out of reason for us to ever imagine we could have a newspaper. We didn't have that kind of money. This little station had a low power, poor management, and it didn't have a network [affiliation]. The absentee managers had given up on any supervision. Early in 1943 the Federal Communications Commission worked out its final yes on us buying KTBC, and there began a long and mostly happy story.

So that spring passed with me knowing that I must leave my brand-new house, which I just cherished beyond everything, and get on down to Austin and take a look at the new business.

---

4. W. Ervin James Oral History Interview, 2/17/78, by Michael L. Gillette, 9–13, provides an example of the political dynamics within the FCC.
5. Wesley and Jim West were prosperous Houston oilmen.

When you bought the station, was it understood at that time that you would go down and get it in shape?

Nothing was really understood. It was just in complete confusion and high hopes. But Lyndon always loaded me up with any jobs that he couldn't do and just insisted that I had the intelligence, strength, and judgment to handle it. He was big on that word, "judgment." So, far from my own conclusions about it, but I went down there late in March with a good deal of trepidation. I got to work on it actually in early April and once more stayed at Mrs. Johnson's house.

Lyndon said, "Write me every day. Tell me what you're doing, how you find things, what you plan you're going to change, and I'll write you. Sometimes we'll phone each other." The use of the long distance telephone was always a scary thing to me; it ran into so much money. It turned out that I spent from late March actually until late June down there, a full three months.

The station was on the second floor of a second-rate building. Actually we were the tenants of the Durham Business School, or of some business school, which, alas, was not any more pleased about having those loud bands there than we were pleased by the quality of the building. It was appalling to climb those stairs into that place of business and see how physically dirty it was. It looked like it hadn't had a janitor in days and days. Aubrey Escoe was the name of the manager. We soon realized that he would have to go. I hadn't been there two days before I realized it was such a tangled skein and there was so much to be done.

It was very hard to figure out what to do first, but I decided the cleanup was the first thing. I knew that nobody in that place was going to have any respect and esprit de corps to get up and get if the place wasn't clean. So I had a staff meeting and told them that. I attempted to get a regular janitor, but I spent one day myself with a bucket full of soap and rags and whatever suitable things there were, washing the windows, while some of them just stood around there with their mouths open, thinking, what kind of person have we got here?

After the cleanup, the next thing was to clean up the long list of accounts receivable. I soon discovered that they were a phantom pretty much, a puff job for somebody preparing to make a sale. Of course, what we paid for the station had been to some extent based on accounts receivable—which didn't get received. [There were] lots of reasons. Some of them were defunct businesses. Some ads should never have been placed in the first time, because they were fly-by-nights, by this time a hundred and twenty days old or more. It was just slack, very slack. The right hand didn't know what the left hand was doing.

On the other hand, unfortunately, it turned out that most of the accounts payable were indeed payable. We compromised on as many as we reasonably could, those that were deemed to be actually payable. We paid them down to the bone until we used up all our resources. At one time, Lyndon issued an ultimatum that he wanted everything paid and all our obligations clean by June 1. It was the fact that Escoe, the manager, really didn't know all that he ought to have known about the accounts receivable and accounts payable and the contracts that finally drove us to the conclusion that we had to get a new manager. So we talked to Harfield Weedin, who had had ten years experience in Texas radio in sizeable jobs and who had stage-managed and announced all of the radio and appearances in Lyndon's campaign of 1941. He was a most attractive man, flamboyant perhaps, but a good personality with a beautiful voice. So he agreed to come with us and to be there by May 17. [Escoe agreed to] stay for a full month after the new manager was found, teach him everything he could.

I can't underestimate the role of Jesse Kellam even from the very beginning before he went into the service. He was a financial adviser at every turn, checked all accounts with me, receivable, payable, new things we had to buy, new equipment. Lyndon kept on sending every penny he could spare. I remember one time he sent a check for $1,500 and attached to it the words, "Now I have about enough left to buy my cigarettes until the end of the month." At one time I wrote him that we had a balance of $84 in the account. Another time he sent me $300 out of his monthly check or bank balance. I called on the three thousand that was owed to me at that time, about all that was due for some time from Uncle Claud's estate in Alabama.

I soon instituted the practice of asking the salesmen to give me a report every week: who had they called on, what had they tried to sell them, did they say yes or no. That was most unhappily received. They really took a dim view of book work. They thought what they had done with their time was darn well their own business. We didn't think so as long as they were on salary. If they were supposed to work eight hours, we wanted them to. But we finally got that ironed out after a few sassy, amusing reports.

Do you think that any of the employees resented the new pace that the new ownership brought?
Oh, yes, they resented it, and they let it be known. It was not abated, although I tried always to win them [over].

Did you ever sense that they resented the fact that a woman was now the boss?
No, I didn't ever feel that.

As far as the staff went, we had this dual process going on. We knew we needed to weed out; we needed to get new people who were our people, who were can-do people. We needed to wait until the manager came to start that process, and at the same time the draft was nibbling at us. Two people were called up by the draft and more were going to be in doubt, and their time was uncertain and short. Harfield soon hired John Hicks to come with him as program director, and he was going to get there by June 1. So we had set the date of June 1 for a new start.[6]

---

6. Harfield Weedin recounted working with CTJ in Harfield Weedin Oral History Interview, 2/24/78, by Michael L. Gillette.

Lyndon said we ought to advertise that. No matter how little money we had, we just had to get it from somewhere, for an advertising campaign to be divided between the *Austin American* and the country weeklies with particular attention to the weeklies covering the coverage of KTBC, and especially those in the Tenth District. Don't forget the other side of the coin. Alas, on reading the correspondence, I thought [we needed] billboards, just a few within the city limits—I'm against it myself—and also amused to see that it was in a letter back that Lyndon wrote me that he says, "I do not think billboards are wise." He also thought that the new manager, Harfield Weedin, ought to write—and here he gets a little grandiloquent—a thousand letters to the civic and business leaders in Austin.

To start out fresh in the world, we thought we'd better have a nicer-looking location, which meant a move, and some nicer-looking furniture. We decided we'd like to rent space in the Brown Building, but we had to go through the long red-tape process of getting the priorities for whatever materials were needed. We started it the very minute we made the decision, kept after it, herded it through all the bureaus, and finally got it about the middle of May. Our furniture was just awfully beat up. I decided on some pieces that could be refinished, repaired, a piano, a few desks and things. I finally decided I had to have two desks and seven chairs.

In one of those letters you wrote and discussed the possibility of hanging three pictures of the men that you admired most in different branches of government.
Oh, yes. We wanted something for the walls. We were getting this new furniture and having other furniture done over, and we wanted everything new and bright, but also cheap or free if possible. You can always get a picture of the president, even if you just go buy one like the post office has. So I asked Lyndon to arrange to get us one of those, and if he didn't think it would be in bad taste, that I'd love to have one of the Speaker and of [Justice William O.] Bill Douglas as my favorite two from other branches of government. Then a good sure thing to get—and this was probably free, because they probably had some extras— I went to see Max Starcke⁄ and got pictures of some of Lyndon's beloved achievements in his early years in Congress relating to the dams. I think we got one of Buchanan Dam and of the administration building and of some power lines going over the mountains with some beautiful yucca in bloom down there at the base of them.

If it hadn't been for the help of friends on every front, we never would have made a go out of that station. We did have a lot of friends in Texas, in New York, everywhere, who were helpful to us, beginning with Ed Weisl,[8] who knew most

---

7. Max Starcke was general manager of the Lower Colorado River Authority.
8. Edwin Weisl was a prominent New York attorney.

everybody and could help us on every front in how to apply for a network [affiliation]. Ed Weisl actually opened so many doors to us, made so many people feel that this was a competent, able young couple who would fulfill their obligations in the community and do a good job whether it was in politics or in business. We may have tried NBC first. We wound up by making our big push to get CBS. We did get it.

What was the issue here? Did you have to represent a large enough market in order to attract network affiliation?
And the coverage of another CBS station could not be close enough to interfere with their sales. We had to choose a network that didn't have a contract with anybody close enough to us to serve them. We soon began to feel that to get higher power and to go nighttime probably would not be possible for the duration [of the war]. "The duration" was the term that was on everybody's lips in those days. We kept after it and got it as soon as we could.

There again, I guess the increase in power was in part determined by whether or not it would interfere with another station in the same vicinity?
Yes, and very much getting the priorities for some kind of materials. I'm more and more amused to go back through that old correspondence and to see the costs of things, a matter of which I was very cognizant, as all my friends knew and still know. For instance, the big heavy equipment for which we have grown so used to paying enormous prices, I look back and see that when we ordered a Gates Series Deluxe Console, it was priced at $830, and that we ordered two microphones for fifty-five and an analyzer for seventy-five. I had to learn an awful lot about technical material. I learned it, got it down to some sense of understanding, and then promptly forgot it within a few months. Everything turned out to be more [expensive].

And salaries. We'd been paying an announcer twenty dollars. He was called up by the army; we had to get a new one. We had to pay him twenty-five a week. The program director, John Hicks, that Harfield Weedin thought was excellent and he wanted to get, was making seventy-five a week. He thought with the great allure of living in Austin—and it does have allure—maybe we could get him for fifty. I think we finally got him for sixty-five a week. When you think of it in terms of today, it really rocks you. But the funny thing was that I had a picnic for all of the employees and their wives and, in two cases, their husbands. We had two women, Jane Mabel and Louise Vine. I had a picnic. I bought all the food for nineteen people, cooked it all myself out at Mrs. Johnson's house; cost twelve dollars. We had it out at the marvelous, cold, cold spring there at Austin that all of us old-timers love so much, Barton Springs.

This picnic was to celebrate the fact that Harfield Weedin had come to join us, and we just wanted to give everybody a feeling that this is a clean slate, a new start. We're going to forge ahead. We can all do it together. We recognize the problems. That was the front we tried to present to the advertisers in town and also to those people to whom we had owed bills and whom we finally got paid.

Do you recall any aspect of your education in the radio business that you learned from other station owners about the business?
Or people who were knowledgeable about it. Oh, yes indeed. I went to Abilene. I saw Bernard Hanks.[9] Paul Bolton was helpful every step of the way.[10] Roy Hofheinz came up, and he was very helpful. He was something of a genius in that field, as in so many. Colonel [Paul] Wakefield was a delightful man.[11] I happened to have known him longer than Lyndon had, and he had some great ideas about how we must be the first ones to catch and interview any celebrities that came to town. With the war bond drives and because it was the capital of the state, there was a trickle, if not a stream, of celebrities that came to Austin. Then he suggested reading human interest stories over the radio.

There were just a lot of things to clean up. There was the ASCAP [American Society of Composers, Authors, and Publishers] contract and INS [International News Service]. We had bought an expensive library that we got very little use out of it. It was called the Standard Library. We were able to resolve that contract and ship back the library. Physically packing it up was one backbreaking job.

Did you yourself get involved with the programming, or were you more interested in the business?
More interested in the business probably. I should have been more interested in the programming. I really wanted it to serve the community and fill its needs and make money and be respected and deserve respect. For the actual programming, I can't remember having had a lot to do with it. One little bit of programming that I did suggest was that we give a little vignette of news about a war hero, particularly a local one, from time to time. There was one lady from somewhere in our district who had six sons in the service. There were some kids in Bastrop carrying on a house-to-house campaign to collect grease and nylon hose.

In the back of my mind was always the Tenth District and Lyndon's job. There was a lot of that, too. People would call me with messages to give to Lyndon about their husband who was trying to get in Officer Training School, or [they] had not heard from their son who had been missing in action for a long time. The more determined and courteous but persistent congressman can hurry those things up. The answer may not always be yes, but you can get an answer.

---

9. Bernard Hanks was a principal in the Harte-Hanks Newspapers.
10. Paul Bolton was a longtime KTBC employee.
11. Paul L. Wakefield was a journalist who held various governmental positions and rose to the rank of major general in the Texas National Guard.

So you really had sort of a district office there?

In a minor way. I had always had a district interest. Lyndon was interested in everything that happened. We never wrote more regularly to each other during a separation. One time I got a seven-page single-spaced typewritten letter from him, full of about that many things to do. Always the tenor of it was setting deadlines to get things done, always a deadline so short that I couldn't meet it: "Get all of the bills paid up by X date. Get into the Brown Building by X date. Set a time when you think you can get out of the red."

He was big on staff meetings, too. We had several of them. He wanted us to show the people who worked for us the financial statements to show them why it was so urgent to keep down expenses. The station had lost five thousand dollars the year before and fifteen hundred in January and fifteen hundred in February. So that's what we came into, and we needed to make all these improvements. At the same time, we didn't have vast capital to outlay. So we had to call on them for long hours, hard work, a lot of enthusiasm, a lot of team spirit, and mostly they came up with it after we got the new group together. Lyndon would use very graphic expressions, for instance saying, "In order to raise a good crop, we must plant good seed corn." That is, we had to spend this money to pay the bills, get a good reputation, put in all the new equipment, move into a new building, get our ASCAP license going and a good news service, and try to get on a network.

He seems to have learned a great deal in a hurry, too, about how stations should operate.

Oh, yes. As the modern expression is, he was "a very fast study." He learned it all quick. He talked to everybody he could that knew something about it, and we had lots of friends and so many friends in those days who were willing to be helpful. He also was always talking about such things as cutting down expenses on water and lights and telephone and insurance, briefly, until we could afford them. He always wanted us to have a budget and know what to expect our next month's expenses were. At the same time, he warned me several times to go on and load up and spend the money on certain things that might become impossible to get as the war went on. Maybe they wouldn't, but against the chance that they would, he wanted us to have a good in-depth supply of tubes and necessary equipment.

Every now and then in a letter I would mention that "Now it's ten thirty and I guess I'll go home to bed," or maybe that I'd say that "I was here until eleven last night." They were long days. As I look back on it, I'm just real pleased to think that I tried that hard and learned that much.

HOME AGAIN

Finally, sometime in late June, I got to go home—home being Washington, which I was just so anxious to see—with some sense of satisfaction in the months' activities and in the hope for the station. Actually, it turned out to be August before we got in the black. I remember very well the first amount of money we got was eighteen dollars in August, and I used it to go get a much-needed dental repair. The nerve had been killed in one of my front teeth, and it was all black, as you may have seen in some of the pictures, some of the campaign pictures. So I had a new tooth put in.

It was such happiness to be back at home in Washington. Our back porch always in the summer was a center of activity. It was great big, screened on three sides, ceiling fan, lots of comfortable furniture. At some time, there arrived in it as a gift from Tom Clark a great big double chaise lounge. We covered it full of pillows, and everybody headed to it. Then there was a swing and a lot of canvas chairs. Everything was sort of cheap and inexpensive, except our chaise lounge, but we didn't know that.

[The porch] looked down onto a beautiful green garden where the people who had originally owned the place had planted a long border of peonies, and every spring they came forth with their glory of pink and rose and white. Then there was quite a lot of hillside rocky area which was a natural rock garden. That reached up to an iron fence which separated us from our neighbor, Dr. O. E. Reed, with a huge elm tree that shaded the whole backyard for many years before it died.

That backyard was a scene of just much happiness during the years from 1942 to 1960, although at this time, in the summer of 1943, we were just really settling into it.

But Zephyr had already acquired a good deal of a reputation among our friends as a good cook. We were always having company; it streamed through the house. In summertime, homemade peach ice cream was one of our favorites.

9

War Years, 1943–1945

Lady Bird's responsibilities multiplied in the war years. After her work in the congressional office came the purchases of KTBC, a home in Washington, and another home in Austin the following year. In addition to overseeing a business and maintaining two houses, she now hosted more dinner parties and houseguests than in previous years. Sam Houston Johnson, LBJ's alcoholic brother, often lived in the Thirtieth Place home for months at a time. Lady Bird's constituent and social activities as a congressional spouse continued, but she finally had the opportunity to assume yet another responsibility, that of motherhood.

NAVAL AFFAIRS COMMITTEE: "WORK OR FIGHT"

Lyndon always hit the ground running, and 1943 was a passionate, full-blooded year, a year of using himself at full capacity in which he was terrifically committed to the work at hand. That work was getting on with the war. He was angry at the delay, inefficiency, red tape, foot dragging; that became evident both in the military and in the private sector at home. He was at war against it, using as his tool the Naval Affairs Committee.

Lyndon got the chairman to appoint a committee to investigate naval personnel itself to make sure that able-bodied men who could go to sea were not sitting at desk jobs. But the main focus of his wrath and his main effort at that time related to absenteeism, which had gotten pretty high. "Work or Fight" was the slogan of the day. Something like out of ten men, nine plus would show up for work in war plants or other places, particularly in war plants, and that was what he was concerned about. He wrote a really marvelous speech in which he got the navy to say the number of battleships or carriers which could have been built with the man-hours that were lost through absenteeism. Then he talked about the ghost ships that never got there, that didn't show up to protect the men at whatever the crucial battles were of that day. It was effective. It also put him at cross purposes with labor and with some of his good friends, like Jim Rowe. But he wrote scorching rejoinders to them. I remember one particular phrase, something like, "If we don't clean house ourselves now, some more people later on "are going to clean house and they're going to break a lot of precious things as they throw around them."

"A REVOLVING-DOOR HOTEL"

All during the war years, our house was kind of a revolving-door hotel. We expanded it just as far as it could go, making the third floor into a fairly acceptable guest room and bath that housed a long train of servicemen and women, secretaries, staff, friends from home. Hotel rooms were scarce. It wasn't at all unusual to get a call from some constituent saying, "I just can't find a room. Can I come out and stay with you?" If there was a place, the answer was always yes. Dorris [Powell] came up from Karnack and visited me for nice long stays, one time bringing her thirteen or so–year-old daughter. My various Alabama kinfolks came up. Many of our good friends would stop by for a night or longer. There was one delightful period when Jake and Sugar Pickle were in Washington for a few days and John Connally and Bill [Deason] and Lyndon, and they had a domino tournament which lasted for every day they were all together.

A whole stream of the old NYA crowd and all of our old friends passed through the house. 1943 was the summer that the NYA died, leaving us with all its sweet memories and an inheritance on Lyndon's part of trying to get jobs for any of the people in there that the draft didn't gobble up right away. The NYA was not really needed anymore because the war needed so many young men and women, and war plants needed them. There wasn't that slack in the economy that had brought the NYA into being. Jesse Kellam would come through every now and then. He'd gotten out of the NYA and gone into the navy. He was a married man with two children and just at the breaking point in the age. He didn't need to go. He'd even been in the other war. But he was determined to go and sold his house in Austin. That was a blow, I expect, to his wife, that gentle soul, and it was to us. We'd looked forward to being his neighbor out there on the river sometime.[1]

One time Lyndon and I looked at each other, and one of us said laughingly, "Some of these days somebody is going to come up there and going to stay, and I'm going to think you know them, and you're going to think I know them, and neither one of us is going to know them!" Well, it finally happened once about like this: A young voice on the other end of the telephone line gave his name and his rank—he came from somewhere in the Hill Country of Texas— and said, "I'm just passing through and I don't have a place to stay, and I remember when I saw you all out at Buchanan Dam you said, 'Come and see me sometime,' so could I spend the night?" I said, "Sure, come on out." He was a nice-looking enough young man. We took him up, and I felt sure that Lyndon,

---

1. Like Kellam, the Johnsons had purchased a waterfront lot on Scenic Drive in Austin from Charles Marsh, but they later sold it before building a house on the property. CTJ OHI 10.

when he came in, could identify him further. I told Lyndon all about him, and he couldn't. [The young man] was up there on the third floor where all our visitors stayed. But everything he mentioned was something that we knew, and he said, "You remember, I drove the boat that time y'all came out to Buchanan and Senator Wirtz was there." He rattled on and on, [naming] several people who did always come with us out to Buchanan Dam. But neither one of us could remember this serviceman who had been driving the boat and working, no doubt, for the LCRA. It was all very nice and warm and happy, and he went on his way the next day. I don't think he ever knew that neither one of us could remember him.

In the parade of the years one of the recurring dates was always the arrival of Aunt Effie for a visit. She would come to see us about twice a year and stay two or three months. It added up to a total of about a fourth of the time of the year, or perhaps a half. Then she would go back to Alabama to visit other relatives. She loved the spring in Washington, and she loved the fall, too. Because one of the greatest treasures of her life, one which she passed on to me by osmosis I guess, was her delight in flowers and the burgeoning earth and the beauty of the world around her. So I treasured my little gas coupons and I always carried Aunt Effie just about everywhere I went in the car, even if it was just to the Safeway grocery store.

Mrs. [Sam] Johnson also came to visit us every year. That, too, was a time for celebration. It was especially nice if they could come together, even in our crowded household, because they became great friends. They loved to talk about their respective families and old times and history and art, and it was a most satisfying joy to me that they liked, appreciated, and respected each other so much.

Would Aunt Effie become part of the working family or the household? Would she be pressed into service to help the congressman?
No. Aunt Effie was much too gentle and retiring. Work, unfortunately, was not a part of her life. She was a very intelligent woman, but she was the result of too much sheltering in her young days on the part of her father and her brother. She wasn't acquainted with work enough, even the work of handling her own business affairs, which were handled entirely by Uncle Claud, and that was a great deprivation. One should be made to work or at least encouraged to work. In her young days, she had played the piano; she had painted and done the polite, artistic things that a young woman learned. Somehow my mother escaped that.

Aunt Effie was also a great reader. But she had many physical problems, many of them real and some of them perhaps imagined. I don't know quite where the line was. Her eyesight was poor by this time and her reading limited. She was not blind, but she was sight impaired. I found out about and secured for her recordings for the blind from the Library of Congress. They were available, and it was a great thing to choose the ones she wanted and get them installed in her room by her bed.

So her routine was just to stay out on the pretty porch or upstairs in her room and talk to whomever had the leisure to talk to her. As I look back on her life, I am grateful for the many good things she contributed to my life, and I'm sorry I didn't do more to add to hers. Yet her own life had been impaired by not being pushed, forced into the world more in her younger days. But she was a good conversationalist and had opinions on everything.

Did these opinions coincide pretty much with Mrs. Johnson's opinions?
In a great degree, yes, although she perhaps had wider-ranging empathy and compassion for people in general. Mrs. Johnson was oriented very much toward taking care of her own family, and it was from Mr. Johnson that Lyndon got his care for the poor and afflicted and the common man and his just real down-to-earth affinity with them.

Sometime during the summer of 1943, I went to see our old friend Dr. Will Watt in Austin and got the big news that I was at last pregnant after eight and a half years. We were very proud and happy, and so was Dr. Radford Brown, my doctor in Washington. I'm sure that he felt the same sort of a sense of victory and elation that I did, because he cared about his patients. I had started going to him some three or so years before. Dr. Brown was one of the nicest human beings I ever knew and one of the most admirable. He was a great figure in my life and a marvelously professional, empathetic, delightful man. I daresay, except for his knowledge and his guidance, some of the physical problems that had kept us from having children might never have been overcome.

1901 DILLMAN STREET

Circumstances caused a large west Austin duplex to be available for a quick and quiet sale. Houston contractor Warren S. Bellows had provided 1901 Dillman Street for his mistress, who ultimately committed suicide in the bathtub.[2]
Sometime during that late summer and fall of 1943, the tide of niggling opposition against Lyndon came to a peak in the person of, alas, Mayor Tom Miller, our loved friend. It came about over the purchase of a house in Austin. A house went on the market under rather unusual circumstances, which caused it to be at a reasonable price. It was a part of an estate, and it belonged to the woman friend of a wealthy man. She had died. The man was most desirous that the house be sold quickly and the whole circumstances hushed up for his reputation, for his family, for everything. It was just one of those things that were right below the surface, known, but not to many. The mayor had an option on buying it; he had let it lapse. The lawyer called Lyndon up right away and said, "You ought to get it." Lyndon, flush with the feeling that he was going to have a

---

2. Harfield Weedin Oral History Interview, 2/24/83, by Michael L. Gillette. Weedin also describes Tom Miller's reaction upon hearing that LBJ had purchased the Dillman property.

family and have a business in Austin, decided that he would take this other jump. So we bought the house and incensed the mayor.

1901 Dillman had charm and was a happy part of our life for a good many years. It was a duplex, and as the years went on, we enlarged it and enlarged it as we did everything we ever had. It became the local Austin address of any number of secretaries who really lived the biggest part of the year in Washington. When they would come to Texas, they very often but not always stayed with us. For poll tax purposes that was a good permanent address.

Our side was upstairs where you walked into a large living room with a huge picture window that looked out onto a nice bending live oak, the hills in the distance, for what I could see of them, the rapidly building up area in front of us. I had my first oil painting given to me by my brother Tony. Perhaps it was a primitive of a Mexican village and a snowcapped mountain in the distance. Adobe houses and a street and the snow-capped mountain, probably Popo [catepetl], in the distance. Very soon we got our second one, which was a Porfirio Salinas,[3] from Edmunds Travis. It still hangs in the ranch house in the den over the fireplace. Salinas soon became Lyndon's favorite; he gravitated to his paintings because he felt they expressed the spirit of the Hill Country, which was so much home to him.

The backyard was huge, a marvelous place to raise children in. One of the stories of our life was that Lyndon was determined to get the backyard, which looked rather scraggy in spite of nice trees, planted with nice St. Augustine turf grass. He just wanted a beautiful backyard. He wanted a barbecue pit made out of stone. He delivered his desires with a deadline, of course, and I said, "But, honey, it's hot." The right time to plant grass is late October or maybe get it in the ground early sometime in March. He said, "Oh, it will do all right, it will do all right." He was so insistent that we went on and got it planted, and I was almost hoping it would die. Well, the heavens opened up and those bountiful rains came, and the grass prospered and did beautifully. It was just a great laugh for everybody.

He commissioned me and Nellie to get the barbecue pit built. We didn't know a thing in the world about barbecue pits. We didn't want to know anything about them. Nevertheless, we rounded up somebody who built the barbecue pit and got it done in jig time, and I think we used it once. It turned out to be quite a lot of trouble to build that fire and get it to exactly the right temperature and put out the meat. The ingredient that we omitted was the man of the house who was going to do the cooking. We had innumerable marvelous picnics, but we would either make fried chicken and ham or stuff in the kitchen

3. San Antonio artist Porfirio Salinas painted Texas Hill Country landscapes in the 1940s, 1950s, and 1960s. Collectors of his work included Sam Rayburn, J. Frank Dobie, John Connally, and LBJ. John and Deborah Powers, *Texas Painters, Sculptors and Graphic Artists: A Biographical Dictionary of Artists in Texas before 1942* (Austin, TX: Woodmont Books, 2000), 442.

and bring it outside and serve it on tables, or else we would have some local barbecue person drive his wagon up into the backyard and set it out.

One of the accusations that Tom Miller raised was "Where did you get the money?"
Absolutely, and that is the one that was bandied around on everybody's lips: where did we, on the salary of $10,000, suddenly turn out to be able to buy a radio station, and then later on a house? That was the beginning of the first strain of troubles that we had had. Always before that, we had been the young white knight on the horse and poor as Job's turkey, though that was never the case as far as I was concerned. But it's just that what I inherited from my mother was in my daddy's hands and I wasn't in need of getting it. I was perfectly glad to leave it, but the time had come when we could make use of it.

Was this more of your mother's money than the inheritance that you got when your Uncle Claud died?
I frankly do not know, but both of those two strains entered into it. All of that was coming to fruition. From those two sources there was a sizable amount later on, but that's a story for a couple of years down the line. I made a detailed accounting of the whole thing and where it came from. In any case, there was a lot of talk going around the town, because the mayor was a talker without a peer. Nobody ever won an argument with him.

Lyndon wrote him a long and absolutely masterful letter. He asked me to read it and add what I wanted to in it, and then I did. It was a letter about two or three days before the mayor's birthday, and it was wishing him a happy birthday. That was all quite true, because we cared about him and we weren't about to turn loose of him, and yet we were hurt and angry. Lyndon, explaining to him where this money did come from, wrote,

> The latest statement that you made that has caught up with me was that you, quote, "could not understand where my wife was getting all her money." We paid about five thousand cash and made a vendor's lien note for the balance. We borrowed five thousand from our friendly, ethical bank with which I've done business all my life, and we got it at a decent rate of interest. It is a demand note that will be paid off as soon as another note Mrs. Johnson owns comes due. The other note, Mayor, is in the amount of twenty thousand which represents a part-payment from her father for a part-interest in her mother's community property.

When he handed it to me, I wrote up above his draft: "Mrs. Johnson's mother died twenty-five years ago and what finally descended to her three children was administered by their father. For the good old American right of passing on your life's earnings to your children, I have no apology to make, and I imagine it is one of the things you were working for, too, Mr. Mayor," because Mr. Mayor set a great store by his son Tom.

I think the mayor ameliorated his insinuations. His concern about where I had gotten my wealth diminished. This angry feeling between us did not last, certainly not on our part. But words have wings, and especially rumors, and once they are afloat, they never die. They circle around and around and come back to haunt and hurt. Buck Taylor, who was not a man of consequence and did not live in the district, was soon making noises that he was going to run against us the next summer. What the mayor had to do with actually hoisting him on the scene I don't know. I think by the time Taylor got going, the mayor was back as our staunch friend. But the question of where did the money come from followed us with Buck Taylor, later on with Hardy Hollers, later on with others, all through the years, coming to a head, actually, in 1946.

LBJ IN THE TENTH DISTRICT

It was a balm through the years to Lyndon to get back home. All of that period for him was a passionate, intense, often angry time. He was very impatient with bickering between the services, red tape, and bureaucratic holdups and all that. He could get bogged down in Washington, and it did him good to get home. Lyndon's program when he went home to the district was to go to every post office in the district. As he wrote somebody, that meant visiting a hundred or more small towns and less than thirty days to do it in. So he wasn't at home very much. When he got home to the district, his eye was on next spring: Would there be an opponent or wouldn't there? After having gone to Congress in April of 1937, it was this year that we then began to hear the first real rumblings of discontent. He was determined to put in a vigorous fall to avoid a harder spring. In his letters, Lyndon would often repeat the phrase "Time is the most valuable thing you have; be sure you spend it well." And yet he himself was sometimes one of the chief breakers of that rule. He would get interested in somebody who was not all that important, or he would get interested telling a long story and be late for a meeting, which would, of course, have a lot of people on edge.

The Tenth District was a very intimate, homey place. Everybody called Lyndon by his first name. Everybody brought their problems to him. Individual problems are the bricks and mortar of the building of a congressman's reputation and whatever he stands upon. He opened his office on Mondays of every week in room 718, the Brown Building, and he'd take all comers. Mary Rather, his secretary then, said he'd sometimes have as many as eighty or a hundred people come in each day, maybe in a group, maybe by ones. Didn't have any regular appointments, just sit and wait your turn. I rather expect they might let a few people in the back door, but mostly that's the best way to try to do it. Sometimes he wouldn't get home until nine thirty or ten at night. Then the other four days of the week he would go out over the district, speaking at a bond rally here or service club there or all those hundred towns.

How did he come away from these full days of meeting with constituents who brought problems to him? Did these sessions tell him something about the district that he felt was important?

Sure. He would try to help them solve their problems or explain the government's position to them. Lots of times he could help them; sometimes he couldn't. And oh, sometimes it was very painful because people would just plain want to get their son out of going to the army at all. You were helpless. Also, you were a little ashamed and embarrassed for them, and at them. But oh, there were so many times when you could help them. When just your knowledge of the labyrinth of Washington machinery could find an honest answer to what seemed to be their insoluble needs.

He flourished on those times in the district. They were exhausting, but he was stimulated by them. It was just a constant thread of going through these ten counties and these hundred or so towns. I remember the phrase often used in the Hill Country about "The best fertilizer for any man's ranch is the footsteps of the owner." Certainly, the best fertilizer for the career of a congressman is to put his feet on the streets of all of the area that he represents and shake hands with the people.

We defeated Buck Taylor with no trouble, getting 70 percent of the votes, losing Washington County by a fairly narrow margin. Lyndon called me that night about midnight disappointed with the results, but I wasn't. 70 percent I'll stay with anytime. As it happened, I do think that was one of our high points. Nobody had contested us in 1938, 1940, and 1942. Now here in 1944 we win by 70 percent. Most of the other times when we had a contest, whether for the district, the Senate, or the nation, our portion of the Tenth District vote remained somewhere between 61 and 65 percent almost all those years until the last time.

LYNDA BIRD

Whatever Lyndon was doing, I was cozily getting things ready for our son's or daughter's arrival in March. I remember the focal point of the so-called nursery. In that small house a room had to serve lots of purposes, but baby was going to have a room. The best thing in it was a white wicker bassinet on wheels that Jimmie Allred gave us. It was very big and very elegant, with ribbons and pillows. I cherished it then and for years to come. Later, Luci and many children of other favorite families used it. It was well seasoned with the close intimacy with lots of loved children. But the height of its life was to be a taxi around the house when our children got big enough to push it. They would put each other or friends in it and go barreling around in that house at 4921 Thirtieth Place. It is now at the LBJ Library in somewhat limp condition.

One Sunday morning, the nineteenth of March, I felt the time had come to go to the hospital. I had my little suitcase packed, and I said to Lyndon, "Let's go." Aunt Effie was there visiting us on one of her long visits. Mrs. Johnson had come up to participate in the arrival of her new grandchild. They were cozily visiting with each other. We were all getting ready to enjoy the spring beauty of Washington. So I said, "Lyndon, I think we better go to the hospital." About that time he received one of those interminable telephone calls, and he got on it. I was patting my foot in the car, for one of the rare times rather put out with him because he didn't hurry off the phone. Finally he came and we went to the hospital. He stayed awhile at the hospital, but neither he nor I was anxious for him to stick around. The customs change, and this business of fathers staying to be of assistance was not in at that time. I think doctors wanted them out of the way. I certainly did, because I soon began to feel like it was no time to put my best foot forward and try to look attractive and have my lipstick on. So he spent a large part of the day driving around with Tom Clark, as he later told me. We all thought the baby wouldn't be born until the next morning. I think the doctor did ask him to come back later that night, and Lynda Bird was born before midnight; I don't really have any idea when. Lynda Bird was a big-boned child, seven pounds seven ounces, long, big hands, feet, head, lots of black hair. Not pretty, highly vocal, opinionated from the beginning. It was later that she became really a beautiful physical specimen. She took after her father in her stature.

Was he worried before she was born?
No, I don't think either one of us were worried. It was a momentous occasion, but it just didn't occur to us that anything except the best could come of this. Although I feel sure that all the time he had been expecting a boy, he never talked about it to me. I had, too. It was quite a surprise when it turned out to be a girl. We hadn't even considered it. He never had expressed to me that he would be disappointed if it was a girl. He had been very careful about that. But we had talked about boys' names. We had not talked about girls' names. It was Mrs. Johnson who just the night or two before I went to the hospital had said, "Well, now what if it is a girl? What are you going to name it?" We both had a blank stare, and she said, "Why don't you name it after both of you?" I guess she prudently thought this might be the only one. So she said, "Name it Lynda Bird, and spell it with a "y." That suited me fine; I loved it.

One of the letters he wrote at the time said that he wanted to name her Lady Bird after you, and that you said no.
Oh, it's bad enough to perpetrate a nickname like that, or any nickname usually, on a child. I would not want to be a party to it, although I long ago made my peace with my own.

Was he a proud father?

Oh, yes! He was calling right and left as soon as the news was available. We did stay a bit longer than usual in the hospital. In those days, one was supposed to stay in the hospital about a week. I brought home with me a tyrannical baby nurse who stayed for a couple of weeks. I give myself small plaudits for knowing how to handle children. I remember the absolute horror I felt on the day when it was finally this lady's day off and I saw her disappearing down the street, growing smaller and smaller in the distance. There in the bassinet was that squirming red infant that I was totally responsible for. Anyhow, we made it together. Mrs. Johnson, poor dear, got a childhood disease of all things for a woman who had raised five children—I think it was mumps—and had to be confined to the third floor. The doctor said that that was catching and that we must by all means not be exposed to her for a while. Maybe that is why I actually stayed in the hospital several days longer.

MY OWN BACKYARD

When we bought the place there was one tree, an apple tree, at the right rear of the yard. In the course of years, I planted a weeping cherry closer to the house, and then on the opposite or left-hand side, I planted a pink dogwood and then a white dogwood. The four trees formed a square. Across the rear of the yard was a fairly deep flower bed in which I had some marvelous peonies left over from the original owner of the house who had been a nurseryman or had a nursery-man in his family, because these were great specimens and gave me eighteen years of joy. Our next-door neighbor and I would confer over the back fence about when was the time to put out pansies in the fall or put out more grass seed, which we did twice a year, about September and March. I always planted zinnias. I only planted things that were easy to grow and would give me a lot for a little work, because in spite of the good help I had, there was always twice as much work as I could get around to doing.

A storm blew down my apple tree. It was flat on the ground. I called a nursery and got the [nurserymen] out there. I was determined to prop that tree back up again. They looked at me like they thought I was crazy, but if I was prepared to spend the amount of money—which wasn't huge, but to me it was sizeable. So we just dug a big hole, replanted that tree, and firmly put stockings on it and supports on it. And I lived to see it there until I left the place in 1961. I had such affection for that backyard.

It was the spring [of 1944] that we had our first victory garden. Bill Deason planted it, and it was in the right-hand half of our little backyard, probably thirty feet square. Never were so many beans and tomatoes and black-eyed peas especially, even a few messes of corn, raised in such a small plot of ground. Bill Deason did it magnificently. Later on, when he wasn't there, I did it happily and less well. But we ate out of that garden from probably about June on until we were still getting tomatoes when frost came in early November. There was a little tiny back porch that opened off of the kitchen, and you went down some steps, and we had a round table that came from the old ladies, and we just let it sit out there until finally after six or eight years the rain finally rotted it, but we'd had our pleasure out of it. You could get about six or eight around it. Zephyr would fix us many a good meal from the garden. We would serve surprised constituents such things as black-eyed peas that were grown right under their eyes a few feet away.

When Bill Deason got married, his reception was at your house.
Oh, yes, yes. Lyndon was a great part of the life of his staff, and he loved the members of his staff. And almost without exception, they loved him and remained his close friends from beginning to end. We participated in their weddings in some way or another, gave the reception, or Lyndon was best man. In this case we were absolutely overjoyed to do it, because we just loved Bill and we came to love Jeanne. But at the same time, Nellie Connally and I had a "Gee, what are we going to do?" feeling. When our husbands were busy or out of town, Bill was always there for us to lean on to carry the heavy suitcases, to move the furniture, to escort us out at night, anything. So we felt like it was saying good-bye to him in a way. But nevertheless, he had been a bachelor a long time and so marriage was highly due.

"THAT MOMENTOUS CROSSING"

I remember one night in June being waked up by a telephone call about three or four a.m. It was the sort of call you know is a great moment, good or bad. I could tell from Lyndon's expression that it was something tremendous and dramatic. He did turn to me for just a moment, because, of course, I was wide awake, and tell me what it was. Then he was listening to every word. American troops had landed on the coast of Normandy. It was D-Day. Having been poised in England for an indefinite period of time, they had made that momentous crossing. Our friend Bill White was with them writing about it, and our friend Earl Rudder was with them, leading [the Army's Second Ranger Battalion], scaling the cliffs [of Pointe du Hoc].[4] The reason for its success was because they had gone up in an area that the Germans had not really considered that anybody could. But the [Rangers] scaled the most difficult cliffs. The invasion gave a new shot in the arm for unity.

---

4. William S. White covered the D-day invasion for the Associated Press. For an account of James Earl Rudder's command of the Second Ranger Battalion at Pointe du Hoc, see Thomas Hatfield, *James Earl Rudder: From Leader to Legend* (College Station: Texas A & M University Press, 2011).

Meanwhile, I was at home, getting acquainted with Lynda Bird and never feeling very at ease tending to a baby, but liking her very much and very interested in her. I was less mobile after she was born. The back porch became the center of my leisure, and the backyard the center of my work, together with going to the grocery store and all the other marketing. I was the purchasing agent for a growing family, and it included a good bit more than just husband, wife, and children and staff, as the years went on.

There was one delightful diversion. I was asked to christen a submarine in Portsmouth, New Hampshire, in July. It had the unlikely name of USS *Tench*. I asked Mary Clark to be my attendant; those things were fancy in those days. We went by train up to New Hampshire and went to the shipbuilding yard. There it was on the ways, ready to slide down in. There were admirals and servicemen and everybody spic and span lined up in attention, and [the ceremony included the] national anthem and prayers and a gift of, I think, records from me to the servicemen for their recreation time on the submarine. I smashed a bottle of champagne over it with great difficulty and a horrible grimace, and the pictures are nothing to rejoice over, except those that are posed. Dear sweet Mary was the most delightful of companions, and it was a marvelous break from a vigorous four- or five-month-old little girl. It was the big outside world, and for once I was sort of the center of attention. I must say I enjoyed it.

END OF AN ERA

[The 1945 presidential inauguration] was held in a place that it never had been before or since, to my knowledge: the porch of the White House, the one where you walk out of the Blue Room and those two lovely circular steps go down to the grounds. It was a cold, dreary, bitter day, and it was a very brief ceremony. I certainly thought nothing of the change of place. No doubt, in retrospect, it was because the president, then in the thirteenth year of office and actually only about three or four months before he died, must have been a very worn and weary man.

It was a bitter cold day, gray and spitting sleet. Lyndon and I started to the ceremonies, and the ticket on our car windshield permitted us to park, but a good long ways away. We got out and we walked, and a car drove up beside us and said, "Get in." It was the man I really came to know as Senator Bob Kerr. He was then governor of Oklahoma. Every governor was always invited to the inaugural. That was the very first time I remember him in our life. He became one of the staunchest friends.

We went on up, and we watched the ceremony. It was brief. Later on, I had an odd across-the-years return to that [inaugural ceremony] at a reception in the White House to which I had invited all of the Roosevelt children and their children, and a great many of them came. I was standing this time inside the White House, inside the Blue Room as I recall, close to the windows that become doors and open out onto the porch, with James [Roosevelt]. He said that [in 1945] he had just flown in from his military service for the ceremony, and he had not seen his father in quite a long time. He was shocked by his appearance, thin and pale and wan.[5] I certainly did not know that he was a sick man there in January of 1945 as I watched.

The two dominating things in the year of 1945 that I remember are just what everybody else remembers: the death of FDR and the end of the war. Aunt Effie was visiting us. She was downstairs listening to the radio, and I was upstairs. She came to the foot of the steps and hollered up at me, "Lady Bird, President Roosevelt is dead!" My first reaction was just a quick flash of anger. Now that doesn't make any sense. But I think perhaps it's not an unusual thing if you depend on somebody a great deal, and everybody that I knew had a sense of dependence on him. He was our leader; he was a father figure. We felt everything was going to be all right, or as close to all right as could be, with him at the helm. You just got mad if such a person was removed from your life.

I just flashed back, "That's not right; you haven't heard it right," which was unnecessarily rude of me. Then I immediately flew to the radio and every station was full of it. There was nothing else on the air. Soon you had to believe it. My thoughts would have gone immediately to Lyndon. I know I would have felt like I wanted to comfort him. But he just was not comforted by me or anybody for a little spell. Then the most curious—I don't know how to describe what befell our circle of friends, the city of Washington, and the nation to a sizable extent. It was a period when everything ground to a stop, of almost paralysis, and of wanting to know every detail, and then of finally, gradually coming to. The days all seemed like Sundays for several days. The next day Lyndon and I went out to Helen Gahagan Douglas's.[6] I don't know that we even called and said, "Could we come?" It was just a time when close people got together, and I know that off and on for the next twenty-four or forty-eight hours we were with close people who had loved him and believed in him. Tommy Corcoran, I think we were with. I remember Jim Rowe and Libby being there. You huddled together for warmth.

Then the day when the body reached Washington and when the cortege moved down Pennsylvania Avenue, Lyndon did the oddest thing. He stayed in bed all day, and he acted like he really didn't even much want to have me around. I told him, somewhat timidly, that I was going downtown and stand on the

---

5. CTJ described James Roosevelt's recollections of his father's condition at the 1945 inauguration in her diary entry of July 16, 1964. Johnson, *A White House Diary*, 179–80.

6. Helen Gahagan Douglas had had several responsibilities during the Roosevelt administration, but in 1945 she was a Democratic member of Congress from California.

street and watch it pass. He said something sarcastic like, "This is not a circus, you know." But I still wish I had gone. I'm mad at myself for not going. Not that you didn't share being at home listening to the radio. You did. But it would have been a moment to absorb and share right close on the street.

Do you think he felt hurt that he hadn't been invited to that funeral?
I think he probably did, because he had a curious dichotomy about funerals; they really just laid him out. They were emotionally exhausting and physically exhausting, but, on the other hand, he wouldn't miss them. If he was at all able, he went to them. This, of course, was private, and he was not included, but he was pretty small-fry. He was still just a member of the House. He considered himself personally close, and he must have been in a way by the number of times that he went down there, because they were really quite frequent.

In one of those letters to Jim Rowe, LBJ wrote that "Washington is just not the same place that it was."
Oh, yes. There were a lot of the close devotees of FDR who never could see in any successor, no matter how brilliant and wonderful he might have been, their shining star.

That's just the way with close friends and staff people and folks like that. But it took a while. Lyndon was soon close to President Truman. He had known him before. But I remember him going out on the ship called the *Williamsburg*. There would always be just stag parties, poker parties, and he would have with him folks like Bob Hannegan. chairman of the Democratic National Committee. They would enjoy some relaxing moments on the ship. The president would take with him his close friends. He would have with him his close friends like Fred Vinson, who was also a very close friend of Lyndon's, and his secretary of the treasury [John W. Snyder], and Clinton Anderson, who became his secretary of agriculture.

The image that we have of you during the Roosevelt period was a close-knit group of lively, intellectual, aggressive, New Deal–oriented people who were a reasonably close group. Did this group of your friends disperse after Roosevelt's death?
Oh, no. We clung together. Many of us have remained together ever since, in my opinion: Jim Rowe and Libby, his wife; Tom Corcoran; for ages Ben Cohen. Every one who were old FDR people, their friendship remained. The luster was somewhat off. I think they will all remember it as their special day in the sun. Those of us that were in an elected public office and had our constituencies, we still had our job to do. It remained in our memories forever, but we went on with the day's work. Your words are exactly right. There was a lot of midnight oil burned, a lot of feeling that we can roll up our sleeves and remake America. It was a heady time to be alive and to be in government.

Did President Johnson become more conservative in the years after FDR's death?
Yes, I expect so. Of course, it really is representative democracy, and Lyndon represented first a district and then a state that was more conservative than he was. For a long while they were in love with FDR, but then he had plenty of opponents in Texas. We are a little bit more conservative in Texas. The miracle is that Lyndon survived successfully for such a long time in Texas. One of our friends, speaking nationally, said, "Lyndon, you took us about as far as we could go and farther than lots of us thought we could." Thought we could or would, I'm sure.

In retrospect, I have the feeling that the year 1945, particularly after Roosevelt's death, after the urgent necessity to get on with the war had come to an end, there was just sort of a miasma of uncertainty and not exactly the winter of your discontent and certainly not stalemate, but still a waiting period. It wasn't one of the most glittering times of our lives.

President Johnson voted for the Taft-Hartley Act[7]?
Yes, he did. People trying to write about him must be concerned about just how liberal or just how conservative is this man. Which is he? The fact is that he wanted everybody to work and be willing to work. At the same time he didn't want anybody to be without, and he voted for school lunches and he voted for food relief for Europe and Asia, as I recall. He voted for Taft-Hartley. And he was very, very strong on everything for national defense and for the strength of this country. So where does that bring you out? I guess it brings you out an old-fashioned, middle-of-the-roader, a mixture of conservative and liberal.

A SERIOUS ILLNESS

A week after Germany's surrender, Rep. Johnson led a congressional delegation to Europe, ostensibly to study naval assets that could be transferred to the Pacific theater. The trip, which lasted almost a month, gave LBJ a graphic impression of the war's devastation.
When [Lyndon] arrived back [from Europe],[8] he brought with him Jerry Wilke,[9] a darling young woman, who was with the Red Cross, had been stationed in

---

7. The Labor Management Relations Act of 1947, which prohibited secondary strikes and the closed shop and authorized the president to block national emergency strikes.

8. LBJ was one of five members of the Naval Affairs Committee to report on the transfer of naval assets to the Pacific theater. The other members of the delegation were F. Edward Hebert, Michael Bradley, Sterling Cole, and William Hess.

9. Jerry Wilke had worked in LBJ's 1941 Senate campaign. Virginia Wilke English Oral History Interview 2, 3/18/81, by Michael L. Gillette. As CTJ left for the hospital, she asked Jerry Wilke to host a previously scheduled dinner for Sam Rayburn that evening in the Johnson home. Virginia Wilke English Oral History Interview 1, 3/3/81, by Michael L. Gillette.

Europe. He had seen her over there. Her period of service [was over, or it was] about time for her to come back. He just picked her up and brought her back on that plane. He had made it a point to get in touch with every service person he knew personally, particularly anybody from Texas, and bring back word from them and give it to their parents later on.

All of this I absorbed later. All that I absorbed when he first got home was that there he was, home, and I was glad to see him. He had brought Jerry Wilke with him, and he had a whole batch of presents. But I was very, very sick and not wanting to admit it. I'd been feeling ill for a couple of weeks, had called the doctor, only got his nurse, and she knew how overpressed and exhausted he was, and she said, "Is it an emergency?"

I said, "Well, no, I don't think so. I think I'm probably pregnant." So she said, "All right, I'll put you down for Tuesday, two weeks from now," or something like that. I said, "All right," because I didn't know that it was an emergency. As it turned out, the day Lyndon got back I was really miserably sick. I remember wanting to be joyous, wanting to express my happiness that he was home. He wanted to show me some presents he had brought me, and I didn't much want to look at them or anything. I really had to exert all the power I had to maintain my composure and try to be happy, because I never have wanted to admit it if I was sick, and it just seemed like such a beastly time to be sick.

That night, in the middle of the night, I really thought I was going to die. I didn't want to wake Lyndon, who was exhausted. I got up and just crept into another bed. But I was torn between wondering whether I just had to tell Lyndon to get up and call the doctor or not. Finally I must have gone to sleep or passed out. The next morning I felt even worse. I told Lyndon I didn't feel well and just good-bye. But he didn't know how sick I was. So as soon as he was out of the house I picked up the phone and called the doctor and told him how I felt and everything. He said, "I'll be right out." Then I did pass out. Zephyr or somebody came in the room, they told me later, and they were just very much upset and they phoned Lyndon's office.

The doctor got out there in a few minutes. He had called an ambulance on the assumption that he would need it. I remember trying to tell him the symptoms as they were loading me into the ambulance. As I rode along, I remember thinking the oddest string of thoughts: isn't it wonderful if I am all this sick that there is an ambulance, and there is this fine doctor, and that I'm on the way to the hospital, and I'm going to be taken care of. I also remembered having bought a dress and paid more for it than any dress I had up until that time, and wondering what somebody else who couldn't pay for that ambulance or buy that dress, what they would do when they're presented with a situation like that, and sending up a prayer of thanks to my father and my grandfather and my very hard-working husband that I could buy that dress, and hoped I got to wear it later on, and that I could ride in that ambulance going to get help as quickly as possible. Ridiculous, random thoughts, particularly the dress.

They took me down to the hospital. It was a ruptured tubular pregnancy. I think the name of the tube is called fallopian; pregnancy that doesn't make its way to the uterus but gets stopped in the tube and necessarily gets bigger and bigger and then bursts, which means that blood poisoning would set in and you would die if you didn't get an operation. So I was real sick. I remember it quite well, and it went on successively for several days, with high fever and a couple of bad ups and downs. Particularly, I had lost a lot of blood and had to have a couple of blood transfusions. There was none of the proper type in the hospital because, I guess, in the war years it was being used so much for returned servicemen. So they asked Lyndon to see if he could find a donor right quick who was the proper type. He got Congressman John Lyle, and then he got a visiting friend of ours from Texas, Irving Goldberg.[10]

But I wasn't still quite out of the woods. I had some peculiar reaction, and I passed out and scared myself and the doctor, and had the oddest sensation of falling down, down, down in a bottomless hole. Sometime in the middle of the day, Lyndon came to the hospital to see me, not called by anybody and not his habit at all. Once he was reassured that I was going to live and be all right, it would be his natural custom to just stop by in the evening when he got the work done. This particular time, the doctor knew how sick I was, and I felt I was very sick, but nobody had called Lyndon. He said he just had the feeling that he wanted to go see me. And oh boy, was I glad to see him, because it just felt like a lifeline, just something to cling onto, a reassurance.

But that's a long way around to tell you how I felt about Lyndon's getting back. Actually, when he had talked so much about his trip that night before, and when he had shown me the gifts, I was just in no shape to take it in. Then life did run on so quickly after I was out of the hospital. However, I came to know that it had been a hideous, horrible, stomach-turning trip, and he had seen so much misery and degradation and cruelty that it had just been emotionally exhausting. He went to Munich and Dachau[11] and the underground city of Berchtesgaden and just a whole lot around over Europe, saw the devastated cities. I think it strengthened forever his determination that nothing like that was going to happen to us. I felt the fallout of the trip and his horror of the whole thing. If he had been determined to have a strong national defense before, he was even stronger afterward. Yes, the whole thing just turned his stomach. He was horrified by all of it, everybody's cruelty to everybody else. I recall just an

---

10. John E. Lyle Jr. was elected to Congress, Fourteenth District of Texas, in 1944; Irving Goldberg, later appointed by LBJ to the Fifth Circuit Court of Appeals, was a staff member of the Naval Affairs Committee in 1945. Their oral histories refer to donating blood to CTJ. John E. Lyle Jr. Oral History Interview, 4/13/84, by Michael L. Gillette; Irving L. Goldberg Oral History Interview, 4/10/81, by Michael L. Gillette.

11. Although the other members of the delegation went to Dachau, LBJ and Donald Cook did not go. Donald C. Cook Oral History Interview, 2, 10/1/81, by Michael L. Gillette, 32. Also see W. Sterling Cole Oral History Interview, 2/5/87, by Michael L. Gillette.

aversion to all the misery that he saw. I can't particularly remember that he said the names of any particular areas. For the succeeding two weeks or so, all I thought about was staying alive. So I didn't absorb and digest all of that as I should. I'll always feel kind of rooked out of it, because that was one of the world's greatest experiences, if a hideous one, to be over there and to see it so quickly after the war and to contrast it with the happy security that we have up until now enjoyed. That must have been very strong in his mind. I guess only in the time of the Civil War had we ever known anything like that, and then it was not the whole land. Then it was just the South.

When I got home from the hospital in late June, I had to stay upstairs for a couple of weeks, and I couldn't lift anything that weighed much at all, and that certainly included Lynda Bird, who was a lively, running-around little fifteen-month-old. I would just have to scream for help from the cook or the nurse when she was with me and about to pull the furniture over or hurt herself or something. I remember, I'm pretty sure, that Aunt Effie was still there, because I remember Lynda Bird very early, before she could certainly have understood much about what Aunt Effie was reading, would just love for Aunt Effie to read to her. I have a mental picture of her climbing up those stairs. She was a chubby little girl and a very strong little girl. She would be getting up those stairs partly on her knees. She could always get where she wanted to get from an early age, if not very gracefully. She was just chugging up the stairs is the best way to describe it, and she would be saying with every step, "Read, Effie. Read, Effie. Read, Effie." Aunt Effie, up in her bedroom, would cuddle her up on the bed and would pick up almost any book and just pretend that she was reading, making up the story as she went. Because she could make up better ones than she could read probably, and her eyesight was very poor. But Aunt Effie adored her, and I'm glad that she had at least better than two years of knowing her.

Lynda was really a very amusing child, and when she wanted to express her displeasure she had several mannerisms. She would lie down flat on her back and cover her eyes with her hands and just be stiff. You just knew that she was saying no to everything you wanted her to do. And another one, she would bend over and put her head on the floor with her little hands. That means she just didn't like a thing you were saying to her about do this, do that, or show Uncle So-and-so whatever tricks we wanted her to perform. Lyndon used to take her bottle away from her or make out like he was going to take it away from her, and oh, she would just laugh, because she didn't think he was going to do it at all.

Lyndon was very proud father, and for the time that he spent with Lynda, he was very interested and very easy around her. I can't say that he spent a lot of time with her, though. Something that I think he chided himself with unduly in the last years of his life, because she certainly managed all right.

Then we dropped the bomb and Japan surrendered, and the news flashed all over the world. For the second time in the year, the city was shaken, this time in a very different way. It seems odd to think that what people did was everybody got in their car and drove and drove and drove and just blew the horn, just thousands of vehicles going up and down the streets of Washington, some of them just screaming and crying, "Hallelujah!" But everybody blowing their horn and the streets just crowded. This time I was right there with them; he wasn't there to tell me that it wasn't a circus. I was in my car. Maybe I got somebody to take me, because I couldn't drive for about six weeks after I got out. But I was in the car, in the crowd, feeling the juices of the victory and the wild elation of everybody around me.

KTBC

Did you, now with this young baby, take a less active role in the station?
Yes, a less active role. I was not spurred on by necessity. We had waited a very long time for a child, and Lynda Bird was just an eye-popping miracle to us. My thoughts turned to taking care of her and helping Lyndon's career in Washington. But every week I got the salesmen's reports, and there were years and years when I signed all the checks and knew what big decisions needed to be made and had the opportunity to say something about them and sometimes did.

I don't know just when it began to enter Lyndon's head that when Jesse Kellam got out of the navy, that he would sure be a wonderful man to go to work for us at KTBC. There began for us a long period of breathing a sigh of relief about that business. In the hands of Jesse we felt that it was secure. At least he would look out after it with great industry and very great integrity and devotion to us. He made it possible for us to continue in public service, knowing our living was taken care of. That was a kind of freedom that is just the best thing that can happen to a public servant in my opinion.

Our little fledgling radio station sent its top newsman, Paul Bolton, to cover the United Nations in San Francisco. He stayed out there for days and days and covered it from beginning to end. I was proud of doing that. We were pretty small to have done such a thing, but we always strove to be the top news station in town. Paul had quite a following and a great reputation for integrity and ability, if not for a particularly good voice.

To ensure that any additional competition of KTBC's was friendly, LBJ assisted a group of friends in launching KVET, its name reflecting the fact that its owners were returning veterans. Among them were John Connally, Jake Pickle, Willard Deason, Ed Syers, Edward Clark, and Robert Phinney. KVET used KTBC's transmission tower.
My own impression of KVET was that our having done pretty well in the radio business was just like a bunch of friends are out hunting blackberries. You find yourself a good patch and you're doing real well and say, "Hey fellows, come on. There's more here to pick." Lyndon was always thinking of his boys, who by this time were surely men—what was going to happen next to them. I think he had a lot to do with selling them on the idea of seeking this franchise and going into

this business. He was a person with a good deal of vision, and you could see that this was a coming industry and a coming city.

There's been a lot of skepticism about separate ownership, because KVET owners, some of them, worked for KTBC, and the fact that they lived at Dillman Street.
Oh, yes. Skepticism all over the lot.

Why don't you sort out how separate they were, if in fact they were separate, and who owned what?
Well, of course, they were separate. It was their business. I'm trying to remember who "their" was. I'm pretty sure that Jake [Pickle], Bill Deason, and John Connally were part owners, and Ed Syers and Bob Phinney.

Didn't you have any fear that this would cut into your market?
No, it was really a growing industry and a growing city. I certainly didn't have any fear. I know somebody was going to. It might as well be somebody that you knew and liked. I remember going over there and seeing their facilities. Part of it was in a very old and quaint building.

Lyndon really had a long vision all the years that I knew him. He was always looking to the future, thinking about not just the future of his family but of all those returning servicemen and what were you going to do to put them back to work. It had been such a gigantic job to gather them together, and now we were going to have to disperse what we had put together. Letters were pouring in from mamas, "Get my son home," and "It's time. We need him on the farm. Papa's sick and about to die," and everybody wanted to get their son out of the army lickety-split. As a matter of fact, we dismantled it much quicker than Lyndon thought we should. I remember hearing him say over and over that we make these gigantic efforts, and then we think it's never going to happen again. We dismiss everybody and disarm and wind down too soon, not holding back enough strength for whatever may happen.

10

"A Grinding Occupation," 1946–1947

Lady Bird's inheritance made the purchases of KTBC and the Dillman Street property possible, but her sudden wealth also gave LBJ's conservative opponents a campaign issue. As rumors of the Johnson's personal enrichment while in public office circulated, LBJ delayed his entry into the fray until three weeks before the primary election. During this time Lady Bird compiled the financial records documenting the sources of her recent assets.

In the postwar years, LBJ's poor health required frequent hospitalization. For Lady Bird, this period was marked by two personal transitions: the loss of her aunt Effie and the birth of her second daughter, Lucy Baines Johnson.[1]

THE 1946 CAMPAIGN

1946 was the first hard campaign for the House of Representatives that we had had since the initial one in 1937. Actually, it was the only one. It was one that left a kind of a slur, a dark mark on our life, overridden, true, but it did exist for all the rest of time. Accusations by our opponent, Hardy Hollers, about Lyndon's affluence and enrichment of his friends, accusing him of owning everything from, in most instances, apartments, bloomed and proliferated. We were supposed to have owned quite a lot. A particular one that they said we owned was the Travis Apartments.[2] Then there were breweries we were supposed to own; I never quite understood which breweries. Fortunately they didn't yield any income. And [there were rumors that we owned] KVET radio station and some big properties in Arkansas; just a whole lot of rumors floating around. All those things, once let loose into the air, little gnats continue to sting and annoy. It was

---

1. At age sixteen, Lucy changed the spelling of her name to Luci.
2. John B. Connally to LBJ, 5/24/46, LBJ Library. For a discussion of Hollers's accusations, see Robert Dallek, *Lone Star Rising: Lyndon Johnson and His Times, 1908–1960* (New York: Oxford University Press, 1991), 280–84.

the first time that we had not been the young challenger, the fair-haired boy with nothing against him, the common man's friend and a poor boy.

All of this talk, both sub rosa and out in public, about Lyndon getting rich sometimes had its funny side. I remember two occasions: One was when some good friend got questioned. Didn't he think this was pretty skeptical? Didn't he sort of look with a wary eye at Lyndon's getting so rich? This fellow replied that he didn't give a damn if [Lyndon] had made a million dollars and if he had stole every penny of it. That put an end to the conversation. Then another funny thing was that I got a letter, and I got many like this, but this one was so in earnest and so plaintive and so innocent. This woman wanted to come down to Austin to put two or three of her children in school, and she couldn't find a place to rent anywhere. She knew we owned an apartment house there and couldn't we please manage to let her have an apartment in it? She wasn't meaning to accuse us of anything that we ought not to do.

Why do you think Hardy Hollers emerged as a candidate? Weren't the opponents trying to find a really strong opponent?
Yes. Obviously they were. John Connally has an interesting letter on that, but it's a little too long to repeat. [The opposition] was, in general, supposed to be conservative people, anti–New Dealers, oilmen. Somehow or another they lit on Hardy Hollers. He was seeking support as early as February, and by April he was making speeches at the Austin Rotary Club and all around. Hollers delivered his opening address in Austin in May and from then on out things revved up. He was spending lots of money in ads in the country newspapers and speaking on the radio once a week. A whole bunch of our friends were just calling on us, just pleading with us to come home and stay. Lyndon did send me down there, I forget just exactly when, but "send" is the right word.

When we headed down to Texas in June to start the 1946 campaign, we went by car. Lera [Mrs. Albert] Thomas and her two little girls were with us. Lynda and a nurse must have been with me. We were quite a crowd. We may have even been in two cars going tandem. But I remember distinctly that we got together to spend the nights. By this time it was more motels than it was tourist homes. I said, "Listen, I want to go by Alabama and see Aunt Effie." She had left just shortly before, like a week before, knowing that I would be going to start the campaign. For some reason—not that she was sick enough for me to think that I wouldn't be seeing her again, but she certainly had been declining—I went by there, and that's one of the things I'll always cherish. She got to see Lynda one more time. She was just crazy about Lynda, and Lynda was crazy about her. She was a remarkably animated little girl and very interested in people and bits of information and lots of curiosity. So she just bounded in to see "Appie." By that time, Aunt Effie may have been in one of the long series of sanitariums, as they were called, or hospitals to which she went.

In Austin, I was trying to help open a women's division, calling on old friends like Marietta Brooks. Bess Beeman's name has got to be in capital letters. She's the one who carried the petition and got about twenty-three thousand signatures. She worked on it in tandem with Jake Pickle. Dorothy Plyler was a strong right arm in that time, and so was smiling little Jerry Wilke at the front desk, getting everybody off to a good start. Sara Wade, a friend of Willie Day Taylor's, was just about the best telephone operator that ever was. She could handle six of them just like James Dick playing the piano and participated in several of our campaigns.

The women were definitely an auxiliary and not the main force. They would listen to what the more knowledgeable folks had to say. Marietta Brooks was chairman. Mrs. Bob Long may have been vice-chairman—at least she had an important role. She was always president of some women's civic club. There was an elderly lady of very considerable prestige, Mrs. Taylor, who made a speech for Lyndon. We considered that a coup. What the women's organization did was to write letters to all of their friends in every walk of life in the district, address campaign literature, get their little boys or friends to tack up posters on the trees along the roads or put up placards in the store windows of the merchants. That took a nice smile, and if you are a bill-paying customer of that particular merchant, you were likely to receive a better welcome. I am sure there must have been two or three ladies who actually spoke for Lyndon.

I remember particularly one women's meeting in the ballroom of one of the hotels. Every woman that we could get in touch with to lure a sizeable crowd came. There were women of considerable significance on the platform to speak. There was Ouida Ferguson Nalle, the daughter of the former governors, and Mrs. Jane Y. McCallum,[3] and quite a few others. Then I remember distinctly seeing a simple little housewife with a fresh, very unsophisticated sort of country face, and I thought, oh, this poor lady; how is she going to hold her own in this group? I was just shaking with fear. That poor lady [gave what] was probably the best speech there, because she was talking about her experiences as a mother in the war. Johnny went to the war; Johnny got captured. She wrote the Red Cross, she wrote everybody in the army, she got sent from here to yonder to yonder making inquiries. Nobody could tell her where Johnny was. There was word he was in this hospital, that hospital, in a prison camp. Finally she got in touch with Lyndon, and somehow with dogged determination he tracked down Johnny. So she told us the story, "I remember Johnny." She wasn't aware that she was being dramatic, but I remember that as a perfect little vignette of what a congressman does, small bits of service to the people back home that are not small to them. They matter a lot.

---

3. Jane Y. McCallum was a leading suffragist, educational reformer, and Democratic Party activist.

Also one of the main jobs that women did was to divide up the telephone book of the major towns and just get on the phones on election morning bright and early and just phone, phone, phone, phone. Just take page after page, introduce themselves briefly and courteously, and say, "I hope you're going to the polls today and vote. If you haven't made up your mind, I urge you to think about my candidate, Lyndon Johnson." Then others could furnish cars and go by the old folks' homes, as we thought of them then—nursing homes—anywhere where people were rather immobile. I do not know whether we were sophisticated enough to start out ahead and get absentee votes to people who were housebound.

Lyndon held his fire for a long time, much longer than [I wanted]. I got nervous; I got itchy. I was really alarmed by such people as Everett Looney getting alarmed. I was wanting him to come on down there. I was in Austin. May was progressing on into June. He did finally set July 6 as the date when he would come and make his opening speech.

He asked me to dig up every bit of information I could out of wills, check stubs, what I paid in inheritance taxes, just everything that I could about my own finances, where and when I had received Alabama money and what I had done with it. And I did. A large part of my work in Austin was not in addressing envelopes and getting out pamphlets and posting up placards, as it had been in other campaigns, but it was just digging into [the] reams of correspondence that had settled Uncle Claud's estate, whenever it was finally settled. Aunt Effie, of course, was still living. [I compiled documents on] when she had given me how much money, how much I had received from my father to apply against what my portion of my mother's estate was. I had a very large, thick folder of information which I got. I made the thorough acquaintance of copying machines at that time. I used to go to Miller Blueprint and get things copied. I may even have made a trip to Alabama to go back through such records as I could. At any rate, when I had been in Alabama I had made loads of copies and notes in the settlement of that estate, and I had dug all those up and compiled an enormous and very conclusive bunch of evidence of where money came from and where it went.

I remember very well that opening night. It was one giant blast on the night of July 6, in Wooldridge Park. I've often thought if I were to ever write just a tiny little chapter on politics, I would maybe name it "Memories of Wooldridge Park." It was a traditional place in the capital city of Austin where every politician either kicked off or wound up his campaign. I don't know what the agora was really like in the life of so-called democratic Athens, but I gather it was a place where everybody went and spoke their piece. Wooldridge Park was where you went to speak your piece if you were a politician in several decades of Texas life. It was a lovely, bowl-shaped natural amphitheater in a very green park with live oaks in it, and an old, old [bandstand]. It was a glorious night. There were people stacked as far as you could see, not room enough to sit down or climb up in a tree. Different communities would have banners; they'd just say Lockhart,

Luling, San Marcos—loads of San Marcos—Johnson City. People would come in caravans from the surrounding areas, just the ten counties of the [Tenth District]. I think there were delegations from every one of the ten counties.

It was the custom in those days to ask a whole lot of people that the community looked to as leaders, everybody from the mayor to the big businessman to one representative from the blacks on the platform and maybe one from the Latins. You would get anybody with a title and a position of prominence in the community. You were likely to have a very impressive roster behind you. Lyndon decided he would march up there on that stage with nobody except him, me, and his mother, who lived there in Austin. By that time she had lived there for several years. We had dressed up looking as dignified and simple as we could and marched up there, just really strung up to a pitch. We were very thoroughly prepared to answer any charges. I was even geared to stand up and start rattling off the facts and figures, and I carried this huge file in my arms up onto the stage.

Lyndon had a great sense of timing, a sizable sense of drama, and he was "putting in his stack," as he would have expressed it, and he thought he would either knock him out of the ball park or else he would be in for a long, hard summer.

In the speech he said, "Those that want to come up and shake my hand, do so, or if you want to, come up and examine my financial statement."
He certainly did!

Do you recall his reaction to the speech?
We all felt a great sigh of relief. We've done our best. We have done what everybody has been after us to do for about two solid months. That is, come home and tell it like it is and try to rally all our friends and take the reins and charge forward. I think we felt that our best had been good. I know when I walked down that slope into the basin of Wooldridge Park and looked around at that crowd, I just began to feel this is going to be all right.

Did anyone actually come up and look through the financial records?
No, not a soul, and I remember being sort of disappointed. Of course, it [would have] been almost impossible to have plowed through it. You were looking at [photocopies] of everything from canceled checks to contracts of purchase, to wills, to inheritance taxes paid, and letters from my daddy stating how much would be coming when, and letters from Uncle Claud and Aunt Effie.

It must have been a good feeling to have this sort of an aura of suspicion dealt with head-on.
Oh, great. Just great. A great relief. For years that file, which was finally encompassed in two or three thick and bulging cedar red envelopes, reposed in the

bottom shelf of our little library at 4921 Thirtieth Place in Washington. They're dispersed now; I don't know where they are. I would love to lay my hands on them. But I think we got them out later in checking back on various things, and they gradually got dispersed.

So the big cannons roared, and we began our campaign on July 6. One good thing about it is we had only three weeks for the campaign, because election day was the twenty-seventh. It wouldn't have been possible to sustain the rate of effort we put into it otherwise. It was a tremendous crescendo of effort, out of which some specific pictures emerge. Lyndon would go to ten or twelve towns a day, a good deal of driving in between, make speeches, and then there would be a major rally at night in a fairly large town. He'd go to Blanco and Johnson City and Round Mountain and Cypress Hills and Marble Falls and there make a size-able speech. Meanwhile, we had our good friends answering some of the charges. Ed [William Edward] Syers[4] answered the one about us owning KVET and pretty much refuted it in the minds of people who could bear to give up the idea. Then Lyndon would go down to the other end of the district and talk at Bertram and Liberty Hill and Andice and Briggs and wind up at Burnet. Then down toward Georgetown, where he would cover Florence and Briggs and Jarrell and Bartlett and Schwertner and whole lots of little bitty towns that I can't even remember the existence of. I wonder if they're still on the map. This was all salted and sprinkled through with daily talks with his office in Washington. Once or twice at least he had to return to Washington in those three weeks to vote on some-thing urgent.

Did you travel with him on any of these campaign stops?
Some of them, not as many. Now I wish I had just shared every bit. I guess actu-ally I just wouldn't have been that tough.

When he would come home at night, would he recount the day's campaigning to you?
Usually he was too weary. He would recite some of the problems. He would say, "What phone calls have I had?" I would do my usual thing of unpacking [the] suitcase and packing it again if he was going to be gone overnight. The things they did were so redolent of our American past, like a church picnic and an American Legion rodeo and a barbecue, which was likely to be stag, or a fish fry of Veterans of Foreign Wars.

There was one point late in the campaign when there was a big deal about Hardy Hollers having free barbecue or free hot dogs and Cokes for everybody who came to the park. In what I must say was both a thrifty fashion and some-thing of a poor-boy style, Lyndon said he couldn't afford that, but he just had a letter from some of his good friends in Elgin who said they had a mighty fine

---

4. Syers, an Austin advertising executive and World War II veteran, was one of KVET's owners.

watermelon crop that year, and they were just going to bring him up a whole truckload of watermelons. Would everybody please come out to Pease Park and just get ready to have a good old-fashioned watermelon eating?

There were a lot of colorful things about campaigning in those days which I remember with nostalgia and affection.

Another incident that sticks in my mind was at a little town called Dime Box, where there were some black folks standing out in the edge of the audience. Lyndon invited everybody to come up and shake hands at the end of it, and they didn't come up. He said, "Come on, y'all, come on. Shake hands." And they came up. And he got a pretty angry letter from a good friend who said nevertheless he was going to vote for him, but he sure did get himself into a peck of unnecessary trouble "shaking hands with those niggers."[5]

What was his reaction to it?
Placating, not sorry he did it. He didn't read the riot act to the man that wrote it and say, "You have got to change your ways," nothing like that. But he went right on doing what he wanted to do.

Lyndon got a movie star, Gene Autry, whom somehow in the course of our work on radio we had come to know. Lyndon was helpful to him in his service plans, opened some doors to him to get to meet people in the Air Transport Command. They liked each other, and he agreed to come and help us for a day. I do not think he knew what he was getting into. It was one terrific blockbuster of a day. He stayed at our little house on 1901 Dillman. We went to about seven different rallies in Austin. He shook more hands than he ever knew existed, and of course everybody was absolutely thrilled to see him. I'm sure a lot of little boys wanted his autograph. He had on a flamboyant and very attractive costume. We've all laughed about that day since when we've met, as we have a number of times through the years. I remember him finally getting back to 1901 Dillman and taking off his boots and looking up at Lyndon with a kind of a wry expression, part amused, part incredulous, part "How could you subject me to this?"

Did he sing while he was there?
I am pretty sure he sang "Back in the Saddle Again," one small song perhaps at each one of those rallies.

When you had all these people coming into your house constantly, day and night, how did you manage to keep food and drinks in the icebox?
[*Laughter.*] It was a very casual affair. We always felt that the job at hand was so much more important than the precision of the service or the quality of the food that we just did the best we could. And actually our household help was

---

5. Noah Alberts of Dime Box wrote to LBJ that he could lose votes by inviting blacks to shake hands. Noah Alberts to LBJ, 7/21/46, LBJ Library.

just as elastic and just as interested and just as devoted to the ultimate outcome of our various causes and campaigns. I'm sure it was hard on them, but
it was also a kind of a game to see how well they could do it, and they did it
mighty well.

VICTORY AND RECUPERATION

Finally came the big day of July 27. For us it was a big victory. Lyndon defeated
Hollers. He had about forty-three thousand and Hollers seventeen or eighteen
thousand. When it was over we went to the Hill Country to rest. We went to
Wesley [West]'s ranch. We began going to the ranch, first Lyndon alone and then
both of us, and Neva [West] would come up. That began a very long and good
friendship. One of my favorite views in all the world is around his swimming
pool at sunset and the hills in the distance. You can see the cattle and very often
the deer. It's a spot that's remained close to my heart, and I really think the seeds
of Lyndon's wanting to go back to the Hill Country to live grew from that.
Perhaps they had been in his heart ever since his boyhood.

There was one delicious little moment when Lyndon took Stu Symington
and Paul Porter to the West ranch.[6] Wherever Paul was there was laughter.
I remember Paul wearing chaps, and I daresay he was the only person anywhere
around that was wearing them. The ranch people would have been wearing blue
jeans, real beat-up and old, and khaki pants, and boots that looked like they had
been worn twenty years, and a hat that was greasy. There he sat up on the fence,
just making everybody laugh, and of course Stu had an air of eternal elegance.
The Wests liked them both. It's marvelous to be young. There was a lot of spirit
and a lot of fun.

The Blanco County Fair and Rodeo resumed its gala carryings-on. It had been
closed off during the war. They hadn't had it since 1941. So Lyndon was asked to
lead the parade, and he said he wanted to carry his little girl on the saddle in
front of him. Lynda would have been two and a half in late August. She was sitting on the saddle in front of him as he led the parade through Johnson City.
There were a couple of old-timers sitting on the curb, and this story came back
to us. One man said, "Well, you can see old Lyndon has rode before." And the
other one, the local wit, replied, "Yes, but not lately."

Lyndon more and more, as I look back on the years, after enormous periods
of exertion, his body finally reached the point of exhaustion. The physical bill
came in, and he was sick in the fall. He went to the hospital in Austin with a
bronchial infection. All his life he had chest troubles, bronchial troubles,

---

6. Stuart Symington was Assistant Secretary of War for air until September 1947, when he
became the first Secretary of the Air Force. Paul A. Porter had held a number of government
positions in the 1940s, including chairman of the Federal Communications Commission for
two years until his resignation in 1946.

respiratory troubles. He then went up to [the] Mayo [Clinic]. I don't know how long this went on. He mentions in a letter that it was six weeks or two months of not being worth much. Jim Rowe wrote to me at one point, speaking of Lyndon: "I found him older and tireder. For Pete's sake, slow him down."

Did he seem older to you?
When you're around more or less constantly, you do not notice it so much. I cannot say that he did. It was in the last years of his life when he no longer ran off from me when he walked. He used to take such long steps and so fast that I couldn't possibly keep up with him. I would come huffing and puffing along behind. In the latter years he moved slowly, and then I knew he was getting old.

Did you try to slow him down?
Oh, yes.

How would you do it?
All unsuccessful, and I don't remember that there was a great and wily range of them. But I would just tell him how life was fun, and he'd last so much longer and he would be able to enjoy other years so much more if he would take thirty or forty minutes to eat instead of five, and if he would get regular sleep and not push himself. But there was always this fact, in a campaign, of every district man, every county man, they would get you for their twenty-four hours. They wanted to make a good record, and they wanted to introduce you to all those people they had been trying to sell on you and trying to convince that you were an outstanding, able, interesting, wonderful young man. You were their product; they wanted to sell their product far and wide. They didn't realize that, when you got on that plane or in that car, you went on to doing exactly the same thing down the road, and they could go home and go to bed for two days. So it was a grinding occupation. This year, 1946, I feel sure there were at least three times when Lyndon was in the hospital, maybe more.

"A GRAY FALL"

Finally, Lyndon was back at home from Mayo's. Then came the real blow of the year, the nationwide congressional elections. The Republicans gained control of the Congress for the first big time in sixteen years. They got lots of seats in the House, a good deal more than they needed for a majority. That, of course, meant that Speaker Rayburn would no longer be Speaker. Joe Martin[7] was the next in line. We liked him fine, but it was just a great big void in our world for the Speaker to no longer be the Speaker. It was a real blow. I think for a while he

---

7. Republican member of Congress from Massachusetts.

actually toyed with the thought of just declining to be the minority leader. He did accept it in the end. The Democrats all got together and took up a collection and bought him a Cadillac to replace the one that he had had the use of all the years as speaker.

It was a gray fall with the shadow of the new Republican regime for Lyndon, and for me the realization that Aunt Effie was probably in her last illness. She was in a hospital in Birmingham. I got word that she was not doing well at all and that perhaps I had better go back to see her. By this time, I was not feeling a bit well. I was in the very early part of the pregnancy that resulted in Luci, but I didn't really know it yet. It wasn't confirmed. But I did go and had a several days' visit, which troubled me very much, because I did not think that she would survive it. Aunt Effie, poor dear, could eat very little, and the hospital was a repelling place. I went for hours each morning and each afternoon and maybe back at night. What she actually had I do not know. I think [the diagnosis] was cirrhosis of the liver, which is so very unfair because that's something that you associate with heavy drinking and eating. Aunt Effie, for heaven's sake, had eaten like a sparrow and had never had anything to drink. It may have been some form of stomach cancer. She had all of her life been an invalid, but it was obvious that this time she was a very sick woman, and I was very troubled.

After spending Christmas in Austin, we went back to Washington. I distinctly remember getting out at the front door of 4921 Thirtieth Place NW, with that innumerable bunch of bags and things and everything that accompany you when you have a two-and-a-half-year-old child. I was feeling pretty wretched really, and immediately somebody came to me with the news that Aunt Effie had just died. There was the problem: Shall I go to Billingsley? If I'm going to get there for the funeral I will have to leave today. I had at that point already had one very serious loss of a child, a miscarriage, and several other episodes. I called my doctor and he says, "I do not think you should." It's one of those things that you're never really happy with the answer. It is probably wiser that I did not go. On the other hand, I will always be a little sad that I didn't. Aunt Effie was buried in Billingsley right beside Uncle Claud and right beside her mother and father in a cemetery which I visit every summer that I go to Alabama. Actually, it's getting so that a lot of my visits to East Texas and to Alabama involve going to different cemeteries. This is a very country and rather sweet little cemetery. I remember Lyndon saying when I took him there once that he liked it and he wanted a tombstone just like that. So the year 1947 began with a major change in my life, Aunt Effie's death and the departure of a long and gentle influence.

LYNDA AND LUCI

Lynda was just a never-ceasing source of amazement and amusement to us. She had a little snowsuit with ears like [a] rabbit's on the top. I would take her down to the Capitol and to her daddy's office and show her all of the great men in the Hall of Heroes, especially Sam Houston and Stephen F. Austin. I have loads of pictures, both movies and stills, of Lynda Bird running through the tulips around the fountains and standing under the cherry trees, of me holding her up in the branches. That camera Lyndon gave me really did yeoman service. Lyndon, for all that he protested that he hadn't seen enough of his children in their growing-up years and he didn't do enough toward raising them, was not forgetful of that. One Saturday he took her to the circus and to the zoo one Saturday. He said she was a mighty curious, interested little girl and never stopped talking.

We started Lynda Bird to a nursery school. She was three years old that March. She and Mr. Sam were great friends. He would always talk to her when he came to see us. He had that amazing quality of not talking down to children but of acting like they had something in common and were the same age. He brought us some gardening tools and told her that they were going to make a garden. That garden never came into being, at least not by their mutual efforts, but they sure did have a lot of happy conversation about it.

I was just real pleased, also surprised, that apparently I was going to have another child. My doctor was even more surprised than I was because of the tubular pregnancy and the loss of one tube. We felt sure that we were going to have a boy. We talked about names. My very favorite would have been after my father, Thomas Jefferson Taylor, any portion of that, or all of it. I also considered Bill Douglas a little bit because he was a good friend of ours. I admired him very much. So did Lyndon. Their ways eventually became strained, but most of our lives together we were close.

I was looking for the baby the last week in June. As that week wore on and she wasn't born, it was a pretty tiring time. Finally, dear Dr. Radford Brown said, "There might be some complications here. We'd better go on and induce this child." So he put me in the hospital on the night of July 1. I remember walking the hospital corridors and going through the ritual of having the castor oil and all that. Then Luci was born uneventfully the next morning about dawn some-time. As I began to come to, I said something hazily about how is he, because it was firmly rooted in my mind that we were going to have a boy. Lyndon had included words about baby brother when he'd be writing the family and telling how Lynda was responding to the prospect. The doctors came in and said, "You have another fine little girl." Well, there was about one moment when the bottom dropped out of the world. But nature is wonderful; it was with me just about one moment.

Did you want a boy as much as he did, or did you want one just because you knew that he wanted one so badly?
I think it was just because he did and because it was a natural, rounded fulfill-ment. It is a long-term matter of sadness to me that there is nobody really to carry on the Johnson name, since it goes through the male line. Nor is there

anyone to carry on the Taylor name. I have a nephew, but he has only girls. So really there is no one of either side of the family.

But Luci was pretty from the beginning and made her place so readily in our hearts and lives. When I took her home, I believe I put her in the front room. We had just three small bedrooms on the second floor at that dear old house on Thirtieth Place. Ours was the largest, and then there were two that shared a bath. Luci [was] first in the familiar wicker basket that Governor [Jimmie] Allred had given us for Lynda and then later on in a baby bed which we still have. It was a very placid addition to the house, a much gentler addition than Lynda Bird had been. It was really a happy summer.

What was Lynda Bird's reaction to the baby sister?
Curious, interested. She was secure enough never to imagine that this child could threaten her, and she didn't. I have delightful pictures of Lynda Bird carefully inspecting this little creature curled up in a blanket in my arms. Ruth Taylor[8] came up and spent a while, and I can remember sitting on that screened porch, which was such a part of our lives on Thirtieth Place, looking out at the succession of summer flowers, and at the victory garden, and letting Luci have some fresh air and later taking her out in the baby carriage.

DECORATING

Our house in Washington was really a very modestly furnished house. I was beginning to think about improving it and making it better, and oh, how I did want to. I would take the income from Alabama and go to see Miss Genevieve Hendricks, a very excellent decorator there in Washington whom I had met through a course she gave on decorating at the Congressional Club. Miss Hendricks took one look at our living room and said, "You need a great big couch against that wall and then a big mirror behind it, because it will increase the size of the room. And you just must put some sort of a mantel over that hideous red brick façade there," which we did, a frame one with some nice molding. On top of that I began to put the Doughty birds, which dear Neva and Wesley began giving us at each Christmas sometime along about here, a pair of Doughty birds which are now priceless, except, alas, that years of many visitors and, as time went on, active children, sometimes played havoc with those delicate pieces of art. I soon had a lovely historic scenic print on the walls of the small, modest dining room and a nice English Duncan Phyfe dining table. From 1947 all through the fifties, this was a thread of my life to improve bit by bit. I was filling out slowly my Chippendale chairs for the dining room, or buying a handsome secretary desk for the living room, a couple of more pull-up chairs for the living room. Just as fast as Alabama

8. Ruth Scoggins Taylor was T. J. Taylor's third wife.

would yield a little money from timber or cotton, I would go down and place it in furniture.

I really didn't aspire to antiques. It is funny; I did not spend nearly as much money as I could actually have afforded. I felt that I could spend all of the Alabama money, and I always did it on something of a permanent nature, like an improvement at KTBC or furniture for the house. I would have been furious at having spent it on something like the grocery bill. Lyndon always took care of that, all of the business of living, and I took care of the business of long-term investments and/or the few personal indulgences that we permitted ourselves.

Speaking of the grocery bill, he seems to have had people over for dinner an awful lot back then.
Constantly, and it was a great pleasure and frequently a challenge. Fortunately, Zephyr was an excellent cook and elastic. Some people have said that she just didn't have the best disposition in the world. I didn't find it so. She was always ready if Mr. Johnson wanted to add four people or six people on an hour's notice. She could always take something out of the deep freeze. Or maybe if one dish was a little short, she'd stretch another one or add another one. We canned. We put up as much as we could out of the garden. There was a marvelous market to which we would go and buy fresh vegetables and fruits in season and just eat them like gluttons and also put them up. I did the shopping myself at the local Safeway. It was Lyndon's joke that I would spend two hours trying to get something for two cents less, which wasn't quite true, but I still was very much aware of what everything cost. To go back through checkbooks of that time is really amusing.

Do you think you were too thrifty during this period?
It certainly didn't seem to hurt me any. [*Laughter.*] But I do think that I could have stood up better beside some of the society that he thrust me into if I had spent more on clothes and cared more. Caring is just as important as spending, because it's just as much a matter of grooming and accessories as it is of the initial cost of whatever the dress is. That always mattered so much to Lyndon and not enough to me. It took me a long, long time to see the error of my ways. I really think he was very forgiving in lots of ways.

You two seemed to have been opposites in one sense, you being thrifty and he on the other hand almost extravagantly inclined in terms of buying something for somebody or spending money on this or that. Was this a problem?
No, not really. He only bought when he could. As long as he was making two eighty-seven a month as a secretary or ten thousand a year as a congressman, he, too, was thrifty. But he made quick decisions and he spent what he had quickly and, yes, rather lavishly.

He was always buying presents for others.

Yes, and it gave him great pleasure. He loved to see the women that he cared about dress up in dresses and then parade out in front of him and he said, "Let's get that one." Then he'd say, "And let's get that one." And he said, "Nope, that's mule color. You're all the time trying to get thin and what do you want to put on something that's so full it makes you look fat anyway?" He always had extremely positive opinions about clothes. I remember one funny time when he took me and Gene Lasseter to New York. He bought a hat for me, and it was a way-out, extraordinary hat. It was sort of a turban of various shades of satin. It was really a very handsome hat if you wore it with a lot of distinction. I said, "Lyndon, I just don't quite know whether this will do or not. It's a lot of hat. Do you like it?" He said, "Like it? I like it so much I'm just scared they don't have two." They did have two. The funny thing was he then turned around and he got one just like it for Gene, not realizing that it would be the bane of women's existence to show up in the same identical hat. However, she lived sixteen hundred miles away, and so we never met wearing the same hat.

FORRESTAL'S PRESCIENT LETTER

Lyndon, from his vantage point on the Naval Affairs Committee, had become quite close to, and quite admiring of, Secretary [James] Forrestal. We would go out on the *Sequoia* with the secretary and a small group at night down the Potomac. Loved it then, loved it later. One of the most beautiful things that ever happened was the rides on the *Sequoia* about sunset and getting down to Mount Vernon and stopping and everybody on deck being very quiet. A voice that later became a tape gave a brief salute to the first president.

As my six-weeks appointment with the doctor approached and we were getting ready to go to Texas, we got another invitation from Secretary Forrestal to go out to dinner with him on the *Sequoia*. Lyndon, of course, accepted immediately. For once I wasn't eager to go, because a move is always a trauma to a woman, especially with two small children, one of them just six weeks old. I was in the throes of packing. We were actually going to leave the next day, or maybe it was two or three days off. But we went. We got there and got out of the car and started up the gangplank at the *Sequoia*. We didn't see the secretary. That's not surprising. He was often delayed. But we noticed a startled expression on the face of one of the congressmen or somebody high in the navy. He said, "Well, hello, Lyndon, glad to see you." But you could tell that we weren't expected and it was a very odd feeling. After a few minutes when the secretary didn't come, Lyndon said, "Look, we had an invitation from the secretary to come to dinner. I wonder if there could have been some mix-up." This man said, "Well, we'd love to have you. Please go on with us. But the secretary had told me several days ago I could use the boat tonight."

We felt sort of silly, so we didn't go. We got off, and we went home. The next day we had a very prescient handwritten, hand-delivered letter from Forrestal, in which he said, "Dear Lyndon, I'm sorry about the mix-up last night. I can't blame it on the staff. It was complete aberration at the top. Maybe I'd better get the hell out of here. Maybe I'm breaking up. Love to Lady Bird, and I'll ring you before you go. As ever, Jim." He made quite an impression on me. He was such a hard-driving, determined, intense man, I thought, an extremely intelligent and gifted public servant, but high-strung. I don't know how long after that it was when he went to the hospital; maybe it was months. As we all know, he plunged to his death from his hospital room in the tower of Bethesda Naval Hospital [in 1949].

AN ELEGANT "VACATION"

All during that spring [of 1947] and as summer wore on, there was the recurring theme of "Are we going to run for the Senate next year?" Also, Lyndon mentioned several times to me and in letters to friends that we might take a little trip after the baby was born and Congress was out and after we got to Texas. We were dedicated to going to Texas as soon as I was up to it, which we expected to be about six weeks after the baby was born, if Congress was adjourned about that time. I had all these lovely visions of some glamorous foreign travel. Marvelous ideas began to hatch in my mind of Paris, of Rome or Rio de Janeiro. There was word of taking John and Nellie [Connally] along. All of that was fine. All my life I never could get enough trips. Little did I know how this trip was going to turn out when it came about.

So the question of our "vacation" came to a head. It turned out that we got in the car, Lyndon and John in the front seat, Nellie and I in the back seat. And what we actually did was ride all over south Texas [laughter], stopping to visit a whole roster of people who naturally were the jefes in any presumed political future. We were really testing the waters for 1948. As soon as we would get in the car, Lyndon would turn the radio to KTBC and the volume as high as it would go. I would stick my fingers in my ears and away we would go. He wanted to see how far [the station] would reach. Unfortunately, it reached an awful long ways. [Laughter] He was impervious to loud noises if he was interested in them. I was irritated by loud noises always, whether they were something I really wanted very much to hear or not. He and John would talk politics, individuals and issues, and Nellie and I would sit in the back seat and laugh and laugh, with a certain wry note to our laughter, because we both had the same ideas of an elegant vacation. This trip probably lasted around ten days.

One of the things we did was to go down to Houston, where we went to see Jim West's garage. It was absolutely unique. A great big garage, all underground. It would make a fantastically wonderful retreat against bombs in case of a war. I rather think that's what he had planned it for. Clean as any bathroom I had, but lots of vehicles in it and lots of things stored: groceries, equipment, supplies of all sorts. It may have been the first bomb shelter that I ever experienced. He liked gadgets.

After an altercation with a local power and light company, he told them to cut off the service, and he built his own power plant in the backyard. He also had a communications system at his ranches that was extremely sophisticated and advanced for those times. He could just talk to oil rigs all over.

Did this trip yield any conclusion with regard to running for the Senate in 1948?
I would say only a tentative conclusion and a rising interest in it. It was my general feeling that after a goodly number of years in a job, Lyndon always began to be a little restive and thought, "I have sucked this orange dry; I have gotten all I can. I've learned all I can." I think perhaps—he was moving in that direction. Certainly he hated to hit the cold water. It would mean so much hard work for all his friends.

Money was by no means the big horror that it has now become for a politician, but it was certainly a great big obstacle.

Was part of the purpose of this trip to determine whether or not he could get the backing?
Sure, sure. It was testing the water. And it's my feeling that John was a moving force in pushing him forward in a number of these elections. I know that I was not scared; I could take it or leave it. But I had more than willingness, a certain eagerness.

So we had our vacation and we laughed a lot about it. It drew us closer to the eventual decision, although over and over when Lyndon covered the district—and, believe me, he never failed to cover the district—he was asked that question at every turn. At every one he kept his own counsel and said he'd cross that bridge when he came to it.

Congress did go back into session in November, but to move back would have meant that we'd have to move again to come home for Christmas, or spend Christmas in Washington. And Christmas was always terribly special to Lyndon and to me, and so I made the decision to stay down there with the two little children. After all, it wouldn't be more than five weeks or so. I went through the laborious process of getting the children both dressed up and looking as pretty as they could and me in an evening dress, and going down to Christianson-Leberman for a formal posed photograph, which I later had made into a miniature on ivory for Lyndon's desk. That was my Christmas present to him that year, and it stayed on his desk until he died.

We had a party at 1901 Dillman after Luci's christening, which took place at St. David's Episcopal Church on the twenty-seventh of December. We had asked Daddy's wife, Ruth, to be a godmother along with Mary Rather, hoping that that would make Daddy feel good. Our always-loved Senator Wirtz was godfather. He had sent her an exquisite little china angel when she had been born, and we'd told him that we were going to ask him to be godfather.

St. David's has held a lot of my life, from my confirmation in the Episcopal Church back in 1930 or 1931, when I first started the university, then the baptism of both of the children and the confirmation of both of the children. Charles Sumners with his beautiful organ voice, the presiding churchman, has been present at all those functions, and then he remained in our life long enough to make a prayer when Lyndon's body lay in state at the LBJ Library. He, too, is gone now, but he was a loveable part of my life.

11

"The Hardest Year of Our Lives," 1948

The year 1948 began with the familiar pattern of Washington's annual rituals, even as the drama of a pivotal election loomed on the horizon. Republicans saw their opportunity to retake the White House from FDR's vulnerable successor after sixteen years of Democratic rule. Truman's assertion of federal control of the oil-rich Texas tidelands, the submerged coastline extending 10.35 miles into the Gulf of Mexico, and his civil rights proposals met strong opposition in Texas. Lyndon Johnson, in his votes and speeches, defined his differences with Truman's Fair Deal to reflect the views of his increasingly conservative statewide audience. He voted for the antilabor Taft-Hartley Act and opposed federal legislation to create a permanent Fair Employment Practices Commission, prohibit lynching, and eliminate the poll tax. His vigilance at the onset of the Cold War found expression in his advocacy of national defense. His support of a seventy-group air force, which translated to more than twelve thousand planes, advanced his philosophy of preparedness while fueling the Texas economy with its aircraft engine plant and numerous air bases. His record in the postwar years made him eligible to compete for the Senate seat again in 1948.

LBJ's tumultuous victory over Coke Stevenson, by a margin of eighty-seven votes, is a familiar saga, steeped in political lore and controversy. Lady Bird Johnson's narrative recounts her own transformation in the course of the campaign as she overcame her shyness to assume an active role in supporting her husband's candidacy. Moreover, as she gently nudged him forward in the political arena, she revealed both an appetite and a determination equal to his own.

1948 went on with its usual milestones of the White House congressional reception. It usually takes place in about February. All the wives looked forward to it happily [*laughter*], and all the men looked forward to it with a grimace. At least that was the case in our household. I guess Lyndon was still renting white tie and tails. It was years and years before we ever bought one. Another annual event, one that he relished much more and participated in very actively, was the Jefferson-Jackson Day Dinner. This year it took place at the Mayflower Hotel.

We'd have small dinners with awfully good talk. I remember my favorite was to get about eight people together, and if I could have Speaker Rayburn, as I frequently did, it was always just real special. I remember one time Bill Douglas and Mildred were there, and Mr. Sam brought his date, the attractive Mrs. Davis, a widow. He kind of specialized in widows. And Marietta Brooks was visiting me, and I believe Houston Harte[1] was in town.

Did LBJ usually plan these dinner parties or did you plan them?
He would tell me whom he wanted to have, and then I would fill in. He was the instigator of most of our life, both business and social, but I also urged and slipped in my own plans.

Chief Justice [Fred] Vinson and Roberta were a part of our lives then, a great friend of Lyndon's, marvelous Kentucky stories, good salty conversationalist, and good judgment, and a great friend of Truman's. Roberta was a marvelous storyteller herself, stories just a little bit on the risqué side, and much prized by all the women who got to join. It's really something to reflect on how soon we came to know the biggest people in town, what good friends they were of ours.

When Truman appointed him chief justice, the word got on the radio sooner than Mr. Vinson wanted it to. He was rushing home to tell his wife, who did not want him to go on the court, because never, never, never could you make any money on the court. As great and powerful as that job was, she wanted after many years of public service to finally land in some job where you would make a good living and store up something for your old age, or illness and death. Truman appointed him, he accepted, it got on the radio, alas, too quick. She heard it going home from the beauty parlor. She went home and got in bed and began to cry, and at some point, the chief justice phoned the Speaker and Lyndon and said, "Y'all have got to come and help me." They went over there, and they asked me to join them later. They all tried to console her and reassure her that it was going to be all right. But, oh, it was a very difficult time.

THE DECISION

I really don't know whether Lyndon was consciously getting ready to positively go for the Senate or whether he was just testing the water and dipping in a foot into the cold water tentatively. I suppose deep inside he had made up his mind.

---

1. Houston Harte was a principal of Harte-Hanks newspapers.

I really don't think he knew until the final moment that he made the plunge. The time was drawing near in Texas when we had to make a decision. Bill Deason wrote us that Claude Wild said we just better go ahead and announce immediately. He didn't think O'Daniel would run. That was one of the big ifs in the situation. In early May, Lyndon wrote Senator Wirtz that he was going to come to Texas any day and he sure did want to talk with him and decide which course to follow. He told John Connally he wanted to see him too. But at the same time, he had Warren Woodward already going around to helicopter firms, talking about how you would rent one and on their safety.[2] As a member of the Armed Services Committee, Lyndon had looked at demonstrations of helicopters. It's interesting to speculate whether at that time seeds were planted in his mind about what he would do later.

He went to Texas the first week in May. How one wishes across the gap of years that you could remember exactly how a decision this important happened! I don't. I've heard Lyndon tell this story that he went down there very undecided, very much aware of how difficult it would be to raise the money, particularly since if he lost this one, it was out, gone, no House job to go back to. Not like in the campaign of 1941, which was a special election and no need to resign. Also, he was aware of what a cruel, demanding schedule you have to keep up, day after day, across this huge state, and how physically draining that would be. And also what you have to ask of your friends, many of whom just don't want to be called on to do so much. You feel like a dog when you ask them to do it, and you feel worse when some of them say they'd planned a vacation then in some other place, when they don't do it. So he was far from straining at the bit to run.

This is the way Lyndon has told it to me in the years since. Somehow, he found himself in a hotel room with a group of young men. I'd love to be able to remember every last person he said was there—John Connally was, and I'm sure he was the ringleader and had called the meeting. Joe Kilgore.[3] I think Posh Oltorf.[4] I don't remember who all, but it could hardly have taken place without Bill Deason. Sherman Birdwell was probably there. A whole lot of his comrades in arms through the years. Lyndon raised all these objections, and they knocked them down like this: "We've just gone through a war where everybody was demanded to give his all. How have you got the right to say you won't endure all this and make all this effort? You're the best we've got. This is what you do

    2. Memorandum, Warren Woodward to LBJ, 5/3/48, House Papers, box 98, "Helicopter—Schedule," LBJL.
    3. Joe M. Kilgore was a member of the Texas legislature and later served in Congress.
    4. Frank C. "Posh" Oltorf, a member of the Texas legislature, became the lobbyist for Brown and Root. R. L. Bob Phinney, who also attended the meeting, remembered that Jake Pickle, Stuart Long, and Jesse Kellam were also there. R. L. Phinney Oral History Interview, 9/19/68, by Paul Bolton, 16–17.

well. You can win or you can spend everything you've got trying and face up to losing."[5]

In a manner, they shamed him into being willing to undertake no matter how heavy a load. He said he picked up the phone to try to call me and tell me that he was going to walk out of the room and announce because he wanted to share it with me and didn't want for me to just hear it on the radio. But I wasn't at home. I have a memory that I was over going through the vast and beautiful possessions of Mrs. Evalyn Walsh McLean, who had died, one of the great hostesses of Washington forever. Her possessions were going to be auctioned. When I got home, I got the message to try to get in touch with Lyndon immediately. He had hit the cold water, and he asked me to load up the children and join him as soon as I could. This was May 12.

So I began to shift gears into moving two children and such household as I could back to 1901 Dillman. Naturally it required a few trips to the various doctors and lots of decisions. It took us until the twentieth. I guess we left on the eighteenth because in those days we went by train, and it was two full days. I loved those train rides. We'd get a stateroom or at least two little bedroomettes and make ourselves quite cozy. Lynda, who was old enough then, would run up and down the aisle of the train. Luci would very peaceably lie on the bed.

I knew pretty much what we faced. I was eager for it and got off the train with those two children ready to hit the ground running. One piece of good news came right after I got down there. Senator W. Lee O'Daniel announced that he would not seek reelection, so that was a long sigh of relief for us. Lyndon opened his campaign—no surprise—in Wooldridge Park with a big rally. The campaign in a nutshell was peace, preparedness, and progress.

Our campaign headquarters were opened by John and Charlie Herring in the old Hancock Building, an old Victorian edifice of some faded magnificence. It was a fine old house that was almost at the stage of being condemned. But it had been a great house in its day. Claude Wild was the official campaign manager, and Marietta Brooks, no surprise, was named to head the women's division. Men were pretty much in charge. Women were always relegated to getting out the campaign literature and addressing the envelopes, licking the stamps, and putting on the teas. But Marietta was a good leader and she had been active in so many club groups. She did know a lot of people around the state in women's organizations to appeal to, and to haul me around to, to attend teas. She was

---

5. Jake Pickle remembered that a persuasive argument was the need for a liberal or progressive voice in the race to counter the Dixiecrat movement. J. J. Pickle Oral History Interview 2, 6/17/70, by Joe B. Frantz, 16. John Connally recalled resorting to another tactic to persuade LBJ to run. The group agreed with him that he should not run and proposed instead that Connally be the candidate. Connally, *In History's Shadow*, 113; Stuart Long also described a proposed Connally candidacy. *The Nation*, October 19, 1964, 236; also Horace W. Busby Oral History Interview 1, 8/23/81, by Michael L. Gillette, 17–21.

not a bit timorous. She'd just as soon talk to a bunch of men, labor leaders, as not. We were making our steps into active participation.

The women's job was to get the poll tax list from the county or district man always and get a bunch of ladies over at a little social and pass the list out and everybody would check, say, "I know this family," "I know that family." Then they would put their names by them, and they'd distribute postcards. They'd write them a little personal postcard at the meeting, or else they'd promise to take X number of postcards home and do it there. Then everybody that was left over on the poll tax list, if they didn't know them personally, they'd just divide the rest up. The idea was to get an intensive, personal-contact campaign, just an endless chain of personal greetings, and where you couldn't do that, just to get a message in the hands of every voter, signed by somebody. How well that worked depended of course upon the initiative and follow-through and devotion and organization[al] ability of all of these women. Some of them were top-notch and worked like beavers, and some of them turned out to be more shy than we had thought or less diligent or got sick or went on a vacation. So it's hit and miss. But the energy that was poured into this on a volunteer basis, for nothing but love and affection and belief in the candidate, was absolutely wonderful. That is one of the places where I could be useful. One of the main jobs of the wife of every candidate is to thank, to thank the volunteer workers in the campaign office itself and to thank the women out all over the state. That was something, to the extent I could, I tried to do. It was easy to do because people were giving you hours of their life, most of them free. You look now at the amount of volunteer labor you had and you're just amazed. I remember one little boy looked at his mother and said rather plaintively, "Mama, when are we going to have something to eat besides Post Toasties?" She would work so long in the volunteer office, she'd get home at night and just put a bowl of cereal on the table.

Was there considerably more activity from the women in 1948 than there had been in the 1941 campaign?
I think so. There was increasing women's activity from the time we first entered in 1937, when there was very little, then beginning probably in 1941, certainly by 1946, and increasing greatly ever since.

Perhaps the war had a good deal to do with that.
It did. Women got out of their homes by necessity, economic necessity, patriotic necessity, and took paid jobs and volunteer jobs.

HANGING ON A THREAD

Then came one of those desperately painful events in our life. Lyndon went up to Amarillo and made a speech, and then he started on the train to Dallas. He had Warren Woodward with him. Woody reports that Lyndon had one tremendous chill, and he was just shaking the berth down and saying, "You got to get me warm; pile on more blankets. Get in close to me and rub me." He could have some of the most frightening chills in which you'd almost think he was going to shake the bed down. Then he would rise from that couch of pain and get up and go do what he had to do for a while.[6] Lyndon had kidney stones which plagued him for decades of his life.

The next day, Wednesday, the twenty-sixth of May, he was going to meet with Stu Symington in Dallas.[7] There was an air force ceremony there; an award was going to be given to Jackie Cochran. Perhaps Stu also received one, or maybe as secretary he was just awarding it to Jackie. She was very much a part of our life in that time. We had been to a glittering cocktail party that she had given in her suite in one of the Washington hotels earlier that spring. She always had some powerful men around her, and she was just as capable and just as tough as about any of them, a woman of great energy and lots of records in flying. She was either the first woman to fly a certain kind of aircraft or the first one to break a record, and always striving for one more achievement in that field.

Lyndon was supposed to make a speech in Wichita Falls, but he was just in too gruesome pain to go on. He had fever of 104 degrees and severe abdominal pain. They took him to the hospital in Dallas. Claude Wild announced that Lyndon was in the hospital suffering with kidney stones and that he'd had them for several days. I shiver to think how long he may have had it and endured it. I wasn't with him for those few days preceding it. I was in Austin that Wednesday morning. I took a flight up to Dallas to join him as soon as I could and walked into the hospital just as tense as could be. There was the sweet and calming presence there of the editor of the Wichita Falls paper, Rhea Howard, who was our dear friend for decades.

I understand that one of the problems was the question of whether or not to release news of this illness to the press.
Lyndon always just gritted his teeth and hated like—he just was against releasing that sort of thing to the press. It had to be told. I think Claude Wild asked Lyndon whether he could or not. It always made Lyndon mad. He was always wrong about it, in my opinion. Everything gets known.

The story that others tell was that then he was upset because his people had gone ahead and released this news in spite of his orders not to and that he was threatening to resign from the race.
All of that is quite likely. Oh, yes, he was; he was at that point, I remember. He talked that part of it over with me as soon as I got there. He just said, "I can't go

---

6. Warren Woodward's account was recorded in Warren Woodward Oral History Interview 1, 6/3/68, by Paul Bolton.

7. The meeting concerned the status of Sheppard Air Force Base. Randall B. Woods, *LBJ: Architect of American Ambition* (New York: Free Press, 2006), 201.

on like this. I might as well resign now, because the doctors tell me that I have got to have an operation and that I will be out of commission for at least six weeks. By that time it will be into July and the campaign will be lost." Was it Shakespeare? A message was sent by a soldier on horseback. The horse lost a shoe, the horse couldn't run very fast or not run at all. The man didn't get there in time to deliver the message. The battle was lost, the war was lost, the kingdom was lost. So it really just hung on a thread.[8]

By the merest chance, Stu Symington called the hospital to talk to Lyndon and got me. What he said was, "Jackie Cochran is here. She has a plane." He told me the kind. "She flies it. She knows Mayo's inside out, and her good friend there is Dr. Gersh[om J.] Thompson [Sr.], who does kidney stone operations, a very new technique where they don't cut you open. They just insert some long calipers way up inside and crush the stone and pull it out and have you up in a week's time. You've got to call Jackie. You've got to put Lyndon on that plane. You've got to make him go."

Well, that was not as easy as it sounded. First place, the [Dallas] doctors there were pretty stiff-necked and unfriendly about it when the suggestion was first made. That is a trait of the profession. I really don't remember how we worked it out, but I think it was through the kind offices our good friend, one of the doctors at Scott and White, to whom we explained the situation and got his help. I remember his palliative efforts.

I did call Jackie; I asked her if she could call Gersh Thompson. She was a woman of action. She said, "I will call him immediately. He can do this. He has done this on—" and I think she said on her husband, Floyd Odlum, who was incidentally a very considerable figure in the financial world. He was the head of the Atlas Corporation. She was a salesman and a pilot and a registered nurse and all sorts of things. She said, "We will be there," within the hour or something. They gave us a short deadline. Then I had to go in and talk Lyndon into doing this. I never tried so hard for anything in my life. But I just thought to stay there was hopeless, and he was utterly miserable, and we would indeed, whether we resigned or just petered out, lose the race if we couldn't get back into it quicker than six weeks plus a little.

Was he reluctant to do it?
He was in such misery, he didn't know what he wanted to do. He just wanted to be released from that misery.

Was there a conspiracy among you and Warren Woodward to keep the press away from him, to keep him from resigning from the race in despair?
Yes. We just didn't want him to talk about what he was going to do. We certainly didn't want him to cross that bridge before we had to. We got out quick through

---

8. Benjamin Franklin includes the proverb in *Poor Richard's Almanack*.

the back door. We really just got out of there with such speed before the reporters were hot on the trail. I don't really know whether we were "released" from the hospital or whether we just simply ordered a stretcher and ordered a car up to the back door and just walked out.

There were some personal friends who carried the stretcher out.

We went to the airport. The plane, a very fast plane, was big enough to have a very comfortable berth-type arrangement, maybe a double seat that had sheets and everything on it for Lyndon. Jackie had some medical equipment on there, too. She was at the controls, and she was loving it. Woody had flown during the war. He was just admiring the adventure and the plane. Lyndon was pretty heavily sedated by that time. Every now and then Jackie would come back and leave Woody or her copilot or somebody at the controls and do something to alleviate the pain. I do not know how long it took us to get to Mayo's, but not long. Gersh Thompson himself was at the foot of the steps to meet us. He was a very top doctor. I think Jackie had been very helpful to him in many ways.

I actually issued a statement from the Mayo Clinic, saying that Lyndon was making satisfactory progress but it was unsure when he would be released from the hospital. That was after he had gone into surgery, which was just as quickly as hospital routines and tests would permit. I felt that it would be more intimate, personal, and would elicit more sympathy for me to do it. It would be straight from the family, the next best thing to Lyndon doing it. I didn't mind. I just wanted to tell them exactly how it was, because I really had enough faith in Dr. Gersh Thompson. It was our only hope anyhow, so you might as well settle for your only hope.

As soon as the pain ceased, as soon as the stone was crushed and removed, Lyndon just bounced back with an enormous sense of revival and partly just in admiration of this doctor who had done something in a brief matter of minutes or hours with the prospect of being released from the hospital in five or seven days and being on his feet and ready to reenter the arena. It was just like a gift of five or six weeks of life. I won't say he was euphoric, but he may actually have been. I felt like a thousand pounds had been lifted off of my shoulders, and I was pretty euphoric.

He and John Connally were at odds with each other during this period because of the initial release to the press.

In almost every serious and terrible campaign, there was a time when Lyndon would think, "This is hopeless and I want to get out of it." John never wanted him to get out of it and was always impatient with him for considering it. And yes, they would get mad at each other, because John wasn't carrying the load and didn't suffer quite as heavily as Lyndon did. My sympathies were with Lyndon. At the same time, I just did not think there was any sense in belaboring the press or anybody else.

"THE JOHNSON CITY WINDMILL"

Lyndon recuperated in Mayo's, stronger day by day, but also more restive and wanting to get back on the job. The big news that happened while we were at Mayo's was about the helicopter. A bunch of Lyndon's friends led by Carl Phinney and General Bob Smith of Dallas had gotten a hundred former servicemen to put in some money to get a helicopter to put at Lyndon's disposal for twenty days. They had figured that it wouldn't cost any more than a statewide network broadcast, and it would enable him to get to all of the little towns in Texas, or as many as possible, and save hours and hours of driving time. Besides that, it would attract attention. I think *Time* called it "the biggest gimmick in Texas politics since the hillbilly band and the free barbecue." I clearly remember standing in the backyard at Dillman and seeing it go right over and Lyndon lean out and wave. It turned out to be a highly personal machine, painted red, white, and blue, and had "Lyndon Johnson for U.S. Senate" in letters as big as possible. It became a trademark. He called it "the Johnson City Windmill."

It was the middle of June when Lyndon began really using the helicopter. The first day was just four or five stops; it began with Terrell and Canton and Lindale and ended the day in Marshall. Where I was known, I would sure try to be there. I was there every time he ever was in Marshall. At first he would keep on announcing that he was going to cover every section of the state in this helicopter till that got pretty firmly established and repeated everywhere. The next day he went through a lot of my territory, and I remember those scenes: Jefferson and Gilmer and Pittsburg and Daingerfield and Linden and Atlanta and wound up the night in Texarkana, where he had a really good rally. It jelled into a pattern of six to nine stops a day, which was the biggest tour de force that we ever went into, certainly up until that time.

In the course of the campaign there were two helicopters, a Sikorsky and a Bell, and two pilots.[9] The one that we became really quite close to and have remained so ever since was Joe Mashman, who got quite caught up in it himself. There were times when Lyndon would be so utterly weary and his voice would be so exhausted and croaky that he would say, "Tell them about me, Joe."[10] The helicopter had room for two passengers in it. That other fellow had to be a combination speechwriter, bag carrier, coordinator; he just had to be everything. Mary Rather wrote that Lyndon had already worn out two grown men who took turns traveling with him. The first one lasted a week and the second one dropped out on the fourth day. "We've just rushed a third man to Texarkana to take over

---

9. See interviews with the two helicopter pilots: James E. Chudars Oral History Interview, 10/2/81, by Michael L. Gillette, and Joe Mashman Oral History Interview, 3/28/74, by Joe B. Frantz.

10. LBJ apparently had Joe Phipps, who flew on the Sikorsky, tell the crowds about the candidate. James E. Chudars Oral History Interview, 10/2/81, by Michael L. Gillette.

there tonight." She said she would take on the last eight days of the campaign. I don't think that worked out.

The advance man, that adventurous and sometimes luckless individual, had to go along in a car with the suitcase and arrange where the helicopter was going to land in each town and where it could obtain the proper kind of gas. The usual thing was to land on the courthouse square if you could persuade the city fathers and the merchants around the square to rope off enough space. The advance man had to be a persuasive and busy fellow. He had to get the permission of everybody to do that. Or you could land at the fairgrounds, or at a football field, or perhaps at a park.

The advance man also had to arrange for a crowd in each one of those five, six, eight cities in which Lyndon was going to land. He dealt with our leader in that local city, who might or might not be highly interested and capable. He would get out flyers or leaflets. He would hire little boys to deliver one to every house, or maybe the women's committee there might do it. The women's committee especially was called on to make telephone calls to everybody. Then you would have a sound truck with Lyndon's name and some campaign material written on it, and it would tour around all day long telling about the candidate was going to land at two thirty on the courthouse square, whatever the case may be, and come and listen to him, see the helicopter. You had to be careful that it was all right with the city fathers to use a sound truck, because some cities had ordinances against them. I remember there was some East Texas town where a strong friend of ours got such an ordinance repealed for one day so he could use the sound truck.

Then you better make sure that you covered the local radio station and got them to do two sorts of things: cover it as a news story, because indeed it was a news story, and also, if necessary, you might have to pay for some short spots saying that the candidate was going to land where and when, and come listen. Then you had to go to see the newspaperman—it was usually a local weekly— and you very much hoped that it could get out in the next one and not be deferred until six days later.

Then sometimes arrangements would be made to address a local service club just long enough to have a bite of lunch and meet that segment of the populace. The advance man had to make the decision on whether it was best to speak where you actually got out of the helicopter or to jump in a car and go quickly to a place where you could draw a better crowd. The name of the game was to draw a crowd, to spend as short a time as possible, cover as many people as you could, shake a lot of hands, get in the helicopter, and hurry on to the next place. Sometimes they would crank in an hour or so rest in the afternoon. If Lyndon had a good friend in that town, he might do that. Of course, there was always a decision as to what town to spend the night in. Usually they would try to make that the largest town in the area and have a rally there and really work toward a big crowd.

Lyndon would have all sorts of things that he would demand from his advance man. For instance, if it was a real set-up rally covered by radio at night, he'd want to make sure that the speaking stand was of a suitable height for him, and he practically had to do everything from squat to stand on tiptoe. Sometimes there would be a twenty-five-watt lightbulb way up on the top of the building, and then sometimes there would be real good lights right down over his speech. The one thing that annoyed him the most was to place him in such a position that he was far removed from his audience, because he wanted that first row of seats right where he could look right down into the eyes of the people and grip as many of them as he could with his gaze, which he roved backwards and forwards across the crowd. Personal communication, intimate contact, was what he strove for and what he was best at.

Woody—Warren Woodward—was one of the principal advance men. I think that Mack DeGuerin and Harvey Payne and Sam Plyler and Dick Connally and probably Hal Woodward, Woody's brother, were also advance men. In some instances, a district man may have acted as an advance man. Lloyd Croslin was always one of the staunchest and most reliable district men. I expect he doubled sometimes, and so may have Cecil Burney in Corpus Christi, whose wife Kara, an extraordinarily nice and high-class woman, no doubt had a lot to do with his meetings.

There were lots of adventures connected with the helicopter. They were in East Texas, I believe at New London, when he was going to land on a school grounds. Suddenly, as it was about to land, a swift hard gust of wind came up and almost swept it into the school building. They barely avoided a life-threatening wreck just by luck and the Lord and a good pilot. Another adventure in the helicopter was when he was scheduled to land on the roof of a filling station, of all things, which seemed a highly perilous thing to do. But it was done. It's remained a piece of campaign lore ever since.

Was the helicopter an attention getter?
To cover ground and to attract a crowd were its missions. One main mission was to get him from town to town, all those little towns that you couldn't possibly cover in this vast state that extends for a thousand miles from Texarkana to El Paso and then just as far from the Panhandle down to Brownsville. Also, interestingly enough, the helicopter drew a lot of children, and therefore, a lot of women, because the mamas went out to take the children. Lyndon always was particularly interested in getting the support of women; he was a believer in their ability as helpers and as voters. He made an especial appeal to them. This was perhaps an unexpected bonus from the helicopter.

The crowds got better. In the early days, sometimes even in the helicopter, he'd only have a hundred at a stop at a little town. But he spoke of seven hundred at Athens and fifteen hundred at Jacksonville as we were winding into the last of June. Things were really picking up. The first three months were the most exhausting campaigning I've ever witnessed or been a part of. The amount of travel, the miles covered, the time consumed in going over this huge state is just absolutely mind-boggling. At one time, he made at least ten talks a day, and I've heard him speak of thirteen.

Was there any effort made to limit the number of speeches per district or per day?
Constantly, constantly, and often a losing battle, because as Lyndon would get overworked, his voice would get hoarse and his patience thin. He was a less salable product. Some of his natural warmth and buoyancy would be gone. But it's hard for the local campaign workers to evaluate that ahead of time against the fact that they want him to see this one more group. In the course of these months, he lost twenty-seven pounds.

IN A GROOVE

If the mood at the time that he went to have the operation in Rochester had been desperation, it gradually escalated in the course of June to enthusiasm and satisfaction and high hope. By July, everybody was just feeling, never assurance, but that at least we were there in the running and had a strong chance. By this time Lyndon was really in the groove and enjoying it and sometimes speaking far too long for his own energies and sometimes for the crowd. Most of the time, he could tell their mood and respond to it. When they got restive, he would cut it off. But some of his folks would send him a note and suggest that was enough. He might or might not get heated. I used to send him notes, too. Often he would read them out to the crowd, to my embarrassment and their amusement.

Lyndon began to take out after Coke. He was never much one to attack his opponents, but seeing his real strength, he decided he had better. He just began to use a satire on Coke—who smoked a pipe almost constantly—and asked him a serious, deep question. He would look solemn and take a few puffs and give you a Mother Hubbard answer. And so Lyndon was exaggerating that in his little satire. He'd say, "How do you stand on the seventy-group air force?" Then he would mock Coke by replying something like, "I believe in constructive government." Somebody in the crowd came up and gave Lyndon a corncob pipe. Actually, before the campaign was over, that happened about a dozen times, so he used those pipes as props. They used to show up around the house for a long time. I finally emptied all the drawers.

How did you perceive the choice that the voters would make?
Naturally, purely subjective, but the governor had many of the attributes of the traditional Texan: rancher, tall, lank, silent, conservative, well-known, all of those were some of his advantages. However, you'd be hard put to find anything daring, constructive, or imaginative. At least I did not see him as coping with a

changing world, as a man of today and tomorrow. I thought that was Lyndon, with youth and vigor on his side.

We began to have real good crowds. They'd go from a few hundred to five thousand. Lyndon, it became obvious that he was getting more buoyant as time went on, if he could get any rest at all, that is. He'd get the folks into the act by saying, "Anybody here seen any other candidate? Raise your hand." A few hands would go up maybe. He'd say, "How many of you have shaken hands with any other candidates for this job?" Then he would go on to say how he was going to try to see every last one of his future employers, and he thought anytime you hired a man for a job you wanted to look him in the eye and size him up, and that's what he was there for. He began to refer to Coke, without naming him most of the time, as a stand patter and a sit-it-outer, just smoke his pipe and wait for whatever [might] happen [to] go on and happen.

He spent that last week going to the big towns: Fort Worth and Waco and San Antonio and then a big day in Houston with little side trips to Pelly and Goose Creek and Baytown and Pasadena. And then Friday in Dallas, in the suburbs. There was a big luncheon given in my honor by the Dallas women's division. Something quite important happened for us when former governors Jimmie Allred and Miriam Ferguson came out for us and urged the election of Lyndon as senator in a radio broadcast from Austin. Both had let us know earlier that they were for us; I think this is the first time that they announced it. They were saving that ammunition for the last.

A MEETING WITH MA FERGUSON

It had been my job at one point during this campaign to see Mrs. [Miriam] Ferguson[11] and solicit her help. Lyndon sent me to see her all by myself. He used to send me to do the most extraordinary things which I had neither the talent, nor the background, nor the wish to do, by a mixture of persuasion and making me believe I could. He'd say, "You mean that you've got two degrees from the University of Texas and you can't do that?" It was real funny. But I went to see her at that house on Enfield. At that time, it was a much more attractive house, because no rent quarters had been built on the back and the lawn was well kept. It was a very nice house. It's at almost the crest of a hill where the road divides into a Y, white stucco, old-fashioned, but a home of some grace. She was a highly interesting woman. She was no figurehead. She really and truly got out a little black book, which one had heard about all one's life. She went through it and said, "Yes, I can write this one. I will write that one. This one will be very helpful to you." This was much earlier in the campaign. By this time, Governor Jim Ferguson was dead, but she also had been governor.

---

11. Miriam A. Ferguson, wife of impeached governor James E. Ferguson, served two two-year terms as governor of Texas, beginning in 1925 and 1933.

Anyhow, she was helpful and in a very pragmatic way, and I felt like I was seeing a Texas legend.

Could you see any tangible results of her work?
I can't really assess that, but I just feel sure that in deep East Texas, which had been one of their strongholds, that we did. That plus the heavy work that we did there in the beginning of the second primary, opening in Center; I think that swung a lot of that for us.

As throughout our life, it was really an unfair division of labor. I didn't work nearly as hard, nor was the strain nearly as hard, but I did have a very divided life and a terribly full one. I'd spend hours down at the campaign headquarters thanking all the workers down there, doing my share of writing letters to people who had been helpful, and urging others on, and bringing down cookies and coffee for a break, and either doing the things that needed to be done for two children, like taking them to the doctor or arranging to get some little friends over to play with them, or going to the grocery store and stocking up, the usual domestic business of life. Answering the telephone, being the go-between to Lyndon, passing on messages and/or advice, all of those are part of the grist for any political wife's mill.

Very little is clear-cut in politics, and something that is endemic with a campaign is confusion and jealousy and backbiting and everybody wanting to get the ear of the candidate. That is another place where I could be mildly useful. If they couldn't get to Lyndon, I was a good deal more accessible, and they could say, "Tell Lyndon so-and-so," and I would make little notes in shorthand on the back of envelopes in my purse, or I usually had a shorthand book around with me. So I was a conveyor for those late nights when I finally got to see him or over those endless cups of coffee that I would bring to him in the morning. Sunday was a kind of escape valve. Usually he managed to get home or someplace to rest on Sunday and plan strategy for the next week, if you can call that resting. It would be meeting with the chief supporters and evaluating what had been done and planning what was to be done next.

"A SLOUGH OF DESPOND"

July had been an ebullient month, with a certain satisfaction, never assurance, but hopeful and feeling good about it. We were in for a shock. As we always did, we voted late in Johnson City and then went in and thanked everybody at the headquarters for all their long toil. Then we went to a hotel suite to listen for the results. So many campaigns and so many waiting-out periods have gone through my life I cannot honestly remember the scene. But it very frequently was the Jim Hogg Suite at the Driskill Hotel, and I think that's where it was. Walter Jenkins would have set up a blackboard. There would be a number of telephones. People would be telephoning in the vote in such-and-such a town or such-and-such a district as Johnson this, Stevenson this, [George] Peddy this, and we'd write it up. Then another district would be phoned in. And then the Texas Election Bureau would send a total. We'd be listening to the radio, listening to the telephones, writing up on these blackboards. I would be ordering up coffee and sandwiches or, as the night wore on, scrambled eggs and bacon. People would be coming and going.

The outcome of it was a staggering difference in favor of Coke Stevenson. He wound up with 477,000 votes and Lyndon 405,000, and Peddy a very respectable 237,000. So we woke up to a situation of being 71,000 behind our opponent in a runoff. Could we pick up that many? The bottom dropped out. We were as low as I ever remember. We met that afternoon at the Dillman Street house with some of the old regulars: John, Senator Wirtz, Everett Looney, Charlie Herring, and several others. We all sat around and talked about what to do next.

Do you recall LBJ considering dropping out of the race?
Oh, yes. That happened more than once in our political life in times of apparently impossible tasks. He was depressed; he was exhausted, depleted. So was I. I wasn't depressed, no; I was exhausted and depleted, but mad. [*Laughter.*] I just wouldn't have any part of dropping out. I don't think he really was ever going to do it or wanted to do it. I think he wanted to see how much we would be willing to put into a second go-around against those formidable figures. I made myself a rare speech. I said I would rather fight and fight and put in everything we could and get all the more money and all the more hours and lose by 50,000 than lose by 71,000. If we could reduce it to 40,000, let's strive for that, and maybe we could bring it down to 25,000, and, just possibly, we might barely win.

It was a slough of despond. It was bleak. But there are also moments of levity. Thank the Lord we were still young. Lyndon had to leave almost right away because President Truman had earlier called a special session of Congress.

Did he consider having to be away during part of the critical campaign period a further setback?
I don't know. I expect he did. I personally think it might have been a good thing because it took him away from the scene for a while. It removed him from spreading his feeling of despondency and gave him a chance to think it over.

So the last week of July 1948 found Lyndon, me, and all his campaign workers in the mood composed of dogged determination to slog it out, to reach every possible success that could be, and spurts of adrenaline that produced just superhuman work. I don't remember a prolonged period as intense in my whole life as between July and way on up into the late fall of 1948. By whoever's congealed wisdom it was, we pretty soon came to the conclusion that, one, Lyndon had not worked enough in the cities, and so we made the decision to do that as soon as he could get loose from Congress; second, we just must work on the Peddy voters. It was because of that that we decided to open the second primary in the little East Texas town Center, because that was his home area, and we had tested the waters and received a lot of friendly feeling from over there.

Did they set out to woo the Peddy votes right away?
A large, big, juicy morsel right out there. I am sure we did because that had been Claude Wild's strategy all along. I really don't think Lyndon ever thought that he would win without a runoff.

Two of the things particularly bore Lyndon's stamp. One that he just harped on us before he left to go back to Congress was to write a thank-you to every one of the county and district women and suggest that the women take over, quit waiting for the men to tell them what to do, get lots more active. Second, he urged us to write thank-yous as thick as we could to all of his staunch supporters in the Tenth District, because the Tenth District had voted for him 65 percent. He used it and hammered it that the people that knew him best voted for him. Those are four major guideposts as we launched into the long next month.

Several things happened that were good luck for us. Coke Stevenson decided to go to Washington to learn about foreign policy. He devoted really quite a short time to that important project. He went up to about a three-day session and made calls on Senator Connally, Senator O'Daniel, I believe, and Bob Lovett, under secretary of state. When he emerged, the newspapers lit on him like a duck on a june bug. He had rather a bad time of it and emerged somewhat shaken. They also asked him over and over, how did he stand on the Taft-Hartley Act? He said, "You'll have to check my record on that. It's plain." But he could not say what the record had been. They kept on asking, "Well, just give us the gist of it." Some of them said they looked for it and couldn't find it in his record. I'd say that was a sizeable minus to him, that and the fact that he expected to emerge as a foreign expert in such a brief time.

Lyndon did not stay in Washington long. He returned in early August and began his work in the cities, met in Fort Worth with all his campaign workers to help map strategy for going everywhere. He hammered on Coke's generalities and used the phrase "wouldn't stand up and be counted." He challenged him on all sorts of controversial issues like Taft-Hartley and the seventy-group air force and something not quite so big but very hot in Texas at the moment: a possible raise for teachers' pay. He himself came out strong and clear on all those things and made some and lost some.

WOMEN TO THE RESCUE

Meanwhile, women, including me and Marietta especially, did follow Lyndon's directive and got more active.[12] We took a trip to Corpus Christi with Elizabeth

---

12. Another description of CTJ's and Brooks' travels, including an automobile accident, is Marietta Moody Brooks Oral History Interview 1, 8/10/71, by Joe B. Frantz.

Odom and attended a meeting of the women leaders. These events would be a combination. Somebody would stand up and talk after refreshments had been served. We would tell people what they could do. They could send a postcard to all of their church list or their Christmas card list or their club list. At that time, women were very much involved with all sorts of study clubs and social clubs. Now that they work so much, that's less and less a part of our culture. And very importantly, they could form well-organized teams to take people to the polls on Election Day, just load up their car, make two or three trips. Organize it about who was going to do what. We had some good organizers. Not to say there wasn't some friction between them from time to time; that seems endemic in a campaign. But I all my life have tried to be unaware of office friction, cross currents, or enmities, and mostly I just saw a great combined striving for Lyndon.

Our schedule was absolutely frenetic in the last three or four days. Marietta and I went down to Houston. I had to screw my courage to the sticking point because that was a big meeting, arranged by Mrs. Jimmie Allred. Judge Sarah Hughes[13] addressed the group. We also went to a dinner where all the Harris County councilmen and commissioners and the mayor and mayors of smaller surrounding towns were there. Then we went to a big reception at Baytown. We heeded well Lyndon's demand that we get out and do things on our own and not wait for the men to tell us what to do. Marietta and I went to Dallas for a big meeting with Julia Brydon and the women's division there. We went to a big coffee in Fort Worth. We went to a ladies' tea in Columbus. We traveled by automobile mostly. We used to just buy five gallons of gas at a time so we could campaign at every filling station. I'd always go through the filling station and shake hands with everybody there and introduce myself and, if they would let us, put up a poster in the window of the filling station.

Were they usually receptive?
Yes, they were. Maybe a little startled, but receptive. We also had a hammer and some nails, and we'd stop along the way and put some of those posters up on an oak tree that happened close by on the right-of-way. Those things really lined the roads in those days. We didn't go at such tremendous speeds but what we could see them.

We talked a lot more; it wasn't just shaking hands and moving around. Marietta talked well, effectively, and liked it. I talked scared, I don't know how well, and didn't like it a bit. But I was determined to do it. I just wasn't going to consider not doing it, because I did get good response from people, and they at least thought I was sincere, as they expressed it, if nothing else. It took me a long

---

13. State district judge Sarah T. Hughes of Dallas would later serve as a federal district judge and administer the presidential oath of office to LBJ.

time to get around to realizing that I was going to have to say more than "Thank you for inviting me to this barbecue."

We wound on toward the last day of the campaign. The final crowning event was to be this rally on August 27 in San Antonio right in front of the coliseum. It was going to be a combination birthday party for Lyndon and a rally. He courted San Antonio assiduously over and over because he had lots of friends there. If you worked at it hard enough, you could turn out the San Antonio vote; you could get the people to the polls. That is what he felt had not been done in the first primary. We had, I think, lost San Antonio. He considered it traditionally a strong place for him, and that was a slap. He wasn't going to do that again without exerting everything he could to prevent it.

En route to that rally, Marietta and I were going to attend a tea at Seguin put on by Lyndon's old San Marcos and NYA friend Wilton Woods and his sweet little wife, Virginia. They had invited every lady in Seguin to come to this tea. Marietta and I set out with our little suitcases packed. We were going to spend the night in San Antonio after the rally. Marietta was driving. There had been a light shower. The road was a little slick. Apparently an oil truck had been ahead of us and had been dribbling some oil. We ran into a particularly slick spot; she lost control of the car. It was apparent we were going into the ditch. I'll never forget the next few seconds—and they were only seconds—and we did careen right into the ditch. I think the car turned over several times. I remember hitting the top, hitting the sides, hitting Marietta herself with my arm, with my shoulder, my head. Just like a ball in a box that you're shaking: bam, bam, bam.

Finally we came to rest in a pretty deep ditch, with the nose of the car pointed up at the road and the back resting at the bottom and sides of the ditch. I tried to open the door and I couldn't, but I could run down the window. I looked at Marietta, and it was obvious that she was pretty bad. I couldn't tell if she was unconscious, but anyhow, she was very shaken. I not so much. I climbed out of the window and scrabbled up the steep bank of the ditch and stood up on the shoulder of the road and began to flag people down.

I never will forget my amazement. I felt sure that the first person going by would stop for me. Not so. I remember a lone, nice-looking, youngish woman gave me a startled, frightened glance and picked up speed. I was just openmouthed. The third or fourth car did stop. It was a very old car driven by an old gentleman, a farmer. He said, "Anything I can do for you?" I said, "Sure is. You can help us get out of this car and just take us into the closest town. How close are we to Seguin?" He told us, and it wasn't many miles. He said, "I'll take you into Seguin. I'll run you by the doctor's office." So, with his help, we managed to get Marietta out of the car.

Was she conscious at this time?

Yes, and she was helping us. But she was hurt, and she was letting us know she was hurt. We half led, half carried her and put her in the car. I remember thinking, oh Lord, here it is Friday; the voting is tomorrow; I wish I'd voted absentee. I made myself a promise never to let that happen again.

I was a mess. I was scratched and dirty. My stockings were all torn up, and my dress was ripped a bit. We bounced along in this old gentleman's car with Marietta moaning and me saying to myself, "I wish I had voted absentee." We got to the doctor's, and he examined us and said [to me], "You're all right. I do not find any broken bones. I can turn you loose, but I'd better hospitalize Mrs. Brooks." And he did. I just saw that she got into the hospital. I'm sorry; I just left her there unattended. Meanwhile, I had phoned the Wilton Woods. It was almost time for the tea. They came down and rescued me, and we thanked the old gentleman. To this day, I regret that I don't know his name. I'm sure that I introduced myself and solicited his vote. But I was shaken, too, although I was not seriously injured.

I said, "Virginia, I want to take a bath, and I've got a dress in this suitcase I can put on, but you're going to have to give me some stockings." We shined up my shoes a bit, and so I was in the receiving line about twenty or thirty minutes late with a big story to tell, and a little bit wobbly, but all right. After we finished the tea, someone drove the Woods and me on over to San Antonio. Thank heavens I didn't have to drive. I got dressed for a big final night. That was the night of my debut on speaking to a really large group. Not much of a speech indeed, but the biggest I had made up to date. I had notes and did it impromptu, and it was just more of my evaluation of Lyndon from the years I had known him and how I had seen him represent the Tenth District and what sort of a human being he was.

Meanwhile, I had told whoever was there in charge, John Connally or Claude Wild, not to dare let Lyndon know what had happened because it was going to be all right. All I was going to have was some bad bruises. So we got through that evening, and we shook hands with a jillion people, and San Antonio showed its love for us. It was a big warm successful rally. We went to bed for a very short night.

When did LBJ find out about the accident?
As late as I could arrange. I imagine sometime during the day, because he was just too weary that night to observe the bruises. They mostly became more apparent the next day and then went through a marvelous variety of changes from black to purple to green. When I got up, I was appalled at how bruised I was. Fortunately the bruises were in places that they didn't show. But for more than six months, in fact nearly close to a year, there was a huge black place that became hard as a rock on the right-hand side of my right thigh down close to the knee. I didn't realize that a bruise made a hard place, but it sure did.

Lyndon decided to stay in San Antonio and just visit with his precinct managers and local people all day long in an effort to see that people really did get out to the polls. He set no little task, I will assure you. He just said, "I want you and Mama and Rebekah and Josefa to take the Austin phone book and divide it up four ways"—he may have cut Sam Houston in on it—"and just sit at the phone all day and ask everybody to go to the polls." That was a gargantuan job, but it was a very much smaller phone book then, very, very much smaller. But we pretty much did it; we phoned all day long. I was very stiff, but not too stiff to lift the telephone.

I went back to Austin. The car being in no shape, I drove home with Lyndon's sister, Rebekah, and her friend Anne Bird Nalle. As we went along, Anne Bird quipped, "One of these days we will get our just reward, a form letter beginning 'Dear Friend.'" [*Laughter.*] It was an absolutely natural response, and it's probably exactly what happened. But I thought, oh, dear, if you were just on the other side of the fence and knew that you were trying to write thousands and thousands of those letters, you'd realize why some of them didn't say, "Dear Anne"; Anne Bird would have been the correct thing to call her.

"TENSE AS A VIOLIN STRING"

My recollection is that once more we stayed in a hotel suite for days and days. I would expect that it was the Driskill, and we would meet in the Jim Hogg Suite. Downtown there was a better liaison with telephones and votes coming in and newswires and all like that. Sunday morning's *Dallas Morning News* said, "The Senate race looks like a photo finish with Stevenson holding a slight edge, but LBJ threatening to overtake him." We didn't get the Peddy vote in Harris County. We did get it in the East Texas counties. In those days, city votes were not as formidable as they now are. Former governor Miriam Ferguson wired all of her supporters that "it's important that all Johnson votes be counted and returned in present close contest. As soon as the votes are canvassed, wire results Johnson headquarters collect."

So the vote just began to swing backwards and forwards for the next days. On Sunday night, the twenty-ninth, we had a 693-vote lead over Stevenson on revisions and additions from three counties: Harris—the biggest—Duval, and Childress, a very mixed bag. Stevenson lost no time in beginning to criticize the returns from Duval, which had been his stronghold in every previous election that he had run in.

What was your mood over the weekend? Did you, LBJ, and the others in the organization feel that you were going to win? In 1941 you had a lead and saw it evaporate.
We were tense as a violin string. I don't think there was any feeling of assurance anyway. I just know, sharpened by the experience of 1941, we weren't going to fail to have our supporters there in X box whenever anything was counted. I remember in a far northwest county, Jacksboro, I believe it was, there was a very elderly judge of the voting box who made what was undoubtedly an honest error of transposition. Let us say Lyndon had ninety-four votes, and the judge recorded it as forty-nine. Later on, a recount may have showed that, but meantime, there

had been sworn returns. When you've got 254 counties, and at that time a lot of them were very rural, there is room for errors, just unintentional human errors. So we wanted extreme vigilance to make sure that we got our honest shake.

Then on Monday Stevenson regained the lead, pulled back up to 119, with about four hundred votes said to be still out. By Tuesday it did look hopeless, because Stevenson was leading by 349.

At some point in this, George Parr did make the statement that "Yes, we all voted for Coke Stevenson in the last election." They had voted for him every time. "But he promised to name a [district attorney] down here,[14] and he didn't keep his promise. He's no longer our friend and we're against him. You bet we voted for Johnson."

Did you observe any contact with George Parr during that campaign, particularly in those closing moments?
No; there very likely may have been telephone contact, but never anything personal. I think our relation with him was greatly exaggerated. He's had a relation with everybody who ever was in politics. Lyndon had a natural affinity for Latins, and he had a respect for Parr, because, as a leader of the Latins, he had the reputation of trying to protect them and help them. Yes, he did try to also get them to vote a certain way. The only thing he ever asked of us was to get him some tickets to the Kentucky Derby one time, because he knew we were good friends of Senator [Earle] Clements [of Kentucky]. This was years later, and I think that was the extent of his attempt to control our actions.[15]

Then Stevenson's lead began to be chewed away at. Twenty-five more counties were reporting official returns, and then one would call back and say that wasn't official; they had found some more somewhere. Lyndon was harping on that a canvass is to correct errors made by precinct officials who work under pressure and report their votes at the end of a long, hard day at the polls. So canvass them and count them. That went on all week: Sunday, Monday, Tuesday, Wednesday, Thursday, and by Friday Lyndon was in a seventeen-vote lead and by Saturday issued a victory statement. Stevenson didn't comment. Texas Election Bureaus gave Lyndon a lead of 162. The *Dallas Morning News* was calling for an investigation by the state senate investigating committee, and Lyndon responded by asking for an investigation by the FBI.

Then the next big hurdle that loomed before us was September 13, when there was going to be a State Democratic Executive Committee meeting in Fort Worth. Lyndon began to get out word to all of his friends to come to that. Normally those things can be very sparsely attended by the old pros, but he just

---

14. South Texas political bosses George Parr and Judge Manuel Raymond of Webb County had wanted Stevenson to appoint James Kazen Laredo district attorney. Robert A. Caro, *The Years of Lyndon Johnson*, vol. 1, *Means of Ascent* (New York: Alfred A. Knopf, 1990), 190.

15. According to Robert A. Caro, Parr credited LBJ with helping to secure a pardon in 1946 for a income tax conviction in 1932. Caro, *Means of Ascent*, 191.

wanted to be backed by flanks of friends. Lyndon asked that Mrs. Alma Lee Holman of Taylor and [attorney] Jerome Sneed Jr. of Austin be appointed to the subcommittee canvassing the runoff votes. That was about the time that we moved our whole tattered battle formation up to Fort Worth for the State Democratic Convention. That really did turn out to be a contest in a Roman forum. I felt like one of the Christians. [*Laughter.*] Oh, dear.

Then we had all the bad luck that you could imagine. Everett Looney was injured in a traffic accident. He was our main legal staff standby. Senator Wirtz was the wise guidance, but Everett Looney was out there in front doing major talking for us. He got hurt. Then somebody [Jerome Sneed] who was for us collapsed in the lobby of the hotel. They didn't know whether it was a heart attack or what. So he was out of commission for a while.

The secretary of the Democratic committee, Vann Kennedy, announced that Lyndon had an eighty-seven-vote lead, and Wirtz moved that the subcommittee accept that count. So that is a scene in the hotel I will long remember. You could cut the tension with a knife. Coke Stevenson had a very impressive countenance, kind of dour, a big, tall, silent man who smoked a pipe all the time and looked like a stage character out of the Old West. You could look around and you could count your friends and you could count your enemies. Then there were some that you just didn't know which way they were going to come down. There was a recheck, and Lyndon still got an eighty-seven-vote majority.

After each of the two sides had a chance to present their statement to the executive committee, then the executive committee voted, twenty-nine to twenty-eight, to proclaim Lyndon the Democratic nominee. Then the minority group gave notice of an appeal, and then before the vote was announced, one member withdrew and asked that he be counted as not present and not voting, thus tying the vote. To this day, I don't know who that was and don't want to know.[16] But a member had been absent on the first roll call. Several people tried to locate him because we knew that he was for us. If we could locate him, he would vote for us. He had to go to the bathroom or use the telephone for some terribly important personal reason. If we could just locate that man and bodily pull him back in, we would once again break the tie. So there are lots of funny stories about the folks that went in search of him. Some of our friends since then have taken great pleasure and with much gusto recounted how they found him in the bathroom and hauled him up into a standing posture and got him onto the floor. [*Laughter.*] All through the years we have met many people who claimed to be the one who really cast the deciding vote.

I think it was Charlie Gibson, wasn't it?
I think maybe it was.

---

16. According to Robert Caro, Mrs. Seth Dorbrandt changed her vote to present in the hope that a tie vote would allow the courts to decide the matter. Caro, *Means of Ascent*, 348.

Early portrait of Claudia Taylor, ca. 1915. *LBJ Library*

Lady Bird and her Aunt Effie Pattillo. *LBJ Library*

Thomas Jefferson Taylor Jr., Lady Bird's father, at the Brick House after 1934. *LBJ Library*

Eugenia
Boehringer and
Lady Bird near
Austin, ca. 1930.
LBJ Library

Lady Bird Taylor (far left) with friends near Austin, ca. 1930s. *LBJ Library*

Portrait of Claudia Taylor, 1934. *LBJ Library*

Lady Bird and Lyndon Johnson on their honey-moon in Xochimilco, Mexico, November 1934. *LBJ Library*

Lady Bird Johnson and her movie camera, June 19, 1941. *Austin American-Statesman*

Sam Rayburn's birthday party, January 1953. Left to right: Miss Lucinda Rayburn, Lady Bird Johnson, Dale and Scooter Miller, Sam Rayburn, Hale Boggs. *LBJ Library*

In Nice, France, after the November 1956 NATO Conference. Front, left to right: Sen. Richard Russell and Lady Bird Johnson; seated in back: Rep. Homer Thornberry (second from left); Eloise Thornberry (fourth from left); LBJ; Walter Jenkins (far right). *LBJ Library*

Lady Bird Johnson campaigns in Texas in 1960 with Ethel Kennedy and Eunice Kennedy Shriver. *LBJ Library*

Lady Bird Johnson recording her White House diary, November 15, 1968. *LBJ Library, White House Photo by Robert Knudsen*

Lady Bird Johnson with Head Start children in Montevideo, Minnesota, September 20, 1967. *LBJ Library, White House photo by Robert Knudsen*

Lady Bird Johnson, Mary Lasker, and Mary and Laurance Rockefeller planting a tree at Hains Point, Washington, DC, April 3, 1966. *LBJ Library, White House photo by Robert Knudsen*

President and Mrs. Johnson at the airport in Ohakea, New Zealand, October 19, 1966. *LBJ Library, photo by Frank Wolfe*

Christmas in the White House Yellow Oval Room: Lady Bird Johnson, President Johnson, Lynda Johnson Robb with infant Lucinda Robb, Luci Johnson Nugent with son Lyndon Nugent, Yuki in foreground, Mary Rather next to Christmas tree. December 24, 1968. *LBJ Library, photo by Jack Kightlinger*

Lady Bird Johnson with her grandchildren at the LBJ Ranch, December 22, 1980. Left to right: Lyndon Nugent, Jennifer Robb, Nicole Nugent, Claudia Nugent, Mrs. Johnson, Lucinda Robb, Rebekah Nugent, Catherine Robb. *LBJ Library, photo by Frank Wolfe*

Did you feel like you were going to win that vote?

Yes, by that time I was beginning to think that the committee was going to come down on our side. So the convention delegates overwhelmingly approved Lyndon's certification, after [the executive committee voted] twenty-nine to twenty-eight again. Then by a voice vote Tuesday night, that was proclaimed, and Lyndon and I were presented to the delegates. Lyndon made a brief statement, and we drew a sigh of relief. I guess we must have slept well on that night. This was the night of the fourteenth, seventeen days after the election.

But we slept too early, because sometime in the middle of the night some partisan of Coke Stevenson got in the car and drove over to East Texas to the home of [Federal District] Judge Whitfield Davidson and got him to issue a restraining order against the certification of Lyndon as the Democratic nominee by the Texas secretary of state. That order was granted at 6:20 in the morning in Harrison County at Judge Davidson's sister's ranch. So they traced him down, knew where he was, lit out, and found him sometime I guess between midnight and six a.m., because it's a good little drive from Fort Worth.

Was there any reason that you know of why they went to Judge Davidson?

I should think there was a very good reason. He was about as conservative a judge in the entire state and a good friend of Coke Stevenson's. It also happened that he had been intertwined in my own early life, but that comes about later. He set the hearing for September 21, once more in Fort Worth. Then he enlarged the restraining order, telling all the county judges and clerks and sheriffs and election boards that they must not distribute ballots for the November election carrying Lyndon's name as the Democratic senatorial nominee.

So it moved undeniably out of the field of election committees into the field of lawyers and judges. The hearing was going to take place on the twenty-first and that was five or six days off. I don't know how we got through that week. But the sample ballots that excluded Lyndon's name from the ballot were made up. That was the time that we had to begin to think about what we would do if we lost the case before Judge Davidson. So we called on Jim Rowe and some of our friends back in Washington: Thurman Arnold, Francis Biddle.[17] I'm sure that Abe Fortas appeared in there somewhere.

I really don't remember how we could have survived those three or four days between the sixteenth and seventeenth on up to the twentieth, but Lyndon, John, and I did go back to Fort Worth for the hearing before Judge Davidson. That is one scene that is printed very clearly on my mind forever. We were in his courtroom in the morning, seated close to the front. Our lawyers were there and a fine array they were: John Cofer, John Crooker, James Allred, Raymond Buck, Everett Looney, Alvin Wirtz, L. E. Jones, Dudley Tarleton. One of Stevenson's

---

17. Thurman Arnold, a former New Deal counsel and federal circuit court judge, was in private practice in Washington. Francis Biddle was a former attorney general.

principal lawyers was Dan Moody, a former governor and a formidable opponent. Our lawyers made a motion for dismissal based on the grounds that the federal court lacked jurisdiction and said that any claims for fraud should be tried in a state court and an investigation should be extended to the entire state. Judge Davidson made a very strange off-the-record suggestion that we just run the election all over; put both names on the ballot and just run it all over.[18] Lyndon, of course, responded that he had won it, and he just didn't want to have to win it twice, and that he had a legal right to the nomination and to have his name on the official ballot. "To barter away that right would be to stultify myself and result in betrayal of the Democratic Party and the Democratic votes of Texas."

Did Judge Davidson appear to be partisan or objective?
Well, this is where the interesting drama came in. We were the defendants, because Coke Stevenson had brought the suit seeking an injunction. Judge Davidson came in, looking very dignified, and in a very unctuous, almost saccharine tone of voice, said, "The defendant's wife I have known all my life. When I was a young practicing attorney just out of law school, one of the first employments that I received was from her father, and I represented him for a good many years and respected him highly."[19] At that point, Senator Wirtz leaned across me to Lyndon and John, whoever was over there, and said, "I'm going back to the hotel and pack my bags and leave for New Orleans." That was where the court of appeals was. That was where you would go to seek a remedy if you lost at this one. I think he said, "Tell Jimmie Allred or Everett Looney to take over, and I'll be in touch with you later." And he very courteously departed from the courtroom. Judge Davidson went on to say, "But the evidence is so overwhelming that I cannot look with favor upon the defendant's plea in this case." So that's when he said he decided in favor of maintaining the injunction, enjoining the Secretary of State from certifying LBJ as the Democratic candidate for the Senate. Lyndon was known as an FDR supporter and somewhat of a young liberal. I'm sure Judge Whitfield Davidson just couldn't abide that. So whatever Lyndon's cause was, he was doomed before Judge Davidson

Did you ever ask your father about Whitfield Davidson and whether or not this was accurate?
Oh, it was a fact. I remembered it. His name was well-known in our household. I smiled at him when I came in, and he'd smile back, but it was just a greeting; that was all.

---

18. See L. E. Jones Oral History Interview 1, 6/13/69, by David McComb, 26.
19. Davidson had also described his longtime relationship with the Taylor family in a letter to LBJ eleven years earlier. Witfield Davidson to LBJ, 4/12/37, LBJ Library.

Down in New Orleans Senator Wirtz asked Judge Joe Hutcheson for a staying order. Hutcheson denied the motion for a stay, saying that a single circuit judge did not have that authority. So there we were with another setback. Our next step was that Governor Allred went up to Washington to consult with Thurman Arnold and others, and Wirtz was going to join him right away.

In the course of this long, drawn-out fall, I was at some ladies' coffee and ran into a friend that I hadn't seen in a couple of years. Let us assume she had left Texas for a while, because she certainly was not very well informed about what was going on. She said, "Lady Bird, what are you and your husband doing now?" I threw up my hands and said, "I wish I knew!" Everybody in the room just collapsed in laughter.

TRUMAN'S CAMPAIGN TRAIN

About this time Truman's campaign train came through Texas. How on earth we ever separated ourselves from the morass that we were in to go and stand on the back of the train and smile I don't know. But Lyndon did, and so did Wright Patman and Johnny Lyle and Maury Maverick. They met him in San Antonio and came on through Austin. They had made speeches all the way along from San Antonio and San Marcos. They stopped in Austin and had a big rally. I was there, looking up at Lyndon on the back of the platform with a broadly smiling Truman. I recall, to my chagrin, actually marching up on the platform, not once but twice, and shaking hands with President Truman. Tom Clark had called me up and had me do it. Then I had meekly gotten down again, and Lyndon saw me. It was very hard to say no to Lyndon, and you couldn't shout above the crowd that "I've already been up." So poor Truman had to endure still another handshake and picture of me.

Lyndon always wanted to get everybody in the act that he could. He saw the man who was running to succeed him [in Congress], Homer Thornberry. He called to him, "Come on up here, Homer." Homer got up there, and about that time this train pulled out, headed for Georgetown and Temple and Waco and so forth. Homer didn't have any money in his pocket, hadn't meant to go, didn't have a car meeting him at the other end. But Lyndon lent him some money and arranged to get him a ride somehow or another at the other end. There was humor even in the midst of all the tension.

Truman received a tremendous welcome everywhere he went in Texas.
Oh, he did! He did receive a marvelous welcome! And yet, this was a very chancy campaign, and there were a lot of people scared to appear with him. There was no general feeling that he was going to be the winner except in his own heart and in those close around him, I guess. But with every stop that feeling must have been reinforced, because he did receive marvelous welcomes in Texas as he went on up toward Dallas and Fort Worth and through

Georgetown and Temple and Waco and Hillsboro. The final speech I think was in Bonham, the hometown of the Speaker. He endorsed LBJ as the candidate along the way.

On the twenty-eighth of September, Justice Hugo Black ruled that Federal Judge Davidson did not have the authority to interfere with the state election and stayed the temporary injunction barring Lyndon from the ticket. He had in his office Governor Dan Moody speaking for Stevenson and then Lyndon's counselors: Jimmie Allred, Thurman Arnold, Abe Fortas, Alvin Wirtz, and Hugh Cox. Black did state that [the ruling] was subject to review by other members of the Supreme Court, but at that time the court was out of session. It was the custom for individual court members to hear things that had to be heard immediately.

Two days later he signed the staying order clearing the way for the secretary of state to put Lyndon's name on the ballot. That was just nip and tuck because those ballots had to be gotten out to all the 254 counties well ahead of election day. By October 5, the Supreme Court did approve Justice Black's action putting Lyndon's name on the ballot. The election was November 2, so for all practical purposes, it seemed actually that the endurance contest was over.

I look back on that little house in Austin, and I think, gee, that was mighty close quarters to have that much tension in. I hope we got those children out to Mrs. Johnson's house some. At any rate, 1901 Dillman had the insulation of the most marvelous backyard there ever was, so maybe that was their chief solace. I had promised them a slide. They already had some marvelous swings, which I had built them a previous year. I had promised them a slide when the campaign was over, and they kept on wanting to know: "When was the campaign going to be over?" [*Laughter.*]

Senator Wirtz felt that we were in no shape to think further or to make further statements. He thought Lyndon's temper might finally have reached the point where he had better have some rest. At Wesley West's suggestion, we went out to his ranch without leaving word with anyone. Just one or two people knew where we were because we were so dead beat that we just didn't want to see reporters. We wanted to remove ourselves from the scene and sleep for about seventy-two hours. We took Mary Rather with us perhaps and one or two secretaries. There was warm sunshine. We were lying around the pool getting sunshine and thinking that we were lost to all the whole world. Our host was not there on purpose. He wanted us to be there. He'd sent up a cook. He was guarding our presence faithfully from anybody. All of a sudden we looked up. I saw a pair of boots looming up right in front of my eyes and I followed on up, and here was an enormous figure of a man, very portly, with a huge belt with a great big map of Texas as a buckle, studded with stones, and an impressive-looking hat. I caught my breath, and I exclaimed something, I don't know what. He said, "I'm Jim West, Wesley's brother. I just wanted to see if you all were comfortable." [*Laughter.*] And I explained, "So kind of Wesley to let us come out here. We really did want to get away from everybody and everything for a few days' rest." He said, "Huh. Should have come to my place. It's twenty-five miles from the front gate to the house." [*Laughter.*] In other words, if you wanted to be really totally sealed off, his place had that much insulation. Wesley's was less than a mile or so from a road that was traveled very little.

But nevertheless, a few people knew we were there, and, miraculously enough, in the morning we would find a load of papers and a very select bunch of little messages lying on the front porch. I think that was Melvin Winters,[20] who would drive out there about daylight and not even tell anybody where he was going, deposit them, and turn around and go back. We've always laughed about it and credited Melvin with it anyhow. It's the sort of kind thing he would do.

"A GLORIOUS FIRECRACKER"

Lyndon dropped a large load of work on me just as 1948 was winding up to an end. About the twenty-first or twenty-second of December, he came in and said that John and Nellie were indeed coming up [to Washington] to take over for one year as his executive assistant, and that he had rented them an apartment. Would I please go out and furnish it and get the furniture moved in? They were going to arrive on Christmas Eve. But I somehow managed it. I usually could skin down things in my own house to some extent. I went back to R. Mars, the contract company down close to the Capitol from which came so many of these inexpensive leather pull-up chairs that are good for a dining room and bridge tables. I wound up in my life having probably two dozen of them, as I've given them to various folks. Part of that two dozen was about six or eight that we bought to go in a little apartment, and two tall white chests of drawers and a double bed and two single beds and some sparse furnishings and a sofa. Just some quick stuff and big talking to the people at the stores to get them to deliver them right away. In those days, they were less busy and more human and more obliging, as I look back on it.

How and why it was decided that John Connally would go to Washington again as executive assistant?
I imagine it was probably a pretty considerable selling job on Lyndon's part, because by this time John felt that his future lay in Texas, in law. He was already established. He was in Wirtz's law firm at that time, and he was manager of KVET. Lyndon felt that he would do a much more competent job with John at his side to get things all organized and going. Neither one of them looked beyond one year; from the beginning, that's what the arrangement was.

---

20. Melvin Winters was a Johnson City contractor who was a close friend of the Johnsons.

So we rolled around to Christmas Eve, and that is when the clouds lifted and we just had one glorious evening. Lyndon found a pink-cheeked, smiling Santa Claus downtown complete with his suit, brought him home to hand out the presents about seven o'clock in the evening at 4921 Thirtieth Place. The tree was never so full. We had over all the office force and their wives or husbands or dates and their children. So it was a glorious firecracker of an end to probably the hardest year of our lives.

12

LBJ in the Senate

As the 1940s came to a close, the nation's rightward shift intensified. If Truman's progressive domestic policies incited conservatives' ire, the loss of China and the stalemate in Korea also weakened his party's standing among voters. Now that Lyndon Johnson represented the entire state of Texas, some of the president's most vocal and influential critics were among his prominent constituents and his potential rivals.

Johnson's extraordinary emergence within the Senate was only partially due to the vulnerability of his predecessors. He quickly became the prize student of the body's most knowledgeable and powerful members. He could not have had more inspiring tutelage, for statesmen of uncommon stature dominated the United States Senate in the 1940s and '50s. Yet navigating the competing demands of his conservative electorate and the imperatives of party loyalty would require all of LBJ's considerable political skill.

January of 1949 began with the usual fanfare. Congress convened on the third, earlier then than it is now. Lyndon was sworn in as Texas's junior senator. We always said we occupied the seat that had been used by Sam Houston. Lynda Bird and I were seated in the gallery. She was not quite four. At the same time, there was a petition protesting Lyndon's election filed with the Senate Committee on Rules and Administration by some of Coke's backers. Senator Connally and Frank Myers[1] issued statements expressing support and refuting the charges. Finally, on the last day of the month, the Supreme Court refused to hear Coke Stevenson's appeal from the lower court decision. That ended his last legal recourse in the disputed election and the last shoe dropped on that centipede.

Did the fact that the drawn-out contested election and court challenges dim the realization that he really was moving from the House to the Senate?
It did rather, yes. It took the edge off of some of the exultation of it. There's no doubt about it. All of those circumstances carried their darkening shadow, just as his entering the presidency was under the darkest shadow of all, such a painful

---

1. Senator Francis J. Myers of Pennsylvania was the Democratic whip.

way. So it was not then exactly one great big celebration after another as he stepped up the ladder.

Was that sense of exultation restored when you realized that he was going to be a senator? Do you recall if and when that happened?
Actually right after he got sworn in, really and truly sworn in, and I began to think: six years, six years. Besides just this one summer ahead when I can draw a free breath, I can draw more or less five free breaths of summer, five summers.

MEMORABLE SENATORS

I wonder if old people always look back upon the past as the time of giants. [Do they just imagine] that people were more able then? I think it is perhaps true. But I really do think you could make a case for the Senate having been a powerful and able body in the government of this country during those years, more so than now.

[Among the Republican senators] Lyndon had a lot of awe for Ohio senator Bob Taft. We were far from ever intimate, because he was a colossus, and we were young and just beginning. We looked at him from a distance, but we knew we were looking at somebody great. Lyndon always had enormous respect for George Aiken of Vermont, partly for his character and ability, partly for his age. They were worlds apart geographically, but very deferential, at least on Lyndon's part. Styles Bridges was a New Hampshire Republican that was a good friend of ours. Styles was about as conservative as they come, but very able and had a very handsome blonde wife. He and Lyndon perhaps recognized a similar strain of leadership in each other. He visited us in Texas early on. Lyndon always admired Margaret Chase Smith of Maine. He was a little scared of her. You couldn't make her do anything. You might be able to persuade her. She was quite arm's distance, but I would class her as a friend most of the time. Then someone who dominated a certain part of the fifties in a fearsome fashion was Joe McCarthy from Wisconsin. That was a tragic story for him and for everybody. He was Irish, likeable, tough, but he had sort of a dark and brooding look. There were a lot of folks that were scared of him, and later on there was a time to be scared of him.

We became friends with Hubert Humphrey early. He had the most loving and outgoing nature. In 1948, his role in the convention and his general philosophy would not have made him a favorite of Texans and of Lyndon's constituency, to put it mildly, but a dear man. He and Muriel were young, more or less our age, and we early developed an affection.

Estes Kefauver of Tennessee practically belonged on the stage. He was very Lincolnesque in appearance. Everybody will always remember that coonskin cap and his battles with the Crump machine.[2] He used a Senate investigating

---

2. Edward H. Crump had been a member of Congress and mayor of Memphis.

committee as a vehicle and a very good one. He was investigating crime. He was a very engaging character with a lovely wife, Nancy. We went to their house a time or two. We were never close, but you had to like him. He was a warm, attractive, funny man. A good human being. Lyndon was more a team player, and Estes was not.

One of my favorites was Rhode Island senator Theodore Francis Green, who was already older than time and who stayed quite a long time. He was an archetype New Englander. Lots of stories about how close he was with his money. He recognized Lyndon from afar as a leader. He began early to like him, and they began to talk and listen to each other. One of the great adventures of my life was going through Senator Green's home, where his ancestors had gone to China in the early clipper ships and brought home Chinese export of lovely dishes of all sort and furniture and art objects. On the walls, he had portraits of generations of Greens who had had important posts. There was an odd sort of friendship between him and Lyndon because they couldn't have been more dissimilar. He took embassy parties seriously, particularly if they were ones that touched on his committee or things that concerned him. Oh no, he wouldn't stay late for legislation. One time I went and sat next to him at [a] party. Lyndon later found out about it. He didn't get home till about ten o'clock, working hard on a bill that Senator Green wanted passed that he had left in Lyndon's hands, saying this really meant a lot to him. [*Laughter.*] Lyndon liked the tale so much it was worth the time.

[Among the western senators] there was Carl Hayden of Arizona, who was a landmark in the Senate, already at that time quite elderly, but still with years ahead of him. He had been representing the state of Arizona since it entered the Union, which was in 1912. He was enormously respected.

Oklahoma senator Bob Kerr soon became one of our great favorites. He was big and tough. There were some things about him that were rather like a Baptist preacher. He was also a consummate and successful businessman, but he was really beautifully at home in the Senate. When somebody would ask Lyndon as president, "If you had your wish, what would you ask for?" he'd say, "I'd ask for Sam Rayburn back as Speaker and Bob Kerr in the Senate," when he needed to get something done. Bob Kerr was very much against drinking, anything, anytime. He didn't like Lyndon to have a drink. I can't say that he made a sale on that one, though. His wife Grayce was a beautiful woman, a big woman just as he in stature was a very big man.

Warren Magnuson, who was in the Senate from Washington State until this January of 1981. [He had been] one of Lyndon's early friends in the House of Representatives in the war years and the bachelor who couldn't be corralled into marriage until finally in our years in the White House when he finally did. We used to have a few vacation weekends with him and his ladylove of the current time.

Oregon senator Wayne Morse and Lyndon crossed swords so many times. They were such enemies in many ways, and yet I heard Lyndon make the remark that every Senate ought to have a Wayne Morse. I was bowled over, because at that time he was really fighting Lyndon on something, and I said, "Why?" He said, "Because he believes with such zeal in what he does believe in, and he gigs a lot of us and reminds us of the other side." He was a staunch friend in some things, educational matters, or labor, one or the other. He was pretty irascible and in a way liked to fight for fighting's sake. But Lyndon had a lot of respect for people who were seldom on his side.

You had to admire Tom Connally, but he could really cut anybody up. Tall, handsome, quick on his feet and with his tongue. He was a masterful man. Not warm. I suppose a lot of people were a little scared of him. Connally was one who was used to wielding power and loath to turn loose of it. He and Lyndon were a bit like the old bull and the young bull, with lowered heads regarding each other. But he was mostly kindly to us, and Lyndon was always respectful to him, and on that basis they got along. Mrs. Connally was a beautiful woman, the only person I've ever known who was married to two United States senators.

The Deep South doesn't get any deeper than Mississippi. Lyndon always just liked James Eastland fine, although Eastland just couldn't stand some of Lyndon's views on civil rights and so forth, but nevertheless, personally, I liked him and his wife real well.

Louisiana senator Allen Ellender had a lovely wife who died early in our acquaintance in the Senate. I remember him chiefly as having an annual luncheon of seafood that he himself cooked. He cooked a whole lot of it in his apartment and then he would bring it down to his office and finish cooking it. Then he'd serve it there in his office with help from the Senate Dining Room and invite nothing but women. This was a reversal of the usual trend of the day.

Bill Fulbright of Arkansas was our friend for many years and our opponent for later years; interesting, handsome, but very often winding up in opposition to, and with just an edge of bitterness toward, a lot of people. He had one of the nicest wives in the whole Senate, Betty Fulbright.

Walter George of Georgia was one of the giants. Lyndon always sat at his feet in a figure of speech. He just thought for judgment, for justice, for knowledge, you just couldn't beat Walter George.

Lister Hill of Alabama was the most courtly, typical southern senator I knew. Both he and his wife were my dear favorites. He did so much for health and medicine. He had that background in his family. His first name, Lister, is after a man who invented antiseptics,[3] I think. We would go to a cozy dinner at the Lister Hills' and very southern cooking.

Clyde Hoey of North Carolina used to wear what Speaker Rayburn called a claw hammer coat and always a flower in his lapel. In appearance, he was just

---

3. Hill's father, Luther L. Hill Jr., was a prominent Montgomery heart surgeon. He named his son after Joseph Lister.

straight out of central casting for a southern senator. He was smart and a born raconteur. He could tell the most marvelous stories.

Lyndon was enormously interested in Russell Long of Louisiana, because [Lyndon] used to have a standing request when he was a young secretary to a congressman that whenever [Russell's father] Senator Huey Long took the floor that one of the elevator boys or somebody get on the phone and tell Lyndon and he would go at a run from his office over to hear Senator Long. So we met Russell early, knew and liked him and his wife, Katherine. She just didn't stay in Washington very much of the time, though.

Burnet Maybank was a delightful and charming man who amused Lyndon. He liked him very much, but he never could understand a word Maybank said. He was from Charleston, South Carolina, with the deepest accent I have ever heard. South Carolina does have a unique accent for me, a real southerner. We liked him, everybody liked him, but we hardly ever really knew what he was talking about. They would just go through a whole conversation, which Lyndon didn't understand, or so he said. Maybank was a member of an aristocratic old South Carolina family, and he was one of the men in the Senate that you looked up to.

Harry Byrd of Virginia was an archetype to me. Lyndon and I had enormous respect and affection for him. His Sunday lunches down at Rosemont were an annual thing that I'd just get mad as hops if I didn't get to go to. He was a great proponent of the national parks. The Blue Ridge Mountain Skyline Drive probably wouldn't have been there except for him. A bunch of his friends used to give every year a small log cabin as a birthday salute to him placed on the Appalachian Trail, a spot where walkers could stop if they found themselves on the trail too late and they could spend the night or they could stop in a storm or just get out of the weather. They called them Byrd houses.

Then without a doubt the one single man that Lyndon looked up to the most was Dick Russell of Georgia, for his brain and his ability. I cannot overstate Lyndon's admiration for him and his desire to listen to him and learn from him. They were staunch friends. You could only know Dick Russell if he chose to know you. He didn't go places socially much. Not having a wife who would make him, he didn't have to go to these big cocktail parties or receptions. He would choose only a small group, preferably people that he worked with, and usually a sprinkling of southerners. [He] could be the most wonderful storyteller when he chose to. It's a painful story to think that he developed this lung trouble and lived with it for so long. I'm glad I knew him all the years I did, but I saw him going downhill. In good times and in bad, his character would keep him working when he probably ought to have been home or in the hospital.

LBJ AND THE OIL INDUSTRY

Texas was growing up around us. Every time we went up to Washington and came back, it looked like Texas had grown. The Speaker used to say, "Texas is just like a great big sixteen-year-old boy, just a-eating and a-growing." By late 1950 we were seven million or so. We were already changing from the agricultural, rural world that we had represented in 1937 into a much more urban state.

We were necessarily becoming more involved and concerned with industries like the petrochemical industries along the Gulf Coast and the oil industries. Lyndon was never much at home with the fraternity of oilmen. In general, his friends were among the independents and not among the big oil companies. He always recognized the fact that the independents were the wildcatters, the fellows who took the chance, who went out and dug holes in new fields and came up with a lot of dry holes and lost millions and finally hit something and made lots. They were colorful, much more gamblers. Lyndon represented them well because already the 27½ percent depletion allowance was beginning to be nipped at. We were already besieged on all sides by states that didn't have oil wanting to lower that allowance, saying it was a tax advantage that we shouldn't have. A phrase that you heard a lot was "America is the arsenal of democracy." We in Texas would follow it right up by saying, "Texas is the arsenal of America, with its oil and its chemical industries and synthetic industries."

One of the most controversial things was that President Truman proposed to reappoint Leland Olds to the Federal Power Commission, and that raised a big storm. Everybody who was an oilman, especially independent oilmen, considered him really the black beast.[4] The communist thing was rising to a boil during that year. Lyndon was never favorably inclined toward Olds; however, he was a pretty judicious fellow. He didn't want to lynch folks. He found himself in strange company.

Another endless, dividing issue was [the question of state or federal control of] the tidelands. [Legislation reestablishing state ownership] came up to the Congress for a vote and passed in a way that was pleasing to Texans and Louisianans and people from Florida. I think we got about what we wanted out of it, but Truman vetoed it, to the rage of Texans. He did tip his hat in the direction of Texas by recognizing their unique claim, but he said that the Supreme Court had disposed of the legal question, so that was the end of that. I suppose it was just too obvious that Congress couldn't pass it over his veto. Lyndon was on the side of the Texans naturally. On the other hand, it wasn't a thing that he was going to live and die by, as other things have been in his life and as it was to Price Daniel.

A VACATION CUT SHORT

It was in June, 1950, when we got off on a little vacation down to the Greenbrier with the Thornberrys, with whom we had become increasingly fond. We just loved going down to White Sulphur Springs. It's some of the most beautiful

---

4. Olds advocated federal regulation of natural gas production.

country the Lord ever made. Lyndon liked to play golf when he could. We were walking from the golf course back up toward the hotel, and we heard over the radio that South Korea had been invaded by North Korea and that President Truman had asked the Security Council to call on the United Nations to expel North Korea, and that he'd ordered the U.S. Air Force to the aid of South Korea, and indeed authorized the use of American ground troops with the United Nations. So we all just looked at each other and thought what we ought to do. We knew the answer. We cut short our vacation and got in the car and drove back to Washington. Lyndon the next day wrote a very strong letter to President Truman, commending him, and used some fine phrases. He had a nice letter back from President Truman thanking him.

All of this added fuel to Lyndon's feeling about the synthetic rubber plants. He thought as long as the threat of communism hovered anywhere close to Indochina and Malaysia and all that part of the world, as long as there was unrest or instability, we didn't want to get rid of our capability.

Did LBJ think that the conflict would spread if it were not contained?
Yes. Oh, yes. Indeed he did. Lyndon was always concerned about the spread of communism as far back as I can remember and until he died. He just thought it had to be stopped there, or, once fed, it would go on to gorge itself. It was very real and lasting and omnipresent to him. The temperature of the country went up and down. We'd all be very excited and concerned for five or ten years. Then we would forget about it and think those people who were concerned about it were looking for communists under the bed.

Important things began to happen in Lyndon's life after we got back from the Greenbrier. President Truman had committed United States troops to working under the United Nations to expel the North Koreans from South Korea. Lyndon made [a] speech in which he bore down strongly on the necessity for all-out effort, strong defense, unity of purpose for keeping defense prices down so we could get all the materials that we needed, and get them quick. Quick, quick, quick was the story of his life. He wanted to achieve anything that he thought was worth achieving fast.

Senator [Millard] Tydings, the chairman of the Armed Services Committee, appointed Lyndon to head up a watchdog subcommittee to ride herd on the military and on the manufacturers of munitions, to try to see that the services got their money's worth, to make sure that all the contracts were handled with the dollar in mind.

How did LBJ happen to be named chairman of that committee?
I'm quite sure that he went to Tydings and sold him on the necessity of such a committee and, without saying "and I ought to be the chairman," made such a good case for the need for it that it just became apparent to Tydings that here is the man to head it. Committees work that way.

Lyndon went to see President Truman, talked to him about it, asking his advice, because Truman himself had handled just such a committee so well not too many years [earlier, during World War II]. It's frightening to think what a short span of time that was between the end of that war in 1945 and the beginning of this Korean conflict, just time for us to get rid of a large part of our defense mechanisms. One of the things that beset us all was the need for haste, haste, haste. Here we were, involved in trying to furnish our NATO allies with supplies and conduct the war in Korea, and everything needed to be done yesterday.

He thought if [the committee] was going to get the job done, it would [have] to be impartial and with cooperation between Democrats and Republicans. It could not be any witch hunt; it just had to be a judicious holder of the line and overseer. Papa was going to look at it good and hard. There was a tendency for a congressional committee to have a kind of inquisitorial aspect to it; it became a thing of dread for a person to have to go before one. He really didn't want his to be like that, because he wanted to get something really done about it and not just fry a lot of people.

The big bedrock of Lyndon's interest was national defense, and [his] watch-dog subcommittee [tried] to root out and control waste, mismanagement, graft, corruption, to make the taxpayers' dollar go as far as it could. It was concerned with the failure to stockpile various strategic metals like tin and prices going sky high on everything we had to buy for the military; on passing the draft bill; on trying to find 4-F men or women who could replace men at desk jobs and free a lot of physically fit men for combat duty. A lot of grist came to his mill. Lyndon must have been about as welcome in most military circles as a skunk at a Sunday school picnic. But he wanted to make sure that the taxpayer got his dollar's worth and that the defense effort moved forward with speed and efficiency. He was just a born enemy of mismanagement and slowness and inefficiency.

Time *magazine did an article on him, "The Texas Watchdog."*
Yes. If you did a graph on Lyndon's arrival on the national stage, the summer and fall of 1950 would be a time when he made a decided appearance on the national stage.

How did he react to this publicity?
I don't think he paid all that much attention to it. It was a tool to accomplish a cure of the ills that he was attacking. He used the phrase about wanting to "turn the spotlight on profiteers." He was very much concerned about the rising prices on the defense items we bought, the engines of war. He said the prices were getting so out of hand that they just made any cost calculations an empty, tentative guess. What he was trying to do was to get the makers of planes, tanks, and munitions to clean their own houses. Just hold them down by letting them know that there was somebody looking out there.

COLD WAR AMERICA

If 1949 had been a happy time for us and in retrospect for the country, in 1950 there were rising clouds and frustration, particularly as the year wore on. The war was continuing in Korea and getting more and more painful. President Truman was talking about universal military training, the draft. People, particularly Texans, were mad at Dean Acheson.[5] They were concerned about the take-over of communism in China. "Who lost China?" was a phrase you heard a lot, and Russia was always looming in the background.

Then, the most ominous [development] was that the Chinese communists entered the war in Korea. General Douglas MacArthur sent out headlines that "it's a new war." Truman declared a state of emergency. Lyndon's committee went into high gear more than ever, and he was calling on us to end the circle of confusion. We'd been selling [defense-related] plants [to private industry] at a very small amount on the dollar and then buying them back at a high price. It appeared at times that the left hand didn't know what the right hand was doing in the military establishment.

As November came along, the ugly mood of the country manifested itself in the election. There was a general distrust of Congress and government, especially against Acheson and the State Department. In that election, Republicans won a lot. Scott Lucas, the majority leader of the Democratic side, was defeated. So was Francis Myers, the whip. The most spectacular election was an ugly one in which Richard Nixon defeated our old friend Helen Gahagan Douglas. That was my first memory of him. It was the first time that I remember ugly tactics, like cutting pictures and pasting them together. That was used also against Millard Tydings of Maryland. A picture came out purporting to be of him in conversation with Earl Browder, who was the head of the Communist Party.

The defeat of Senator Tydings and McCarthy's involvement in it became a cause célèbre and occupied a lot of front-page news. The ugly mood in the country increased. 1950 and 1951 were contentious years.

Congress met early in those days. It just went straight to work within the first week [of January]. Lyndon was elected whip. Senator [Ernest] McFarland of Arizona was elected majority leader. As Democratic whip, [a] lot of Texans thought that it meant Lyndon would just be an arm of Truman and took a very dim view of that, because Truman had plenty of detractors in Texas. This was only a little over two years after he had won, but he had plenty of people biting at him, and he bit right back. [*Laughter.*] Being whip also increased the hours and the strain. It brought some new figures into his life, at least in more common daily contact: Les Biffle, who was secretary of the Senate, and Felton Johnston, whom everyone called Skeeter, who was secretary to the majority. It was a learning process, just like being a congressman's secretary was a learning

---

5. Dean Acheson was Truman's secretary of state.

process to being later on a congressman. He didn't miss a point of it. He tried to know just as much about everybody, their personality, their record, their prejudices, and their regional bent.

THE TRUMAN PRESIDENCY

By all odds, the biggest donnybrook of the scene was boiling up between Truman and [General Douglas] MacArthur. They were approaching a confrontation over the Korean War. Truman was talking about a truce. MacArthur was ignoring him. Somehow or another, there was a letter from MacArthur criticizing Truman that became public.[6]

Then came the bombshell. Truman fired MacArthur, dismissed him from command in that field, recalled him. The country was in an uproar. Our mail was angry. Texans particularly can get more incensed than most people, and MacArthur was at his height as a public hero, an idol to some. He was a glamorous character. Poor Truman had hardly a defender at first. And up spoke Senator Kerr, who was afraid of nobody. It really was one of the bravest political actions I ever saw.[7] MacArthur came home. He addressed a joint session of Congress. I have never sat through a more dramatic stage appearance; I was utterly thrilled. I wouldn't have given my seat to any constituent, no matter how big.

Do you recall LBJ's reaction to the firing and the speech?
I think he felt that the president was within his rights all along because this country does provide in the Constitution for control of the military by civil authorities, and the president is the commander in chief. However, he deplored anything that produced that much division in the country.

Then MacArthur testified before a joint committee hearing, which went into his activities at length. He testified that it would have been a hundred percent different if the Chinese Nationalist troops had been used and if they had used all-out air attacks. He denied that these all-out air attacks would have brought Russia into the war. At this point, the joint committee called on other great military figures. General Marshall challenged MacArthur and said it would have put us in jeopardy of [a] third world war. General Omar Bradley, for whom the

---

6. Rep. Joseph Martin, who had requested MacArthur's views, read the general's letter in the House chamber. Richard H. Rovere and Arthur Schlesinger Jr., *The MacArthur Controversy and American Foreign Policy* (New York: Farrar, Straus & Giroux, 1965), 170–72.

7. Kerr's April 11, 1951, speech appears in *The Congressional Record*, Vol. 97, part 3, pp. 3640–41. Also see Ann Hodges Morgan, *Robert S. Kerr: The Senate Years* (Norman: University of Oklahoma Press, 1977), 110–11. Tom Connally and three Republican Senators, James H. Duff of Pennsylvania and Leverett Saltonstall and Henry Cabot Lodge of Massachusetts, defended the principle of civilian control of the military. David McCullough, *Truman* (New York: Simon & Schuster, 1992), 844.

country always had a deep, warm respect, said MacArthur's plan would have put the United States in the wrong war at the wrong time with the wrong enemy.

Senator Russell very often wrote the script for the biggest action in the Senate, [but he] declined to get out front with the banner. He did not seek any limelight. So the MacArthur debacle began to cool off. MacArthur toured around the country a good deal. By the time he got to Texas, there was nobody ready to start following him on a march to run Truman out of office, at least not before the proper election time.

All of this brought us to an important date toward the end of March 1952—the Jefferson-Jackson Day dinner at the [National] Armory [in Washington]. My brother Tony and [his wife] Matiana were our house guests and went with us to the dinner, and Lyndon and I sat at the head table. At the end of Truman's speech, to my complete surprise, he said that he was not going to be a candidate for reelection. That was a blockbuster. It opened up the Democratic field to all sorts of possibilities. I don't remember what Lyndon said that night except that [the announcement] stopped a lot of us in our tracks.

Is this something that stayed with him over the years?
Oh, you bet it did. He always set that [dinner] as the point at which one would have to make up their mind whether they were going to run or not.

His own announcement was such a blockbuster that I wonder if he ever made the parallel.
Oh, indeed, oh, indeed. Many years later he asked me to look up that date and to get the speech.

It's amazing when you look back and see all the things that President Truman started and pushed. Like Moses, he couldn't get us through to the promised land, but did his best, and later [legislation] like Medicare and civil rights did get passed. Of course, he took his share of hard knocks on both of those. Truman launched or tried to launch a lot of things that just didn't come to fruition. He tried to begin a Department of Welfare. That didn't come about until Eisenhower's time. The Postal Department was already in some trouble, but as we know it now, it was just nothing of any importance. But he tried to reorganize it along more businesslike lines. And a truly long-range thing that he did was his Point Four program, technical aid to underdeveloped countries. That was something that had a lot of appeal to Lyndon because he could have written the old proverb "Give a man a fish and he'll eat for a day; teach him how to fish and he will eat for the rest of his life." He was a great believer in self-help and in training, in the high hope that people were trainable and could pull themselves up by their bootstraps.

Lyndon liked Truman, and he liked him better in perspective, as the years went on, as so many people did. But he was very much aware of Truman's unpopularity in Texas and how hard it would be to elect him. [Truman's] stand on the tidelands [controversy] had made it difficult for a lot of Texans to rally enthusiasm for him. The issue was blown up out of all proportion. To listen to the anger, you would think we were snatching the last bit of education from the minds of the schoolchildren of Texas, and that tidelands had furnished every dollar for their education.[8]

Was this hostility transferred to Texas political figures who had supported Truman?
You bet it was. And the FEPC also was something that they were scared of, also socialized medicine. From July and August into the fall was a period of great pressure on politicians who were in [office], and Lyndon was right at the front of it because he was always doing something. He had voted for more spending bills than a good many of the Texas delegation. There was some that just didn't vote for any, like old [congressman] Clark Fisher, who represented actually the district that we moved into. We were about a mile inside Gillespie County, a fact that we could not help but did not speak of. Aunt Frank and Uncle Clarence had simply settled here, regrettably, and nobody had gotten the county lines changed, because Lyndon always voted in Blanco [County] from the beginning, as I still do.

He seems to have been very discouraged by the political developments.
Oh, he was! Because we were going to waste our strength in fighting each other. The tide was against the Democrats, and it was a very conservative tide. There were times when he was running against a large part of the Texas feeling.

IKE VS. STEVENSON

Even with the MacArthur uproar on the decline, the country was still in a frustrated mood. There was only one person who was a shining knight and that was Ike. Everybody was courting him. Various people were making calls on Eisenhower; would he run for the presidency as a Democrat? Would he run for the presidency as a Republican? Could he be persuaded to run anyhow by anybody? Our friend Sid Richardson was one of those who urged him, hoping for the Democratic Party. Eisenhower's name began to show up on those early primaries in New Hampshire and New Jersey and places like that. He finally came out with a statement that he would run on the Republican ticket if he heard the clear-cut call to political duty.

What was LBJ's opinion of this attempt to draft President Eisenhower?
He was unremittingly and forever a Democrat. He took no part in the attempt that I can recall.

---

8. Revenues from the state's oil leases of the tidelands supported public education in Texas.

There was talk of backing Lyndon as favorite son [in 1952]. Every time that word was mentioned, he repeated that the only job he wanted was the one he had. This was a walking-on-eggs season. He wanted there to be peace in the Democratic Party and the Democratic convention. He didn't want to be in the middle of a brouhaha. It was natural and inevitable that there would be a swell of support for our mentor and dear friend the Speaker. The Texas delegation did start a movement for him. The Speaker, somewhat like Lyndon, was just not talking. Dick Russell, the great senator in Lyndon's estimation, was also a very likely candidate. Russell had expressed a real willingness, even an ambition, for it. The Russell candidacy was for real. The senator thought, "It's now or never." I think he really epitomized the soul of a large segment of the conservative Democratic Party, particularly of the thirteen southern states. He had a deep doubt that the nation would ever accept a southerner, somebody as conservative as he was, but I believe he really wanted to make that try. It was something of a heartbreaker.

Was LBJ in on the genesis of Russell's candidacy?
I don't know. It becomes very hard sometimes to stay out of primaries. It was his lifelong effort to wait until the candidate is chosen and then fight as hard as you can. There's no doubt that he admired and loved Russell. I do not know whether they ever met and talked it over or not. If it happened, I wasn't in on it. This is sad to look back on, because Senator Russell was fighting what was doomed to be a losing battle and he was putting everything into it, including his heart. Not getting his party's nomination for the presidency had an effect on him. It just wasn't the time for a southerner to make it to the presidency. He really felt he could. He made the statement that he could defeat Eisenhower.

The Democratic convention in Chicago was one of the worst of the many fights that we have had. At first, Adlai Stevenson was uncertain and said he had no desire for the presidency. Other candidates were Kefauver; Russell; Averell Harriman,[9] that indefatigable man; and Senator Kerr, who was very close to Lyndon, too. There were two delegations from Texas and a regular donnybrook between them. [Texas governor Allan] Shivers's friends were opening a strategy to have an uninstructed delegation go to the Democratic National [Convention]. Harriman withdrew in a gentlemanly fashion when Truman's own alternate delegate cast his vote for Stevenson, so that cinched it for Stevenson. He chose [Senator John] Sparkman [of Alabama] as his running mate, and there we were. We knew it was going to be a hard fall and a campaign in which Lyndon always knew he was going to support the nominee, but in which his heart was not high about it.

The polarization in Texas is remarkable. We can get more polarized than most people anywhere. There were the liberals on one side pulling at him. There

---

9. Diplomat W. Averell Harriman had been ambassador to the Soviet Union and Great Britain and secretary of commerce, and would later serve as governor of New York.

were the conservatives on the other side, some of them writing measured, philo-sophical, reasoning, earnest letters, and some of them writing insulting, threat-ening [letters]. Both sides were insulting and threatening. But there was a particular audacity to some of the very wealthy people of Texas who would write and say, "If you don't answer this satisfactorily within a satisfactory period of time..." They didn't say exactly what they were going to do to you, but they were going to see that you never got elected to anything as big as dog catcher ever again in the state of Texas was the general trend of it. Nobody gave you credit for trying to think what was best for the whole state in the long run. Lyndon tried to be soft-spoken and placating to the insulting letters, but he could dish it out himself when he was pushed too far.

A lot of folks who cared about Lyndon were very strong for Eisenhower. They gave their advice but were not going to push him and shove him. [They] sent him their earnest recommendation that he better consider long and thought-fully whether his future wouldn't be better served to be out of the state when the [Democratic] nominee came and to have nothing to do with him and preferably to announce for Eisenhower.

Were Rayburn and LBJ trying to get Shivers to promise that he would support the party nominee, whoever it may be?
I think that that is a fact. I can't say why I think so, because Lyndon was always on the side of avoiding a fight, a rift in the party, chaos in it. Once it was inevi-table, he would sign up and go with whatever side he thought was right. He tried to mediate them.

Texans were getting all excited about whether they would support Rayburn or Dick Russell.

Did LBJ think Shivers would support the nominee?
I believe he thought if we didn't shove him too far, he might stay in the Democratic Party and maybe just go fishing, not get out and actually urge peo-ple to vote for Eisenhower, which, of course, is what he finally did. I think Lyndon hoped up until the very last that he would just be quiet. When Shivers did go to Springfield after the nomination and talked face-to-face with Adlai Stevenson, who told him that, yes, he [Stevenson] was for federal ownership of the tidelands, the jig was up. That's when we knew there was no containment for Shivers. He was going to go for Eisenhower and take everybody with him that he could. On the other hand, he was going to see that the Democratic nominees were on the ballot. There were actually as many as three Democratic parties in Texas. Well, one of the biggest brouhahas that ever was.

At some point in August, Lyndon made a newspaper statement, "I am for Stevenson and Sparkman and the Democratic Party, and I hope all loyal Democrats in Texas will vote for them. I am urging all my friends to do the same." It was a simple, straightforward statement. He always coupled it with the fact "that I disagree with Governor Stevenson on tidelands and on several issues, but that doesn't make Eisenhower right on all issues." He said that "you have to remember that most of the people—the farmers, the working men, the poor folks—have been better served through the years by the Democratic Party than by the Republican Party."

Adlai expressed his appreciation to us promptly after Lyndon came out for him. All in all, it was about as painful and frustrating a period in Lyndon's political life for the wear and tear, knowing that you were going against the grain of what a lot of your friends wanted you to, and feeling that it was something you ought to do and must do, and yet it was very hard to do. Particularly when you didn't think it was going to result in success.

October of 1952 saw the campaign, such as it was, get into full sway. There were Texans who just couldn't take Truman's stand on tidelands, on FEPC, on Taft-Hartley. There was a strong tide running for Eisenhower. You were really bucking it when you went against it. However, there were those who bucked it. Lyndon with the Speaker and Wright Patman were the main three that I remember that put an organization together on a shoestring and covered as much ground as they could. Lyndon made speeches all over Texas for Stevenson. It was hard to get an audience, hard to get your friends out. He talked to his usual constituency [about] the Farm Home Administration, about the programs on REA[10] and agricultural loans and soil conservation. He talked with the Rio Grande Electric Co-op and the postmasters, who were always a big part of our political life. Then he spoke over the Texas State Network, where he came out loud and strong: "I will support the entire Democratic ticket in this election. I believe in rural electricity, soil conservation, flood control, farm price supports"—all the things the party had been supporting for years, and particularly heavily underlined a strong defense. He covered East Texas with Wright. They went to Paris [Texas] and the Lone Star Steel plant and Hughes Springs, Linden, Atlanta, Texarkana, Jefferson.

Lyndon harped on the economic issues and on peace and preparedness, and he talked about what it would mean to Texas to lose Rayburn as Speaker and to have a lot of good old southern committee chairmen like Senator George and Senator Russell and Senator McClellan replaced by Yankees. He quoted the price of Texas cotton and calves and agricultural products in all the Republican administrations, winding up invoking the Depression with poor old Hoover, whose ghost was still—you could always get a response from an audience in those days. And he spoke of Nixon presiding over the Senate.

Lyndon talked on the phone with Russell trying his best to get Russell to come out for Stevenson. He finally did. It was a beautiful statement, lost in the Texas papers to some degree. Somebody finally took out an ad about it.

---

10. Rural Electrification Administration.

What arguments did he use with Russell?

I feel sure it was unity and "The Democratic Party from the White House to the courthouse is more important than any one man," and "All the programs you and I have jointly stood for together through the years will be gutted, undermined, at least they'll suffer from a Republican victory."

When Lyndon got word that Adlai was coming to Texas, he met him, traveled pretty much across the state with him, in Fort Worth and Dallas and San Antonio at the Alamo, which is sort of a ritual, as was going to Uvalde to see the old former vice president Garner. That is a meeting I would have liked to have been a fly on the wall listening to.

Was he reluctant to go around with Stevenson?

Oh, of course he [was]. He knew what it cost him. On the other hand, he just could not go fishing, or find it inconvenient, and remain a good staunch Democrat with a Democratic future. Loyalty was spelled in capital letters in Lyndon's life from beginning to end, and loyalty demanded that he stay with Stevenson, although they were very different. Lyndon respected him and liked him, but he was just a world apart. However, Lyndon put the best face on it and described it in a way that would appeal to Texans by saying, "He's a straight shooter who tells you what he thinks and puts all his cards on the table."

The election came with its landslide for Eisenhower and Nixon, carrying many southern states, including Texas. Going against the tide, Henry Cabot Lodge was defeated by young Jack Kennedy [in Massachusetts]. Price Daniel was elected handily, and also Henry Jackson, who was to play a part in many years with us.[11] One big impact for us was that McFarland lost to Barry Goldwater [in Arizona]. That was a personal sadness and an opportunity for a forward step for Lyndon.

Can you recall how he reacted to McFarland's defeat and whether or not he moved right away to get support for the majority leadership himself?

I know that it began to be talked about right afterward. I believe it was Russell who first came out for him. I don't know whether Russell called him or he called Russell.[12] One of the southern senators advised him to touch base with Senator Eastland. Jim Rowe was our pipeline to another segment of the philosophy of the Democratic Party. He said, "I want you to know the liberals are going to get the knife out for you." Lyndon was interested in it early, but he was also, as in so many steps upward, skittish and uncertain and would go hot and cold on it.

---

11. Price Daniel was elected to the Senate from Texas; Henry Jackson was elected in Washington.

12. Jack Hight, a member of LBJ's Senate staff, cited Russell's belief that LBJ was the only senator who could unite the body's liberal and conservative factions. Jack Hight Oral History Interview, 1/9/78, by Michael L. Gillette, 6–8.

Do you think that he felt that the position itself was precarious? Scott Lucas[13] had been defeated previously and now Ernest McFarland.

You would have to observe the short tenure of several of the former leaders, majority and minority. But also there were forty-seven Democrats, and a very mixed-up bag they were. There were New Dealers and Fair Dealers and a particular little group of southerners who had been New Dealers in large percent, but in some strongly not, like Hill and Sparkman, and Russell Long might fit into that. Then there were the old-line conservatives, led by Harry Byrd, or perhaps the spokesman would be Russell. Then there were the northern liberals. So it was a very diverse group to try to ride herd on. In my opinion, [Lyndon questioned] whether he could satisfy all of that wide range of philosophies, bind them together, make a team that could do a good job out of those forty-seven highly individual, "every man's a king" senators.

As Lyndon approached the possibility of becoming minority leader, he formed his philosophy of it. He would unite the Democrats in the Senate—all those forty-seven fractious people—on common ground just as much as he could. Give everybody a chance to speak out, be the loyal opposition. Lyndon early came to the conclusion that he was going to cooperate with the Republicans on foreign policy and a strong defense. He would support Eisenhower when he could and not just oppose for the sake of opposition. Somebody told him—I wouldn't be surprised if it were Russell—"Just talk as little as you can. Just don't have something to say on absolutely every issue, particularly not something in opposition to the administration," and, "Lay your ground on economic issues and on the good achievements of the past of the Democratic Party"—like REA and soil conservation. That philosophy, as he carried it out, gave him a lot of satisfaction. He often looked back on it as one of the best times of his life. He said it was easier to get a minority to work together than it was to get a satisfied majority.

---

13. Formerly Senate majority leader from Illinois.

13

A Senate Wife

With Lyndon Johnson's elevation to the Senate and his rapid rise within the Senate, Lady Bird Johnson acquired an ever widening network of significant associations. While she and her husband were making influential new friends in Texas and Washington, many of their young allies from the Roosevelt years were ascending to positions of increased authority and influence.

Her husband's promotion advanced her own lifelong process of learning. The endless succession of Washington social activities gave Lady Bird opportunities for intellectually stimulating discussions and exposure to a world of cultural sophistication. As a Senate wife, she met many of the personalities who would play significant roles in her White House years. The Senate Ladies' visit to Winterthur introduced her to Harry du Pont's collection of American antiquities; he would later help her continue Jacqueline Kennedy's endeavor to acquire desirable period furnishings for the White House. The Johnson's party for Bess and Tyler Abell after their elopement in 1955 foreshadowed many social events during Lady Bird's tenure as first lady. Bess would become her social secretary, while Tyler would serve as chief of protocol. Finally, the opportunity to share the experiences of Edith Bolling Wilson, who had been first lady a half century before Lady Bird would inherit the role, must have given her a perspective that few women could provide.

THE LIFE OF A SENATE WIFE

Did moving over to the Senate increase your constituent responsibilities?
It certainly did. It increased my constituent responsibilities and gave me a different beat, because the Senate Dining Room and the Family Gallery of the Senate were my principal beat thereafter. To go through the Senate chamber itself when the Senate was out of session and point out chairs where illustrious senators had sat was also something I enjoyed doing, and just to take people through that great old vast Capitol. You could get lost in that place. Little circular staircases about two feet wide show up in unexpected places and wind on up.

Way down in the basement was the crypt that had been built to receive the body of George Washington and Martha, and it never had held them. There were all sorts of odds and ends down there, like a marble bathtub that had been imported from Italy for President Taft. It was about four feet deep, looked like a Roman [bath tub], huge and about four feet deep, but unfortunately too narrow in the beam for President Taft, so it never got used.

I can still close my eyes and see the Senate Dining Room. At that time, it was a very beautiful room of excellent proportions with a slightly concave ceiling, decorated by Constantino Brumidi, the Italian artist who spent twenty-five years working on the Capitol. Later, most regrettably in an effort to enlarge it, they lost all sight of the ceiling, and I think it wound up in a cloakroom or something. But in those days it was an intimate chamber. You felt a certain sense of pride at being there. There was one table in a corner that belonged to Senator Pat McCarran; nobody would have taken it over.[1] There were certain things that were served. For instance, a senator would bring up a batch of the favorite food of his home state perhaps once a year, some crab, some shrimp. For a while I think we presumed to bring up some chili from Texas and offer it to the whole Senate. The specialty of the house was bean soup.

Did LBJ eat there very often?
Oh, yes, because he wanted to eat close to his work. He would dash down and wolf his meal and get back. I spent thirty-eight years trying to get him to dine leisurely, for the good of his stomach, and also for the pleasure of a conversational meal. But I never really made a sale. He said, "If you had worked your way through school like I did in a full college course of four years in two and a half years and carried a forty-hour work week," then he'd rattle off all these things he'd done, "and had twenty minutes to eat, had to walk clear across campus, eat and get back in twenty minutes, you would eat fast too."

Well, certain habits do stick, and that was one.

As the wife of a senator, I was asked to participate more in embassy tours as a hostess. I took great pleasure in taking constituents to them. I reached a policy decision not to put my name on something unless I was really going to it or going to contribute time or money or something substantive. Because I would get one of these embassy invitations that would say "under the patronage of" and list a couple of Supreme Court justice wives or cabinet wives, and I would think, sure, those ladies would be standing at the door to receive for the entire time along with the hostess of the embassy. Or maybe they would divide themselves up among the five or six embassies that were on view. So I would take my constituents by the hand, and we would march around from embassy to embassy,

1. Patrick McCarran (D-NV) served in the Senate from 1933 to 1954. He chaired the Judiciary Committee and the Internal Security Subcommittee.

and not very often did I run into any of these ladies. [*Laughter.*] It took quite a while to dawn on me that you sometimes lend your name to things and that is all of it, which was a practice I did not like.

A custom of those days was stag parties, no longer so much a part of our life, but a lot of serious business and a lot of jocular fun, I gather. I was not there, but I'd get reports from Lyndon. There were always a bunch of things that were conducted by men and for men. There was the White House Correspondents' Dinner and the Radio Correspondents' Association [Dinner], followed by the Alfalfa Club Dinner and something called the Touchdown Club, and then the Young Democrats. I wonder what they did in those days about women members of Congress. But a great many things were stag. Sometimes when Lyndon would attend a stag dinner, I would invite all the women of his office or any women that I could think of whose husbands I knew were at these dinners. That old house of ours, with Zephyr in charge of the kitchen, really did furnish a lot of good dinners.

There were many devices for women to use their daytime hours, and one of them was called the Washington party, at which there was a celebrity table and a style show. We could spend three hours in the middle of the day doing that. It certainly was not deeply rooted in the mores of the custom [to use] your time for some public service thing. We tipped our hats to charities and agencies to help in a cultural and medical way by buying a few tickets, but it certainly wasn't the all-consuming thing that it became in the decade or two later.

What caused the change?
I don't know, but it's certainly a good change. We had made such a strenuous effort from December 7, 1941, to the end of the war and on for several years. We'd done without so much; we'd worked so hard. We'd been so determined to win that we were just happy to relax and just live it up.

Ladies' luncheons and teas were part of the pattern of life. So many social things have changed. We hardly ever have ladies' luncheons anymore. A tribal ritual was a style show. Every ladies' luncheon or every ladies' benefit of any sort was likely to have a style show hooked onto it, ladies parading down the walkway in fancy clothes. Hats, hats, hats. Gloves. One thought a lot about clothes in those days. Maybe we still do, but we allow ourselves a good deal more diversity now. There was quite a lot of sameness in those days. Your spring hat was almost sure to have flowers. Dresses were at a very unattractive, mid-calf length, and we all looked matronly and older.

The wives of all the members of both House and Senate who came in the Eighty-First Congress got together in what was called the Eighty-First Club. I joined at its very beginning. It had some fun members whom I enjoyed through the years; Betty Ford was one of them; Eloise Thornberry was another.[2] We were

---

2. Eloise Thornberry was the wife of Texas congressman Homer Thornberry.

remarkably [nonpartisan]. We laid all those things down at the door and got together and had fun, and were very intent on educating ourselves and getting a little more culture. So that met once a month and that was a lot of fun. We always went to luncheon at some attractive place. In those days, the town was full of what were likely to be called tea houses, which had no relation to afternoon tea, just lunch and dinner with accent on being quaint. Mrs. K's Toll House Tavern was a favorite.

The most fun of all was the Senate Ladies Club, which met every Tuesday. The wife of the vice president was our presiding officer. If there ever was a loosely organized club, that was it. What we knew about *Robert's Rules of Order* was not very extensive, but it was the best place possible to pick up vignettes of history. We all wore white Red Cross uniforms. A whole lot of us met and made bandages. If we knew how to sew, we could do layettes for the infants of servicemen who were in need. If we knew how to crochet, we could crochet afghans, shawls. If we knitted, we could make socks for veterans, particularly in hospitals. I am an ignoramus in most of those fields, so I just made the bandages and listened, listened, listened because it was a great way to learn about the wives of your husband's colleagues, and therefore about the states they represented and the men themselves. A very diverse group we were.

Politics stopped at the door. You'd be sitting by somebody whose husband you knew was pretty much of a mortal enemy of your husband, but we never let it bother us. I've heard some marvelous tales, particularly from the old-timers, from women whose husbands had been in the Senate years before and who, when their husbands died or retired, were likely to continue on in Washington. "Once a Senate wife, always a Senate wife" was our motto. Later on it became a little strained in several ways when there were some divorces. I don't remember any divorces in those days. One lady, whose Senate husband was long since dead, had moved into the Dakotas or Nebraska as a little girl and had lived in a sod house. She talked about the blizzards. You would just pick up little bits of American history with all its regionalism and all of its color that were just fascinating.

Mrs. Lucy George[3] of Georgia was one of the best storytellers, and hers frequently had a racy edge to them. We all brought our lunch in brown bags or else we ordered a hamburger or a sandwich. During the course of that time, we all acquired mugs with our names on them. As people began to travel more, each wife returning from an interesting trip was likely to tell about her experiences. That was our little program. I heard some wonderful stories that way.

Did all the Senate wives participate?
Not by a long shot. There were the steady and the faithful. The young and giddy were not much interested, because you could very well laugh at this and think it

---

3. Wife of Senator Walter George.

dull or not stylish. It was far from dull to me. We always had a good crowd. It had some relation to whether the wife of the vice president took the job seriously, showed up every Tuesday, kept on urging us on, reminding us of the special dates and how much we accomplished this year as in comparison to last year. One of the most faithful and one of the nicest ones we ever had was Pat Nixon. I don't think she missed a Tuesday unless she was out of the country with her husband. I, too, acquired that job later on. We took it rather seriously.

Did you have any particular favorites among the Senate wives?
Oh, indeed! Mrs. Lister Hill was one that I was always fond of. Mary Ellen Monroney was and still is someone I was always fond of, and Ivo Sparkman.[4] All the southerners. I gravitated toward the southerners, but I did get exposed to, learned, and liked a lot of those from all over the United States. For instance, Mrs. Prescott Bush from Connecticut and Mrs. Leverett Saltonstall from Massachusetts.

There were certain things that marked the calendar, year in, year out, and for us in the Senate it was the time when we had the party honoring the first lady, whoever she was. All former first ladies were invited to it and all the cabinet members' wives. It was a very gala occasion. The Senate wives who had charge of putting on the luncheon outdid themselves year after year in the color of the tablecloths and the displays of flowers and the food that they would get brought up from their [native states]. For instance, Maryland was always likely to give some wonderful crabs. Louisiana would be sending shrimp. I think I brought up some pralines.

In May 1953 our Senate ladies took one of the most memorable trips. We went on the train to Winterthur in Delaware. It was such fun to ride up on the train. Then we were taken through that marvelous collection of early American china, furniture, art works with, fabulously enough, the company of Mr. Harry du Pont himself. We all went around with our eyes out on stems, listening to the story of two centuries of American good living. Nobody in the world more qualified to talk about it than Harry du Pont. Little did I know that later on he was going to figure in my life and not from a distance, which it certainly was this time.[5] Then all the Senate ladies, between thirty and forty of us, all lined up on the steps down into the garden and had our picture made. Then we were his guests for lunch. We sat out on the terrace. The dogwood was blooming, and the trees were lovely.

---

4. Mary Ellen Monroney was the wife of Oklahoma senator Mike Monroney; Ivo Sparkman was married to Senator John Sparkman of Alabama.

5. Henry F. du Pont served as chairman of the Fine Arts Committee for the White House during the Kennedy years. While CTJ was first lady, he also served on the Committee for the Preservation of the White House.

WASHINGTON'S SOCIAL SCENE

April and May were always the busiest times of the year. Indeed they were in spite of Lyndon's being so terrifically hardworking. In the spring months, it was quite likely that we would go out three or four times to dinner, mostly to some of these business-type dinners, and then I might go to a tea, a luncheon, and a cocktail party besides. I began to be able to get Lyndon to take us occasionally to an embassy, the Mexican Embassy, for instance. He somehow seemed to think that it was much more important than just about any other embassy.

Jefferson-Jackson Day dinners were a big thing during a whole decade, or so they seemed. That was one of the days of the year when you had to be there. We bought as many tickets as we could. Always, year after year, the same two hard-working cohorts, Lindy Boggs and Carrie Davis, the wife of a congressman from Tennessee,[6] ran the dinner. Lindy, a figure in political life from the moment she hit Washington, was so capable and so suave, she could get anybody to do anything simply by being so nice. You knew she would come back and do as much or more for you sometime. We had a cocktail party for all of the Texans who came up for the Jefferson-Jackson Day dinner.

The most glamorous event of the spring of 1949 was the Tom Clarks' dinner for President and Mrs. Truman at Anderson House. It is this great old mansion on Massachusetts Avenue. It looks something like a European palace or a monastery: high ceilings, broad stairways, imposing drawing rooms. By this time it had become the house of the Order of the Cincinnati, the descendents of the officers of the Revolutionary War, a very high-class club all through the years. They did lend this place out for a sum to have a few very exceptional parties. The Clarks had a party there for President and Mrs. Truman. The tables were decorated with delightful little miniatures of a whistle-stop train. I sat by General George Marshall. I had seen General Marshall many times and met him in gatherings many times, but that is the one and only time that I was ever side-by-side with him for as long as an hour and a half. It was a red-letter day in my life: the house itself, the company. It was mighty big time for a little girl from Karnack.

Like a great many congressional wives, I was always in search of soaking up what there was to be had in Washington to learn from. I liked new things, so I lived it all as much as I could. I went to the Australian Embassy to a reception and went to the ambassador of the Netherlands' party for Queen Juliana and His Royal Highness Prince Bernhard. I admittedly liked the glamour of those things. If they were daytime events, you could go without your husband and with a number of other Senate wives who were in the same position without feeling conspicuous. On the more intimate scene, Scooter and Dale Miller[7] had

---

6. Lindy Boggs was married to Louisiana congressman Hale Boggs and succeeded him after his death. Carrie Davis was the wife of Tennessee congressman Clifford Davis.

7. Dale Miller, son of lobbyist Roy Miller, was a popular Washington lobbyist from Texas.

one of their big cocktail parties. Administrations came and went, and figures surfaced in Washington and rose to prominence and then declined, but Dale and Scooter went on and on.

By sheer chance, I'm sure, and somebody important dropping out at the last minute, I was invited to Mrs. Tydings's house for a small luncheon for Lady Astor in 1951. Mrs. Woodrow Wilson, the widow of the president, was there. She was a handsome woman, full-bosomed, feminine, and likely to wear a big black velvet hat.

Had you met her before?

Yes, at things like the Jefferson-Jackson Day dinner, but I had never sat down at a table of about eight or ten women before with her. I sat there appropriately tongue-tied and listened to them while Mrs. Wilson, at everybody's request, would talk about their trip through Europe right after the close of the war, and where Lady Astor would talk about campaigning in Great Britain. She was a member of Parliament. It was a rough game. She had quite a reputation for wit. While she was running for election, she was making a speech. Some man in the crowd said, "My son's as good as your son." She looked at him and said, "Probably so. It depends on which one of my sons you mean. I've got three sons. If they were shipwrecked on a desert island inhabited only by savages, come back one year later, one of them would have been put in the pot and eaten for dinner, another one of them would have gotten himself elected big chief medicine man, and he'd be running the tribe. We're all different."

ANNA ROSENBERG

One of the interesting new friendships came about when Anna Rosenberg was nominated by George Marshall to be his assistant [secretary of defense]. She was immediately jumped on by the communist-scare folks as having been a member of the Communist Party. Lyndon espoused her cause. I don't know quite why in the first place; I think because of General Marshall. When he met her, he became a great admirer of hers. I remember him saying that there were fourteen Anna Rosenbergs in the New York telephone book, and there was no proof in the world which one of those Anna Rosenbergs had attended the Communist meetings. Somebody had. Lyndon skillfully handled the investigation, knowing how not to rile or put off southern senators or extremely conservative senators who might be against her before she ever walked in the room. She really won him over. He liked ability and patriotism, and she had both of those in high degree, in my opinion. She was one of the smartest, toughest, most interesting people who crossed our path and remained a lifelong friend. Lyndon really always felt that lots of women were as smart as lots of men. He did not labor under any delusions that they were necessarily gentle, velvet creatures.

Anna Rosenberg came and spoke to our Congressional Club. I was asked if I could get her to come, and, of course, I appealed to Lyndon, who gently said it would mean a lot to him if she did, and she came. I cannot think women's teas were exactly her natural habitat. On the other hand, she would put a judicious value on the good opinion of congressmen's wives, so it wasn't all that hard for her to come.

TREGARON

One of the most glittering events was to get invited to Mrs. Joseph Davies's home, Tregaron, for a small lunch where there were not more than eight people. It was a great and handsome house and superb grounds. She had brought back worlds of art objects, which she kept in the house, more elegant things: jade, paintings, Fabergé, beautiful things. Mrs. Marjorie Merriweather Post Davies was the daughter of the Post family that really launched cereals into the American diet. But they began with a drink called Postum, not cereals. That was their first product. Postum was for everybody who didn't want coffee because of the caffeine. All children in my time drank Postum, at least all the children that I knew. I never touched coffee until I was in the university. Mrs. Davies always served Postum along with coffee after dinner at her house. One butler would carry Postum, and one coffee. Predictably, the Postum didn't get many customers.

She began to reminisce. She told a fascinating story about how her father came in from his business day one evening and, in sitting around the table talking to his family, said, "Well, I certainly did meet a wild man today. There's a fellow named Henry Ford who has got this bicycle shop. He says he's going to produce a horseless carriage, and he wanted me to help finance him." She said that apparently he was thinking about it, and he did not know whether it was just a wild scheme that would come to nothing—and it did have some appeal. He was uncertain whether he was passing up a great chance or whether this was just a ridiculous fluke. Well, he came down on the side of continuing to work on his cereals and did not back Henry Ford. But he certainly did perfectly all right in his own fiefdom.

An annual event for several years was a garden party at Tregaron. It was always in a beautiful part of the spring, possibly May. Joseph Davies had a Russian dacha—bungalow—on the grounds which was completely furnished with things they had brought back from Russia, furniture and household arts. He took me out there himself. Just the two of us strolled out there and went through it, and he just talked about it.[8]

---

8. Joseph Davies, a lawyer and diplomat, had served as ambassador to the Soviet Union, Belgium, and Luxembourg in the 1930s. He named the estate Tregaron after his mother's village in Wales.

One night we went to a dinner at Tregaron. The table looked absolutely foot-ball-field long to me. We had gold plates. I think that's the one and only time I have ever had a gold plate. It was just a museum house. Mrs. Davies's whole life was something that will not be repeated. There's not that sort of money being spent on living anymore. I'm glad I had a glimpse of it.

ROSEMONT

Another annual event of the spring was Sunday dinner at Rosemont, Senator Harry Byrd's home at Berryville, Virginia. That broad veranda, that white-columned house looking out to the Blue Ridge and to the apple orchards stretch-ing in front of us, will always stick in my heart as one of the loveliest events of my life. Right by the front gate there's a sign, "Welcome, drive in," which was both marvelously hospitable and in the light of today very daring. I'm sure a great many strangers did drive in and just drive around the circular path, because it was a beautiful drive lined with dogwood.

He would have a party every spring for his friends in the Senate. Obviously it would take more than one party. He probably would have two or three. They were always on Sunday. It was always lunch, fried chicken and crab meat. We had mint juleps out on the front porch. I shall always remember him as he was on those days, a most marvelous host, always standing on the front porch to greet us. How he got there for everybody I don't know. He would wear a white ice-cream suit, if the weather was warm enough. There would be a mixture of a few newspapermen, the more stable and important type, a few local Virginia gentry, his several sons. He had had only one daughter. She had died tragically not too long before we began going to Rosemont. His wife was only once a part of the gathering in all the years that I went. She was an invalid, although she did not die until the mid-sixties. Every room in the house I would walk through lingeringly and look at the family pictures and just absorb it. He was a proud conservative without apology, a courtly, staunch friend. He and Lyndon under-stood each other, liked each other from the very beginning, and were very fre-quently at odds philosophically and voting-wise.

RECIPE FOR A PARTY

We did go to an occasional black-tie dinner. One was at the Belgian Embassy, in honor of Sam Rayburn. Sam Rayburn was almost as hard to catch for a dinner party as Lyndon was—not that anybody was trying to catch Lyndon then. But if it was for Rayburn, that meant with a little hopeful, big-eyed longing from me, we would go.

The recipe for a Washington party is: first, you catch your lion, and then you send the invitations out that you're having it in honor of so-and-so, and then all of so-and-so's friends to go because it is who it is. Of course, the biggest lion in those days was an unlikely but wonderful subject, the Speaker, Sam Rayburn, very socially charming when he wanted to be. He went to some of those parties, and he was the lion at some of those parties. It all depended on how well he liked the host and hostess.

We gave a lovely reception in the Carlton Room for Bess and Tyler Abell. It was a beautiful party, [not] to introduce [Bess and Tyler] to the whole bunch of people that they already knew but to give a special stamp to saying this is a new marriage starting among two families that matter in this town, and we care about both of them. Bess was the daughter of our staunch dear friend Earle Clements and his pretty, gentle wife. And Earle made it possible for Lyndon to be majority leader in many, many ways. [He was] so knowledgeable and smooth and easy and staunch. When Lyndon was off in these long absences with illness, Earle had stayed there and kept things running. He had been a very popular governor of Kentucky and at that time was senator from Kentucky.

Tyler was the stepson of Drew Pearson and the son of Luvie Pearson, two of the most interesting figures in all of Washington in my whole life. I was crazy about them.[9]

We had a kind of a love/hate relationship with Drew. Every now and then, he would cut Lyndon up in his column, and every now and then he would praise him. By and large, I thought Drew had really meant it in all those years when he was exhorting us all "to strive to make democracy live." I thought he really meant it, so I went along with him. He looked like a sophisticated Britisher with his sort of aristocratic face and bristly mustache.

I remember that Bess's mother, who was one of these gentle, planning Southern ladies, would ask Bess to help Lynda smooth her way a little bit. We went to the beach one day, spent the day, Mrs. Clements and Bess, who must at that time have been eight or ten years older than Lynda, and Lynda was kind of an awkward eleven in this year, and Luci eight. Mrs. Clements was helpful and nice to my children, as she was to everybody. I could see that Bess was a very bright, capable young woman. I did not foresee at that time that she would one day be my right arm, but all of that was to come in the future.

A dinner party at our house in those days was likely to have a mixture of Stu Symington and Abe Fortas and Don Cook, Bill Douglas, the Tom Clarks, the Speaker any time we could get him, Fred Vinson, Dick Russell, Warren Magnuson, Bob Kerr, and George McGhee. They were always interesting, and practically everybody that we knew went on to have a sizeable job in one way or another. Lyndon early became a friend of Phil Graham's of the *Washington Post*. Paul Porter used to call our house his favorite saloon between the Capitol and home.[10] He'd stop by and have a drink with us a great many evenings, always with a good

---

9. Drew Pearson was a syndicated investigative columnist and broadcaster.

10. Paul A. Porter, a former member of the Federal Communications Commission and diplomat, practiced law in Washington with Thurman Arnold and Abe Fortas.

story. A characteristic shared by all the Kentuckians that we knew was the ability to tell stories most marvelously. That was true of Paul Porter in aces. Chief Justice Fred Vinson from Louisa, Kentucky, could sure spin a yarn. Our dear friend Senator Earle Clements had that talent, and the best of all was Vice President Alben Barkley.

Everybody who will remember us in those years knew that we lived very economically. But we lived well in that we had always a good cook, always a bountiful table, and lots of company and lots of pleasure in the company. There were always visitors from home and lots of casual dinners for staff, newspaper friends, and other senators. I was purchasing agent for the house, and it's interesting to look back on prices in those days, like a case of Old Taylor for sixty-four dollars, I. W. Harper for fifty-nine. We always drank Scotch, but a lot of people did consume bourbon in those days. Nobody that I recall drank wine except at weddings.

Lyndon often had to stop by several places before he would get home. All kinds of conventions and gatherings would come to town and try to get their congressman and, of course, the congressional leaders. Lyndon had a marvelous way of dropping into them, working the crowd from front to back, howdy-ing and shaking and getting the goodwill of the group for having gone. Possibly before he'd get home, he would have attended two of these, or even more. I had many chances to get to talk to some mighty interesting guests before he would get there. I must say, he and the guests would take over after that, and they were heavily slanted toward men, because there were a lot of men who would come to town on important business and not bring their wives. So we often sat down to a group where I was the only woman or maybe eight [men] and just two or three women.

THE TEXAS ESTABLISHMENT

We saw a good deal of the Texas [congressional] delegation. It was a close-knit organization all the years that we were in it. We would go to dinner at Gene Worley's at least once a year, and they were always absolutely gourmet affairs. We'd have crab in the backyard, just tons of crab, or we would have Mexican food. If it was wintertime, everybody would eat far too much. It was purely Texas talk at those, and Texas newspaper people and House members.

Once a year, it would fall my lot to take the leadership in putting on a Texas ladies' luncheon. I think the delegation was at that time twenty-[four]. That meant deciding where to have it, what the menu was, phoning everybody, keeping track of how many were coming and their guests and so forth, and priding ourselves on the choice of the place or feeling we might have done better. If you had any managing instincts at all, and I was not a natural leader, but once I took a job, I think I did it with reasonable organization. In any case, I did my share in that. We women of the Texas delegation were a very cohesive lot.

The whole delegation, men and women, would get together socially for cocktails or dinner, and the women just at lunchtime. First and last we'd go to practically every one of our houses. In the spring we went to cocktails at the Fritz Lanhams'. He was always the one who would read on March the second this marvelous letter from [William Barrett] Travis [at the Alamo], and he would read it in such a voice that you would be practically tearful and ready to grab up your own musket and go forth to fight when he finished.

We became quite close to the Homer Thornberrys. There began that delightful little interlude of playing canasta at the home of either the Walter Jenkins[es] or the Homer Thornberrys or our house. We would have a casserole and some salad, and then we would settle down to canasta. Lyndon was not very much for playing games. We lured him into a game one night, and we didn't wind up that game until about one thirty or two o'clock. From then on he was hooked. For about a couple of years, we did this about once a week, rotating where we would go. It was our night to just be utterly relaxed. I loved them.

Was he good at canasta?
Oh, yes, and terribly competitive, and loved it.

We were pretty faithful members of all the Texas-rooted things, the Texas State Society and the [University of] Texas Exes. The Texas Exes got together on March 2, the day of Texas Independence, every year forever and ever. I remember the Texas State Society barbecue [in 1953]. The big achievement was getting [Gene Autry] to come to entertain, because he was still a big figure and he was truly our old friend and a very nice man. It was a huge barbecue. Everybody had on ridiculous western costumes. All the Texas folks turned out en masse. Gene Autry arrived with his big hat and big smile and lots of joking about the time that he had exhausted himself trying to get Lyndon elected. He sang "Back in the Saddle Again." We had red-checkered tablecloths and long receiving lines and about a thousand guests. Lyndon was president of the Texas State Society. We had a silly cheesecake picture of about five of us women, including Scooter Miller, Jean Daniel,[11] and me, holding up our legs in a dance. Imagine! We had on stockings that had a little velvet map of Texas with the capital marked with a tiny rhinestone. The aura of the thing was just great.

THE YOUNGER SET

Lynda Bird used to say to me with a sad little smile, "Mama, Washington is made for congressmen and their wives, but it sure isn't made for their children." And that's true, because nobody ever included the children in invitations; that

---

11. Wife of Senator Price Daniel.

is, until dear Hubert and Muriel Humphrey finally asked us to come out and bring both the children, which we did with delight. They had children about the same age, and they had the best time. The Humphreys had of a family room in which there was a jukebox that you fed quarters and it played music. That was for the children's entertainment—for the adults if they wanted, but mostly for the children. They did just love their little piece of the action.

The Congressional Club would annually have a children's party. They were always rather grim affairs to which the children were not exactly thrilled and delighted to go, because they had to get all dressed up. The little girls had to wear white gloves and learn to curtsy, and they danced. You practically had to rope the little boys into going. I don't remember any glee on the part of the children whenever they had to go to those affairs, but we mothers thought we were doing our best. As I look back, I don't expect I got very high marks as a mother. I tried to do things with and for the girls. Were they sensible, helpful? Mrs. Gladstone Williams's class was in manners and in dancing, and in learning how to introduce and be introduced. The little girls had to wear white gloves, and the little boys just had to be hog-tied to go.

Lynda Bird's birthday and Luci's birthday, by the time she became three or so, were big events, and we'd have the children of our staff. I'm afraid there was nothing terribly original about them, just wacky hats and a big cake and anxious mothers. But I have them duly recorded on film and sometimes show them to my grandchildren without the applause that I think they're due.

We began having a party for the children of the Speaker's friends, because he just made a point of always getting to know everybody's children and trying to be an individual to them. He always noticed them, asked them questions, treated them like his friends and like adults. Lynda just thought he was her friend, and she was annoyed when Lyndon wanted to monopolize the conversation with him, because she wanted to. [*Laughter.*] I think it is the only time I ever saw Lyndon spank her was when he was trying to get her to leave the room and let him talk to the Speaker about some important business—and she wouldn't. He finally just took her out and spanked her, much to my horror and anger.

Did you ever spank the girls?
Goodness, no. My father would have thought I had become a barbarian, because the few times that my father wanted me to do something and made it clear, there'd be no question of not doing it. He was a forceful man just from his looks. So could have Lyndon have been, in my opinion.

I had dug my heels into the ground and resisted getting pets for the children. I had just bought new rugs for the house at 4921 Thirtieth Place NW. Oh, I was so proud of them. Lynda must have been about six, and Luci about two and a half or three. Luci wanted [a dog] so bad. One day Lyndon went down into Virginia on a Sunday or Saturday—without us, and fortunately for the outcome. He found this place that he had heard about that was a dog kennel where they had beagles. He went in and bought an adorable little beagle, put him in a box and brought him home and put him down in the middle of the living room and called Luci. I remember to this day her opening up the box, big-eyed, and then looking up at her daddy with this worshipful look. All the angels in heaven were never happier or more ecstatic than she was over that.

There was a little girl named Evelyn Coleman, who lived across the street [in Austin]. She was possibly Luci's best friend at that time. Luci began early just presenting herself at the door of the Colemans and asking if she could go to Sunday school with them. Luci was only four years old, but she always had a great interest in going to church and Sunday school even at that young age.

Luci has always been a seeking child, somebody who was looking for the anchor of religion, for a close relation to spiritual things, to whatever was right, and whatever her role ought to be with her fellow man. I remember one time when she was a little bitty girl she looked up at me—it was a period of time when I was having a series of health problems and did not go to church very much, just couldn't get myself up, get dressed, and go. It was always a matter that the woman of the family takes the lead. She gets the husband up usually and makes him and the children go. Well, I wasn't playing that role to Luci's satisfaction, and she looked up at me and she said, "Mother, don't you think it'd be more deasable [desirable] if you and Daddy and Lynda and I went to church every Sunday together?" [*Laughter.*] How about that for a put-down?

The children were consuming a happy part of my life. They usually had their dinners at the kitchen table, served by Zephyr, because Lyndon would come home at such varied and uncertain and often late hours: nine o'clock one night, seven thirty at the earliest, sometimes eight, sometimes even as late as ten. That's no routine for children. So I would give them their supper at the kitchen table. There was a little drawer on one side of it. When I was out of the room or Zephyr was not looking, they would simply empty their vegetables into that drawer. [*Laughter.*] I hate to think what it must have been like when Zephyr some day opened it up.

As I compare my children's lives now with mine, I am keenly aware that I had the great privilege—and I expect it was also a loss—of having good help. I didn't have to take care of the children any more than I wanted to. I spent leisure time with them. I took them to the doctor; I took them shopping and to get haircuts. But I didn't have to guard them every minute because I had nice little Patsy [White] there doing that. When she was off, Zephyr would, with an eagle eye and a stern voice, but a very loving heart.

In January 1950, I went to Ben Murch School to see the principal and talk about Lynda entering. Ben Murch was about two and a half blocks from where we lived, and I could look forward to her beginning walking [to school] by the time she was seven or eight. It never occurred to me to do anything else but a public school at that time. I grew up in a society where everybody went to public school except children who were troublemakers or who were children of broken homes. It was a good enough school as it turned out. Although the school wasn't far, Lynda still had to cross Connecticut Avenue. So until she was bigger, for several years I would carpool.

Was the President interested in Lynda's education when she first started out to school?
No, and that was his loss, which he often repeated very much. [He said] that all credit was due to me for raising the girls. That's not so, but the compelling nature of his job did mean that he spent very little time with them, although when I read his letters to his mother and on various occasions, I see that he was aware of so much about them.

Lynda Bird, at that time six years old, about six, looked very much like her father, was growing quite tall. I had her hair cut in a Dutch bob. I can't say that it was a most becoming possible hairdo. In fact, I can't look back with pride on the way I dressed my children. They look back with laughter and chagrin and outdo themselves in dressing their own little girls.

Were these dress and hairstyles their own ideas?
No. Actually part happenstance I suppose. I would just take her to the beauty parlor and we would emerge with something, and that's what it was for quite several years. They had a number of look-alike dresses. Luci was very pretty and amenable and gentle. She was like a sweet little lamb or kitten for the first five years or so of her life.

I got the children's portrait painted by a lady named Jean Reasoner. Luci couldn't have been more gentle and adorable when she had her portrait painted. Lynda couldn't have behaved worse. She sat up in her chair and growled at us. She was eating cereal and flung some of it at us and finally put her little head down on the high chair top and went to sleep. [*Laughter.*] I don't know where that portrait is today. I had it for many years, and I would give a lot to retrieve it. It looks very much like her oldest daughter, Lucinda, looks. Incidentally, Lynda got the same lady to paint Lucinda after the lapse of however many years. Everybody did who could. Miss Reasoner just painted the whole town.

I felt like I had not been a good mother, and that occurred quite a number of times, because Luci would so vastly have preferred to live in Texas and not to have been hustled backwards and forwards from one place to the other. Besides, Luci had an eye problem, which was not corrected until she was, I guess, thirteen years old. I took her to the best eye doctor that I could find.

SPRING AND SUMMER IN WASHINGTON

One of the main things that I remember about every spring was just the sheer recurring delight of living it. The first thing that happened was the willow trees along the Potomac would get this delicate green, a kind of a chartreuse, and that was a harbinger of spring. Then next was the forsythia, although there would likely be a snow even after the forsythia was out. After the forsythia, there were the daffodils all through Rock Creek Park, and that was a wonderful time to walk and take pictures. And then the cherry blossoms around the Tidal Basin. There are two kinds of cherry blossoms. The single ones are sort of pale, fluttery pink ones around the Tidal Basin that consume such millions of dollars worth of film every year and are the trademark of the city of Washington. The double blossoms that are around Hains Point that we many years later were to augment are deeper and pinker and fatter and bloom later. But that's not near the end of the feast. My real favorites were the dogwoods. All the forests in the adjoining Virginia countryside were just like fairyland with white lace spread out through them. Somewhere along the way I discovered the azaleas at the botanical gardens. There they sat without very many native Washingtonians paying any attention to them and practically zero tourists.

Then we went into the summer phase in Washington, which was a quite different feel from the hectic pace of spring. There was a delightful ambience about summertime in Washington for me, totally different from the push and strain of spring and winter.

June just sort of ushered in the feeling of relaxation and take it easy. We had all the office force for a picnic in Rock Creek Park. It was backyard living. It was going down to the big farmers' market, where there would be just huge baskets of vegetables and peaches, and that would last June, July, August. I would go down and get things and bring them home and Zephyr would can them. We would make freezers of homemade peach ice cream on the back porch. I worked in my garden a lot. It was a whole different feel, and you'd make up your mind on the spur of the moment to go down to Watergate and watch a ballet or a concert and occasionally something from an opera.

Watergate meant a very different thing then. Right down there on the Potomac, close to one of the bridges, there was a semicircle, an outdoor amphitheater of seats, probably still there, and a big barge would come pulling up to that place and moor for the summer time, and that would be the stage. Events would take place out there and we would sit on these stone seats under the stars. I suppose [summer] was not any different for Lyndon. It was a really—I cannot overemphasize—first and last a very unfair division of labor.

The theater was always a joyful resource. I loved the theater; I fed upon it. There was a theater in Olney. One of the shiny moments in the year for me was when Sir Lawrence Olivier was there putting on *Richard III,* and I was asked to go and greet him. This was a benefit for the Washington Heart Association fund drive, in which I was vice-chairman of the premiere. I just adored to go out to the Summer Playhouse in Olney and to stop at an old farmhouse that had been turned into a restaurant and have dinner first. This night, though, it was a great play and a very romantic and splendid actor. So I still have and cherish a picture of me and Sir Lawrence Olivier.

When you went out to Olney, did you often go in the company of your husband?
I don't think he ever went. I would go with other Senate or House wives or with members of our staff. Lyndon went to very few plays or movies. I remember he did go to one and embarrassed me highly by crying. It was *Grapes of Wrath* by [John] Steinbeck and one of those highly graphic description of starving people and about the Dust Bowl days in the depths of the Depression.

One time I did get Lyndon and the Speaker to go with me to see a play about our founding fathers in the early days of this country, about the making of the Constitution. It was really the sort that made your spine tingle to see Thomas Jefferson and the Adamses striding across the stage and to hear those great words and think, "Here I am, sitting beside Speaker Rayburn and a senator who is my husband!"

LIFE IN AUSTIN

Washington was an adventure, but I always regarded Austin as home. The things that drew me back to Texas were the business, my father, and just a reluctance to belong to Washington, just the pull of wanting to be at home some and to know where home was.

September always ushered in one of those periods of "Shall I go to Texas? How much of the fall will I spend there?" It was a divided life. I can't say that it wreaked any great damage on our family, though. I would always take Zephyr and Patsy with me. As soon as we came back to town, my gears switched to thinking about KTBC, to going to football games and taking good customers and out-of-town [advertising] agencies. My social life in Austin was not as exciting to me in as it was in Washington, although we did some interesting things, having parties in the backyard for the children. Halloween was always a high point of the year.

I began my household life of making little lists and crossing them out—getting Mr. Erb to work on the trees at Dillman Street and repairing the roof and laying a concrete slab behind the garage. The children could enjoy wheel toys there because there were no sidewalks in those days. Looking back on it, I'm sure my children would laugh if they knew some of the saving measures that I did. But the country did them. For instance, you would collect old wool, absolutely unusable old coats or rugs or things, and sell them by the pound to something called the Olson Rug Company. They would wash them and weave them and you would get back a new rug for a very modest price. I did a lot of painting and hopefully making Dillman more attractive. I put Lynda and Luci in [Annette Duval's] dancing school.

During that period from 1945 to 1952, I must have had several miscarriages. In 1950, I had a miscarriage and went to the hospital in Austin. Lyndon did come down then and stay a few days. I never had a doctor in Austin with whom I had the same rapport that I did [with] Dr. Radford Brown. This was disappointing and saddening, but it was no great wrench in life. One of the main things I remember about it is going back to the house at Dillman Street. The doctor told me to stay off my feet and be very quiet for a while. So I spent a lot of time lying on the sofa in the living room looking out of a big picture window that looked toward the blue hills, one of the beloved ornaments of Austin. Everybody who knows Austin remembers the blue hills.

I was doing the same thing there at Dillman that I had begun earlier at 4921 Thirtieth Place NW, and that is decorating. A Mrs. Ferris was making some pretty draperies in my always favorite colors. I loved chintz. I loved yellow, coral, and she had a beautiful chintz pattern that was extremely inexpensive. We really were beginning to get the place to look very nice. If anybody asked me what I did with my life, in a way I'd have to say I made little lists and then I scratched them out. So a very sizeable part of my life was conservator of what we had and purchasing agent of what we ate, wore, and lived with, as well as had to save and invest.

HELEN AND GENE WILLIAMS

One of the happy things that happened that fall [of 1950] was to meet and hire Helen and Gene Williams.[12] We knew we needed more help. Patsy [White][13] was going to leave us. She was pregnant and had come home to Texas with her husband to settle down and have her baby here. I think she stayed until I got Helen. I remember a sweet and tearful farewell with Luci, because Luci was her particular possession.

We were interviewing folks, and Gene and Helen responded to the ad and came walking in. I interviewed them while I was still not very active, lying around the house in late August. I knew quickly I liked them. They seemed so solid and capable. Helen was just a trifle more aggressive than Gene, but Gene, with his big smile, won you right away. Whatever he didn't know how to do he was plumb willing to learn. So we reached an agreement, sitting in that big, nice upstairs bedroom at 1901 Dillman, and they went to work for us right away. It was one of the good lifelong things, because they stayed with us from August of 1950 until about March of 1969. Life was too good for them in Washington, and so with our blessing they stayed on. When Lyndon left the White House, they came home with us just long enough to get us established and the house set up. They were a big asset to our life. Fortunately, they got along all right with Zephyr, more or less, because we couldn't have done without Zephyr either. I like to remember that I had people for nineteen years, twenty-five years, for as long as

12. For the Williamses' description of the interview and hiring, see Eugene and Helen Williams Oral History Interview, 10/27/74, by Michael L. Gillette.

13. Patsy White had begun working for the Johnsons when Lynda was quite young.

nothing removed them except some important event in their own lives, like getting married or very, very bad health.

Helen took over Patsy's job, which was tending to the children and being the maid, cleaning the house, washing. She didn't do the cooking; Zephyr did that. On off-days she did cook. On Helen's off days, Zephyr did tend to the children and clean the house. Helen was a completely dignified person. She was also very perceptive and understanding and became a loving person as soon as she thought we deserved it.

Gene was a man of many parts. He could work in the yard, he could be a very good butler, although we would never have called him that. [He could] drive the car to Texas or anywhere else. Gene was just a man for whatever needed to be done and one of the most obliging, genial-natured people I ever knew.

Did he chauffeur for you all, too, in Washington?
Not particularly. I always drove and liked to drive. When we finally arrived at the majority leadership, Lyndon of course was furnished a car, and occasionally I would have the use of it. If I needed Gene to drive, he would. One of the funny things he did was break in Lyndon's shoes. New shoes have a way of hurting one's feet a bit, or so the old-time legend goes. So Gene would always wear Lyndon's shoes when they were new, and when they got just a little bit softened up, Lyndon would take them over. We were able to pass on a lot of things to Gene because he could wear lots of Lyndon's clothes.

BRACKETVILLE AND SAINT JOE'S ISLAND

There were places in our lives that did offer relaxation and time to put your feet up and talk. I remember them with velvet warmth. The administration building at [Lake] Buchanan and riding in those boats was certainly one of them. In the early days, we would go to [Ed Cape's] Cape Camp on the San Marcos River, same clear green though. At times it was Charles and Alice's beautiful Longlea down in Culpeper. It became Brackettville. In the last few years it was Camp David. Of course, the ranch was always a wonderful escape valve. Lyndon took people with whom he was doing business to all of these places. He did business, but he did it at his own pace, in a leisurely fashion with a lot of jokes and anecdotes and maybe afternoon naps. The West ranch was one of the best.

The first time I heard of Brackettville I thought Lyndon was delirious. He was sick, but I didn't think he was sick enough to be out of his head. But he was saying something like this, "Oh, God, I wish I could get away. I wish I didn't have to think about all this. I wish I could just go down to Brackettville." I thought to myself, "What in the world is Brackettville?" It would have made sense if he said some coastal resort area. Later on I did find out, and for six or eight years we went many times to Brackettville.

Brackettville is a glorious natural spring, deep and cold and abundant and beautiful, in a natural limestone swimming pool. It's been enlarged to some extent by man, and walks put alongside, and great big shoot-the-chute[14] built, and picnic tables. Huge pecan trees shaded it. It had been an army post, Fort Clark, for frontier defense in the 1850s. The George Browns had bought it long, long ago when it had become declared surplus from the army after World War II and turned it into a recreation spot where they would bring a lot of their friends to shoot dove in the fall and to swim or picnic or rest all summer. They had given houses to several of their closest people, including Senator Wirtz. Other people had bought houses, and many rented houses. These were big, substantial old dwellings built by the army for officers. There would be movies in one of the great old houses on the quadrangle. It was just a heavenly spot for children, because you could roam free, and my children in that [first] fall were a little bit too young to fully enjoy it, but we went each year, either staying in a house with first Herman and Margaret [Brown], later George and Alice [Brown]. Sometimes they would invite us to go down and just use it as we chose for ourselves, and we did some of each.

It was there that my acquaintance with Mrs. Herman Brown, Margaret, grew more intimate. She was the first intellectual woman I had known, just devoured books, the opinions of public men of the day, the issues of the day. She was a good foil for Herman, who was unlike his brother George. He was just the toughest, most opinionated, outspoken man, charming man, but he could really speak wildly on the subjects of labor unions and communism and certain other things. George always spoke gently. When I say that Margaret was a foil for Herman, that doesn't mean that she was gentle. It just means that she espoused different ideas, in conflict with his sometime, but so well spoken, so well thought out that sometimes she would just leave him sputtering. They were a marvelous pair, and George and Alice, in their different ways, a marvelous pair. Both women had a rare knack of creating a house of warmth and invitation on short notice in strange places with considerable use of whatever the local handicrafts were, whatever the history of the place would make important for the household. Margaret was buying local artists' work before anybody I ever knew was.

Another marvelous piece of the Lord's world that we were privileged to go to was Saint Joe's Island, which is a long stretch of beautiful wild coast, one of the necklace of islands that extends down the coast of Texas. It belonged to Sid Richardson. He ran a few cattle on it. Mostly he just went down there to hunt and fish and take a few friends and plan. He had a most remarkable house built on it. It was built to withstand hurricanes, a huge white block of a house with a lot of grace and charm, but very avant-garde. It was very much a man's house, too, with huge rooms. The architect was O'Neil Ford. Sid invited us there a num-

---

14. An amusement park ride in which a flat-bottom boat descends a ramp into the water.

ber of times. You only got to Saint Joe's in a plane, or else you landed at some little bitty Texas coastal town and then took a boat. There was no regular passage over there. You had to arrange for the boat. So when Sid got on this island he was pretty much the lord of those premises. You got off when he got ready to leave. There were no other homes except the homes of his cowboys and the people who worked for him. He had a fabulous black cook, a man who made what he called dollar pancakes. They were very thin and about the size of a [silver] dollar. You just loved to eat a whole plateful.

They had many visitors in the course of the years there, including Franklin Roosevelt, who came to fish. The boat anchored off the coast, and he came in to a dinner there and maybe spent the night. The walls of this vast old house were lined with a fabulous collection of western paintings by Charles Russell, lots of [Frederic] Remingtons, and others. Some bronzes. I think now of all those paintings, and there must have been thirty or more, and what they were worth, and that salt air, and the months of being shut up in what had to be, eventually, a hot house if it was shut. I have to laugh at the care one takes of splendid paintings now, but they survived.[15]

Oh, to walk that beach and just to see as far as your eye could reach nothing of the works of man but just a glorious lonely beach. It was a great thrill. We would come across big blue glass balls. Some of us said that they came from fishermen's nets, and then we said what fishermen and what ocean? At that point, there was great division. Nobody really knew. Somebody said from Spain or Portugal; somebody said from Japan. Somebody hooted with laughter and said the wrong ocean, the wrong side of the world. I really would be intrigued to know where those came from. Once we saw a weather balloon owned, no doubt, by some branch of the U.S. Government Weather Survey, but we didn't know what it was. It was just like seeing an unidentified flying object, and it settled down on the beach and we approached it with great concern, lest it explode.

Was LBJ relaxed in this sort of atmosphere?
Absolutely. He did one thing at a time generally, and if he was working, he was working with his whole heart and mind, and if he was playing, he was relaxing completely, enjoying, teasing, learning from whoever his companions were, or exercising. He was always a great sun lover, and he loved to lie on the beach.

---

15. Many of the paintings are now in the Sid Richardson Museum in Fort Worth.

14

The LBJ Ranch

In 1906, Clarence Martin, a prominent Hill Country attorney, legislator, and judge, and his wife, the sister of LBJ's father, purchased what would ultimately become the LBJ Ranch. The 233-acre tract, including a stone house built by a German family in the 1890s, was adjacent to the property that LBJ's father had owned at the time of his son's birth. LBJ had many fond memories of Christmas holidays at his prosperous aunt and uncle's home. By 1951, however, the Martin house was dilapidated, and Aunt Frank was now a seventy-eight-year-old widow who wanted to sell it.

A HOME SEAT

Lyndon had been going out to Round Mountain to see Wesley West since 1943. I'm sure that the seeds were sown right there on Wesley's ranch, which is a little piece of heaven, really. There Lyndon began to remember his own childhood visits to Uncle Clarence and Aunt Frank [Martin] and began to want to have a home seat. Funny that I didn't have sense enough to see it creeping up on us. I went through life really quite ignorant. But somewhere along the way, Lyndon renewed his acquaintance with [his childhood friend] A. W. Moursund. They had known each other's families forever. They began to see more and more of each other. "Hunting" is a euphemism, because Lyndon liked the company, and he liked sitting around the fire and drinking and talking and playing dominoes and making plans and talking about buying ranches which never did actually get bought. That is, not until he bought the one that is still our ranch in 1951.

Lyndon got home to Texas late that summer, and he went out to Stonewall to see his Aunt Frank. Before late September we had bought the ranch house from Aunt Frank. We traded her Mrs. Johnson's house in Johnson City. By that time Lyndon had paid all that was due on that house and the other heirs, so it was his house. He traded her that and how much money I do not remember, but that enabled her to go in and live close to a doctor and a hospital and friends. She was really getting old.

The ranch house was in absolutely falling-down condition. I remember going by there with Stu Symington one day and the dismay with which he looked at it, too polite to say so.[1] I described it as a Charles Addams haunted house. There were cartoons in the *New Yorker* of those days of a haunted house with bats flying out of it and a witch in the door and such things, and this really did have the bats.

Had you ever been out here before he bought it?
Oh, yes, he had brought me out here as a bride back in 1935, but here it is 1951, and I doubt we had been out more than twice in the intervening sixteen years. Uncle Clarence had died long, long ago, and as a widow she neither had the management capability or the money to keep it up, run it, maintain it. The house was run down; the ranch lands were eroded or ill-used.

Had he talked about buying it for any length of time before he did it?
No, he hadn't! It was a blockbuster! I am not even sure that he talked to me and said, "Would you mind? Shall we? I want to so much." I think maybe he'd made his arrangements and then told me about them. But he told me with his heart so much in it and so happy about it and obviously it was such a fulfillment to him that I would feel like slapping a small and defenseless child for doing what it thought was a good act.[2] So, fortunately, I held my tongue, and it wasn't long before I too fell in love with the idea. I guess it was probably six months or so before I could really be enthusiastic about it at all. We brought the Wests over here, and I remember Neva said, "Well, it is a lovely view, and the trees are wonderful, but I think you had better bulldoze down the house and just use that as your house site."

Did he buy it with the intention of using it as his main residence?
Absolutely. No doubt about that. It was going to be his seat, so to speak, the way the English speak of that. It was going to be home.

Did you have misgivings about leaving Austin, moving from Austin to here?
Yes, I did, but I was born and raised in the country and loved the country. I had misgivings about the children and schools, but our life at that point was already so divided. School in Texas went from early September until Christmas. At Christmas vacation, at the earliest, we would go up there. January first always found us in Washington. So I was going to give the Johnson City schools a chance.

---

1. Symington visited the LBJ Ranch on December 16, 1951, according to the LBJ Chronology.
2. Mrs. Johnson did not exactly "hold her tongue," according to her interview with Jan Jarboe Russell; she screamed at LBJ, "How can you do this to me?" Russell, *Lady Bird*, 161; also Robert A. Caro, *The Years of Lyndon Johnson*, vol. 3, *Master of the Senate* (New York: Alfred A. Knopf, 2002), 422–23.

The first thing Lyndon did was get Senator Wirtz to come out to the ranch with him and go down to the river and talk about building a dam. He wanted to impound some water and have a place where we could swim and where he could pump out of it for the cattle to drink, because he was immediately going to buy some cattle. Although Senator Wirtz was a lawyer by profession, he had a lot of the instincts of an engineer, and he'd poured out his life's blood on those dams along the [Lower Colorado River]. So Lyndon thought, sure, he could give him good advice on where to put a dam. They got horses and rode down to the river through weeds and brambles that came well above the stirrups. All you could see was them seated on the horses. There were many handsome, big pecan trees on the north side of the river at that time. There may have been some more live oaks than there are now. You could scarcely see the highway on the other side, so thick were the trees and also very much the brush. He and the senator enthusiastically chose a place, and that is really my last memory of the senator and Lyndon doing something of a working nature together, their last project.

A SAD TRANSITION

On October 27, we went to a [University of Texas] football game, and somewhere in the course of the game I saw some confusion down on almost a front row. We were up high, and this was down low. An ambulance drove up and took somebody out, but we were much too far to see who it was. That was not so unusual, a player or sometimes somebody in the audience left by ambulance. There was no announcement over the loudspeaker. As we went down the ramp leaving the game, somebody brushed against me and said, "Well, you all sure did lose a good friend today." I said, "What do you mean?" And this person said, "Senator Wirtz had a heart attack, and they think he's dead." It's strange how selfish one is. My reaction was anger: "No, no! He can't! We need him! He can't leave us!" Then, of course, that immediately changes, and you begin to think we must get on out there; we must see if this is so. You have a wave of sympathy for the family. We went through all of that. I'm sure perhaps Lyndon never had that initial feeling that I did, but I remember distinctly that I did, just as I did years later when Lyndon himself had a heart attack, the first one.

So we drove on out to his house immediately, the house we had frequented so many times and sat around for so many good dinners and so much good talk and long philosophical advice and political planning. We were met at the door by Olga Bredt, his secretary, and immediately the look on her face confirmed it. He was dead. It was a devastating blow. He was buried in the [Texas] State Cemetery, which is a tremendously dignified and interesting old place, and a fitting place. That wound up a chapter.

What was President Johnson's reaction to this?

All his life he was desperately moved by a funeral of anybody close to him, the death of anybody close to him, and so this was very, very hard. But I also remember how grateful he was, how impressed he was, when it came out in the senator's will that he had been asked to be one of the executors. I think perhaps that he and the senator's son-in-law were joint executors. It was a position of trust and confidence that Lyndon was proud that he felt that close to him.

"COUNTRY MAN COMING HOME"

We were already seeing a good deal of Melvin Winters and A. W. Moursund. Melvin was one of the genial, wonderful citizens who could be called on to do anything for the community, a good friend and a very kind person. He was primarily a contractor, but he ranched on the side. He knew a good deal about ranching and knew a good deal about building roads. Lyndon immediately enlisted his help in finding him a foreman. The first thing I can personally pinpoint is that I came out to Johnson City to Melvin's place of business on September 27, 1951, to interview a man named Julius Matus that he was recommending for a foreman. Then I feel sure Lyndon also interviewed him.

How did you know what to ask?

[*Laughter.*] Lordy mercy, I've tried to do more things that I didn't know how to do than nearly anybody. It was, in my case, pretty much just a judgment of character and temperament, and would they get along and was he industrious. Lyndon knew a good many more things to ask about the care and tending of cattle.

Lyndon was reluctant to leave Texas this time because of the growing attachment for the ranch. He began buying some heifers from Jay Taylor of Amarillo and Lawrence Hagy.[3] Jay sent us a very sassy picture of some heifers knee-deep in beautiful grass and said, "This is what I have told those heifers they can expect when they get to the LBJ Ranch." It was really so pathetic, because Aunt Frank's land had been ill-used for years, and we were just going into the cycle of the dreadful drought of the fifties. This was by no means a large piece of land; it wasn't more than three hundred acres.

Did he have high hopes for a herd of cattle?

Oh, yes! It was a fascination and a real love of his.

Where do you think he acquired that interest?

I'm sure it was sort of bred in the bones—country man coming home.

---

3. Taylor and Hagy were wealthy Amarillo oil and gas producers as well as ranchers.

Hadn't his grandfather participated in cattle drives?

Oh, yes. In those days, those were the longhorn cattle that were driven up the Chisholm Trail.[4] This was a totally different picture. Lyndon had come to know some of the big ranchers, who loved to brag about their bulls, loved to give you the genealogy of their cattle, swear that this one and that one were the best, and say that there was a certain new strain of grass that was going to be the salvation of the industry.

The first thing I did was to bring Mr. Erb out here. Mr. Erb and I were close friends by this time. He had been working on the place at 1901 Dillman ever since we bought it, so we had had six or seven years of mutual work together. Mr. Erb came out, and I said, "I really would love to work on these trees in the yard and the graveyard; they're so fine." The trees, especially in the graveyard, were heavily loaded with grapevines. There must have been many, many, many truck-loads of deadwood to take out of both places. That was the first thing we set about doing that fall.

Mr. Erb and I also made plans for the yard and got some St. Augustine grass. We had to knock out a star-shaped flower bed and an old fountain, which no longer gave forth water, and a crumbling sidewalk down to the front gate on the south side. We took out most of that and put in grass. We kept the old German-style picket fence, although it was very difficult to get any new pickets made. They were already kind of museum pieces.

I took Jac Gubbels, who worked for the Highway Department out to the ranch.[5] He was a very artistic, imaginative landscape man who did a lot to establish in the idea of propagating stands of wildflowers along the rights of way and making the highways aesthetic as well as functional, something I was later to become very attached to. I knew about him, so I just asked him if he would go out there with me and walk and drive around and see where I thought the road should go after it crossed the dam. Lyndon was big on the dam; that was his project. We went out there and we walked through the grove of trees and laid out the road, a nice winding road from where you would cross the river on the low water dam. You do not now cross it; nobody does. The National Park Service has closed that entrance. But then, as we laid it out at that time, you would climb the hill a bit, and it would wind through the trees a bit until you reached the entrance to the house. The biggest flood in history, alas, changed our rather good plans.

In February 1952 I began the first of many trips to Texas to work on the house. I went somewhat reluctantly, because I had gotten our house in Washington tamed to the point where I was just enjoying it, and I hated to leave the children.

---

4. Sam Ealy Johnson.

5. Jac Gubbels, the Texas Highway Department's first landscape architect, was hired in 1932.

But it had to be done. We had to get the ranch house ready to live in, hopefully by summertime whenever Congress adjourned. Obviously we had not taken the advice of our good friends to just bulldoze the house down. We were making a big gamble to see if we could take this old place and turn it into a livable home for forever.

Max Brooks was the initial architect,[6] perhaps for the first couple of years, but he was head of the firm and was taking the bigger jobs. Fortunately, Max took some before and after pictures of the house, and I wouldn't take a pretty for them. This household job soon fell to Roy White, where began a happy lifelong friendship and working relationship. We had chosen Marcus Burg, absolutely local contractor: Stonewall, not even Johnson City. We got an awfully lot of work done for a very moderate price. I think our bid was twelve thousand dollars.

I went down in gray, bleak February weather and stayed with Mrs. Johnson in Austin. I would drive out to the ranch every day, taking my envelopes full of wallpaper samples and paint samples and Max Brooks's plans. Sometimes Max Brooks would go with me.

We'd walk around all over the house with the carpenters and the workers here and there. Marcus Burg would be with us. All the old German carpenters were talking German, and I couldn't understand them. Marcus would give them directions, and they would look at him, uncertain. Then finally he would launch into German, and they would say, "Ja! Ja!" and smile and nod their heads and go back to work.

What was your objective? Was it to oversee the renovation? To decorate?
Well, you bet it was to just see that everything went like I wanted it. I would choose, hang up paint samples, which we did on pieces of plywood. I would hang up wallpaper samples, and I'd back off and look at them and get the judgment of various friends. I loved having Mrs. Sam Johnson's approval; she would come when she could, but it was pretty arduous.

It's a time that has a very vivid clearness in my mind. I would sometimes have lunch in Johnson City at the old Casparis Cafe, right across from what's now the bank, and what was then, I believe, still the hotel. Oh, they had the best pecan pie in the whole wide world, and their chili was pretty good, too. So was their chicken-fried steak. Or else I would just go down to the foreman's house. Julius Matus, his very friendly nice wife, and several small children were established in what had been Aunt Frank's foreman's house. Mrs. Matus would have me down for lunch. We'd sit around their kitchen table. She always had a good and hearty lunch. I remember the most marvelous jam made out of the local fox grapes that grew along the river and everywhere, along the fences.

---

6. Max Brooks emphasized LBJ's involvement in the restoration of the ranch house. R. Max Brooks Oral History Interview 1, 1/23/81, by Michael L. Gillette.

Sometimes I would stay with the Winters[es] rather than drive all the way back to Mrs. Johnson's. There was one hilarious time when they had told me that they would be away when I got home that evening, but that the key was in such and such a spot, and just come in and make myself at home. I got there, found the key, no problem, but I was not a bit good with making keys work. So I turned, and I turned, and I got to the point of just about cussing, and then I saw the kitchen window. I could barely climb to it if I moved an old box in the yard. I climbed up on that box, raised the kitchen window, started raising myself up to climb through, got part of the way through, and got stuck! [*Laughter.*] I was divided between laughter and near panic. Fortunately, I hadn't been there but a few minutes when up drove Melvin and Anita.

At that time, the three upstairs rooms were just in a row on the east wing, and you went from one to the next to the next. Apparently, privacy was not valued in the early days as much as it had come to be by us. So we cut off a little footage and made a hall on the south side, and let a door into each of those three rooms. We put in one bath, thereby thinking we had three rooms very marvelously served.

There was a huge fireplace in the downstairs living room. I'm so glad that we did not destroy or change the fireplace with its wide hearth that was raised up about fifteen inches, or indeed did not take out the long pieces of hardware from which pots had been suspended, first by the earlier residents, and even by Aunt Frank in her time, for auxiliary cooking. She had a proper kitchen, but sometimes it would go out, or sometimes she said she just loved to cook a big pot of stew or beans over the coals.

We made many changes in the room, however. In an effort to make it look like an English library, they had stained the beams a dark walnut color. The walls had a wainscoting and paneling and a lot of bookcases, which made the room very dark and, to my feeling, dismal. So I ripped it all out and painted everything off-white. I felt it brightened it considerably. We took out a lot of the Victorian detailing; however, later on, bookcases lined the walls once more.

Did you expand the kitchen at that time?
Oh, goodness, yes. That was a must. It has undergone several transformations since, but we certainly improved it.

Incidentally, years before, in the very early twenties, Aunt Frank had put in two bathrooms—quite an elegant feature in Gillespie County in early 1920s—and the tile reached to the ceiling. I'm very glad we did not take that out. Alas, we did take out the old tubs, which stood on very fancy legs, and, even more unfortunately, the lavatories, which stood on pedestals and had very wide surfaces around the edge of them. They would have come in so handy later for all one's toilet articles. We did put in a lot of closets, very much needed and very absent in houses built in those early days.

These trips were to be repeated often from February to July. I would generally stay a week, maybe a little longer, because life was very much beckoning back in Washington, where lots of visitors were coming. I think we were [in Texas] twice in April, and then I was there toward the end of May and in June, getting ready for what we hoped would be the moving in, as soon as Congress was over. And Lyndon was writing me with his usual "Hurry, hurry, hurry, we want to move in as soon as we adjourn." And he was down in Texas several times too, briefly, during the spring.

Did LBJ have an input in the decor?
Very little. He left all that to me, but I sought earnestly to follow his needs, and his needs were not all that demanding.

Is there anything you would have done differently?
I suppose within the framework of our means at that time, and we were always, I especially, wanting to live within our means and not above them, perhaps I went as far as I would have gone. It didn't take us long to find out, though, that we should have added more bathrooms and made things a little more plush. Looking back on it, I'm still full of admiration for the skill of the local workmen and their industry. I think we got an awful lot for our money. I learned a lot, and I'm glad we fell into the hands of Max Brooks.

MOVING IN

I began to call up moving companies and have them come out and give me estimates. I hardly ever did anything that was going to cost much money at all without getting two or more estimates. I got two this time, because we had a good deal of furniture that we could spare, and I was gradually with much happiness upgrading 4921 Thirtieth Place. I bought for Lynda and Luci a new suite of furniture for their two rooms at 4921 Thirtieth Place—a lovely French provincial canopy bed for little Luci, going on five, and a sort of a light-colored Italian provincial—these names mean very little—for Lynda. And so I shipped down the [previous] contents of their rooms. I thought that a good deal of the furniture that I got from the old ladies—the brass bed, some of the tufted velvet slipper chairs and sofa, various things—would be better at the ranch. So a big van took off sometime that spring.

The first thing for Lyndon was always a phone right by the bed, a good reading light, make sure there was an ashtray handy everywhere, and, in the living room, wherever he was going to sit, a good reclining chair, with a good light by it. The bed that was in Lyndon's and my room is the very one that now is in his room here. I had bought it from a Shreveport store in 1936 through my father's account.

One thing we bought that still serves us well and will for the rest of our lives was a good round early American cherry dining table. It had many leaves, and

I think for the very first night we put all the leaves in. They stayed in that way practically until Lyndon's departure from Washington. Then we may have taken out a few of them during his retirement years.

There was also in the van, quite by chance, an executive swivel chair with a brown and white cowhide seat. It had been in one of his offices somewhere. It was placed down by the moving men at the dining table. Lyndon sat down in it the first time. He liked it fine. He said, "I'll just use this one for my chair." And so he did, until many years later it was replaced by another somewhat bigger and better swivel office chair.

It was an accumulation of seventeen or so years of marriage and some purchasing. Even so, there was nothing in the big room with the fireplace except some Chinese peel furniture. Lyndon, who likes to get everything done in twenty-four hours, was exceedingly patient with me.

Would this mean that you would not live at the Dillman Street home?
Well, it was an odd thing. We did not actually sell Dillman until the mid-fifties; I think it was 1955 or 1956. It could always be rented. Then there was an advantage in having a little pied-à-terre in the city of Austin.

Out of all the trips to Texas that spring came the return of an old romance, my love affair with the Hill Country in the spring. It'd been a long time since I'd been in the countryside repeatedly in February, April, May, June, and I saw it all unfold. There's just nothing in the world as green and as new and as fresh and as sure of the revival of the earth as the first green in springtime in Texas. It's just something to be intoxicated with. By summertime, I was as much in love with the idea of living at the ranch as Lyndon was.

Mr. E. H. Perry came out and spent the night with us. He remarked on the fact that there was no mirror in the room. Quite true. Lyndon didn't wait until everything got finished before he started inviting folks. He started inviting them the minute we got there. Mr. Perry sent me a mirror when he returned home, which has remained happily above the chest [I had bought from Betty Long] ever since.

Sam Rayburn said he was glad that LBJ got the ranch, because now he could talk about something besides politics.[7] Did this become a favorite subject with him?
Oh, absolutely. He wanted everybody he knew to come see it. He was full of talk about his bulls and the merits of white-face Herefords, and he built fences by the headlights of automobiles. He was in such a hurry to get things finished that he would drive up behind the fence crew, if they were fixing to stop at sundown, and he said, "How about working another hour, boys? I'll turn the lights on." And, cheered on by his ambition, they did. He had gotten Marcus Burg, who

---

7. Rayburn was quoted in Mary Rather Oral History Interview 3, 1/11/80, by Michael L. Gillette, 16.

had done the house, to build a dam. We did not get the road winding through the trees that I walked out with Jac Gubbels. We used a more prosaic one parallel with the fence. Considering what was going to happen to it, it's just as well we did. When the sidewalk was laid in August, thanks to Max Brooks, it had a very nice little curve to it, winding out to the front gate under the master tree—one of the glorious trees of the yard. Lyndon picked up a stick and wrote in it, "Welcome. LBJ Ranch. August 1952."

We soon established habits. We would buy eggs from some old ladies who lived in a stone house up the road. We planted a garden. I got my groceries at Weinheimer's in Stonewall. I went to visit the Johnson City school where Lynda would begin going in September. And so we settled in to be country folk.

Did you feel isolated at all at first?
Oh, no, no, no. We had constant company. Besides, I was born and raised in the country. I had twenty-one years of background living away from folks.

But after Washington and Austin, it seems like this might have initially felt remote to you.
Just the sort of remote that brought a smile to my face.

What about travel back and forth to Austin or San Antonio? It must have been more difficult then without the highways that we have now.
The roads were good. True, they have been much improved since then, if you call widening them improving them. Lyndon always pointed out the section of road that he had worked on as a young man, and at that time, there was a stretch of it that had not been changed a great deal.

THE FLOOD

But one of the most exciting events of my own life took place in early September [1952]. Lyndon had begun to make trips around over the state. We had company all the time at the ranch. Stu Symington was with us for the weekend. I think it was on a Monday morning that the whole crowd dispersed. Our guests left. Lyndon went down to the [Rio Grande] Valley to make a speech. I put Lynda Bird on the school bus early that morning. There were low rain clouds. This was the first time in that brief period of months that just Luci and I had been alone at the ranch. I do not remember Helen and Gene [Williams]; perhaps they had taken off after a busy weekend, or maybe they were here. That morning it began to rain. It rained all day, harder and harder and harder. Finally, it was obvious that the river was rising. There was no high bridge. All of our married life, Lyndon had told me tales about the river rising and Uncle Clarence and Aunt Frank or whoever lived on this side—his grandfather, of course, and he himself as a child—being cut off from civilization. So I phoned the Johnson City school and got the teacher and Lynda Bird on the phone and said, "Now, darling, I don't think you better come home, because it's just possible that school bus might get there and you could not cross the river. So ask Cousin Ava if you can't spend the night with her." I got that all arranged.

From then on, the day began to take over the quality of one of those suspense novels set in an old English country house during a bad storm. Dark came early. Lightning was flashing in just great sheets. The thunder was rolling across the heavens, and the river was rising. Then, up from the dark staggered Mr. and Mrs. Matus and their children, saying that the water between their house and ours was already [so high], they barely were able to wade through that water and get up here, and they were scared. We were on little bit higher land than they were. So I said, "Come right in. We'll all spend the night together."

We could see that trees were already going down the river. The river was making an awful noise. Between the rushing waters and the rain, it was just like squadrons of airplanes were going right overhead. Noise filled the world. We talked about what we should do if it got up as high as the house. We had all sorts of schemes. One was to saddle the horses and somebody hold Luci in front of them and start riding up to the north to higher ground, although there was nobody, no house, no friends, nothing up there. The only shelter we could find was the doubtful shelter of being under big trees. We decided to stay in the house. By that time it really was pitch-black night. We kept the coffee pot going all night. We ate I don't know what, probably just grabbed soup on the run. We decided when it was bedtime that somebody had to stay awake all night long, and we would take turns sleeping, and somebody would go out with a flashlight and approach as carefully as possible to see where the water was. Actually, what proved by all odds the best vantage point was the upstairs porch. And the flashes of lightning really lit up the whole world, so that the flashlight was a silly thing if you just wait for the lightning.

The night was full of marvelous drama. It was like having a front-row seat on one of nature's big explosions. It reminded me of Wagnerian music, *Götterdämmerung*.

And yet I was just terribly sorry because I knew it was going to wreak havoc on a lot of people's houses and fences and cattle and topsoil. As it turned out, indeed it did, including five lives lost. Out of the black night here comes Cousin Oreole [Bailey],[8] her gray hair streaming in her eyes and just looking like a wraith, and she was just bending over with grief, saying "Oh, my new stove! Oh, my refrigerator!" Alas, she knew they were going to be washed away. She had had a dangerous time getting here, because the same sort of a waterway that almost prevented the Matuses from getting here two hours earlier flowed

---

8. Oreole Bailey's name was spelled Oreale in the family's genealogy. Her mother was the sister of LBJ's paternal grandmother, Eliza Bunton. She married James W. Bailey. Rebekah Baines Johnson, *A Family Album* (New York: McGraw-Hill, 1965), 127.

between her house and ours, and she said that she walked in water up to her shoulders. I can't quite believe that, because it would have carried her away, but at any rate it frightened her. She got here, poor thing, unassisted and scared to death. So we made down a lot of extra beds and kept hot soup going and the coffee pot on all night, and I tried to comfort Cousin Oreole, but her new stove or refrigerator was the pride of her life, and she just knew; she'd say, "Oh, my new stove! Gone down the river!"

I was pregnant at the time, and when one is absolutely helpless and something awful is happening, at least I often have nervous reaction or feeling like laughing. I just wondered what is the best costume [in which] to flee before the flood. I wondered what on earth I should put on and should I pick up Luci and carry her in my arms and start walking up to the northward.

Well, we stayed right here, relatively snug in our beds. In the classic tradition of the suspense story in the English country house during the storm, the phone went out rather early on, about seven or eight o'clock that night. Miraculously, the lights never went out. We did check to see where the kerosene lamps were, because most country people keep them handy. And we did have kerosene, good wicks in them, and we knew where the matches were and plenty of flashlights. So we were prepared in a fashion.

Somewhere between sixteen and twenty-six inches of rain fell in less than twenty-four hours. It had begun at a fairly moderate rate on the morning after school started. It had gone on all day. It just became a sheet, a curtainless, staccato, almost bullet force that night. Somewhere along toward dawn, we realized that the rain was stopping. When the lightning would flash, we would see huge trees still floating down the river. We knew enough to know that when no big things were floating anymore that meant the river had crested and was going down. The water crested and stopped right out there at the southwest corner of the fence. The fence was a picket fence at that time. But there was a little pump house exactly there, and it lapped against the edges of that pump house, and it began to retreat about dawn.

When dawn came, it was like looking at a battlefield. What had been huge pecan trees and sizeable live oaks between us and the river, and on the other side, all on this side were gone. Many on the other side were gone. Lots of them were lying there uprooted; many had just been simply picked up like the other matchsticks and carried down the river. The landscape was devastated.

I thought, "When will I see somebody coming to rescue me and what will it be?" Sometime during that morning, Lyndon arrived in a tiny Piper Cub. He had flown up from the Valley, gotten in this little bitty plane, and, to my horror, he had Lloyd Bentsen with him.[9] It was awful if Lloyd, too, was putting his life

---

9. Lloyd Bentsen Jr. was a member of Congress and later a senator from Texas and the Democratic vice presidential nominee in 1988.

in jeopardy, because indeed it was. When I saw him circling, I began to wonder, "Oh, what shall I do, what shall I do? We're all right. He ought not to land. He'll just be killed landing. [There's] no place to land." So I got some sheets and went out in the yard and tried to make the word "OK" outlined, the letters, meaning, "We're okay." And then I thought, "Oh my God, what if he [thinks it] means it's okay to land?" He paid no attention to my poor little sheet symbol and landed somehow or another, came down and saw that we were all right. They landed on that little country lane up there west of the house which was gutted with pot-holes and crisscrossed by timbers, trees. How they found room to land I don't know. He was enormously relieved, except my heart was full of pain for him, to look at this place that he'd already come to love so much, and it was so ravaged. The dam, Lord knows, must have been a complete loss. How much of it was left I don't know, but it had taken an awful battering from timbers.

How about Cousin Oreole's stove?
Whew! There was water in Cousin Oreole's house up to three or four feet. Everything was soggy, awful. Big things were lying on the floor. Down at the Matuses, the mattresses had floated out the door and floated down and landed in trees way down the river. They recognized it by the ticking. It wasn't worth using. Much of their furniture was sadly damaged or unusable.

Did LBJ go down and look at the trees?
Oh, yes. He was supposed to go to an important and long-planned barbecue in the Valley, which he had just taken time off from, but which he knew he was going to try to get back to. So he looked; he didn't stay long. He reassured himself that we were all right. He was going to make arrangements to get A. W., Melvin, or somebody to come in and try to get to us, coming in through back roads or rather nonroads, across pastures in pickup trucks. Then he got in that little Piper Cub and started to leave and couldn't take off—too muddy, too many trees across the road. They crashed into one; I don't know how much damage it did to the little plane. They got in a pickup truck and somehow made their way out to higher ground and got back to where they could catch a really feasible plane and return to the Valley.

It was somewhere along about this point that I looked up and saw Mr. Arthur Stehling,[10] who was a very dignified, sedate gentleman, on horseback, in a business suit, looking not at all like he was trying to rescue somebody from the flood. He'd come down from what we now call the Double Horn Road, which was then a little one-lane dirt road. I had an almost giddy inclination to say, "Doctor Livingston, I presume?" [*Laughter.*] He said he'd heard about our

---

10. Stehling was a Fredericksburg attorney, businessman, and political supporter of LBJ.

situation, and he wanted to reassure himself and find out if he could do anything for us, and were we all right? I told him we were, and we recounted all that
we knew. He told us about the neighbors up the river and down the river, the
damage, and five lives were lost, and a lot of cattle. Untold number of trees were
washed out all up and down the river, including, farther down, some magnificent cypresses that it would take a hundred years to regrow.

Then he said he'd go back on his horse. I do not know who arranged it, or
quite how it happened, but predictably enough, A. W. and Melvin arrived in a
pickup truck and loaded in Luci and me and whatever we needed to take with
us. We went to the Moursunds' house to get properly fed and bathed and clothes
changed, and then we were going on in to Austin to Dillman. I think the Matuses
stayed on in our upstairs.

As far as my life goes, I didn't see an awful lot of Lyndon that fall. After the
flood was over, the drought took up again; we had several years of a wretched
drought. The ground cracked open. Sometime that fall I had a miscarriage.
When I began to feel that I was going to have a miscarriage, I called the doctor
I had in Austin, and he was out of town at a football game. It was a Saturday, and
I tried to call anybody in his office and couldn't get a soul. I finally in almost
laughing dismay said I guess I'd look in the yellow pages of the telephone book
and find somebody. I finally wound up in the hospital in Austin, and whoever
could took care of me. Later on I did go to Scott & White and have some further
work done. Scott & White was the landing place for us when we didn't go to
Mayo's. I did have a miscarriage, and so the end of another set of hopes. But it
was in no way actually the result of the flood, because I never suffered any damage or anything, except the greatest excitement and sympathy for all the people
who lost their savings and their cattle and their fences and their furniture.

We were undaunted. We did not for one moment think about walking off
and leaving this devastated landscape. We just began to get truckload after truckload of debris hauled up and taken away and burned. I'm sure Lyndon went
right back to work on the dam. That same dam has had a lot of work done on it
through the years.

TV STATION

Important things that had a bearing on our own future were happening. The
FCC was about getting ready to release plans for the allocation of TV channels
but warned that the freeze was still on all the materials. We had made our decision to go into the television business when we could, but all the material that
we would need to build was frozen, and we didn't have a channel. Now at least
we knew that they were going to start allotting channels pretty soon, and we
were ready to jump when we could. We got our TV permit. Getting the materials
was another matter again. They were still hard to get, but we had applied for our
permit long, long, long ago, and we had put in orders whenever it was appropri-

ate and sensible to do so. We prepared as much ahead of time as we could, and one phase of it that I took pleasure in doing in the previous year is walking all over those hills around Austin in boots and the oldest pants I had, and climbing through the cedar and over the rocks with our engineer, Mr. [A. Earl] Cullum. And finally deciding on Mount Larson as the tallest and best [location for the transmitter].

Was the radio transmitter already up there on Mount Larson?
No, no. It was a new purchase. We bought sixteen acres around the top in order to have a long stretch to put the guy wires in. That country then was practically Indian country, fit only for goats and adventurous picnickers.

Had you already made the choice between VHF and UHF, or did this decision come later?
It came when they told us what was going to be available for Austin, and I think what was available was one VHF and two UHFs, or something like that. At that point, it was not really firmly fixed which one you ought to try for. Fortunately, we tried for what turned out at least for the next twenty years to have been a very good choice.

What was the basis of your decision?
That television was the next thing that was going to happen in communications. There were a few stations already on the air, and those were doing mighty well.

But why did you decide for VHF instead of UHF?
I really don't know. I think it was very likely we took the guidance of our engineer, whom we got to know very well. We just saw him through the years. It's a Dallas firm. He'd been guiding us ever since we got into radio. As a matter of fact, his firm still does, on big decisions. I can remember, on radio, how we happened to decide to try to get both AM and FM, when absolutely nobody was thinking about anything except AM, and that was just because of Roy Hofheinz. Roy Hofheinz, a voice in the wilderness, kept on saying that down the future it's going to be FM; that's what you want. We smiled tolerantly and applied for FM just in case he might be right. He really was a man of vision, an extraordinary person. I don't know whether he had any engineering knowledge or not.

KTBC-TV went on the air on Thanksgiving Day. There was a football game, and for that reason, instead of having Thanksgiving dinner at the ranch, I think we had it at Dillman. We had a very illustrious bunch of folks. Besides Senator Russell, we had both George and Herman Brown, who had with them Dave Frame, and Wesley West came up, too, and Melvin and A. W. came from Johnson City. Jesse Kellam was there, of course, and Paul Bolton might have been. We drove up that precipitous mountain path to the top of Mount Larson and looked out on our beloved city of Austin and the river down below us. At that time, it was wilderness out there. It was a tense time, of course, to see if everything was going to work, if it was going on the air on time and in good shape.

Well, did you have a monitor up there?
Yes, we did. We had a very small building, and we had a set up there. It's my recollection that a bunch of us crowded around it and saw it up there.

Why did you go to the transmitter instead of down to the studio?
I don't know. The transmitter was a very dramatic site, and we put an awful lot of money into it, and it was a dominating place. That's my memory, though, is that we went up there.

Didn't you also buy a television station or have an interest in one in Waco?
We very certainly did buy one, KANG [in 1954]. A good friend of mine from university days, Clyde Weatherby, had been successful in another line of business, car dealerships or real estate, or both. In any case, he had some money to invest. He invested it in a TV station in Waco, but he couldn't make it go. It was having a lot of trouble; he needed bailing out.

Did you have to spend time on this one as well?
No, never a lick. At some point we bought the whole thing or just bought a part of it. There were two stations over there [in Waco]. They were highly competitive, and I think we finally wound up by selling KANG to the other station and getting 27½ per cent of the stock.

ENTERTAINING AT THE RANCH

As the first Christmas at the ranch approached, it was wonderful in a way, but we really hadn't gotten the house fixed up very much. But we put a wreath on the front gate. We had all the family, and Lyndon assumed the role of paterfamilias. I guess it was just a few days before Christmas that we got everybody out there. Of course, the queen of the occasion—for Lyndon and for me, too—was his mama, but from the remaining children of Lyndon's father's siblings, all of those that were still living were there. There were at least three generations there. I think there were twenty-one of us in all. Lyndon sat at the big table that had arrived. All the leaves were put in. We had rolls of pictures made.

Did this family gathering reminded him of earlier ones when he was a youth growing up?
Oh, you know it had to be, and I'm sure that was exactly why he wanted to do it. He remembered all of those, and he wanted to assume the role and gather the clan. I just wish I had done better by it and had had the house all aglow with

flowers and fat, comfortable furniture. There was our rather bedraggled-looking Christmas tree, which the children and I actually decorated together. It didn't profit too much from our inexpert fingers. Then we took pictures by the front door, which had a wreath on it, too. It was a big picture-taking session, and I cherish every one.

My own family came to spend Thanksgiving with us at the ranch in 1953. Daddy and his wife, Ruth; my brother Tommy; and Sarah, his wife. Tony, the one with whom I felt the closet affinity of all, and Matiana. There were our children, sitting down crossed-legged, on the grounds in front of us, in the front yard of the ranch. I'm a little bit too plump, which doesn't speak well for me. There's a warmth in looking back and seeing Tommy's and Tony's faces, even if it is the occasion of a great big deer hunt and they have their kill propped up in front of them, and in seeing Daddy with his three children by the fireplace. I'm glad they shared this old house with us some.[11]

There were some events that went on and on through our life. We had a barbecue dinner for major KTBC clients at the ranch, and I had a party for the ladies of Stonewall. It came as a surprise to me that if you invited ladies that the children that they had at home that they couldn't leave at home all came too. [Laughter.] There was one lady I could always depend on to play the piano, and they would get the singing started. It's a wonderful community. I soon grew to respect it mightily and enjoy it very much.

I think by that time our shooting days had begun. Lyndon shot most of his life, not with any great enthusiasm, but just because he liked to be out in the open with people who liked to shoot. It was social thing with him and a time for masculine companionship and outdoors. I never was the least bit interested in it, but I got a little hurt because I missed out on a lot and didn't get included on a lot. So I was determined to learn; I did. I shot one or two or three deer, and that was very soon the end of it. Certainly it was the end of it in that November day when the President was shot.

President Johnson didn't do any hunting after that?
No. He asked the Secret Service to take all the guns and store them and lock them. We had made so many passes at trying to quit having guns around homes. I can think of at least two important people in my own personal life who I very surely believe would be alive today if there hadn't been a handy gun in their house.[12]

Lyndon jokingly said that he couldn't live sixty-three miles out in the country without breaking the speed limit coming and going into town, so he had to get a plane. And believe me, he did drive awfully fast. He was a skillful driver with very fast reflexes, but he scared the life out of me. And he never seemed to realize

---

11. LBJ Home Movie 25, Fall–Christmas, 1953, LBJ Library.
12. LBJ did hunt on Dec. 31, 1963. Johnson, *A White House Diary*, 29.

how much it scared me, because if he knew how much mental anguish it caused me, I don't believe he would have done it. He would say, "Now, it's all right. Don't get scared. I'm watching what I'm doing. It's just as safe as can be." I said, "I don't like it anyway. Please slow down." I didn't have very much effect, though.

Did he ever have an accident?
No. But we finally got to building an airstrip, in either 1959 or 1960. The person who did it was, of course, our old friend Melvin Winters, who was a road contractor and had great big machinery. Those caliche hills, alas; the good soil was thin. You got right down to the caliche awfully quick, and caliche is very hard and makes a good airstrip. I guess we had the caliche strip before we paved it. We celebrated the paving of it by Easter of the next year.

15

The Loyal Opposition, 1953–1955

On the same day that Americans elected Dwight Eisenhower president, Arizona voters chose Barry Goldwater over incumbent Ernest McFarland, clearing the path for LBJ's promotion as Senate minority leader. Eisenhower's immense popularity in Texas, especially among some of LBJ's most significant supporters, gave him ample incentive to cooperate with the moderate Republican president.

As LBJ began to consolidate his power in the Senate, Lady Bird continued to straddle her divided lives between Washington and Texas, between husband and children. When she accompanied Johnson on trips, staff members and domestic help became surrogate mothers. If she didn't travel with LBJ—and often when she did—he took friends and staff along. Their lives seemed to drift increasingly into different orbits during the early 1950s, but a life-threatening heart attack in 1955 brought them together in the most jarring fashion. His mood swings undoubtedly worsened after the heart attack, but they had plagued him well before then.

DEMOCRATIC LEADER

1953 was a time of big change. The Republicans had won; Eisenhower was going to be inaugurated on January the twentieth. We had lost Senator McFarland in the election. Lyndon, who had been McFarland's whip or assistant leader, was elected minority leader of the Senate. At forty-four, he was the youngest man in years and in seniority to ever hold that. One thing that gave him a lot of satisfaction was that he was nominated by Russell of Georgia, and he was seconded by Theodore Francis Green of Rhode Island, an old patrician, delightful character, so far removed from Lyndon geographically and socially and in so many ways, but always very fond of Lyndon. [He was] seconded also by [Senator Dennis] Chavez of New Mexico. The fact that Chavez was Latin American and from the Southwest added to Lyndon's satisfaction.

Earle Clements of Kentucky was chosen the Democratic whip. A thoroughly nice man, he was so generally liked throughout the Senate.

There we were, opposite numbers to that great Senator [Robert] Taft, the majority leader, who had Bill Knowland of California for his number-two man. But the shocking change was that the Speaker was no longer the Speaker. Joe Martin of Massachusetts was the new Speaker.

Congress opened on January 3. This time there was a knife-edge Republican majority in the Senate of forty-eight to forty-seven, and one independent, Wayne Morse. In some ways it was the best time of Lyndon's life. It's much easier to ride herd on a group of men who are that closely matched. You have more of a feeling of the necessity of clinging together than of fractionalizing out in every one of your varying political philosophies.

Do you think that experience for two years led him to count every vote and touch every base later on?
Oh, I'm sure it did. The necessity of being ever watchful and vigilant, yes, I'm sure it had a lot of effect on him. Another big job that he had was he was put in charge of the Democratic Steering Committee [and] the Democratic Policy Committee.[1]

Did his attitude change now that he was in the leadership? Was it more exhilarating for him?
Yes, I think so. He liked the necessity; he liked the spur. He liked the razor edge and the need to try to lead his segment of the Senate. He was always very interested in the machinery of government, the parliamentary side of it, the committee work as well as the philosophy.

He had two particular guidelines that stand out in my memory across the years. One was to loosen up the seniority rule enough to give every Democratic freshman at least one important committee assignment. He put Stu Symington on Armed Services, Mike Mansfield and Hubert Humphrey on Foreign Relations, John Kennedy on Labor and Public Welfare, and Henry Jackson on Interior. Could he have been affected by his experience with [Albert] Thomas, where by just a mere two months and then by an extremely able operator, he himself failed to get on the [House] Appropriations Committee? I don't know. He carefully chose each one of those men, not only for what they asked for and were trying to get and therefore earning their gratitude but for their prior record of experience and work in that field and achievement. For instance, Symington had been secretary of the air force. I remember him talking about it a lot and being real enthusiastic about it and satisfied with it. Lyndon went through some kind of machinations to get some committees made larger in order to make room for them.[2]

---

1. The Democratic Policy Committee explored compromises necessary to pass legislation as well as determining its scheduling in the Senate. The Steering Committee allocated committee assignments.

2. Robert A. Caro provides an in-depth explanation of LBJ's maneuvers to accomplish this innovation in committee assignments. Caro, *Master of the Senate*, 493–507.

He very quickly made a statement of philosophy on what he thought a minority party ought to do. I think he told them the way he would handle it before he took the job to make sure they really wanted him. He didn't believe it was the business of the opposition party just to oppose. You see what the new president proposes for the country, and then you help him on it insofar as you think he is right. If a bill or a program was for the best interest of America, even if it was a Republican bill, he wanted to help it. He was more pro-American than he was anti-Republican, although he never ceased to be a Democrat.

If it violates your own belief and your party's deep-seated philosophy, then you oppose him. But he was pretty pleased with Eisenhower's State of the Union message in which he quickly said he intended to have a bipartisan foreign policy and to consult with the Democrats on taking major steps. He and Eisenhower got off to a good start and stayed that way. It was a good relationship. Eisenhower soon set up a system of inviting the congressional leaders, both majority and minority, to the White House to consult with him, and Lyndon made the most of his opportunities. He did not feel excluded, and he liked those years. He knew his way around the town. There was a network of friends in just about every place you needed to do business.

But in spite of that, there were some things that Lyndon as the minority leader opposite [Eisenhower] and opposite Taft did to fulfill his role as carrying the banner for the Democrats. He made a speech calling the Republican Party "one of many faces." When you took a look at it, you didn't know whether you were looking at the Republican Party of President Eisenhower or the Republican Party of Senator Taft or the Republican Party of Senator Morse[3] or the Republican Party of Senator McCarthy. He was saying it makes bipartisanship difficult. Nevertheless, bipartisanship was the aim and the guideline of his years opposite Eisenhower.

On January the twentieth, Eisenhower was inaugurated on the Capitol steps, with Nixon sworn in as vice president. After the ceremony there was a big parade and everybody went to their own luncheons. There was general good humor all over the town. Bitterness had seemed to stain the last couple of years of Truman's time. It is interesting to look back on, in view of the warm and admiring light that now shines on him, to my great pleasure.

As the spring of 1953 went on, Lyndon was digging into his job, learning a lot. It was in the first three or four or five months that he came up against Taft like a brick wall. There was a parliamentary matter that Lyndon tried to get something done and Taft smartly slapped him down. Lyndon had not studied his lessons enough to know that you couldn't do it that way. Taft was the old master. I certainly remember Lyndon's reaction to it: that never again will I be caught

---

3. Morse, who had been elected as a Republican in 1944 and 1950, declared himself an independent on October 24, 1952. He became a Democrat in 1955.

ignorant. I may lose many battles, but not because I haven't studied the situation enough. I may not be strong enough to win them, but I'm going to plan them better than I did this one. Lyndon lost completely and he profited from it. He had great respect for Taft from beginning to end.

Lyndon was a very heavy smoker all during this period. I am sure that it was the pressure of being minority leader and facing up to the formidable presence of Taft. It became evident that Taft was going downhill. I remember passing him in the hall and wanting terribly to ask him for his autograph for the constituent that I had in tow that day, somebody with small children. They were just looking at him big-eyed, but I just didn't have the heart because he looked too tired and ill. In June 1953, Senator Taft announced that he was going to give up the post of majority leader because of serious illness. We had known for some time that he had cancer. He was extremely strong and tough to have persevered as long as he had. When Taft did get out, the Republicans chose Bill Knowland of California. He was not the towering figure intellectually that Taft was. He was a very nice man, but ponderous and not an agile mover in legislative maneuvering. Lyndon, in spite of his increasing weight, was always buoyant, fast moving, just a dynamo. He came to feel that he could nimbly dance his way around Knowland.

Would he share those experiences with you when he came home?
Oh, yes, yes. You could just tell it from his looks and mood and talk. He would tell me about it just as he had when he had the early and complete defeat at the hands of Taft when he made up his mind this won't happen any more. He would say, "Let's invite over the Bill Whites," two or three of his chums, maybe some of his staff. That was the setting in which he would talk. I'm afraid I didn't get all the best of it. He liked a little larger audience. [*Laughter.*]

THE EISENHOWER ADMINISTRATION

Eisenhower picked a real business team: Charles Wilson to be secretary of defense, Roger Stevens for the army, and Harold Talbott for the air force. He ran into a good deal of flak on Wilson, who was such a big stockholder in General Motors, that the ghost of conflict of interest, whether it was called that in those days, I don't know, but it was certainly raised.[4] But he was approved, not too enthusiastically, on the tidal wave of Eisenhower's popularity. I guess he could have gotten anybody approved. Oveta Culp Hobby was [initially appointed

---

4. Wilson, formerly president of General Motors, and his wife held $5 million worth of the corporation's stock. Although he ultimately agreed to sell the stock, members of the Senate Armed Services Committee also questioned whether he should be allowed to receive future stock payments as an extended bonus system. Herbert S. Parmet, *Eisenhower and the American Crusades* (New York: Macmillan, 1972), 170–71.

chairman of the Federal Security Agency and soon the first] secretary of Department of Health, Education, and Welfare, and Bob Anderson was secretary of the navy. He had been our longtime friend from NYA days, where he'd been on Lyndon's board of advisers. We were so glad to welcome those two Texans, both old friends, to the Washington roles they played. Lyndon made a point to be helpful to them in every way he could. Oveta had already been head of WACS, but he took her under his wing, introducing her to all the senators and escorting her to her confirmation hearings.

Also in the early spring, the Johnsons, those nonparty goers or givers, had a party. We really had a great big, fancy, beautiful party at the Carlton Hotel for the two Texas members of Eisenhower's cabinet. It was [Lyndon's idea]. I was much more responsive rather than initiatory, and I don't recommend that one bit. I was late coming to be a self-starter. But I was real proud of this party, and I worked hard on it. The old Carlton Hotel was then, and I expect still is, one of the most elegant settings in Washington. Oveta was absolutely elegant and cool, and her husband[5] older, sage, wry, and witty. Everybody in town was there, probably a quorum of the Senate: Vice President Nixon dropped by with Pat to pay his respects to his president's cabinet members. In fact, we had a large quota of Republicans there: the Speaker, Joe Martin; the Joe McCarthys were there.

What is your own memory of President Eisenhower?
Extremely affable and easygoing. At the same time you had the feeling this was a commanding man and you would not have crossed him with impunity. You knew that he could rise in majesty and swat you down. I liked him. But he was ideal for Lyndon and the Speaker to work with. They respected each other; both the Speaker and Lyndon had a great respect for the office itself. In some ways, [the Senate leadership] was the job to which Lyndon was most suited in his entire life; that and the National Youth Administration, which he just ate up like cake.

Did you have any relationship with Mrs. Eisenhower?
No. I went to innumerable parties for her, and later on in our own tenure in the White House, I made every effort to get every former first lady to come to parties there. She responded more than anybody, and, what's more, she called the staff members by name: the butlers, the waiters, the people she'd known, and I liked that about her.

It was an odd time in American history. Everybody was crazy about pink.

Everybody had to try wearing bangs. The feeling toward her was extremely warm, affectionate. Yet both she and later Mrs. Truman were so unlike their

---

5. Former Texas governor William P. Hobby.

predecessor Mrs. Roosevelt. Maybe the country needed a surcease from striving with its darker side, its troubled lives, which is what Mrs. Roosevelt had specialized in.

FIRST IMPRESSIONS OF THE KENNEDYS

I remember Jack Kennedy as one of the young bachelors who became the subject of a lot of newspaper stories, glamorous stories—particularly in the society pages—because of his handsome boyish good looks and his family background. I remember some sense of sympathy from time to time because we'd heard that he had serious back trouble, that it happened to him as a result of war injuries when he swam a long time carrying a comrade, and that his back bothered him badly off and on thereafter, which caused absences sometimes. Lyndon was not only his senior in years of service in the body but [nine] years older.

My first really clear memory [of Jacqueline Kennedy] was a beautiful story of the wedding in a spread in *Life* magazine, lovely pictures of the beautiful bride. She was absolutely the essence of romance and beauty. It said she had been the outstanding debutante of a season or so. She had had a job of ["Inquiring Photographer"] at the *Washington Times-Herald*.

The first time I remember meeting Mrs. Kennedy was when I decided I would ask all the wives of the new senators to come to lunch at my house to meet each other and then have some of the wives of the top leadership and the wives of committee heads. I had all these ladies congregated in the downstairs basement recreation room, which used to be the garage. I was in very modest circumstances, but we were all interested in each other's lives and our husbands' careers and interested in seeing the new members. It's good to get to know the wives of your husband's colleagues. We were all particularly interested in her because she was so young and pretty. I remember her big eyes. I felt, as I expect a lot of us felt, like here is a bird of beautiful plumage among all of us little gray wrens. She couldn't have been more gracious or nicer, but I was aware that my converted garage was mighty simple quarters for her.[6] [*Laughter.*] Afterwards—and I remember, this because it's unusual—I had a nice letter from her husband, just thanking me for inviting his wife to meet a lot of his colleagues' wives. You didn't any more expect a letter from him than a visitation from Mars, but I thought it was very gracious and nice.

Did she hold her own among the Senate wives?
Goodness, she was quiet, sort of demure. We all thought we were looking at a very lovely person. I think she went out of there with more friends than she came in [with]. I think many of us felt that she was different.

---

6. Jacqueline Kennedy's description of this event is in Jacqueline Kennedy Onassis Oral History Interview, 1/11/74, by Joe B. Frantz, 9–10.

LBJ'S SENATE STAFF

We were served by a great variety of people that were just at different poles. Every one of them converged on Lyndon's pathway and put something great and useful and good and happy-making into the pot. Nobody in my life meant more to me than Mary Rather. She was the godmother of Luci. She was one of those beautiful young women who went to work at an early age because her father and mother just didn't have enough means after she graduated from the university. She needed to go to work and she did. She was crazy about working, and she did it so competently. She worked for Senator Wirtz. From Senator Wirtz she passed to us, and she was a member of our family. She lived in our house a lot of the time. Our home in Washington had a third floor, which for many years was unfurnished except for a working bathroom and one or several beds for young people who were in the service passing through Washington or young members of our staff. Always tender, easy, gentle, and yet she would irritate Lyndon because it took her a long time to tell a tale, to recite the events on which he had to make a judgment. [*Laughter.*] And he'd try to hurry her, and she couldn't be hurried. That led to a lot of humor, and sometimes, I'm sure, he must have said things he shouldn't.

Mary Rather's brother and sister-in-law were killed in a tornado that went through Waco, Texas [in May 1953]. They were out on their first little celebration trip after the birth of a child six weeks earlier. They were riding some place. Their car was simply picked up and hurled and dashed around, and they both were killed on the spot. Mary flew down immediately, and the funeral was two or three days later. Lyndon went down to the funeral. She had already written us a sad note saying that she would have to leave working for us and stay there and tend to the children. She was always the one who kept the lists, knew all the *jefes* in every community and all of Lyndon's best friends. She wrote beautiful letters. She was close to us personally, socially, and in a business way; you could trust her with anything. It was just a great stab in the heart to lose her, but of course it was for something that you couldn't try to argue at all. As it turned out, she was to return to us a little later.

Lyndon had [George Reedy] as director of the Democratic Policy Committee, Pauline Moore [as clerk], Willie Day [Taylor], Dorothy Nichols, and Gerry Siegel. In fact, he just kind of moved his team around, and you could see that these two committees, Democratic Policy and the Steering Committee, were becoming his new engines to drive. And Arthur Perry, old, old friend from the Dodge Hotel days, a longtime Washington figure, secretary to two senators. When Tom Connally left the Senate, we inherited him happily. He took over the job of handling mail from constituents back home. He'd been in the [Internal Revenue Service] and with Senators Sheppard and Connally for many years. Woody [Warren Woodward] left us to go back to Dallas to go into partnership with Harding Lawrence in public relations.

My heart hurts when I think of Walter Jenkins.[7] Walter is one of the best human beings that I've ever known and so able and all of the good Christian virtues. Walter had lots of crosses to bear, known and unknown. He was such a plus point in our lives. There was a saying around the office that everything winds up on Walter's desk. That's right. If nobody else could handle it or would handle it, all the hard things finally wound up on Walter's desk.

Lyndon had a great deal of respect for George Reedy; he always spoke of him as one of the "whiz kids." George was real, real intellectual, book smart. Not as street smart as Lyndon needed and would have enjoyed. It's just a sad page in our lives, because Lyndon really loved him and respected him and was proud of him. Then, in the end, it was quite apparent that George resented and was angry and hurt by Lyndon. My feeling about why he ceased to be press secretary is because of his feet. His feet got so wretchedly uncomfortable, he had to have operations and stay off of them for a long time. A press secretary can't do that. And I guess it was the pain that drove him to drink too much. I don't mean that was a lifelong habit; it wasn't. I think it was a reaction to a bad physical problem.

Horace Busby, "Buzz," as we called him, was real intellectual, and I feel sad when I think of him too. Because he was so able and smart, but others in our life were more loveable. Nobody could turn a phrase better. He was a very skillful man with words and ideas and an awfully good friend. He was plagued by some physical problems such as overweight.

Grace Tully, who had been FDR's personally secretary, had befriended us in the early days from 1937 till FDR's death in the spring of 1945. She would always try to work it out for Lyndon to get an appointment if he wanted one with the president. She was a lovely person, and she was left somewhat bereft when FDR died because that had been her life. She stayed on with, I think, the [FDR] Library [foundation] as it was formed for a year or two. But by this time she was out of a job, and she needed something. Lyndon asked her to come with him, which she did for several years. She was a great fount of information, a great companion. We enjoyed her. She was our good friend until she really felt that she was getting old enough that she wanted to get out. We also hired Isabel Brown, the daughter of George Brown, who wanted to have a taste of Washington life.[8] She was as smart as she could be and a pleasure to have in our facility.

---

7. Walter Jenkins was arrested along with a sixty-two-year-old retired veteran at the Washington YMCA on a charge of public indecency. See Woods, *LBJ*, 550; Vicky McCammon Murphy Oral History Interview 2, 6/8/75, by Michael L. Gillette, 30–38; Recording of Telephone Conversation between Lyndon B. Johnson and Lady Bird Johnson, 10/15/64, 9:12 a.m., Citation 5895, Recordings and Transcripts of Conversations and Meetings, LBJ Library.

8. See Grace Tully, Oral History Interview, 10/1/68, by Joe B. Frantz, and Isabel Brown Wilson Oral History Interview, 2/19/88, by Michael L. Gillette. Brown served on the policy committee staff.

FIFTH YEAR CAMPAIGN

Congress adjourned early in August 1953, and Lyndon took out running to cover as much of the state as he could, looking forward to the next summer of 1954, when he would be up for reelection. He wanted to try to reinforce his position as firmly as he could from Amarillo to Brownsville and Texarkana to El Paso, so he wouldn't have to campaign so much in 1954. He got Jake Pickle to go over his schedule, and all of his cohorts were making dates for him for things as varied as the American Legion, the [American] GI Forum, the State Convention of Sheriffs, Old Settlers Reunion, the Texas Farm Bureau, and the Texas State Teachers Association. It seems there's an association for every profession and every sentimental thing. In that campaigning blitz from September to December of 1953, he made about two hundred speeches all over Texas. I didn't go with him a great deal.

One trip I took with him [in October 1953 gave] a fantastic view of Texas. We flew out to Snyder, where Mr. C. T. McLaughlin from the Diamond M Ranch gave a big luncheon for us. There was an oil well in the front yard practically; a very colorful part of the world. In the afternoon there was a party at the Snyder Country Club. All of the local honchos, elected officials, big ranchers, and everybody who was in charge of this and that were there. Mrs. McLaughlin hosted me for another big chamber of commerce affair that evening. C. T. McLaughlin was an unusual figure in our lives: oilman, wealthy man, businessman, highly respected, very successful, very pro-Johnson, good friend from beginning to end. Our life wasn't exactly filled with rich oilmen who loved us. C. T. has given us some choice reminders that speak of their friendship. The tureen that sits on the dining room table when I don't have fresh flowers is one of my favorite pieces forever. It looks like a piece of German work with cows and crops and scenes of agriculture on it.

In November of 1953, I actually got up and made a speech to the Texas Federation of Women's Clubs at their fifty-sixth annual convention in Austin. I was invited by Mrs. Ben Powell, [whose husband was in] the firm of Powell, Wirtz, Rauhut, and Gideon—great friends and standbys. Senator Wirtz, head man in that [firm] until his death in October, but the elderly statesman in that was Judge Ben Powell. Mrs. Powell was my idea of a duchess: tall, imposing, wonderful carriage, wonderful self-assurance, so knowledgeable, and yet she took notice of me, and she was very kind to me. I was duly respectful and regarded with considerable trepidation speaking to that group. But I lived through it.

Did President Johnson encourage you to develop public speaking skills?
Yes. He was always telling me I didn't sell for what I was worth, which I think is a very good phrase, but he meant mostly in terms of "You should dress up more and put your best foot forward in grooming and clothes." But he was also sure that I could speak with assurance if I worked hard enough on it.

I was forced out into the political arena a little bit more. My debut must certainly have been in 1948, but more and more, the office would take the liberty of saying, "If Lyndon can't come, we'll see if we can't get Lady Bird there" to such things as a party of a bunch of women's clubs in East Texas, a dedication of a reservoir or a dam somewhere. I was always glad to go, particularly if it concerned East Texas, because that got me a chance to see Daddy.

"THE LESS BLOOD SPILLED THE BETTER"

It was late the summer of 1954 that another one of the festering problems in the Senate came to a boil, and that was [Joseph] McCarthy. He was a very macho man and very masculine in a frightening way; handsome. McCarthy very inadvisably took a bite out of Sam Rayburn almost to the extent of questioning his patriotism. You didn't do that with Sam Rayburn without him being your enemy forever. Anybody that Speaker Sam Rayburn finally decided was a no-good so-and-so I could not come to like.[9] And McCarthy said—I cannot quote him, but the implication was very strong that General George Marshall was a traitor.[10] From then on, there wasn't anything that he could have said that would have ever washed that out. So that was sort of the gospel for me too, because George Marshall was just a man in whose integrity I had 100 percent confidence in, and that was a widely-shared view. President Eisenhower seldom did anything that you could get really mad at, but he did not repudiate McCarthy when he said that. He did not come to Marshall's aid, and I felt that he should have.[11] I just remember the hot flare of indignation of a lot of folks, including me.

Knowland as majority leader and Lyndon as minority leader had to put together a select committee to investigate Senator McCarthy. I don't think Lyndon ever did anything with greater care and caution and, would I daresay, plotting. He was very determined to get "work horses, not show horses," as he would have expressed it; senators whose reputation was impeccable and whose word would be taken by the Senate without any consideration. No one wanted to be on [the committee], but he just appealed to their patriotism and love of the Senate, mainly. [The Republicans were] Arthur Watkins [of Utah], Frank Carlson [of Kansas], and Francis Case [of New Jersey]. [Lyndon's choices were] "Big Ed" Johnson [of Colorado], John Stennis [of Mississippi], and Sam Ervin [of North Carolina]. Sam Ervin was a great constitutional lawyer.

---

9. McCarthy accused the Democratic Party of "twenty years of treason." D. B. Hardeman and Donald C. Bacon, *Rayburn: A Biography* (Austin: Texas Monthly Press, 1987), 381.

10. For McCarthy's speech condemning Marshall, see *Congressional Record*, 82nd Cong., 1st sess., June 14, 1951, 6556–6603.

11. It became known that Ike's planned defense of Marshall was removed from his speech. Emmet J. Hughes, *The Ordeal of Power: A Political Memoir of the Eisenhower Years* (New York: Atheneum, 1963), 41–42.

There's been some suggestion that LBJ, in addition to naming the Democrats, may have even given Knowland some advice on the Republicans.

I think that is true, and I'm sure in the most courteous and respectful way. He managed it, because it's my belief that he thought we had to get rid of this man, but without making a sideshow of it. The less blood spilled the better.

These hearings were quite lengthy. They went on from late in the summer until the final vote in December. The Watkins Committee did [recommend that the Senate] censure McCarthy. Every last [Democratic senator] voted to censure McCarthy,[12] whereas the Republicans [were] half and half. That pretty much put an end to his career, and it did it with less bloodshed than might have happened. Lyndon's hand was very adroit in that, although he didn't do it with a light heart, because he did not like to see any fellow senator broken, which is really what he did to him. But Lyndon thought what [McCarthy] was doing to the Senate couldn't be tolerated. Senator McCarthy was already a man who drank, but who had fairly recently acquired a handsome, nice wife. Lots of people hoped that that would change his life greatly. I think it came along too late, perhaps.

LBJ's speech emphasized that McCarthy's behavior had harmed the prestige of the Senate.

Yes, it had indeed. It had denigrated it. Lyndon really liked that system of government and the body of the Senate, which he thought was the greatest deliberative body in the world. The fifties were more or less a good time in the Senate. [There] were rough spots, but generally a good time.

PRIORITIES

As I look back upon those years, I get a lot of black marks. I'm a little bit too plump, which doesn't speak well for me. I should have put those children on a diet and been a more determined mother, or else I should have gone to every last one of those speeches and towns [on] the map of Texas. Instead, I just tried to do both things, straddling between going with Lyndon and staying with the children and not doing a very good job of either, which is intensified as I look in a picture album and notice that the big family living room still had makeshift furniture in it. I don't how long it took me to get that room properly furnished nor how Lyndon managed to be patient that long, because patience was not his long suit. But one divides the hours of one's life as best we can.

---

12. John F. Kennedy did not vote on the censure. Robert A. Dallek, *An Unfinished Life: John F. Kennedy, 1917–1963* (Boston: Little, Brown, 2003), 189–91.

My 1954 date book lists repeated visits to Dr. Radford Brown all the way from early February through the end of March, and then one the sixth of April that was scratched through. That must have been the spring that I now remember through the mists of time as being the last of about four miscarriages.

Lynda acquired an illness that was hard to diagnose. I think it was in the late summer, perhaps August, September. The actual symptoms were exceeding lethargy and spasmodic, uncontrollable movements, jerking. It really was a most concerning matter. Our doctor there in Austin just could not handle it. We must have made eight or ten trips to Scott & White. But we got on the trail of it, and adversity can sometimes be looked back on with a warm feeling. That is, if you win, and we did win. Because Lynda Bird and I were together so much when we were shut up in the car. It was fully a three-hour drive. We'd sing a popular song called "This Old House." We would just rattle it off together. She had a pretty good voice. I had a horrible voice, which did not deter me a little bit. We would stop at the Stagecoach Inn [in Salado] and have lunch going or dinner returning.

Of course, I was very worried, and Lyndon was somewhat impatient and made me mad because he wasn't as understanding as he ought to have been with something that doctors couldn't get to the bottom of. It was just strange. I think it left a lasting mark on Lynda in that her handwriting is still very bad from those involuntary, spasmodic movements.

The doctors said she just mustn't go to school. She must not be subjected to any stress. So she didn't go to school in September or October. I think finally in November they had her start half-time at St. Andrew's, a little Episcopal school where they would recognize her difficulty and give her special care and attention. By Christmastime she was quite all right again, and it was just all an episode in the past.

That was the sealing of the close relationship with Willie Day Taylor, because when I couldn't be with Lynda, Willie Day would. Willie Day would take over even in Texas for a while, for instance when we went back up [to Washington] for the last of the McCarthy episode. She was on Lyndon's staff. She had been married years earlier and divorced. She loved children and was good with children. She particularly loved these two children and bossed them. And they needed both love and bossing.

We saw almost none of Lyndon that fall [of 1954] because he was covering ten or twelve or more western states for senators who were up for reelection, which in a way made it easier for me to have all those trips to Scott & White with Lynda Bird.

So you didn't go on any of those western trips?
No, not a one of them, and I feel that I missed a lot, but I had a lot. In that particular fall, it was very clear the important thing was to be with Lynda.

THE MAJORITY LEADER

1955 was a very important year for us. When the Senate convened in January, Lyndon was elected majority leader by a very narrow count. There were forty-eight Democrats and forty-seven Republicans and Wayne Morse. Morse voted with the Democrats to organize the Senate. Wayne Morse was the burr under the saddle of countless people, leaders and presidents. Lyndon always chafed as much as anybody else under his recalcitrance, but he also respected him and liked him. The majority leadership was to us a stepping stone beyond all others. Lyndon and Speaker Sam Rayburn were good folks to have at the helm in a time when their philosophy was that the opposition party is not supposed to just oppose. It took a lot of skill to manipulate those waters, and those two gentlemen really had it.

When LBJ was elected, were you proud of him?
Oh yes, I thought that was great recognition. I was proud of him. I do not think people really understood the awe with which Lyndon regarded that job and later regarded the presidency. I also felt [he had] a sense, "Am I up to this? Can I do it? Well, I'm sure going to give it the best try anybody ever did." His ego, which certainly did exist, just did not believe he was the smartest fellow in the world who could handle easily all those things. He just thought he'd have to work twice as hard as the next fellow to competently conduct it.

Lyndon had an absolutely marvelous majority leadership office, which I had a hand in decorating by the simple matter of going down into the bowels of that vast building, the Capitol, along with a decorator who had worked for me at my little ordinary house, and finding some old discarded, handsome things of another era, andirons and fire tools. One, for instance, was a really handsome brass fender to go around a fireplace. It could be shined up with great effort to be quite beautiful. There was a fireplace in this marvelous office. We asked if it were possible and safe to use the fireplace and got the word yes. It was just too much trouble; nobody had done it in years and years. So I said, "Let's just on occasion do it when we have a social gathering there. You stay down there so late. You do have people drop over for drinks and serious conversation. It would be nice if Zephyr would bring down some good little nibbles and we could have a fire." My decorator found a few handsome pieces here and there. And it gave that office the look of distinction.

The year 1955 was just full of forerunners of physical troubles. Among his many problems was this business of having to wear a brace on his back because of a disk problem. He was unusually tall from the hips up, and this just was one of the things that plagued him. In January we took the train Mayo to have some kidney stone tests. Lyndon and I thought we'd live it up, so we got a bedroom on the train. We sat there and looked at each other in opposite seats, and we said, "We ought to celebrate." So what we both did was order a glass of milk.

Lyndon was fighting overweight and fighting having three or four drinks at the end of the day, because of the stress of the day, and I was always fighting overweight. But nevertheless our favorite drink was milk, so we decided that we'd just sit there and have a glass of milk and look out the window.

Was it ever determined what caused his kidney stones?
No, no. If medical science knows, I don't, and I don't think they do. They told him to omit a few things from his diet, actually things that he never ate anyways. Something about the chemical makeup of the body which I don't understand and I doubt they did.

It was something that plagued him in his early life, but I don't think it bothered him from the presidency on through until he died, did it?
I don't believe so. It seems like the Lord "tempered the wind to the shorn lamb" in those days, and we had generally pretty good health.

At Mayo we did have some work on kidney stones, and it was a full-scale operation, I guess, because it was in a certain spot. In 1948 they had been able to reach in with forceps and crush it, but that all depends on where the kidney stone is lodged. It took us a long time to get out of Mayo. When we left Mayo, we went to the ranch to recuperate, and that is when they [ratified] the SEATO Treaty, which is always one of the odd little footnotes of history.[13]

There was one little, tiny bit of finding the world of travel and recreation. Lyndon had lived a life of work, work, work, with which I had gone along, big eyed and enthusiastic. But early that year we went to Florida with Tony Buford[14] and August Busch, and Earle Clements. It seems to me that Senator Smathers of Florida was a moving figure in that trip. That was the time that we met Bebe Rebozo, the great friend of Nixon, whom we liked. I believe it was the time when A. W. Moursund came over and joined us and looked at us like we were idiots because we wanted to sit out in the sun and get a suntan. That is what A. W. had been avoiding all his life out riding for cattle. Finally, he did consent to sit on the top step of the beach house with his hat pulled down over his face the best he could, us all laughing.

1955 was also the year that we took almost the one and only vacation my children can remember taking with their father. We went to Daytona Beach with a bunch of congressmen. They had something called the congressional baseball teams, which were largely figments of the imagination. But they went down for "spring training" to Daytona Beach. Daytona is one the most beautiful beaches in the world, and we really just lived it up, and the children just remembered

---

13. The Southeast Asia Collective Defense Treaty created the Southeast Asia Treaty Organization, which would provide the justification for the U.S. intervention in Vietnam.
14. Buford was the Washington representative of Anheuser Busch; August Busch was the CEO.

that. You'd be surprised how important it was to them to be with their father on a vacation. You rent some sort of a beach car that was low to the ground and that any number of folks in bathing suits could sit in, cling to, manage to stay on top of, and we did that. It was very much of a family time and a laughing time and something that we obviously should have done more of, since it meant so much to the children.

"EMBATTLED AGAINST DEATH"

The date was July 2, Luci's eighth birthday. She was, of course, going to have a party. And who puts on the party? Mama. Lyndon was going down to George Brown's place called Huntland [near] Middleburg, Virginia, which was our paradise. We adored getting to go to Huntland. It was an old–Civil War, red brick house way out in the country. It was well staffed, casual nevertheless, had a swimming pool, beautiful gardens.[15] The Browns lived there for a few days, weekends, maybe at the utmost sometimes for a week. They used it as a retreat for themselves and their friends and made it available to us at times. Lyndon went down there with George and a bunch of their special friends. I stayed at home to put on the party, which always included about ten or twelve little girls and boys.

When the party was close to over, I got a call from Middleburg from a member of George's family—it may have been George himself—saying that Lyndon was sick. The local doctor had been called. He said it looked like a heart attack. He wanted him to go into Bethesda immediately. They had called an ambulance. Lyndon was in it and en route to Bethesda, and I should go out there and be prepared to meet him. So I went out and met the doctors, arriving in a pretty good state of ignorance. I was told to stand close to a certain entrance. They were in touch, by what I don't know, but they knew that he would arrive in X number of minutes.[16]

A doctor, who had been in the [Army Medical Corps] and who had lacked a number of months [to fulfill his service obligation] when the war was over, had been called back to duty to finish that time at Bethesda Naval Hospital. He was a heart specialist; his name was Willis Hurst.[17] There was also a young doctor on duty who Lyndon always called "the little doctor."

---

15. For additional information about Huntland, see the oral history of Isabel Brown Wilson, who happened to be there when LBJ suffered his heart attack. Isabel Brown Wilson Oral History Interview, 2/19/88. by Michael L. Gillette.

16. Frank "Posh" Oltorf and Dr. James Gibson rode in the ambulance, which doubled as a hearse. Frank Oltorf Oral History Interview, 8/3/71, by David McComb.

17. Oltorf and J. Willis Hurst indicated that several LBJ staff members, including Walter Jenkins and George Reedy, were also present at the hospital. J. Willis Hurst Oral History Interview 1, 5/16/69, by T. Harrison Baker; and 3, 11/8/82, by Michael L. Gillette.

We stood by this entrance, and all of a sudden the rear doors of the ambulance opened. Lyndon on a stretcher was brought in. I looked at him; he looked just like himself. I was enormously relieved. I don't know what I expected. The doctor was bending over him, taking vital signs. Then in a minute, two and three [doctors] and a [then] whole clutch of doctors were bending over working on him.

The first thing they said, "Senator, you are going to have to give up cigarettes." And he said, "I've got to?" The doctor said, "Yes, absolutely." And he said, "Well, give me one more."[18] And the expression on his face as he smoked that cigarette was really quite marvelous, because it was the ultimate enjoyment and drawing out of the pleasure into lengthening moments. He did not have another cigarette for about sixteen years. He reached in his pocket and handed me his billfold. I think he also told me where his will was. Then the doctor looked up at me and said, "I must tell you he may go into shock any moment." I had never seen anybody in shock. I thought, "He looks just like himself." Then he began to go into shock and became as gray as the cement sidewalk; my first experience with anybody in shock. I was horrified. He was no longer Lyndon. He passed the cigarette over. I cannot tell you whether he was conscious or not, but it was a totally different person.

Meanwhile, there are more and more doctors doing more and more things. They put him on a big trolley and wheeled him into the intensive care unit and told me I could wait right outside the door.

From the first moment I became acquainted with Willis Hurst, I just had a hand-in-hand feeling for him, and it was a great gift from the Lord that he happened to be in that place at that time. He had trained under Dr. Paul [Dudley] White, a cardiologist at the top of his field. I learned later that Willis had been one of his favorite students. He is a Georgia man. As soon as they had put all the tubes in Lyndon that they could and done everything that they could in that state of the art to stabilize him, Willis came and talked to me. He said, "Your husband is a very sick man. I have seen men who are sicker than he is get well, and I have seen men as sick as he is die. All that I can tell you is that every hour, every day that he responds to treatment and that he lives is a victory. And the first twenty-four hours is the biggest victory." I said, "I am going to be right here."

I asked them where could I spend the night, and they showed me to a room close by. I called home to let Zephyr and Luci and Lynda, if she was there, know that I would not be home, that Daddy really was very sick; so for them to just send up prayers and love, and not to worry any more than they could, because

---

18. Oltorf's recollection of LBJ's response to ban on smoking from the doctor in the ambulance is more colorful: "I'd rather have my pecker cut off." Frank Oltorf Oral History Interview, 8/3/71, by David McComb.

they just had a wonderful bunch of people working on him. I called his mother. I made such staff calls as I thought should be done. In the few seconds between his arrival and going into shock, he had told me who to call. He was a very in-charge, forethoughtful man even in that situation.

I felt embattled against death and absolutely enraged that it could dare to overtake me and my husband. He was forty-six; I was forty-two. My thought was, "We are not through yet; we've got things to do. We've got each other. This can't be. We're going to oppose strength to strength and beat it." I think that is a universal reaction.

Do you think the girls were ever conscious of the severity of the situation? They were pretty young.
Eight and eleven. Lynda must have been; Luci, probably. I'm sorry to say I may not have helped them enough; I may have kept them more in the dark. The simple fact is that I did not leave the hospital for any length of time. I did call them on the telephone and talk to them every day. I got Willie Day Taylor, God bless her; she was already my great reliance with the children.

So the gist of it was that he stayed in the hospital about six weeks, which was the current practice for anybody with that serious a heart infarction.

And you were there through most of that time.
Yes. I went home to get a nightgown and makeup. After he began to get better, he began to want better food. As soon as food was acceptable for him to eat, Zephyr and I went to work, providing him with all of his favorite things within the limits of what he could have. So I was a kind of a taxi service between home and the hospital.

The phone calls we [received] were so very wonderful; important, loving calls, jillions of them. Then this poor little tailor called, just wondering if he was going to be fixing up about five hundred dollars' worth of suits for a dying man. Lyndon had gone to the tailor two or three days before and had bought a dark blue suit and another suit. It must have taken a considerable amount of nerve, but the tailor called me and said, "Mrs. Johnson, did you want me to proceed with those suits?" I said, "I'll have to get back to you." This must have been about the third or fourth day. I wouldn't have done it the first twenty-four hours or the first forty-eight. But every day Willis would tell me with a mounting beaming smile, "Every day is a victory. Every day that he lives and is improving means that he is going to come back all right." So about the third or fourth day I repeated the poor little tailor's question. Lyndon smiled sardonically, "Tell him to go ahead with the navy blue one anyway. Whatever way it goes, we'll need that one." [*Laughter.*]

When the Senator's mother came, he was still in the hospital at that time?
Oh, you bet. And her first plane flight, I think. Their closeness was a very strong bond indeed, because not only was he her first child, but he was also her reli-

ance. He was the strength in her life. He was the one who helped take care of all the rest of them. It was just like his death would have been just an incalculable loss to her.

We reached home from the hospital on August 25, two days before Lyndon's birthday.[19] He set a childlike importance by his birthday. I think we came in Wesley West's plane and landed at Fredericksburg. From then on, life was a roller coaster of gloom and depression or else elation. As Lyndon began to recover from his heart attack, his whole thought was concentrated not on possibly being a candidate for the president but whether he would be strong enough to resume duties as a majority leader. Was he up to that? Could he take it on? Or should he resign?

Periods of depression go with heart attacks; it is absolutely a clinical response. All that fall Lyndon was not immune. His face was very drawn. He was down a good deal of the time. I remember sitting there in the living room one of the few times that we were alone, just looking at him. His face was just a picture of gloom, and my thoughts went to a cabinet off of the kitchen where there were about six deer-hunting guns. But it was a deep gloom.

During that time dear [Dr.] Jim Cain[20] came down from Mayo to see us at the ranch, and Willis Hurst came from Atlanta and laid out a routine for us.[21] They were two of the best friends that anybody ever had. How fortunate we were to have them in our lives. On doctors' orders, Lyndon lost lots of weight. When he went into it, he went into it hammer and tongs. Juanita Roberts had been a nutritionist in her first career. She knew an awful lot about fat and calorie counting. She got us a scale for the kitchen at the ranch, and we used that all the time. We did an awful lot of substitution. We gave him desserts, which he simply just yearned for, made out of egg whites and artificial sugar, which was pretty new then, and mashed up frappé fruit. He ate more vegetables than he'd ever done before. We learned to broil a roast. I learned what Juanita had already mastered, the art of a varied and fairly interesting but very low-fat, low-calorie diet. It really denied him almost everything that he really liked, which was something heavily sweet or juicily fried. But he just attacked his overweight like it was an enemy, and he did lose, lose, lose. Unfortunately, a lot of it was in the face, and that became drawn. When you lose a lot of weight very quickly, it leaves your face gaunt and older-looking and far from the buoyant image of health that you want to project. He did fill it out. He did get a suntan. He did look much more fit by the time he was back in Washington.

---

19. For a detailed account of LBJ's recuperation at the LBJ Ranch, see Mary Rather Oral History Interview 1, 12/10/74, by Michael L. Gillette.

20. Cain was Alvin Wirtz's son-in-law.

21. James Cain Oral History Interview, 2/22/70, by David McComb; Hurst Oral History Interview 3, 11/8/82. by Michael L. Gillette, 8–9.

It was a period of ups and downs. A part of him realized that life is so temporary that you had better start doing some of the things you'd put off, the pleasures of family life, the pleasures of comforts, even luxuries. That's when he decided to put in a swimming pool, and we put in that swimming pool in jig time in the fall. As he was recovering, he had just a necessity to be building a fence, digging a tank, building a house. He couldn't stand inactivity. He decided to build a guest house, so we did. It was very functional: four bedrooms, two bathroom, combination kitchen and dinette.

1955 was a crescendo year in our lives. There was a lot of love and interest and concern expressed for Lyndon by his fellow senators and by a lot of people. That would have been the most important of all, to have his fellow senators express their feeling. He even had a wonderful letter from Bernard Baruch and letters from a cast of characters you wouldn't believe during that heart attack and the long recuperation.

16

"Toward the Liberal Side," 1956–1959

LBJ's 1954 reelection gave him a six-year cushion before facing Texas voters again. His battle with Governor Allan Shivers for control of the state's Democratic Party machinery in 1956 provided additional political leverage. In an uneasy alliance with the liberal-labor faction, LBJ mobilized his grassroots organization of county and district men to defeat Shivers's forces at the precinct and county conventions. Johnson now had greater latitude to chart a course as a national Democrat. His refusal to sign the Southern Manifesto criticizing the Supreme Court's Brown v. Board of Education *decision marked the turning point in his embrace of civil rights measures.*

The 1958 congressional elections increased the Democratic majority in the Senate from a margin of two to fifteen, but unifying this large divergent majority proved challenging. In his last two years as Democratic leader, he faced mounting criticism from both the left and the right. No wonder Lady Bird Johnson preferred 1956 and 1957 to the two years that followed. Realism tempered the presidential ambition of both husband and wife. For once, her reluctance equaled LBJ's. Yet she prepared herself for the inevitable campaign by taking a public speaking course.

There were several strands running through our lives in the end of 1955 and in the years 1956 and 1957. One was the strong sense of how good it is to be alive. There's nothing to increase the hot rush of pleasure in living like a close brush with death, which Lyndon certainly had experienced. The other force was the battle in Texas between the liberal and conservative forces, neither one of which Lyndon thoroughly satisfied, because he was on the path to a more liberal attitude, particularly toward civil rights. There was a great outpouring of affection and of comradeship for Lyndon when he returned to the Senate in January 1956. I breathed a sigh of relief because I thought he was good for the Democratic leadership and he would be failing to take the jump if he didn't [continue].

1956 was a year of mounting confrontation, with [Governor Allan] Shivers having come out for Eisenhower, as he was heading all along and we felt he would, and

Lyndon going to be nominated as favorite son. We had a real head-on collision with Shivers, which was painful and wrenching to us and possibly to him, but which was inevitable considering the digression of their philosophies. It had an ugly side to it. Texas is a very conservative state. It is an odd thing that Lyndon not only survived but prospered so long in representing Texas. The happenstance that he was about six feet four and looked like people's idea of a Texan had something to do with it. And folks would say, "Oh, Lyndon, I don't go along with a lot of his ideas, but he sure does love Texas." And for that they forgave him much. Both Lyndon and I got some bad telephone calls. It was unsettling and unpleasant, but you can't die but once.

In March, Senator Johnson announced that he had not yet made a decision to go to the convention as a favorite-son candidate. He was quoted in the paper as saying, "The response from Texas on this has been almost entirely favorable. The response from Lady Bird has been much less enthusiastic."
I never thought I could really affect it, and I was not against it. It is just that I didn't want it to go any further. I didn't want him to be a candidate for president or set his heart on it or get too bound up in it. But lots and lots of states have favorite sons. They don't necessarily get very far.

In those years there were meetings of the district men representing the different state's senatorial districts. We had a good man in nearly every area except some West Texas areas, where we were without support. So they would all come to the ranch, and we would sit around under those oak trees and go from one to the next: What's the condition of your district? What have I done that is good for them or that makes them mad? What are your problems? It was a good way to keep your finger on the pulse of the state.

Did you enjoy that kind of political talk?
I certainly didn't walk out on any of the sessions. I sat at the edge and listened and took it all in and enjoyed it. I had my own judgments. I mostly went along with—there were occasions in our lives in which I had very strong opinions and voiced them. But I was a soldier in the ranks mostly.

One time when those district men were there, a terrific rain storm came up and the river rose. At first it was mostly a matter of laughter—if the river rises then we are all caught here. Have we got enough beds? I was busy counting all the beds in the house and in the guest house. We had three houses in which we could have put people. What you need most in a situation like that is an unlimited amount of coffee and drinks and at least a ham and a good deal of meat. You can always get vegetables and things out of the deep freeze. Just thinking that you were at the mercy of the weather was really an exciting thing. Lyndon would call the Department of Public Safety or the Highway Department who had their eyes on all the roads, whether you could cross or not, bridges. We finally got word that "you are going to have to get out of there by five o'clock, or you may not be able to get out of there for the next twenty-four hours." I think some stayed; most went. But it made for a funny, exciting, kind of frontier-like meeting.

THE 1956 PRESIDENTIAL CAMPAIGN

The first national convention I ever went to was in 1956. It was so crowded, so confusing, so much running to and fro. Conventions I could do without forever, and I pretty nearly did. It's amazing that anything purposeful and wise ever comes out of them. I just did not like the atmosphere then or ever. Small points that I remember about this one: we had a box in which I sat with Mrs. Sam Johnson, Lyndon's mother; Lyndon was up on the stage most of the time. There was an awful lot of conferring. People were always in and out, in and out. I remember coming to our hotel room terribly late one night. Lyndon was not with me. Somebody else was with me, though, because you just didn't want to walk around in that place by yourself. And there, sound asleep across the threshold of the door, was a newspaperman who had been trying to get to Lyndon all day long. [*Laughter.*] This person accompanying me leaned over, unlocked the door, and shoved it open. I stepped over him gingerly, and we shut the door. [*Laughter.*]

We had a slogan, "We love Lyndon," that was—naturally, red, white, and blue—all over everything, and stickers. In a way it was the nicest convention I was every around in terms of people who cared about you without any ifs, ands, or buts, and great enthusiasm and youth. Not us so much, because he was forty-eight years old by that time. You'd hardly call him young, but he had a whole lot of young supporters. Across the board we had a great sampling of Texas.

For all of my disclaimers that I didn't want him to get the nomination, I took pride in the fact that he did get 186 votes. I remember that flashing up on the big screen in there. It was a smashing victory for Adlai Stevenson, who got over 900, and Harriman got 210.

Lyndon was not interested in the vice presidential nomination. I don't think there would have ever been a chance of Governor Stevenson wanting him to take it. So we went home, but not until Lyndon had joined Rayburn in persuading the Texas delegates to vote for JFK for vice president. But Estes Kefauver won it, and on the western edge of the country in San Francisco, Eisenhower and [Richard] Nixon were nominated easily by unanimous vote.

I remember when Estes Kefauver was coming to Texas. Lyndon would meet him at the town, and he would tell him three or four capsules about what the people there did for a living, what the main industry or makeup of the area was, what degree of conservatism, what they were like. He was going to be in Waxahachie, and he says, "Now this is a word that would give nearly anybody trouble, Waxahachie (pronounced WOX-uh-HACH-ee). Why don't you say it a couple of times?" Estes did, and then he was supposed to go make his speech some hours later. This little briefing session would occur earlier in the day, [because there were] as many as thirteen speeches a day for candidates in those days; a rough life. It was nighttime; they were both bone tired. Lyndon introduced him at Waxahachie. Estes got up and said, "I am so glad to be here in

Waxahachie [pronounced WAX-uh-HACH-ee]. Oh, I'm sorry. I meant say Woxahootchie." [*Laughter.*] And the crowd would just roar with laughter, and Estes was delighted with it. He would drag it out and mispronounce it every which way you could. The people and the press were all equally amused. He was a likeable man, but he was a meteor that flashed across the sky and burned out. He had great personality and great rapport with the press and people. Yet he didn't have long-term staying powers. Too bad.

He had a reputation as being a great womanizer. Is that something that was common knowledge at the time?
Well, I don't know from personal experience. I don't think he found me all that delicious a morsel, certainly. Besides, he had a darling wife, Nancy. She made one of the acute observations about being a political wife. When you first wake up in the morning of a two-week campaign trip around the United States, you don't know where you are, what state, what town. That's the way it happens.

There was a comfortable quality about the 1950s, and Eisenhower contributed to that. It was just a very wide trust and affection across the country for him. A whole flock of senators came to Texas campaigning for Stevenson. [But] it was 1956, and Texas was not going to be for Stevenson. They didn't make much of a dent, but we hosted them; Lyndon introduced them, Lyndon traveled with them, Lyndon worked for Stevenson himself.

A TIME OF HIGH ELATION

Toward the end of November of 1956 came something that was very, very important to me. All these years I'd been hearing these marvelous stories from fellow wives of senators and congressmen who would go on trips to Europe, to far away places with strange-sounding names. I was a natural-born adventurer and traveler in books and in desires, but really never having gone anywhere outside the boundaries of this country except to Mexico. I got my first trip in mid-November after the election of 1956. Lyndon decided that you must grab the day as it passes and wrench from it all the pleasure that you can, not just all the hours of work. He took me to Europe the next year, and that was certainly a result of his change in philosophy caused by the heart attack in 1955. It was a very dear thing for him to do for me, because I don't think he was enormously interested in this NATO Parliamentary Conference.

I had twenty-four or forty-eight hours' notice that we were going on this trip to France. I was trying to get the [Scharnhorst] hunting lodge ready for hunting season, which was just upon us. It just had to be postponed for about a week or so while we went over to Paris. But youth is absolutely wonderful. I didn't know the meaning of the word tired. So I got ready [for the trip] with no trouble, and I got the last details in getting the house ready for hunting season pretty much done, too.

[I remember] the high elation of thinking, "Oh, I'm going to get to go." Senator Dick Russell was going and several more senators, but Dick Russell teamed up with us.[1] In Paris the men would work at their conference in the daytime. Eloise [Thornberry] and I would do things like go to the flea market. I have a brass bed warmer with an elaborate design of holes that was used in some French household and now just stands as a decoration by the fireplace at the ranch house. We both bought some things that were very difficult to carry home. We went on a military plane, as did everybody else in those days. We had the most wonderful military escort, an attractive man that Eloise and I were crazy about.[2] He was equal to every demand. Later on he became the commander of the forces in Omaha; that's the "get there quick with the bomb" unit.

Night was a big time because the men would come home and take us to some fabulous place. They took us to one naughty place where the menus were something we took home and framed and put up in the bathroom of the hunting lodge on the Scharnhorst ranch. We went to the Folies Bergère, where probably all Americans went. I even got to use the little bit of French that I could remember from Mademoiselle's teaching us at Saint Mary's from 1928 to 1930. One night we went to Maxim's, which was at that time the place for food. I still have a picture that includes Dick Russell and is therefore treasured by me. He said, "When you are visiting a different country, eat the favorite food of that country; drink the wine of that country. Don't try to duplicate whatever you are used to at home." Good advice; both my stomach and my daring could stand it at that time. Yet I find it interesting coming from him, quintessential Georgian that he was. He was a marvelous companion. He always knew so much history—more national than international—but a good deal on that side, too. His conversation would be filled with interesting vignettes.

It was cold. [The Suez Canal crisis] had angered the Egyptians, and the Arabs had disrupted the oil flow.[3] Not enough oil was not arriving in Paris to keep the hotel rooms warm. Once more, we were young, and we could just pile on another blanket on the bed and put on a coat, and we got along all right. But I remember how very gray it was and how dirty the city was, alas, in the year 1956, and graffiti, usually slogans, sometimes rather amazing slogans.

It was a thoroughly delightful time, and when the conference ended, Lyndon really went the extra mile by renting a van. Our marvelous military escort was

1. The U.S. delegation consisted of eight senators, including Theodore Francis Green and J. William Fulbright, and eight House members, including Eugene McCarthy and Homer Thornberry.

2. The military escort, William Reynolds, described the NATO trip in his oral history. William Reynolds Oral History Interview, 6/16/75, by Michael L. Gillette, 10–18.

3. Egypt's Gamal Abdel Nasser had seized control of the canal after the United States withdrew its offer of aid in the construction of the Aswan Dam. Woods, *LBJ*, 323–24.

tapped to drive it. We went down to the south of France, seeing the countryside go by. It was quite a long trip. We laughed all the way and saw a good deal. We went to Cannes [and] Nice. We may have even gone to Monaco, in which case the men would have gambled and we would not have.[4]

It was a time of high elation, and high excitement, and I loved every minute of it. I particularly loved flying in that plane over the great cities of the world and seeing all the lights of London and Paris. There were still scars from the war. Particularly in Paris, it looked like no shutter had been painted in twenty years. No building had been cleaned in that long. It looked pretty shabby. But it had romance. It had all the allure that you've always read about in books and all the glittering things you've imagined.

Was LBJ a good traveling companion on occasions like that?
Yes. At least sometimes he was. And he really gave himself up to this, because all politics were over for the moment, and his job was there waiting for him when he returned in January.

CIVIL RIGHTS AND THE ART OF THE POSSIBLE

When the Supreme Court, by a 9-0 decision in *Brown v. Board of Education*, said that separate educational facilities are inherently unequal and that enforced racial segregation of public education is a denial of the equal protection of the law guaranteed by the Fourteenth Amendment, that sounded the clarion call for a lot that was to happen in the succeeding ten to twenty years.

The Southern Manifesto was a sharp dividing line and a big controversy when [it] was signed by a great many Southern senators and congressman in 1956. It was criticizing the Supreme Court's desegregation decision and pledging to overturn it by lawful means. Lyndon and Sam Rayburn both refused to sign it, and they both caught a lot of flak on account of it. The Speaker had a wonderful ability to let it roll off of him like water off a duck's back. Lyndon, who represented the whole state and not one wonderful highly personal, highly devoted district that Mr. Sam had, found it more difficult, but he wasn't about to give in on it.

How did President Johnson react to the Brown *decision?*
Lyndon underwent a vast change. I cannot say exactly when it began. I think maybe he knew mid-1950s; I'm not sure. I know about 1957 it was well underway that he knew that we had to overcome segregation. We had to accept the blacks in law and education and the economy, and this was a growth process with him. It was no sudden strike of lightning.

---

4. According to the NATO trip file and Reynolds's oral history, the group did go to Cannes, Nice, and Monaco. "Treaties—NATO—2nd NATO Parliamentary Conf., 1956," LBJA Subject Files, Box 121.

There are some, Mrs. Johnson, who believe that he always felt this way, but only after the mid-1950s did he see the opportunity to really make it—

Well, that is true, too, because he was telling Virginia Durr for years and years and years, "Virginia, I'll vote for you on getting rid of the poll tax, but I'll do it when we've got the votes, when I can make it stick." The minute Lyndon came into the room, Virginia would beard him on the question of poll tax legislation, which she was dedicated to putting an end to. I'm sure he thought he would do it when it would not cost him his Senate seat or his House seat. He believed that if you've got the ballot, you've got your future in your own hands at least to some extent. He believed in [blacks] having the ballot at an early time and worked to put that into [effect]—when he finally got in a position to exert power. It was a long, long process and was very much a part of "politics is the art of the possible."

When you serve a constituency as a member of Congress, it's a combination of expressing their philosophy and trying to achieve their needs, and at the same time trying to lead, to direct. Now you can't drive them. Perhaps you can persuade, but you grow up in the philosophy of those around you. If you don't express it, you soon get booted out of office. For example, quite a few years before, the first minimum wage bill was passed, which was the lordly sum of twenty-five cents an hour. There were three daring [Texas] members of Congress who voted for it: Maury Maverick of San Antonio, [William McFarlane of Graham], and Lyndon Johnson of Blanco.[5] Both of the other two were defeated in the next election. Texas is not a liberal place. Texas would not be for most liberal stands. When *Brown v. Board of Education* was passed, Lyndon did not get up on the stump and go around beating the drums for it. I don't know his innermost feelings. I expect he had a sense of unease about segregation because of his experience in Cotulla as a youth. He had seen that it was a crippling thing in relation to the Latin Americans, who were also subjected to segregation in his school-teaching days.

During the days of the NYA, Lyndon was very insistent that the benefits of the NYA be used equitably among the young folks, black and white, that were out of jobs and in need.[6] At that time, he became a friend and ally of the heads of several black schools, particularly Prairie View and one or both of those in Marshall, and those presidents remained his friends and advisers. They were canny, sage men for the most part and knew how far a congressman could go or, in those

5. On December 17, 1937, the House voted to recommit the Fair Labor Standards legislation to the Labor Committee. In addition to McFarlane, Maverick, and LBJ, Marvin Jones, Sam Rayburn, Albert Thomas, and Ewing Thomason also voted against recommittal. 82 Cong. Rec., part 2, 1835 (1937).

6. An analysis of the inequity of NYA funding for black colleges appears in Caro, *Master of the Senate*, 731–32. For a significant exchange between LBJ and Gov. James Allred on the issue of equity for black colleges, see Horace W. Busby Oral History Interview 5, 8/16/88, by Michael L. Gillette, 2–4.

instances, how far the director of a federal agency could go. They pushed for everything they could get, and they were not angry and did not exert vengeance for things he couldn't get. He stood well with the college presidents.

I remember one incident in Somerville, Texas, when he went to make an outdoor speech.[7] It was customary, particularly in outdoor speeches, for blacks to come and listen, standing at the edge of the crowd. When he would issue his usual invitation to come up and shake hands, meet the congressman and tell him their problems and their views, they always melted away. This time some blacks in this meeting came up and shook hands with him, and he was just as friendly with them as with anybody else. I remember murmurs and ripples of disapproval and some of his friends saying to him later, "You better not do that. You're just going to lose a lot by doing that." He said that he didn't agree, and he thought their opinions needed listening to. I don't think he lost any friends over it. He was not belligerent about it, placating and persuading, but not really successful in persuading, and they didn't condemn him too much, "Well, that's old Lyndon. You have to put up with a few things."

Then there were our trips with the colored people who worked for us, first Otha Ree, and later on Patsy and Zephyr. They were full of difficulties, because once you got into the South there was really no place where they were welcome to spend the night. I remember one time particularly. Mary Rather was with me and Patsy and one child that had to be Lynda Bird. Finally after dark, exhausted, we reached a town in Tennessee. We saw a motel; there was a sign up, "Vacancy." We stopped; we told him. He said, "I haven't got but one room." We said that's all right. He said it had two double beds. We said, "That's all right, we'll take it." Patsy had her head turned the other way in the darkened car. He said, "I'll take you over there." Mary said, "No, no. Just give me the key, and tell me the number." We went over there and opened the door and went in, turned down the beds. The sheets had not been changed. Mary called him up in a hot huff and said, "The sheets have not been changed!" He was so apologetic. He said, "I'll run right over with some sheets." She said, "No, no, no. I'll come get them." Alas, he had already hung up the phone and before you could say Jack Robinson, or at least before we had the wit to get Patsy into the bathroom, there he was at the door with the sheets. He burst the door open, and there we were: we three adults and one child, one adult quite black and big-eyed. Well, his eyes got big as saucers. Mary grabbed the sheets, said, "Thank you very much!" shut the door in his face, and that ended that. I don't know what went on in his mind, but the desire to rent the last room may have been a part of it. He could always say he didn't know.

Was this a regular occurrence?
It was, and sometimes a very irritating occurrence to me. I remember another time when I may have had both children by this time, little ones, and I needed

---

7. Horace Busby recalls a similar episode in the 1948 campaign. Horace W. Busby Oral History Interview 5, 8/16/88, by Michael L. Gillette.

help. Once more I suppose it was probably Patsy.[8] In any case, it was dark and we were tired, and my help in driving was a young man, a secretary, probably my own age. Maybe it was Gene Latimer; I don't remember. We stopped in Memphis, which was probably the town most rooted in that philosophy. This rather snitchy woman in the office took a look at us. She said, "I don't take no niggers." We were too tired to argue; we knew it was hopeless. We said, "Could you please tell us a nice place where my nurse could stay?" She said, "Well, there's a nigger house across the street. They sometimes give them rooms." Then she looked at me and said, "Who is he?" [*Laughter.*] It dawned on me that she probably thought we were off on a liaison of some kind. What on earth would I be doing bringing the nurse and the two children I haven't quite figured out. And I said in my most dignified voice, "He is my husband's secretary." I think I told her who I was, which she would never have heard of, and so we got two rooms, one for me and the two little children. By that time, I was not a bit enthralled with the idea of being a nurse and tending to them [in] the night. I told Gene, or whoever it was, to mind the children a few minutes while I went over and took Patsy to her room. I remember being quite apologetic about the quality of the room. But they welcomed her, and maybe it was what she would have been used to at home in Marshall. I was furious, but I was also tired and caught. There was nothing I could do except tell them the next morning what I thought of the type of hospitality they offered and be on my way.

But there was humor even in this situation, and the funniest time was several years later, after we had Gene and Helen [Williams], and after we had acquired, much against my wishes, a dog, Beagle. It was always a question to how to get those cars home: who was going to take the cars, and now who was going to take the dog. So Lyndon arranged for me and the girls to go on the train, and he said to Gene, "Now Gene, you and Helen come along and bring Beagle." Gene kind of looked doubtful and shook his head. Lyndon said, "Gene, I know you like Beagle. You're always mighty nice to Beagle. How come you don't want to take Beagle?" Gene kind of shook his head. He didn't say, "I won't do it." He said, "Lordy mercy, Mr. Johnson, hard enough to drive through the South if you're a nigger, much less if you're a nigger with a dog." Lyndon couldn't help but laugh at that.[9]

There was the time that Zephyr, walking home down Linnean Avenue [in Washington], fell on the snow and broke her leg. One of the neighbors went out

---

8. CTJ related a slightly different version of the same story, but traveling with Otha Ree, instead of Patsy White. CTJ OHI 38. Zephyr Wright also remembered a similar incident with CTJ at a Memphis motel. Zephyr Wright Oral History Interview, 12/5/74, by Michael L. Gillette, 6.

9. Gene Williams's version of the beagle story is told in Eugene and Helen Williams Oral History Interview, 10/27/74, by Michael L. Gillette, 7–8.

and put blankets over her and called an ambulance. The people said that this was a cook for one of their neighbors. [The ambulance company] asked if it was a black woman, and they wouldn't come and pick her up. Fortunately she was quite conscious. She told them who she worked for. We got up there as quick as we could. We did get an ambulance, but I just remember how startled and angry I was.

What was LBJ's reaction?
His reaction was to get mad and to take just as good a care of her as he possibly could.

Something occurred in a little town in South Texas that mattered for a long time to us in our relations particularly with Latin Americans. In Three Rivers, the body of a Mexican American soldier, Felix Longoria [Jr. who had been killed in World War II], was returned for burial and the funeral director refused to handle him, to hold the services. His widow's sister-in-law had the nerve to get in touch with Dr. Hector Garcia, a longtime friend of ours, who was an organizer of the GI Forum, a group of returned veterans who were working to improve conditions for the Mexican American communities. Dr. Garcia talked to the *Corpus Christi Caller* and the Texas senators and congressmen and military officials, calling it discrimination, which it emphatically was. The next day even the *New York Times* carried a front-page article by Bill White.

It was an ugly page in Texas history. Lyndon really was angry, because he thought if Mexican Americans can fight for their country, they can be buried in the country they helped make safe and they gave their lives for. Actually, it ought to be said that the little community came to feel that way too; it was just the act of one funeral director. Too bad he made that swift judgment. I wish it could have been handled in a way in which the region hadn't had a shameful mark left on it. However, their attempts to make amends—and they did make attempts—came a little too late. Lyndon had wired the widow and said, "If he can't be buried there, we will see that he is buried with full honors in the nation's cemetery in Arlington, if that's acceptable to you." So they shipped the body to Arlington. The family came. A lot of Mexican Americans felt very warm toward Lyndon for that. I remember going out to the funeral services on the bleakest possible gray, rainy January day, and President Truman had Harry Vaughan, his military representative, there.[10]

THE 1957 CIVIL RIGHTS BILL

As the 1950s passed, Lyndon tended more and more toward the liberal side. He dared to try to lead a little more, and one of the high points in his life was the

---

10. For Horace Busby's account, see Horace W. Busby Oral History Interview 5, 6/16/88, by Michael L. Gillette, 35–43.

civil rights legislation of 1957. 1957 was a razor edge of the division of power, with forty-nine Democrats and forty-seven Republicans. Just think about how many of the Democrats, southerners mostly, tended toward the Republicans. It was a hard role for the majority leader. I especially remember [Shivers's appointment of Senator William A.] Blakley [to fill Price Daniel's seat]. We waited that one out on a knife-edge. He was a mean, conservative West Texan as I remember, but living in Dallas at the time. Lyndon was very glad to get him in the Democratic Party but not really sure that he would go. He did, however, [vote with the Democrats]. I remember a very nice luncheon being given for him in the old Supreme Court room. It had so much dignity and [was] just steeped in history, and it was our favorite place to have a luncheon when we could. I remember Lyndon trying to introduce him to the people who would be working with him, especially his fellow Texas delegation.

Four months later [Ralph] Yarborough, who had been trying and trying, finally defeated Martin Dies and Thad Hutcheson [in the Senate race]. We had a little dinner at our house for the Texas delegation and their wives to listen to the election returns, and Yarborough won. He finally got there. He and I had a common thread in that he was very interested in national parks, very interested in the Big Thicket. I expect we [would] really never have gotten it at all [into a national park], although we did get it in a truncated form, if it hadn't been for Senator Yarborough and his ardent work in its behalf.

We lost dear Earle Clements; he was not in the Senate anymore. He had had to run for reelection himself in 1956, and Lyndon had thrust upon him more work than he should have done in July of 1955. He should have been home mending fences, tending to his own reelection. He had been trying to fill two roles as majority whip and substituting for Lyndon, so Lyndon felt that we bore some blame for that. He had a strong affection for Earle, got along with him so [beautifully]. Senator [Mike] Mansfield he admired intensely, but Mansfield was much more an independent man. So that is the way we began the year, just like trying to ride two nervous horses at once, with one foot on each one, like some figure in a Roman circus.

Jim Rowe,[11] who was certainly extremely forthcoming in all his memos to Lyndon, said he thought this was Armageddon for Lyndon Johnson. "To put it bluntly, if you vote against the civil rights bill you can forget your presidential ambitions in 1960. The important thing about civil rights in 1957 is to pass a civil rights bill which the southerners can accept and which the northerners think is reasonable, solely for the purpose of getting this absurd issue off the Hill for a few years."[12] That did loom in front of Lyndon as one of the two most important things in the year 1957. But he never would have used the word "absurd." I think

11. James H. Rowe Jr., a Washington attorney and former FDR administrative assistant, frequently advised LBJ on issues.

12. Memorandum, James Rowe to LBJ, 7/3/57, LBJ Library.

he was bending in that direction and trying to carry as much of his constituency and the South as he could with him and prevent it just from winding up in a bog in the Senate, knee-deep in words and filibusters.

He was always laying in wait until he could do something about it, because he was not one to tilt at windmills. He got real put out with the wild liberals who would rather shout and proclaim themselves from the highest hill as liberals and then never get anything done and do their best not to inch forward and take that half loaf and rather wallow in defeat and cherish being martyrs. He just didn't have any patience for that.

How about your evolution? Did you keep pace with him? You came out of a somewhat deeper southern background.
I came from the real South. East Texas is just part and parcel of Louisiana, Alabama, Arkansas, and Mississippi. But I was also not charged with the responsibility of leading. I did not have the fire inside of me that Lyndon had. I went along, quite comfortably, and was mildly mad at the ADA [Americans for Democratic Action] for taking out after Lyndon. I think a great part of the country began to change in those years.

I remember the long, long prolonged strain. Early on, he had a cot put down in his office so he could catnap from time to time and be prepared to stay there as late as it took.[13] He let the members know that, regardless of their personal social life, we were really going to go at that thing hammer and tongs. Every two or three days, I would bring him down a set of clean clothes. Sometimes I would bring him down a meal cooked by Zephyr, because eventually you get tired of those Senate meals.

Something I enjoyed very much in the difficult times in the Senate was going down there and having dinner with him, just sitting in the office until he thought there was a sufficient lull of thirty minutes or forty-five minutes to go down to the Senate Dining Room and get a bite to eat. There were always the people who went with us; it was always fun, or at least it was a window on history, a window on the world, to listen to them talk—sometimes a very distressing window.

Did he ever just talk to you personally about the problems of getting the bill through?
Yes, just in the sense that "Here I am walking this tightrope, trying to prevent endless filibusters, trying to get something that the South can live with." He was proud of the South. He loved so many of the southern senators. Just on the basis of his conversations with me, he thought it was best for the South and the future of the South, the respect of the world, its economic progress. All were somehow tied up with it, its peace within the nation and among ourselves. Lyndon really felt that a southerner could not be elected [president]. He felt that prejudice against the South, ill-founded or well-founded, was so deep that it was a chasm

13. LBJ slept on a cot in his office during the filibuster of the 1960 Civil Rights Act.

that could not be closed. It was patently unfair. The Lord didn't distribute brains or patriotism or any virtues that unevenly.

Lyndon's main worry at that time was twofold. Some of these senators were in their eighties; some of them were feeble; some of them had real physical problems. He was scared that some old senator was going to die right there on the Senate floor while we were talking about civil rights on all those long, long nights. Yet at the same time he was determined to hold them in session until some decision was reached. Of course, he did run the Senate with a pretty dictatorial hand, just because he thought that was the only way to run it. He just hated those long, long consumptions of time and those filibusters. And he hated to use [the practice of] keeping the Senate in session around the clock for himself and for the old men in the Senate. But he was determined to make it get the work done, to crank out what it was supposed to crank out, and [in] a fairly timely fashion.

The Senate finally did pass a civil rights bill on August the seventh. Those facts are well known. I remember the door flew open after voting was over, and Lyndon marched in feeling triumphant. He immediately got Skeeter Johnston, who was secretary of the Senate, and a really surprising group. But the bill then had to go to a conference committee. So we weren't over all the hurdles. And Senator [Strom] Thurmond had a one-man filibuster, which beat all the records with twenty-four hours and eighteen minutes, the longest in Senate history. If we were to go back over the *Congressional Record*, we would find that he gave a bunch of recipes for such things as how to cook turnip greens and black-eyed peas. [*Laughter.*] But we did pass it on August the twenty-ninth. I don't know that I ever felt a greater sense of elation.

SPUTNIK

Our lives marched into the fall [of 1957], and some very significant things happened to us. The most significant event was an October evening when Russia put up the first satellite, which was called Sputnik. Jim Rowe and Tom Corcoran came down [to the ranch] to see us. Those two, Lyndon and I, and whoever else was there walked down to the cemetery, the old familiar evening ritual of after dinner, maybe stopping at Oreole's. A great big owl went flying over our heads from the woods on our right toward the river and landed on the closest perch on the left. They are all feathers and float through the air like spirits. We were all looking up at the sky, and we were all thinking the same thoughts. Nobody was talking; it was a very silent, expectant group: what did this hold for us? We'd always looked up at the sky as a scene of romance with stars and the moon in just a dear, familiar part of our world. Suddenly there might be menace in it. Suddenly there might be some unknown thing that could do us harm. We knew it was pregnant with something happening, and none of us could predict what. But it was a night that made a great impact on me, and I was glad to spend it with two people like Jim and Tom.

Lyndon was enormously interested in, drawn to, seized upon, and never left the thought that space could have a great effect on the future of this country. He was on the Senate Preparedness Subcommittee. He lost no time. As soon as he got back to Washington, he started committee hearings on that missile program. What was that thing doing up in the sky? We had programs, drafts on the table to make such an object. Why did the Russians beat us? Why didn't we go to work faster and outdo them and achieve superiority? The people who were trying to do it were going to have a constant communication from him that would not be very relaxing to them.

Then our first satellite effort did get launched at Cape Canaveral in December, but it blew up, which only fueled Lyndon's determination that we were going make up ground and get ahead in that race. He said, "What happened this morning is one of the best-publicized and most humiliating failures in our history." From the very beginning, he felt that it was closely tied up with the future of not only us vis-à-vis Russia but of the whole future.

A PUBLIC SPEAKING CLASS

The public speaking course was one of those many things that my lively friend Scooter Miller forced me into in her very social way. Pretty soon you'd find yourself boxed in, and you wouldn't mind. Scooter was just as adventurous and just as determined as Liz [Carpenter]. I was crazy about her; so was nearly everybody else. She knew everybody from Texas and nearly everybody in Washington.

Mrs. Hester Beall Provensen had a class composed of wives of senators and congressmen and a lot of diplomats and some wives of cabinet members. It went on about once a week for about nine months [beginning in January 1959]. Every one of us had to stand on our feet and make a little talk of three minutes or five minutes. Then she would critique them, and others would critique them. One subject that must have been given to me was a three-minute speech on why Texas is the Lone Star State. [*Laughter.*] It would be fun to go back and see what on earth I said. All I know is that those were good hours, learning various facets of the world with the speaker's club. She was a born teacher, and she is one of the best things that ever happened to me. I was extremely shy about public speaking. I didn't even want to get up and say, "Thank you for inviting me to this barbecue." But she could make you think that there were people out there just like you, and look them straight in the eye. Try and never, never begin with saying how you couldn't talk; they'd find that out soon enough. Always have things that would have warm public interest.

Had you by this time become more comfortable as a speaker?
Oh, yes, much more comfortable. It was not then or ever my milieu, but yes, I was relatively comfortable, because it was easy for me to believe that those

people out there in front of me were very much like me.[14] I didn't have to be afraid of them. I tried very hard to look into the eyes of two or three of the people in the front row, the third row, or catch somebody right, left, straight in front of me, whom I could make eye contact with, because that is one [way] of establishing a rapport, of a point of communication with them.

Did the president give you pointers?
Oh, he was always giving me pointers. For instance, he said, "You drop your voice on the last of the sentence. Don't do that. Sometimes lift it. Sometimes you need to drop it." He had been a former debate coach, and he liked teaching people. He did it all his life. [*Laughter.*]

And Liz [Carpenter] used to say so many things that were helpful. She said, "Just look right out there at them. Just imagine they are all from Dime Box or Rosebud." [*Laughter.*] Those were two towns in the old Tenth District for which I will always have an affectionate remembrance. You might have thought we were making fun of Dime Box and Rosebud; we weren't. We were just saying they are a microcosm of America; they are a piece of us.

MARY LASKER

Somewhere along this time, Mary Lasker[15] entered our lives. She was warm and open-armed to me as well as to Lyndon. It was a natural. She wanted to educate Lyndon and use him in all of her health [lobbying]: let us get the Congress on the right track to supporting it. Her husband had told her one time, "Mary, you can collect any amount of money you can get from our rich friends. You can give everything I leave you. But the fight against killer diseases can never be sufficiently supplied by private means. The government has got to put its shoulder to the wheel. And maybe you can get them to; you can try." She was beginning to do that; a dauntless warrior.[16]

At that time Florence Mahoney was one of her Washington chiefs. Florence had a great old house of much faded grandeur in Georgetown. They used it for a movie, *The Exorcist.* Many dinner parties were held there in which the senators on medical committees were the quarry. They got some of the most cogent, gently applied arguments for fighting killer diseases, as well as some of the most elegant dinners and interesting evenings.

---

14. Hester Beall Provensen occasionally helped Mrs. Johnson prepare for speeches when she was first lady. Bess Abell Oral History Interview 2, 6/13/69, by T. Harrison Baker, 7.

15. Mary Lasker, the wife of advertising pioneer Albert Lasker, was a prominent New York advocate of government-funded medical research.

16. Also see Mary Lasker Oral History Interview 1, 11/10/69, by Joe B. Frantz; and 2, 7/19/78, by Michael L. Gillette.

Mary had many interests in her life. Health held most of her heart, but she was touched by, yearned for, wanted to spread widely, beauty. She was the first person to plant flowers on major streets for New York and to try to get the merchants along the street to support them. She was a big believer in "seed money": getting things started, spreading the gospel, getting others to take it up. But this is a later story that begins about in 1964. She was very dear to me.

LOSS AND SADNESS

I happened to be in Lyndon's office when we had a call from John Connally's brother, Wayne, telling us that [John's daughter] Kathleen had died of a gunshot wound. It was one of the most painful tragedies we ever were associated with up to that time.

Kathleen had been Lynda's best friend for years and years, although Kathleen was about a year older and vastly older in sexual development and social interest than Lynda. Lynda was still wearing saddle shoes and wanting to be a little girl when Kathleen was having dates and was beautiful and had really reached a degree of maturity that was very noticeable to me and to all the adults. We had not seen much of her for a year. She had been going with a young man, apparently very much against her father's and mother's wishes, and it had progressed to the point where she had run away and married this young man [Bobby Hale] in a civil ceremony. She was just sixteen. They had gone to Florida. He had found a job in some sort of construction. I do not know what communications went on between John, Nellie, and Kathleen. I know they were somewhere between angry and devastated.[17]

Then there came a time in the lives of these two young people when they had an argument. Just what happened we will never know. The boy reported that she reached for a gun, which was in their house because they were raised in two families apparently that always hunted, always had guns. A gun was as likely to be in the house as a broom. He was trying to wrestle the gun away from her, but she shot and killed herself. This was the message that Wayne Connally told us in the majority leader's office. We were both stricken, for John, for Nellie, for Kathleen, because we had been around when she was born. We had known her every day of her life. She had lived in our duplex at 1901 Dillman. The children had played in the backyard. It was incredible and hideous that she was dead.

Of course, we went to the funeral.[18] It is unforgettable in my mind. In Lyndon's typical fashion, we were an entourage: Mary Margaret Wiley, Warren Woodward, Lyndon, and I. They had a beautiful house in Fort Worth. John was working for Sid Richardson, and after Sid's death, I suppose, for his estate and

---

17. John Connally's account of this tragedy appears in his memoir. Connally, *In History's Shadow*, 153–60.

18. The Johnsons flew to Fort Worth for the funeral on May 1, 1959.

for Perry Bass. We went to their house. It was somber; it was full of years' and years' accumulation of mutual friends. It was a gathering of people that loved John and Nellie. Then we went to the funeral. We were on one side of the grave, and the young husband and his family on the other side. There was civility, but no closeness, as I remember. There is no recapturing those minutes in that last encounter and no need to try, because with death, that's an end of it.

I remember something that John said to Lyndon, Nellie, and me—just a tiny group of us. It was a brief statement as though he were admonishing us: "When they want to talk, you talk to them." It reminded me of *Romeo and Juliet*, the scene when she tried to get her mother and father to listen to her story about being in love with this young man of the wrong family, the Montagues. They said, "Run on, child, we have serious things to discuss." Apparently she had tried, felt rebuffed, because they didn't seem to understand or listen, at least not enough for her.

This I remember, which casts a little light on Lyndon's nature: when we left the cemetery, we were all in the limousine; every seat was taken up. Somebody said, "Where shall we tell the chauffeur to go?" I said, "I do not think we should go back by the house. We've been there, and we've said everything to them that we can. I think there comes a time when John and Nellie will just want to be together with their other children, possibly some of his family and hers." Lyndon just erupted and said, "I'll tell y'all that if anything like this ever happens to me, I want every one of y'all there, and I want you to stay with me." He was a man that just did not want solitude. He wanted solace in suffering and good friends by his side all the time. Oddly enough, in the very last years of his life, that was not so much so. I think he had passed into either a serenity or just a stilling of the juices of life to where nothing much mattered.

[That tragedy] left many deep impressions on my mind. One of them was if that gun hadn't been so handy, she might be alive today. I do not think the fight they were having was serious enough to have ended in her death except for the emotion of the moment and the presence, real handy, of a gun. And that has repeated itself, sadly enough, in the [death of a son] of yet another Texas governor [Price Daniel]. So my feeling to control the availability of guns stems from many sources, and that's certainly a very important one.

My brother Tommy Taylor, who had been our county man in Marion County in any statewide campaign, and who had been our dear friend, was sick. His trouble was not diagnosed immediately, but I don't suppose it would have made any difference if it had been. It was cancer of the pancreas. I came to know that disease is the most fearful thing that can happen to you. As soon as I heard over the phone what the doctors in Jefferson and in Shreveport, where he had been taken to the hospital, said, I called Jim Cain at the Mayo Clinic. In his very loving but serious way, he let me know that the chances of recovery were very, very slim indeed, if that was the real disease, and the symptoms did sound like it had to be.

It was one of the rare occasions that I was alone at the ranch when I made that call. And so I began to cry, and I went outdoors and climbed up on a fence around the old barn—much has been changed there—and I cried and cried and cried. Nobody there to observe, and I did not feel that I had to restrain myself in any way. And I went in the house and I cried and cried and cried. I really don't know whether I have ever cried since.

You made several trips to Shreveport to visit your brother.
Then Lyndon did at one time, too. He was very fond of Tommy. Tommy was one of the genuinely good people I have ever known, and I'm awfully lucky to have had him as long as I did.[19] It was only after we were grown, though, that we became close, because he was eleven years older than I was, and in my childhood he was always off at school. Mother sent him and Tony to New York to school. He went to lots of schools, but if Mother had only lived longer, many, many things would've been different. She died before he was through college, and I think he finally just got a degree from the College of Marshall, which was right there at home and a small Baptist college.[20] It does not rank at the top scholastically.

LÓPEZ MATEOS VISITS TEXAS

1959 was the year when Lyndon's fortunes were obviously going up in the eyes of many people and a lot of talk about him being nominated for the president. But the most dramatic, the most glittering, the most romantic thing that happened to us was the visit of [Mexican] President López Mateos, his wife, and his daughter, and a sizeable number of his top people.

Came the big day, which was October the eighteenth. Predictably, there was a barbeque in a grove of trees along the Pedernales east of the Ranch. We had a marvelous group of important guests: former president Truman, Speaker Sam Rayburn, Secretary of the Treasury Bob Anderson, who was President Eisenhower's friend and cabinet member.

López Mateos was a very handsome man. He knew that he was important in a way that many American politicians did not look upon themselves as being, a kind of monarchical attitude. Truman or Lyndon would never have had that feeling. So we did our best to make it as classy a barbeque as he might ever see. And, of course, we had mariachi bands. Looking back on it, we should have had some Texas western singers and fiddlers. We may have had them in addition. But we loved mariachis just as much as they ever did in Mexico.

We were walking along from the gathering and about to enter the house, Lyndon with the president and I, following with his wife and daughter. And there was Lupe [Bravo], a Mexican man who worked on the ranch at that time

---

19. Taylor died on October 31, 1959.
20. The college is now East Texas Baptist University.

and still does, just doing some of his work around the house. Lyndon thought the world of him. He said, "Lupe, come over here. I want you to meet the president of your country! At least the president of your country before you came over here to be with us." Well, if you have antennae at all, you can tell you've done something very out of keeping with your guests. [*Laughter.*] Not that Lyndon cared a hoot! Lupe was a good man, and he should've been proud to meet his president. His president should've been proud to meet him! Because Lupe put a good face on Mexico as far as skill and industry and being an employee you could be proud of. It wasn't quite in tune with the president, though.

At that time, the ranch house had three bedrooms on the east wing served by one bath. And I thought to myself, "Well, I'll give the president and his wife the biggest one, and I will give their daughter the next one, and then I will give his secretary the smallest one. And I will tell the secretary that would he kindly go down the hall and use the bath in the west wing, so the three of them will have a bath." [*Laughter.*] After that visit, I then did set my sights to add two new baths and dressing rooms to that east wing, and that was the genesis of that. [*Laughter.*]

The next day it was planned for us to go into San Antonio, and Lyndon thought, "Ah, that's a Catholic country. Bishop [Robert] Lucey is a good friend of mine. I will just put him on the guest list, and we'll all go in and hear him preach in the cathedral the next day." Well, we came to find out a fact we didn't know about Mexico. As an outcropping of that long, long revolution that began with putting Porfirio Díaz out in about 1910 and lasted until 1932, one of the things that Mexican politicians did was sever their relationship with the Catholic Church except for ceremonial purposes. They were married in the church, they were buried in the church, and their wives dutifully and pretty consistently attended church regularly. But as far as going every Sunday, or showing up, or having much public affiliation with a church, they didn't.

We did go to the cathedral the next day in company with all of the women. I am not sure whether any of the men went with us. In considerable haste, something else was planned for the men. So I can't say that it was a great social triumph as far as the skill with which we did it, but, oh, it was a wonderfully bright, convivial time in my memory. Lots of Texans enjoyed it very much, and it must at least have enlarged the understanding of some of the Mexicans.

17

1960, The Point of No Return

Lady Bird Johnson's recollections of the 1960 presidential campaign reflect LBJ's ambivalence—as well as her own—toward seeking the nomination and the "total confusion" of the Los Angeles convention. When a sign painter prematurely unfurled a "Johnson for President" sign on the Ambassador Hotel headquarters in Washington, LBJ ordered the sign removed.[1] He declined to compete in the primaries, relying on his friends in the Senate to advance his candidacy in their states. Yet his two basic calculations were accurate. His only chance for securing the nomination was the possible erosion of Kennedy's delegate support on multiple ballots, and, as a southerner, LBJ's only viable path to the presidency was through the vice presidency.

While Lady Bird opposed LBJ's acceptance of the vice presidential nomination, she apparently did not press her views on him. Moreover, she seems to have recognized that their lives were going to change regardless of the course they chose. Her recollection that John Connally was "irrevocably against" LBJ accepting the vice presidential nomination is supported by Connally lieutenant James Blundell, but Connally's own memoir indicates that he had told LBJ that he had no choice but to accept the offer.[2] Both Connally and Mrs. Johnson emphasize that many of their Texas supporters left Los Angeles feeling embittered and betrayed by LBJ's decision.[3]

Lady Bird enjoyed the scenery, if not the pace, of the presidential campaign. Yet the least pleasant event provided perhaps the campaign's most effective publicity. When a "Mink Coat Mob," which had assembled for Republican Tag Day to canvass voters in the Dallas business district, accosted LBJ and Lady Bird, Johnson made the most of the ugly scene for the cameras.[4]

---

1. James Blundell Oral History Interview 1, 10/29/74, by Michael L. Gillette.

2. Connally, *In History's Shadow*, 162–66. Bobby Baker's memoir also mentions Connally's advocacy of LBJ accepting the offer. Bobby Baker, *Wheeling and Dealing: Confessions of a Capitol Hill Operator* (New York: W. W. Norton, 1978), 125–27.

3. Johnson and Connally had evidently given Texas donors the assurance that LBJ would not accept the vice presidential nomination. Dallek, *Lone Star Rising*, 578.

4. For a detailed account of the incident, see Lawrence Wright, *In the New World: Growing Up with America, 1960–1984* (New York: Alfred A. Knopf, 1988), 24–28.

Late in the campaign, T. J. Taylor died. Lady Bird's grief was compounded by the realization that he had left the bulk of his estate, including her beloved Brick House, to his third wife, Ruth.[5]

I really cannot overemphasize how much Lyndon loved the Senate and being majority leader. It was a very powerful job with an aging, somewhat ailing Eisenhower and that narrow margin in the Senate. It was a great time to be majority leader; the times and the man met. But Lyndon always had a remarkable amount of vision, and he could see that that would no longer obtain if we got a Democratic president, particularly if he was a strong Democratic president. The job of the majority leader would be to implement whatever the president said.

It's not only [a question of] did he aspire to be president, which I do not really think he did. He was deeply awed, deeply uncertain about his ability, his health, his being a southerner, whether that was a good thing for him to do. But that job [he had] just wasn't going to exist if we got a Democratic president, at least that's the way I looked at it and think he did. We were reaching a point of no return, a certain defining of pathways at this point at the end of 1959. So many signs kept on pointing to the fact that Lyndon was going to be a candidate [for president].

1960 was a crowded, crowded year that I do not remember as one of my favorite years at all. The whole year was an inevitable getting onto a greased slide in which you were heading toward this [presidential] race, and there was no stopping. For better or worse, here we go. It would seem strange, but from my standpoint, and I do think to a very considerable degree [from Lyndon's, we were reluctant] to wind up in this race for the presidency. The big obstacle of the southerner being elected, the big obstacle of handling the job of the presidency if you got it, loomed very large for him. He really believed that being a southerner was an obstacle that was divisive and might not be overcome. Not that it was fair or sensible, but it was there.

My overall remembrance of the year is one of total confusion, travel all over the United States, going too far, staying too short a time, rush, rush, rush. I was not happily in tune. However, early in April I did have a little taste of [how] maybe I could get in tune. I went to what was billed as a "celebrity breakfast" given by Theta Sigma Phi, which is a journalism honor sorority to which I had belonged in the University of Texas. This was a question-and-answer; the victim—the speaker—was asked questions by all the members of the sorority. This was in Fort Worth. I found it rather exciting. I was not scared of them; I could think of fairly sensible answers, I thought afterward. [It was] maybe a little taste of what was to come, a primer in the school of learning how to fill this role.

---

5. For a discussion of T. J. Taylor's will and the legal challenges to it, see Russell, *Lady Bird*, 200–203.

More than anything else, I was caught up in a tide that I could not control. And no, I didn't really want to; I had no hunger for the job. I had all of Lyndon's ambivalence about "Is this too hard a job?" I was not enthusiastic. But in that little two hours spent with the Theta Sigma Phis, I felt a certain excitement and challenge [at the prospect of running for president].

We began to make forays out into the country, dipping our toes into the water, into "Are we going to launch into this full scale? Here it is April. Is Lyndon running for the presidency or isn't he?" One time I went to Dallas to a coffee where there were all sorts of miscellaneous civic leaders, PTA, Business and Professional Women, Civil Defense, a cross-section of the country, farmers' wives from Grand Prairie and Cedar Hill, the sort of people whom we hoped would be our supporters. We were trying to encourage people to go into the precincts and be workers for us.

ENLARGING THE CIRCLE

Somebody among our friends assembled a bunch of young businessmen in Houston, thinking that Lyndon should get better acquainted with the younger generation. When he thought of important Houston businessmen, he thought of George Brown and the group that used to met in room [8-F of the Lamar Hotel]. In that meeting with young businessmen in Houston, he met Jack Valenti,[6] I think. They took to each other right away. Besides that, very importantly, Jack took to Lyndon's secretary, Mary Margaret Wiley. He began to come up, presumably to visit us and Lyndon, but very much to see Mary Margaret. That was a troubled courtship because work didn't quit till there wasn't any work left to be done. Lyndon didn't at all expect his secretary to go off and have a date when six o'clock came, or seven or eight or nine. [*Laughter.*] Jack was perfectly welcome into the family and at the dinner table; Lyndon tolerated them going off awhile after dinner.

There was one funny time when mischief got the better of Lyndon. He and A. W. [Moursund] decided to get Jack drunk. I don't know if they wanted to get him so drunk that Mary Margaret would be disgusted and would not have him around anymore and thereby insure Lyndon not having to fill her place. [*Laughter.*] I think they did succeed, but he survived it with good humor, and it certainly did not impair their relationship. He kept on coming to see her. It did take several years to get to a wedding.[7]

Bill Moyers joined the staff [in 1960].[8] My feeling toward Bill was totally affectionate throughout. I remember passing him in the office of the majority leader.

6. Houston advertising executive Jack Valenti joined LBJ's presidential staff after the Kennedy assassination.

7. Jack Valenti and Mary Margaret Wiley were married in 1962.

8. Moyers, a Marshall native, had worked for KTBC in the 1950s.

There was an outer office where there were likely to be a secretary who greeted people and who was always on the phone, and one more desk, and at that desk sat Bill Moyers. He might be dictating letters into a machine, or he might have had a real secretary there taking them. But he would be imperturbably typing language that was eloquent and elegant in the midst of the most utter confusion. Everything except a swinging trapeze would be going on in that outer office, and there was Bill performing so beautifully. I always was intrigued by the fact that he had been a minister. I don't think he ever had a church, but he had finished the course in becoming an ordained Baptist minister. That always clung, although I think it's true that he wound up in an extremely intellectual milieu. Bill was always searching. It was a lifelong, "I love you. No, I don't," relation between him and Lyndon, and perhaps it was more needful on Lyndon's part than it was on his. My feeling is totally affectionate.

Liz Carpenter[9] was just as much my friend and my fellow worker as she was Lyndon's. She was strong enough and tough enough to stand up to Lyndon, and he was honest enough and realistic enough to know that she had so much to offer, even if she was sometimes abrasive. Even if she sometimes wanted him to do something that he was just too exhausted to do or that didn't come natural for him to do. He usually did it, and he might roar at her, but he always loved her and admired her. And I, too, and very much laughed with her.

A RELUCTANT CANDIDATE

Do you have any recollection why LBJ didn't enter the primaries?
Well, I have a very strong feeling about it. [*Laughter.*] I don't remember if he ever sat down and said why he didn't—that was because he was using up all he had being majority leader. That was a full-time job which he loved. I do not think he was planning, plotting, intending, heading in the direction of being president.

I think he was reluctantly and at the last minute propelled into it by the unending faith of Sam Rayburn and the determination of John Connally, and then just maybe the beckoning prospect of it's now or never; maybe I ought to. It was certainly not for lack of knowing how. Not for lack of realizing that if you wanted to become president, you had to work to become president. You ought to be going around the country to every Democratic meeting. Lyndon would have tried to go to a whole lot of nonparty meetings as well if there had been anything in that direction. It seemed to me that he didn't.

There was a time when [the Citizens for Johnson] headquarters were set up. They were rather flamboyant headquarters, I think somewhere on Lafayette Square [in Washington]. Some of his friends rented a building and put up a

---

9. Veteran Washington journalist Liz Carpenter joined LBJ's staff during the 1960 presidential campaign.

sign. Lyndon went down and demanded that the [sign be removed]. He just wanted [the headquarters] operated out of one little room in a hotel, like I think he said Truman had done. You could honestly say John and others had a right to be angry at Lyndon for his continued ambivalence about running. That was pretty painful. He was very reluctant. He'd lived pretty darn close to that job. He watched Roosevelt and Truman from a fairly intimate vantage point and Eisenhower from quite a different vantage point. That's a scary job! It's also one that an honest assessment is bound to make you think, can I—not run and win—but can I live up to all the American people deserve out of that job?

He was a reluctant candidate and not a 100 percent believe-in-himself candidate in his desire to get it and his capability to get it. He took his case to the country by going to innumerable Jefferson-Jackson Day dinners, gatherings of Democrats, but not on television or big rallies of people. I guess [the campaign] wasn't handled as well as it should be.

There were a lot of travels in 1960. We went to parts of the country that were totally unknown to me before. Ed Johnson, predictably called Big Ed, [former] senator from Colorado, had us out to his state for a meeting of Democratic leaders, which Lyndon addressed. I think it was a part of the National Western Mining Conference. We went to Wyoming to a breakfast with the delegates to the State Democratic Convention in Cheyenne. Salt Lake City was a place that made a deep impression on Lyndon. He liked the Mormons. He thought they did what they said they were going to do. I cannot imagine that the Mormons had much natural affiliation partywise with Lyndon, but person-to-person he liked those leaders in that church. Travel, travel, travel, hurry; there was precious little relaxation in that whole year.

I don't know quite what it was that led us to so many western states. I guess it was because Lyndon was less known in that part of the world. But that spring we did go to Idaho and to Spokane, Washington, and to a dam dedication in Pierre, South Dakota. Senator [Richard] Neuberger of Oregon was one of the earliest people who thought we ought to preserve the rights-of-way of the highways for the good of the country and not for billboards, and he dared to raise a flag to that purpose. A good bit later on, it certainly became one of my hopes that we could look at the country on potentially scenic highways which the federal government had helped fund or had entirely funded.

My geographical knowledge of the United States is pretty much a gift from the campaigns of 1960 and 1964. In my own little sack of treasures, it's important. I just loved getting to know this country. I did not like the way in which it was done: hurry, hurry, hurry, hurry, trivial remarks to people and then go on. I would have like to have had some smaller, more substantive meetings and seen more scenery and less folks, maybe, but this was not cut out for my education; it was the political process.

THE 1960 DEMOCRATIC CONVENTION

On Sunday, July the tenth, Katie Louchheim, as women's head of the Democratic Party, had arranged an informal conversation between the press and the candidates' wives. I really didn't have any trouble in participating with the press, because I wasn't scared of them. They could do something to hurt Lyndon, and therefore I couldn't be as open and as at ease as would have been my natural desire. I was aware of that. When he finally began some of the hardest times of being leader of the Senate, the good relationship with the press that he had had as a member of the House and the Senate began to erode, I guess because they kept on nibbling at and trying to find out things that he thought that if he told them would put in jeopardy what he wanted to get done.

But you yourself have always had a good association with the press, even—
I have and better than I deserve. Part of it I must credit to Liz [Carpenter]; part of it [is] I just have no reason to be afraid of them. They can't take away anything from me that I value. They can hurt my husband; there I am vulnerable. Mostly I feel about them like I first thought about them when I took that course in the university in the early 1930s: this is where things are happening. I would like to be in there myself, learning about being a press person, being the one asking the questions.

On Sunday we had a hospitality suite; we stayed at the Biltmore. And there were people streaming in and out of there, huddling in corners, making plans. The next day there was a reception honoring the candidates' wives, given by the California Federation of Young Democrats and the Women's California Central Committee. The next day, which was the twelfth, Perle Mesta[10] had a brunch honoring the delegates' wives. I just went to everything there was that I was told to go to.

Now, the twelfth was the day that LBJ debated Kennedy on television.
Yes, and I never remember a more tense time. You just felt like you were in the arena where one of the great big contests of history was taking place. I knew from the outset that Kennedy had caught the fancy; the fever was up for him. He was young and younger-looking than his years and very articulate and charismatic. I came to dislike that word, but I think it fits. I did not feel hopeful about that; neither, I think, did Lyndon. I cannot say that he came out of it the winner. It really had nothing to do with the substance of the beliefs of one man or the substance of the other man. It was a matter of electric response of a crowd to two people. I remember the tenseness and the desire to support and say you are so much better than, and all that. I couldn't honestly say it. I could see the delegates

---

10. Perle Mesta was a well-known Washington hostess from whom the LBJs subsequently bought "The Elms," their home during the vice presidential years.

being drawn to liking better our opponent. The whole year was not my favorite year. This was something to be gotten through, as far as I was concerned.

Then Wednesday, July 13, the actual convention, was just like being in the biggest circus tent that ever was. Groups from all fifty states [were] huddled together in their separate corners, or front stances, or somewhere in the middle, with state flags and placards and banners, and it's a great show. It is total confusion.

This was the Speaker's last chairmanship. Anybody who's been around on those occasions will remember his gavel falling, his looking out at the crowd, and his ability to finally get order. There was [Dorothy Vredenburgh Bush], a very pretty Alabama woman who, since time began, would call the roll, in a loud, clear voice, beginning with Alabama.[11] "Alabama votes its favorite son, so-and-so." Or, "Alabama casts its X votes for—." It is a big show, followed by great roars of approval or gasps of despair, or sometimes by anger. It's a good show to watch, but it sure is better to be detached than involved.

THE VICE PRESIDENTIAL NOMINATION

It was on July the thirteenth that Kennedy was nominated. There was great discussion that night about whether Lyndon might be offered the vice presidency. He didn't believe he would be offered it and did not want to accept it. He resisted. There was just an in and out, just a coming and going, of the Speaker, John Connally, [and] of course, at all times, Walter Jenkins. [Senator Bob] Kerr expressed himself as against Lyndon's accepting it in case lightning should strike and he should be offered it. John Connally was irrevocably against it.[12] At first, the Speaker was [against it].

It was the best night's sleep that we'd both had in a long time—I speak for myself, and I think that that was the way Lyndon felt—broken too early by a telephone call. I'm a light sleeper, so I woke up quickest to it, and my recollection is that it was John Kennedy's own voice.[13] He asked if he could speak to Lyndon. Then there was a moment's hesitation on my part because Lyndon was so tired, and it was just so marvelous to just be able to rest. But I knew I couldn't, because, after all, he was our party's nominee, so I went over and shook him and said, "Wake up."

Did you think the call was about the vice presidency?
I thought it might [be].

11. Dorothy Vredenburgh Bush, secretary of the Democratic National Committee, called the roll for every Democratic convention from 1944 to 1988. Obituary of Dorothy Vredenburgh Bush, *New York Times*, December 23, 1991.

12. In John Connally's memoir, he states that he advised LBJ to accept the vice presidential nomination. Connally, *In History's Shadow*, 162–63.

13. Betty Cason Hickman's recollection is that she answered the phone call and summoned Mrs. Johnson, who then awakened LBJ. Betty Cason Hickman Oral History Interview 1, 4/10/84, by Michael L. Gillette, 32–32.

Some of the accounts have you telling your husband, "Don't do it," and other accounts have you saying, essentially, yes, that you were willing. It must have been a very, very difficult choice.

Well, they both could be right, because I did not want him to. I loved the Senate just like he did. I did not know how good a number-two man he would be, because he had always been a very free man. In the House of Representatives he was responsible to his 300,000-odd constituents back home. When he became senator from Texas, he was responsible to the ten million of us, whatever we were. But at the same time, he was a free man. He had to implement their will, but he could do a lot toward trying to persuade them of the path that he thought they ought to follow. Ultimately he could just take the different route and then hope that they would follow him. If they didn't, they could jolly well toss him out of office at the next election. But he was much more of a free man than he would be as number-two man to a president.

To assume a new role as number-two man, I didn't know how happy he would be in it. I also knew that the people of the state of Texas would think we'd deserted them, that we'd walked out of them. They would be hurt and angry. So I really didn't want him to. At the same time, it was going to be his life, his job, his career. I was not the fellow that was going to have to do the job, bear the burden. So I just really drew back from trying to influence anything. I just wouldn't dare try to persuade him. So that's about what I said to him. I wanted him to do what he must do.

Do you recall the visit of Robert Kennedy to the hotel suite? He apparently came and told Senator Johnson that there were a lot of liberals who were upset about his nomination and perhaps he should withdraw. That apparently created some bad feeling, which remained permanent in some ways.

That was one of the first incorrect moves then on their part; all the other moves were good. I remember him either calling or telephoning or coming in—and frankly I don't know which it was—and Lyndon saying something like "That is for your brother, who is the nominee, to tell me, and I will wait to hear from him."[14] But the contact from Senator Kennedy was that he wanted him, hoped he would, and was depending on him. I do remember the total confusion of the day. The whole thing was such a crescendo of comings and goings and telephone calls and emotions. A blind man can only feel one part of an elephant and say what it is like. I do not claim any clarity whatever about that. It was just like being inside a rapidly rotating machine. I do remember the Speaker calling back, and he came down to talk to us. Some of these conferences took place in

---

14. The most thorough account of the conversations and events of July 14, 1960, including Robert Kennedy's multiple trips to LBJ's suite, is Robert A. Caro, *The Years of Lyndon Johnson*, vol. 4, *The Passage of Power* (New York: Alfred A. Knopf, 2012), 109–40.

the bathroom. [*Laughter.*] They would leave even me and retreat to the bathroom and talk. The Speaker [was] retracting his own earlier statement and urging him to take it. Some press man asked him why was he doing that. He said, "Because I am a smarter man this morning than I was last night." The Speaker very often had a good way of succinctly putting any position he took.

Do you remember what your own feelings were about whether he should accept?
A certain amount of dismay and sadness and reluctance, also a feeling that "This is not mine. I will not be anything in this except 'the wife of,' and that will be the same. And I must not try to affect the outcome." The world that was so familiar to me had suddenly cracked and fallen apart. We were not going to be in the Senate I had known and loved anymore, especially not majority leader. So I was very far from elated, but it was not my decision to make.

I think I understood it. I wouldn't be surprised of it wasn't old Mr. [Joseph P.] Kennedy that had a good deal to do with this; Papa looking to the South, looking to Texas, adding up feelings of people, wondering what it would take to put his son over the top, and thinking that Lyndon might very well be the one that could make the difference. I also know that that was in Lyndon's mind too. He owed everything that he had achieved in life to the Democratic Party. This might be its greatest time of need. He might, if he put in everything he had, make the difference. Also, he thought in his time being majority leader, he had sucked that orange dry. He had given it everything he had; he'd gotten everything out if he could. That was finished. I know there was some of that in him, his reasoning for accepting it. [Lyndon had] no hatred for Nixon, but just a feeling that the Democratic Party and Kennedy-Johnson would be better for the country than the Republican Party and Nixon.

But in the Speaker's mind apparently there was in his mind a real reluctance to see Nixon president because of an animosity.
Whoo boy, you bet! Ever since Nixon had called him a traitor. That would have been unforgivable and unerasable for the Speaker, and he just couldn't have stood for that man to run his country.[15]

After Kennedy was nominated, Lynda asked her daddy, "I guess nothing is going to happen tomorrow, will it?" And he says, "No, honey." She said, "Okay then, I'm going out to Disneyland." So she went out to Disneyland with her boyfriend. It was that day that Lyndon was nominated as vice president. They looked around for all the family members to get a picture together, and she was not to be found anywhere. Then somehow or another they located her out at

---

15. For Nixon's charge that the Democrats were "soft on communism" and Rayburn's reaction, see D. B. Hardeman and Donald C. Bacon, *Rayburn: A Biography* (Austin: Texas Monthly Press, 1987), 381–82.

Disneyland. [*Laughter.*] That's where she found out [about the vice presidential nomination].

The quote that I remember reading in the Washington Post *was something like, "Usually I'm Daddy's little darling, but tonight I was not Daddy's little darling."* [Laughter.] *How did you feel when he was nominated for vice president by acclamation on the first ballot?*
It was like trying to swallow a nettle: hurt, sticky, spiny. He didn't want the job, but he felt an enormous sense of obligation to the Democratic Party. It had given him, us, every honor it could: wearing the flag for a Democratic Party as a member of the House of Representatives and as senator. It's hard for anybody now to understand how people felt then. There was a sense of party loyalty, of obligation, of belonging because you wanted to belong and of loyalty that it imposed. Then he had to look at the job of majority leader he had loved. He reveled in it. But it wouldn't be the same if he didn't accept that nomination and went back and tried to continue as majority leader. He always liked and respected President Kennedy, but he was the not the sort of member of that team who would just be prepared to happily and wholeheartedly espouse every piece of legislation.

That's my feeling. I know it's not the general feeling, but from a close-up position and the way I felt, the way I thought Lyndon felt, it was a hard thing to do, to leave the job he'd had and enjoyed to take this lesser job. But Lyndon feared that the Democratic Party would lose; Nixon would win, and the Democratic Party would be out for years and years. So he opted for doing what he thought of as a duty and accepting the nomination. That Governor [David] Lawrence nominated him was a pleasant thing for Lyndon, because Lawrence of Pennsylvania was one of the old time Democratic politicians: sturdy, respected, high-class, a fine man in Lyndon's book.

After Lyndon accepted the nomination, some of our very best Texas friends just got in their cars and on planes and left and didn't say good-bye. We couldn't get them on the phone. We tried and tried. When Lyndon called for John Connally, they said, "Oh, he's gone." He had packed up and left and started driving home. I know that his anger was such that he didn't even want to talk it over with Lyndon after Lyndon accepted.

What do you think Connally's resistance stemmed from?
Because he'd pinned his all, he'd pledged his all, to Lyndon to fight to the last gasp. I think John felt a betrayal, dismissal, a good-bye to Texas. He thought they were two entirely different, disparate people. The Speaker upon reflection did not feel that. I guess the Speaker was building on his seventy[-eight years]. He'd been in the Congress longer than anybody ever had and had mounted up a whole lot of experience and wisdom. So the Speaker was ready for him to do it wholeheartedly.

When President Johnson made his acceptance speech, I remember one line from it, "I'm proud to stand beside and stand behind Jack Kennedy."
Yes, and he really felt that way about Kennedy—not everybody around him, not everything related to him—but on balance he had a great respect and admiration for Kennedy. I want to make it real clear it's not that he looked down on working under Kennedy or looked down on the vice presidency. It just wasn't anything he wanted or had ever aspired to, and he had to wrestle himself to do it.

After that you went back to the Ranch. Was it a let-down feeling or an exhilarating feeling?
Oh, it was let down and strange. But a whole bunch of neighbors came and welcomed us, and there was a lot of pumping of hands and slapping of backs and a lot of show of affection. And even that, too, was funny, because about half of that county—the part going to the west towards Fredericksburg was thoroughly German, and they were not pro–Democratic Party. Not many liberal bones in any of them. I think the only time Lyndon ever carried that area was in 1964, as it turned out. But because they were neighbors, they lived with him, they knew him; they tolerated him, as different as he was. [*Laughter.*]

HYANNISPORT

Soon after the Republican nomination, you went with President Johnson to Hyannisport [Massachusetts]. Was that your first trip there?
Yes. My first trip to any kind of what might have been an intimate association with living in New England and with folks for whom that was their life.

And were the Kennedys pretty hospitable?
Yes. I imagine they were, although we were strange to most of them; not to President Kennedy. He and Lyndon had been together in the Senate [for seven years].

But your own relationship to Mrs. Kennedy changed in this, too. You had been a senior member of the Senate wives. You had befriended her when she was a young person. Now, all of a sudden, you were in a junior position to her. Did that come with any kind of discomfort to you?
Not in the least. For one thing, I do not have an overweening personal ambition—to see the world and have interesting experiences, yes, but to have titles and position, no. It's easy to see that she and I came from different worlds socially. Mine was country girl, loving being a country girl. Certainly not used to elegant living, but always I had been the daughter of the biggest man in our village, in our county in East Texas. Well goodness knows, I didn't know a fauteuil from a bergère. Elegance in living had not been a part of my life.

We arrived late at night; Jackie and her sister [Caroline Lee Bouvier Radziwill] were there, and Senator Kennedy.[16] They insisted that we have something to eat, but it was late at night and we'd already had something. I remember she spoke of lobsters, and I thought to myself that lobster is my favorite food, but I'm not going to ask for anything at eleven o'clock at night. The men mostly went off and talked, and I was not a party to it. I just saw this great big, rambling white house and the ocean and thinking what a nice place it would be for a family to have as a summer home, except it would be too cold [in the winter].

Jackie was there resting. This was not long before she was going to have their second child. She was a photographer, as everybody knows. She got out an album to show me some of the pictures she had taken of her darling little girl, and they were really so precious. Her sister was there with her, and they were so congenial. It was a close family life that we were butting in on. It was a charming house, full of pieces of much-used family furniture and some attractive antiques and a lot of pictures of the family doing things. I was interested in seeing all the memorabilia along the walls and the things that the family had done and of the period of time when they were in London in the embassy.

I remember a sense of there being crowds around and a feeling that this was likely to become a tourist attraction. Large quantities of press arrived, and I remember the brother-in-law, this Polish count, a titled man named [Prince Stanislas] Radziwill; "Stas," they called him. He was looking at the press and putting his hands [up] and saying, "Extraordinary, extraordinary" that they should so invade, so beleaguer, so make themselves a part of everything. He was walking around looking like he was in the zoo. It was pandemonium. Press everywhere. If you were tough enough, you could reserve maybe a little privacy, but [the press] were trying to be invasive.

What was your reaction to meeting Rose Kennedy?
Intense interest. Anybody that's got nine children and has been the wife of the ambassador to the other leading country of the world, there's lots about them to be beglamored about. I thought also that although Mr. Joseph Kennedy appeared to me then and always the head of the family, as being a pretty strong dominant autocrat, but yet I thought that lady had her own particular sort of indomitable strength. I was terribly impressed every step of the way.

---

16. Jacqueline Kennedy recalled that she and JFK vacated their bedroom so the Johnsons could sleep there. Jacqueline Kennedy Onassis, 1/11/74, by JBF, pp. 12–13; also see Jacqueline Kennedy, *Historic Conversations on Life with John F. Kennedy* (New York: Hyperion, 2011), 84–85. One of LBJ's secretaries recalls that Mrs. Kennedy all but ignored the guests. Betty Cason Hickman Oral History Interview 1, 4/10/84, by Michael L. Gillette, 49–50.

It doesn't sound as if there was any kind of discomfort in your—
Not any on my part. I did so want to make it any easier for Jacqueline Kennedy if I could, because you sensed that this was not what she had expected to do with her life, that she was in a strange new world, even as I was in strange new world. She was always somebody who was appealing, and you wanted to help her.

THE PRESIDENTIAL CAMPAIGN

Our return to Texas was shadowed by the fact that a lot of our friends felt at a distance from us because of Lyndon's agreeing to go on the ticket as number-two man. That was not what they wanted for him or of him, and there was a distance between them and Senator Kennedy. Lyndon knew he had a selling job to do. He never tried harder in his life to do a selling job.

I remember Senator Kennedy's coming to Houston and talking to [three hundred Protestant] ministers.[17] The appearance before the ministers was a help, a turning point. There was a growing respect. I remember how proud we were of how well Kennedy comported himself with such dignity and solid answers. He said the message we wanted him to say, that we hoped he could and would say, and he did it so well. We were all beaming at the newspaper reports and the feeling among all the folks who went.

I remember Lyndon's great sense of pride and vindication. He was proud of his home folks. He was proud of the way they received him there, and he was proud of Senator Kennedy and his responses, and he felt it was off to a good start.

There was much that was funny about the campaigns with the Kennedy ladies. I do not believe that Mrs. Jacqueline Kennedy went on any of them. She was pregnant; she was not well, and added to the fact that she had a bigger nettle to swallow than I did. So the party usually consisted as me as a host and two Kennedy sisters[18] and one time his mother. We would go to a series of Texas towns after somebody had preceded us on the road to round up interest on the part of radio, television, newspaper, come and interview, come in and write as big stories they could be enticed to write. I did so want those ladies to like and respect and be interested in all these people they were meeting. I've got to say they were very different. [*Laughter.*] One time we went to some West Texas town, and they gave us corsages that were made out of the fruit of the cactus, the prickly pear, a purple, bulbous-looking thing on it. I think the stickers had been pulled. [*Laughter.*]

My sense of the vastness, the difference, the regional characteristics of America was heightened during that campaign and in every successive campaign. Oh, my

---

17. Kennedy addressed the Greater Houston Ministerial Association on September 15, 1960. For an account of Kennedy's speech to the ministers, see Chris Matthews, *Jack Kennedy: Elusive Hero* (New York: Simon & Schuster, 2011), 286–90.
18. Ethel (Mrs. Robert) Kennedy and Eunice Kennedy Shriver.

eyes were out on stems. I liked the small towns in West Texas or in almost any portion of Texas better than I did the big crowds. And they were big in Dallas and Houston. Now San Antonio, it's just not possible for me not to like San Antonio in whatever form. And we did a lot of that with the ladies.

Somewhere along this path, something happened to me that has affected me ever since and has stood me in good stead as the wife of a president later on. I fell in love with the different segments of this varied land. One time, Lyndon and all the whole cortege of press and speakers and everybody that was helping him went to what was billed as a "bean feed." It was very much like a barbeque, except that the main thing that you had to eat was beans with some pork in the pot. All the other dishes—salads and desserts and pickles and everything—were brought by women of the neighborhood, wherever it was. This particular one, in either North or South Dakota, was way out in the country.[19] The main thing you saw were tractors, lots and lots of tractors; it was a farm show. It just reminded you that this piece of America is the bread basket. These great mammoth machines must just go roaring across this rich, beautiful earth. Gosh, I wish I could come back and see it in planting time and harvest time. This is quite a phenomenon.

Then in October especially, we would find ourselves in New England, and we'd pass lots of [roadside] stands with bright colored pumpkins and apples and corn, and you'd see an evergreen forest and hills and a snowy white church spire rising. Gee, it was easy to fall in love with New England. I never expected to, always felt sort of stand-backish about New England. I was wrong. [*Laughter.*] Beautiful and something to love. So it was just a process I enjoyed very much, had lots of respect for, tired me out, felt infinitely sorry for Lyndon because he had to make so many decisions so quick. This time, just for vice presidency, of course, but in the later campaigns even more tough.

T. J. TAYLOR'S DEATH

My daddy had always been in charge. All eyes in the family and the community turned to him when there was a problem. He had always been able to solve it, to come out of it. Maybe not always happily for him, but always to the best interest he could possibly work out for all of us around him: Mother's death, the Depression. Daddy was a survivor and a ruler. 1960 was the year in which my father really ceased to be a towering, powerful man we all looked to. He failed mentally and physically. I visited him four or five or more times during the calendar year, until he died during the campaign in October of 1960. During 1959 and the early part of 1960, some of the best and most revealing visits that

---

19. According to LBJ's Daily Diary, he and CTJ attended the National Plowing Contest in Sioux Falls and an event in Worthington, South Dakota, on September 21.

I ever had with my father took place, unhappily and likely to be with him in a hospital bed. He would talk about his early arrival in Texas and what propelled him to come to Texas, which, of course, was "Go west, young man," to seek his fortune, as the phrase of his youth was. [There was] no doubt that his fortune lay somewhere. Every American youth was going to succeed if he worked hard enough. Some of my best memories are when he was first put to bed, of him talking in ways that he had never talked to me before about his courtship days, his early days with my mother. I was startled and delighted to learn of the effect that she had had on him. So there he was lying in the bed in Marshall, approaching the end of life.

It became obvious early in September that Daddy was not going to live, at least he was not going to be the man I had known since my very first memories. I went to visit him in the hospital, and Lynda and Luci were along. It came as an overwhelming final sadness but nothing of a surprise. In fact, you couldn't even be sorry, because if he were in full possession of his mental faculties, he would have hated being anything but a dominating figure. It was not too sad because he was not Mr. Boss, Cap Taylor, the person I'd always known. He was certainly no longer a dominating figure in that hospital bed, finally having suffered the indignity of having a leg amputated, which is what happened to you in those days if you had what was called hardening of the arteries, a heart condition, a circulation condition. When you are no longer able to run your world, just terrible things can happen. This was none of his fault. I grieved for him early on and said good-bye to him before he died, and those last few weeks were just to be endured. He did not actually die until later on in October.

After the funeral service, the battery in the hearse [carrying him] to the cemetery [died]. This rather long line of cars following the hearse to the cemetery was stopped on the highway. There is just something peculiarly poignant in that. Here was a man running for vice president, trying very hard to help the man he was serving, President Kennedy, in becoming president, [but] stopped in a funeral procession for his own father-in-law. I felt so sorry for everybody around me. There's nothing you can do in that situation except hope, and it's pointless to hope, because people will excuse you for being very, very late at the next place or even canceling it.

He was not buried beside my mother but in a cemetery called Algoma in Marshall, Texas, in the lot that someday will be occupied by the wife of his later years, Ruth. It pains me to think about that cemetery. It's right between a highway split. A piece of [the highway] went straight to Shreveport; a piece of it went the old route to Shreveport. There is the cemetery right in between. Well, can't help those things.

I had the most beautiful, poignant letter a week or two later from Mrs. Bobby Kennedy. I remember it still. Those things do matter, taking notice of the death of your friends' loved ones, whoever your friend is. If you write them a sweet letter or go to see them or express yourself about being so sorry that they have this loss, it's good. I had so many opportunities to learn. I just wish I had felt that I had taken advantage of them. You'd finally emerge a much better person.

"A SEA OF MAD SLOGANS"

It was absolutely the most unexpected thing. You just couldn't dream it would happen. [On November 4, we emerged from a meeting in the Baker Hotel in Dallas] to go a luncheon rally inside the [Adolphus] Hotel. We had to cross the street and enter the lobby and get to the elevator. We were surrounded by a mob carrying banners and shouting. Nearly everybody had a placard up on a stick and waving them. It was just a sea of mad slogans; very obvious they didn't like Johnson; couldn't stand Kennedy. I can't remember what some of the banners said, but they were all very unfriendly and ugly things: "Turncoat" and "[You] don't belong here anymore," something like that. You could hardly make your way because they were so close on all sides of you. They didn't want to give us room to walk. At first I couldn't believe what I was seeing, because this was a tightly packed, angry crowd. These were the people that we had represented since January of 1949. We thought we knew them. Dallas, a very conservative town, had never been a stronghold for us, but they'd always been courteous. And we did have some good friends there. I remember seeing Stanley Marcus[20] walking with us, and I thought, oh good, perhaps he can help, since these are his customers.

It would be easy to be in a mob and get scared because it's an animal feeling there. You just wondered, what would it take to rouse them? What would it take for them to do something really painful, ugly, or irreversible? But I was intensely interested in everything around me, not scared, but well aware of the tensions and of how this could get out of hand.

They were carrying a banner, and somebody was shoving them probably, but anyhow, it knocked off my hat, probably my best hat. That was the nearest thing to making Lyndon mad, but I think that was unintentional. I looked over in the crowd and saw Senator [John] Tower, who was Lyndon's Senate opponent, so I leaned over and told that to Lyndon. Then I recognized a man named [Bruce] Alger, who was the congressman from Dallas. He was the very advent of Republicans in our tightly knit delegation, the very first one.[21]

By this time we were in the lobby [of the Adolphus] and heading toward the elevator, and it was getting harder and harder to move. It seemed like [it took] a long time to get through the lobby. It certainly was minutes, because people were blocking you at every step. Nobody physically hit us; they just hollered at us and showed their banners and said ugly things.

---

20. Owner of the Neiman-Marcus department store.
21. In 1960 Alger was the Texas congressional delegation's only Republican member.

Then all of a sudden I realized that Lyndon was going slower than he needed to. He was a pretty big man, and he could have just said, "Excuse me, please. Excuse me, please. We are going up to our engagement," and just almost forcibly could have parted the crowd. He didn't. It dawned on me that since we were in this hell of a position, he was maybe enjoying it a little bit. Maybe going to let them have their day and show that their day was ugly and give the press time to record it and try to use it, in a strange way, for his own purposes.

We finally got to the elevator, went on upstairs, and walked into a cheering, loving, affectionate crowd, and a total change. But we were shaken and impressed. I don't think we were ever frightened, but we did realize the hostility of a sizeable, articulate segment of this country to Kennedy, to the Democratic Party, to us. What hurt me was that we thought these were our people. These were Texans. We worked for them for eleven years. But we hadn't realized the depth of the differences. I guess it was one of the tensest times I've ever lived through.

THE ELECTION

Did you expect to win by the time Election Day came?
I thought it could be either way. I thought it was entirely razor-edge and up for grabs. But I knew that I couldn't affect it. It's just like being in a big storm. You just do your best to stay safe and not make it any worse.

As Election Day came, was LBJ tense or relaxed?
Very tense, very tense.

This was extremely important to him because his stake in this was that he could take Texas for the ticket.
Either he could deliver or he couldn't deliver, and so, of course, this was crucial for him.

As always, we voted in Johnson City at the Blanco County courthouse, where Lyndon had taken me to vote the first time in 1936. For Lyndon and me election night took place in the old Driskill Hotel in Austin, where so many election nights had gone with us. We were in the Governor Jim Hogg Suite, and a lot of our close friends were there. There was a lot of press there. There was usually a blackboard and one or two people who would be rushing in and putting up figures, and just a whole cluster of phones ringing, and people coming and going, and a lot of confusion. I do remember very late at night, when it finally got fairly certain that Senator Kennedy and Lyndon had won by a tiny majority, that it did occur to me that I ought to say something, just a salute, to our opponents, the Nixons, because they, too, had tried as hard as they could and given it all the strength and energy they had. And I did. I have the feeling that I probably went to bed a long time before Lyndon. He was a good deal more revved up than

I was. You have that all-of-a-sudden slightly deflated feeling; you do not have to struggle anymore. You do not have to gather up that adrenalin from the very bottom of your resources. You can afford to fall apart.

Poor President Kennedy, poor everybody who has to adopt the ways of a strange community when they are running for office and may not like those ways but have to make out like they do. [*Laughter.*] [When Kennedy visited the LBJ Ranch], predictably, he was given a hat by the citizens of Stonewall. It was funny. I watched this all fall because President Kennedy had a very courteous, nice way of accepting gifts and saying something nice and perhaps humorous about them, but never actually making use of them, especially if it was a hat. [*Laughter.*] Indian bonnets, western Stetsons. They went hunting, and we had lunch, predictably, with the Wests, and the [Gene] Chambers, and the Moursunds, and a bunch of staff. Then President-Elect Kennedy left that evening to fly on to Florida.

Was that a relaxed time when Kennedy was there?
No. [*Laughter.*] If you'd been in a pressure cooker for two months, you do not really relax after a campaign as I lived it, and as I saw others live it, until come sometime later.

PALM BEACH

There was a very considerable flurry of planning [for the new administration]. At one point Senator Kennedy invited, and here I'm afraid that he invited just Lyndon alone, but Lyndon, who would always say, "Come and bring your family," or at least "Bring your wife"—that was his general pattern—and he understood that I was invited. Anyhow, we went down to Palm Beach, and they were staying at the home of the senior Kennedys. Mrs. Kennedy had just had the baby not long before, and she was recuperating there. We had been to that lovely place once before when Lyndon was a senator. Mrs. Rose Kennedy had invited him. In fact we were in that house three times, as I recall. It was a comfortable, charming house with a patio. This time Lyndon and Senator Kennedy were shut up in conversation most of the time. I remember Mrs. Kennedy telling me that she had been so busy with trying to plan all this wardrobe that you'd have to have and looking at little samples and swatches, and at the same time trying to get her strength back. She was walking on the beach and getting out in the sun as much as she could. There was a movie in the patio at night, and staff and Secret Service men, as I recall, were invited to take some of the chairs and sit around and enjoy the movie. Except for that, it was talk, talk, talk.

A NEW HOME AND OFFICE

Ever since we went on the air with the television station on Thanksgiving Day of 1952, we had been living in crowded, inadequate, temporary quarters. We just needed a home. At the corner of Tenth and Brazos there was a good, sturdy, ugly building with gray brick facing that had been used by either the YWCA or the YMCA for many years. At this point it was empty and for sale. Max Brooks said, "Let's go have a look at it." We decided to buy it. It would have to be gutted, and I mean gutted. The radio station remained in an adjoining building, and the television station was put into this building.

The top floor, the fifth floor, was reserved for a penthouse apartment for us. We were going to live over the store, so to speak. There was room for a little terrace; that part appealed to me. We would have a little garden out there. It had lots of virtues because there was nothing between us and the capitol of Texas, straight in front of us, off of this little terrace, and the Governor's Mansion to our left, and the old Land Office building to our right. A population of bats and swallows from some surrounding buildings flew around at night. It was an interesting possibility; it offered us more room than we had ever had before.

To me it was important to see what the view would be like from this presumed apartment we were going to have. So Max first climbed a ladder, and I climbed it after him. It was a little bit hairy to look down on five floors of space below you with nothing but steel girders and narrow catwalks. It's amazing that we didn't hurt ourselves badly.

How did you get down?
We climbed up; we climbed down. [*Laughter.*] But we really did. We may have had a camera; we may have taken a picture. At any rate, we got a good eye view of what we would have from the living room windows, from the big bedroom window, which was going to stretch across the whole bedroom. It was pleasing, and there was a lot to be said for it. So we let a contract early in the year.

Actually, we moved in October of that same year, at a time when our life was never more hectic. I got Genevieve Hendricks to come down and stay with me in the early part of this year, 1960, and plan the furnishings of this little apartment. She was a top-notch person. We had really become friends. I valued her. She would recognize the fact that I didn't have all that much money— a lot of her clients did—but that I aspired to better things, and she wanted to get me better things, to the extent I could pay for them. She raised my sights; she educated me as to furniture and the way a house should look. I consider her a part of my making, and I am grateful to her. That penthouse, a very pleasant little place with a rooftop garden, two bedrooms, two baths, a living/dining area and a kitchen, was our pied-à-terre in Austin until I alone bought a house in the late eighties.[22]

22. Mrs. Johnson bought and remodeled a home on Mt. Larson.

18

Vice Presidency
"A Pebble in A Shoe"

In Lady Bird Johnson's words, the vice presidential years were "a very different period of our lives." The 1960 presidential election made them national celebrities. As vice president and second lady, their invitations and opportunities multiplied. But prominence was not the equivalent of power. Although President Kennedy gave his vice president a limited portfolio, the office was essentially a demotion for LBJ. He was now the presiding officer of the Senate, but he was no longer in charge of the body he had led so effectively. Nor was there any apparent avenue for political advancement. The new president had inherited the leadership of the Democratic Party; the vice presidency was a dead end. Not surprisingly, Lyndon Johnson was often restless, bored, and depressed in his new job.

Making up for the loss of power was the opportunity for extensive international travel, a learning experience in hands-on diplomacy. In April 1961 the Johnsons represented the United States at the celebration of Senegal's independence, returning from Africa by way of Geneva and Paris. The following month, they embarked on a long Asian trip, covering Wake Island, Guam, South Vietnam, Taipei, Hong Kong, Thailand, India, Pakistan, and Greece. Mrs. Johnson did not accompany her husband on his dramatic trip to Berlin soon after the construction of the Berlin Wall. In 1962, they traveled to the Middle East, where they visited Lebanon, Iran, Turkey, Cyprus, Greece, and Rome. Trips in 1963 took them to the Dominican Republic for the inauguration of Juan Bosch and later to Scandinavia, where they visited Sweden, Finland, Norway, and Denmark. Their final trip—to Luxembourg, the Netherlands, and Belgium—came in November 1963.

In contrast to LBJ, Lady Bird relished the vice presidential years. Their purchase of the Elms, hostess Perle Mesta's mansion in Washington's upscale Spring Valley, gave the second lady an opulent setting for entertaining. Her frequent role as a stand-in for Jacqueline Kennedy at official functions and the international travel provided a valuable apprenticeship for her years as first lady.

THE INAUGURATION

It was the coldest inauguration in the world, I'm sure. Every one of our friends had a story about it. One of the most elegantly dressed couples I know from Texas started out all dressed up [for] one of the balls. The taxi they were in came to a dead halt and couldn't go a foot farther. Finally they got out and flagged a ride in a truck, which turned out to have been used to carry fish. [*Laughter.*] They arrived at the ball, as you can imagine, redolent of fish, but just loving it. It made a big story for them, just for fun. There was an endless round of balls and a magnificent setting for the actual swearing-in ceremony itself. From Senator Kennedy there was a truly rousing speech that you could be so very proud of. I can remember a touching little moment when Robert Frost was reading from some of his poetry. He was very old, couldn't see very well.[1] It was, of course, one of the most dramatic moments in our life.

No more dramatic to me than the swearing in of the senators. Lyndon had been elected to both the Senate and to the vice presidency. He was there in the chamber and made the required speech about resigning. I was in the gallery watching, and I felt like one of these watchers at a wedding when the preacher gets to that part, "If there is anybody here that knows why this should not be done, rise up now or forever hold your peace." That was the last good-bye to the Senate, and it was an emotion-charged moment. Then we walked out of the Senate and into the new job.

There was a lessening of his ties with the Senate and of his association with them. Each body is always very jealous and guarding of its prerogatives, the executive is, the representative is, and the judicial is, and I can understand that. Yes, Lyndon was sad that he did not see more of the senators.

There were stories that went around Washington of people asking, "How's Lyndon doing?" And then the response was, "Lyndon Who?"
In my feeling Lyndon was never hurt, angry, or disappointed at the principal, that is, President Kennedy, in his belief that he wanted him to take part in everything. Never at any time did he have any cause to feel anything but the president wanted his help, advice, work, and participation. Lyndon did feel that there was some dislike, some withdrawal on the part of some of [Kennedy's] staff toward him. It was a pebble in a shoe. It wasn't a major thing, but it existed, and it made those years less buoyant, wonderful years for him than the years of the House and the Senate. Although, on the other side, there was the learning experience of trips, the feeling that he was contributing something, both in the election and in the carrying out of all implementation, to the man whom he had chosen to

---

1. LBJ held up his top hat in an attempt to shield the poet's eyes from the sun's glare. Dallek, *An Unfinished Life*, 323.

help. I think he also took a good deal of wry pleasure in seeing what fun I was having. [*Laughter.*]

THE VICE PRESIDENCY

I wonder if you could discuss his expectations about what the vice presidency would be like, the degree to which he was either surprised or disappointed or pleased with his relationship with President Kennedy.

As he had been a student of the presidency, so he had indeed necessarily been a student of the vice presidency, and I can't say that he was surprised. But I do think, and he would have very likely stoutly denied it, because it's a loyal thing to say that you just love your job, but I think he had hoped it could be more substantive than it was. None of that was due to President Kennedy. President Kennedy couldn't have been more understanding and perceptive and active in choosing the things that he assigned to Lyndon to do and giving him a very free rein and backup in doing it. That is, he was chairman of the Space Council. He was also chairman of the President's Committee on Equal Employment Opportunity. Then the president wrote him a letter and asked him to be there and take charge of the [National Security Council] whenever he himself could not be there. These were things well chosen to Lyndon's liking. In his early life, rural electrification and the series of dams along the lower Colorado River gave him greatest satisfaction. In his later life, few things ever gave him more satisfaction than this nation's progress in space, with which he had the opportunity to play a sizeable role.

President Kennedy was most farsighted, cooperative, and helpful. He gave Lyndon a lot of leeway. One of the best things that ever happened to it, of course, was finding Jim Webb, who happened to be a longtime friend and acquaintance of Lyndon, who did the selling job of getting [Webb] to take [the space program] over.[2] It really was a magnificent achievement. To me, the human engineering was quite as wonderful as the electronic engineering: getting government and business and scientists all to work together.

My trips had been very limited, but in the vice presidency we traveled a great deal. As early as April of '61, President Kennedy asked us to represent the United States when Senegal's independence from France came about. That was a trip full of panoply and display. This first one to Senegal was an eye-opener, but the biggest eye-opener to him was the one when President Kennedy asked him to undertake a trip to Southeast Asia in '62. We made two separate trips, which included among them the Philippines and India and Vietnam and Thailand and Pakistan. What Lyndon came back thinking about Asia particularly was that such an enormous part of the world's population lived there. He got more of a

---

2. Webb was much closer to Sen. Robert Kerr than to LBJ in 1961. For Webb's account of LBJ's role in recruiting him for the NASA position, see James E. Webb Oral History Interview, 4/29/69, by T. Harrison Baker, 3–5.

perspective on the Western world, the United States and Europe, on which in my growing-up time everybody's history concentrated. We had learned very little about Asia and virtually nothing about China or Africa. But here our first trip was to Africa and then to these Asian countries.

A source indicated that both of you were very much struck particularly by the incredible phenomenon of poverty.
Uh-huh, just revolted. Revolted. Also Lyndon kept on wandering into the little villages of India where you would see so much done by manual labor that [that could be helped by] something just as simple as one motor. Dig a well and get one motor [to pump] some water up, instead of pulling it up bucket by bucket by bucket. Even having a steel plow or a tractor instead of a wooden plow. It was a great learning experience from which he gathered a great deal.

There was one magnificent moment when the president asked Lyndon to go to Berlin in August 1961. The [Berlin] wall had just gone up. I have some marvelous pictures of him in front. It was raining. He was wearing a khaki overcoat, and he stood out in the crowd. And the crowd was absolutely fast and surging. It was that flag on the bumpers of the cars. It wasn't the man so much as the message from America, and you had a tremendous feeling. In fact, in all our experiences the feeling for America was very, very strong, and very respectful and hopeful. I never saw such a mob in my life as I did in Turkey, and it took us I don't know how many hours to go from the airport to downtown, to the hotel in Istanbul. But I did think if that mob, which was so friendly and wild with greetings, if it turned against you, that'd be one of the countries I would least want to be in. Only some years later in South Korea[3] did I see a mob, a greeting, a welcoming of that magnitude and that force.

"NEVER TO RETURN"

1961 was a bad year, a very bad year. Speaker Rayburn had something that he said was lumbago. He said he had a little back trouble. I went out to the airport to meet Lyndon coming back from his Berlin trip, and there was the Speaker to meet him. I took a look at the Speaker, and his face was gray. He had lost a lot of weight. He was never a portly man, but this time his clothes just hung on him. My heart just sank. He was always just the dearest, most wonderful man and gentle with the wives of his good friends, if he liked them—which he very frequently did. He never did put on with anybody, but if he liked you, he was a very courtly gentleman. But this time he was more so than usual. When I got home I wrote him a letter, the basis of which was how wonderful it was of you to go out and meet Lyndon. I didn't say, "I'm worried about you" or anything. But I just

---

3. For CTJ's description of the visit to South Korea in October 1966, see Johnson, *A White House Diary*, 446–51.

said how wonderful it's been, you've been one of the greatest parts of all of our years in Washington, and every time I see you it makes me feel more reassured about my country and happier for myself. I got back really a very nice letter from him, and I think he knew he was saying good-bye. He did leave the next day or two, never to return. He went into a hospital, and it was pretty soon diagnosed as cancer. We made a trip or two up to see him, and he died in November.

Also Senator Kerr died, to everybody's great surprise, because he was a monumental tough guy. You'd think death was a long way off for him. He got sick, went to the hospital. Everybody thought he was on the way to recovery, and then he just suddenly died. That was early January of '63. So those were two things that took the underpinnings out of the House and Senate.

LUCI'S DYSLEXIA

Luci made a change from Ben Murch School. She went on to another junior high for one or two years, and then I finally got her into the National Cathedral School, which was a triumph for me. A year or two earlier, a great thing happened in her life. She had long had an eye condition—now the well-known name for it is dyslexia. But there are many, many forms of that, where what you see doesn't get translated to the brain in quite the way it should. It used to be a puzzle to her teachers and to us that this child that we thought was so bright would not make good grades. The teachers would talk to me about it, and I would take her to the best eye doctors that I could, according to what my peers, the wives of other congressmen and senators, told me was the best eye doctor they'd found. And they'd say, "Nothing's the matter." Finally, she fell into the hands of the doctor who discovered her ailment, maybe after Lyndon became vice president. Janet Travell directed her to Dr. [Robert] Kraskin. [He] figured out what it was, gave her a series of eye exercises that changed her whole life and personality, because she became an achiever up to her very remarkable mental capacity, whereas before, because of this eye problem, she had been stunted, frustrated, and angry. It changed her personality, her rate of performance; it was a wonderful blessing. Whatever he did, it was a boon, principally to Luci, but almost as much to her mother and the rest of the family.

THE VICE PRESIDENT'S WIFE

There is rarely very much in the press about the vice president's wife.
Listen, that couldn't have bothered me less. [*Laughter.*]

What it was like to be the vice president's wife? How did it change your life in terms of the staff you had and various things?
It didn't change my life. I had the same staff I had had at 4921 Thirtieth Place except that I added a gardener and I got myself a secretary. Bess Abell was a

secretary for all purposes: social, business, typewriter, everything. She was absolutely a jewel. I had a lot more company of an official nature. I became the presiding officer of the Senate Ladies' Red Cross, instead of just one of the ardent members who went every Tuesday. In all my years with Lyndon, whatever he couldn't do, he assigned me. It was naturally assigned to me to keep him closely informed on our business back home, because it was really my business. So I still kept up with the reports on KTBC.

We did everything we could to help President and Mrs. Kennedy on that basis, because Mrs. Kennedy was not very well. I had a lot of official parties that Mrs. Kennedy or her social secretary would ask me to have, delegations, some ladies from Japan, Indira Gandhi, the Shah [of Iran], some daughter of some prime minister, just the whole panoply of visitors. I always took great pleasure in that. Instead of just the Texas constituents back home, we began to have a wider range of groups that would come to town. When it was not possible to go to the White House, we could offer them some hospitality. I did see a good deal of the press because Liz [Carpenter] began to work. She worked for Lyndon during the years of the vice presidency and didn't come with me actually officially until after the assassination. But we all found ourselves working together, more or less. Whoever worked for Lyndon was likely to help me out, if needed, and vice versa.

[The Kennedys] asked us to many delightful parties. The parties at the White House assumed a different flavor in that administration, more informal, more gay, more glittering, and frequently more substantive. I'd been to quite a lot of Eisenhower parties and a much lesser number of the parties in preceding administrations. I enjoyed them all, but these did have more grace and glamour.

"A GREAT LEARNING EXPERIENCE"

The vice presidency was a very different period of our lives, somber in some aspects, glittering and gay in others, and a great learning experience, and a sadness from the loss of people like Sam Rayburn and Kerr and less contact with the Senate. I just had the most fun and enjoyed it tremendously. I can't say that Lyndon enjoyed it a great deal, although he learned a lot and we traveled a lot. For the first time, we decided we would just spend everything we could afford and more, because we had lived quite frugally. There was always one more tractor we needed to buy, or we needed to put up a tower for the radio station, or we needed a few more acres of land or something. But this time we decided we would spend it on living, and so we bought a beautiful house, the Elms, which had belonged to Perle Mesta. I shall always remember that house and its lovely grounds with greatest affection. I set about furnishing it, and when Lyndon did anything, he went whole hog. So he was all for it and wanted me to get good furniture, good everything. We had some marvelous parties there on the most fantastically modest budget, because of the ability of Bess Abell and my own staff, which had been with me from Texas for a long time. I was always blessed with a good staff.

I knew the vice presidency was somewhat limiting to the capacities of Lyndon, but that is a built-in component of the job. I don't know how you could ever change it, because Lord knows we tried to learn from it. When our turn came to have somebody that we dearly loved as vice president, we tried to do what we thought President Kennedy had tried to do for Lyndon, and it didn't always work.

There were reports in late '63 that the vice president might not be on the ticket in 1964.
The administration had been pushed, in some ways reluctantly, into a very strong civil rights stand in '62 to '63 in the [James] Meredith episode and Birmingham and the March on Washington and the civil rights speech in June of '63 that President Kennedy made.[4] Obviously, that was going to be a liability in the south. There was strong concern, particularly if Senator Goldwater were the Republican nominee, as to whether Kennedy could do very well in south in 1964. Some of the accounts claim that, obviously, this put the vice president in a very difficult position, because if he was too closely identified with the administration on civil rights, he would in a sense be providing the rationale to drop him from the ticket because he would no longer carry the weight in the election.

What was his response to the rumors that he would be dropped from the ticket? Did he blame anybody in particular for that kind of speculation?
Of course, it was painful, and it was just something to endure. I don't know that he blamed anybody in particular. He knew the general sources. It was not as though you would be losing something that you cherished or wanted. You'd rather walk out of it than be pushed out of it. It was not a good time. He received assurances from the president himself from time to time, but it was not a good year.

---

4. In September 1962, President Kennedy federalized the Mississippi National Guard to force the state to comply with a court order to admit James Meredith to the University of Mississippi. In April 1963, Martin Luther King Jr. led a demonstration protesting Birmingham's segregated facilities and discriminatory hiring practices. The chief of police, "Bull" Connor, attacked the marchers with fire hoses and police dogs. Blacks retaliated. Administration officials and local moderates negotiated a tenuous peace. In June, the Justice Department and the federalized Alabama National Guard forced Gov. George Wallace to stand aside, enabling black students to enroll in the University of Alabama. On June 11, Kennedy gave a televised speech calling for new civil rights legislation. Dallek, *An Unfinished Life*, 514–18, 594–604.

THE TRIP TO TEXAS

What precisely did the president and vice president hope to accomplish on the trip to Texas, and to what degree were they accomplishing it before the unexpected happened?
Lyndon wasn't as much a part of the planning of that trip as he thought he should [be]. It was just presented to him as something that was going to be done, and this aggrieved him somewhat.

I thought he had urged the president to go.
I don't quite think that's right. Governor Connally, I think, had. And there's no doubt about it, he was needed. His popularity was not good at that time, and his popularity needed to be improved. Also fundraising was going to have to start before too long. But I think the trip was good for somewhat more of John's planning than of . . .

There are all sorts of accounts of the split being very bitter between Connally and Yarborough, [with them] refusing to sit in the same car.[5]
Yes, all of that existed. But the odd thing from our standpoint was that Senator Yarborough had always been pretty good about voting with Lyndon's line of what he had wanted philosophically and legislation he had pushed. However, personally we were never close. We were very close and devoted and had years of association with John. It was perhaps just as simple as the fact that John was a good deal more conservative and Yarborough was a good deal more liberal, and their chemistries just didn't mix.

Did you feel that the president was successful in the trip before Dallas?
Yes. The crowds were better. I remember meeting them in San Antonio, and there was a moment when Mrs. Kennedy went out into the group and spoke to a few young Latin American girls, and she was very sweet and gentle with them. And I thought, "Oh, gee, she's going to do it just fine."

Did she speak to them in Spanish?
I don't remember. She had spoken in Spanish the night before to great accolades and applause in Houston. This was just a group of youngsters in the airport— "working the fence," as it is called, something quite new in her life and very old in ours. She was doing it gracefully and sweetly and making a lot of people happy, and I thought, "How nice." It did look like people were turning out in sizable numbers and very friendly. So we were feeling good about it.

---

5. According to Lawrence O'Brien, it was Albert Thomas who first asked President Kennedy to come to Texas. Lawrence F. O'Brien, *No Final Victories* (Garden City, NY: Doubleday, 1974), 155–57. For a full description of the efforts to get Yarborough to ride in LBJ's car, see Caro, *The Passage of Power*, 301–9.

Once the events had taken place in Dallas, there are accounts of a great deal of bitterness on the plane, and that Mrs. Kennedy had wanted to take off, and that there had been a delay.[6]

I know the delay was because Lyndon would not leave until she and the body arrived. He said he was not going to leave until she got there. Can't you imagine how awful that would have been?

There is that much-publicized or alleged incident in which, when the plane landed at Andrews Air Force Base, the attorney general came on board and raced to the front to be with Mrs. Kennedy, and, according to a number of eyewitnesses, President Johnson extended his hand, and the attorney general just ran right by and didn't shake his hand. You're the first person that's ever told me that.

You've never heard that?

No. Can't you understand that his mind was so... One could easily forgive him that.

What specific recollections do you have of that trip back?

Everybody congregated in groups. Naturally you gravitated to those that you were closest to. Somebody would come by and offer us coffee or bouillon or a sandwich. Hardly anybody ate anything. Everybody was wrapped in his own cocoon or nightmare. Lyndon was vastly more alert than I was. Suddenly he looked around, and he said, "This is the president's compartment; let's get out of here." So we went back and sat in the body of the plane, and in just a few moments Mrs. Kennedy came in and, of course, went in there. There was never anybody that wanted to give more deference and assistance than Lyndon. What could matter less than the fact that Bobby rushed on, rushed past, if indeed he did? I don't remember. I know that the casket went off first, and I think that is entirely appropriate.

I remember Lyndon's secretary, Marie [Fehmer], I think, was putting in calls while we were still on the ground. Two of them were to the attorney general to dictate the oath. Then on the way back, we called Mrs. Rose Kennedy. That's another one of those instances where as soon as he could say what he could, which is nothing really except that we'll all pray for our country or something like that, he handed it to me. He was always handing me the telephone when I didn't always necessarily want it. Then he tried to reach Nellie [Connally] to be brought up to date on John. I had been to see her, and she had said that he was going to be all right, and we felt that he was. He was big and strong and tough, but this really laid him out for quite a while.

---

6. After Mrs. Kennedy and the casket boarded, LBJ delayed takeoff until Judge Sarah T. Hughes arrived and administered the oath of office.

Did you have any part at all in writing the statement that President Johnson delivered at the airport?
No, I didn't, but I saw it and read it in several drafts and approved it.

It must have been an unbelievable strain.
It was. It was just a nightmare quality. You didn't think this was really happening. It was also a mixture of anger and shame that your country should behave like that. Particularly, although you can't blame the state of Texas or the city of Dallas for one individual's action, yet there was this horrible feeling that it happened in your own state.

I never in my life saw such a crescendo of activity, never before or after, and such a gathering of forces. On the way, Lyndon sent word to the plane that had taken a great number of cabinet members to Japan, and he got back the answer they had already gotten the word and had turned around. He would have the cabinet in, the Senate leadership and House leadership, and then all sorts of groups of press, ministers. In fact, sometimes my mouth would just hang open at seeing somebody whom I considered practically an entrenched enemy walking into Lyndon's office. He was determined to pull everybody together that he possibly could, because he really was not sure how widespread this might be or how rending. He just wanted desperately to try to unite us and then just to forge ahead with all the legislation that was on the dockets. So it was a tremendous effort to restore order and to bring us together and to wrest from this tragedy whatever we could get of determination to proceed with legislation that had been stalled or was not being successfully completed.

THE JOHNSONS AND THE KENNEDYS

I was not an intimate of Mrs. Kennedy, by any means, but I saw a bit of her. Lyndon actually saw more of her because she was a very appealing woman. I remember when she wanted to get something done, she was absolutely the most graceful person. At the same time, I felt she could also be a difficult opponent indeed if she ever were. But she and Lyndon liked each other tremendously. At least I know he liked her, and I think she liked him, because she gave every evidence of appreciation in several instances.

Another thing that he did for her [that he would not have done] for the State Department, not even, I expect, would he have done it for the president, but because she asked him he did, and that was make a speech. For some reason the president couldn't, and I can't think why [Dean] Rusk or somebody else didn't. But anyhow, she asked him to make a speech vis-à-vis André Malraux [the French minister of culture], when Malraux came over here. That was not Lyndon's cup of tea. But I think he would have done anything she asked him to, because she was really so graceful and charming and persuasive and also apparently very appreciative.[7] I found out a good bit about that quality after the assassination. I received several letters from her.

Let me ask you about President Johnson's relationship with Bobby Kennedy.
It was necessarily made up of many things. It was never close or affectionate. On the one hand you had to weigh Lyndon's [loyalty]. In the life of an old-fashioned politician—and to some extent Lyndon was that—some words are written in capital letters, and one of them is *loyalty*. After he had agreed to be vice president to John F. Kennedy, he had a loyalty to him and to his staff and family and all like that. That weighed heavily with him. He tried to like [Robert Kennedy] and understand him. Their chemistries didn't really mix. On that other hand, everybody had to like his wife. Ethel was a darling, and she had us out to their house a number of times. Then there was this enormous surge of compassion and misery for him when his brother died, and once more a big attempt to understand and like. All of that led to a very considerable output of effort to help him get elected to the Senate. Actually, I guess they were just foredoomed not to ever be good friends.

I remember a couple of instances myself, one of which I thought was very graceful. It was [April 8, 1964,] after the assassination, and it was the funeral of General [Douglas] MacArthur. I just remember it was a somber, bitter cold, stormy day. We were all standing in line down at the Union Station, and I found myself standing next to the attorney general. We waited quite a while and he leaned over to me and said, "You're doing a good job." Then there was a perceptible pause, and with what seemed a real effort he said, "And your husband is too."[8] So he was trying, too, I think.

I remember another time standing in the East Room at the White House. Lyndon must have been president by then. [Robert Kennedy] leaned over and said, "Well, Lady Bird, I hear you're going to make Washington beautiful." [*Laughter.*] I just had this feeling of a little lady over the teacups. But what he didn't know was that, in my opinion, I was several million people, because that is something that is deep in the hearts of a lot of people all over the country. They just want to make their hometown, their capital, their state as environmentally beautiful as they can to live in and work in and play in and be proud of. So multiply me by about quite a few million, and you've got something. No big deal for me, but it is a big deal for all of us put together. I just smiled and said, "I'm going to do my best."

It was sad that they couldn't have been better friends, and they were not. But Lyndon strove mightily, against the very strong advice of a whole lot of his friends, to act in a completely loyal and compassionate manner to every one of

---

7. See Carl Sferrazza Anthony, *First Ladies: The Saga of the Presidents' Wives and Their Power*, vol. 2, *1961–1990* (New York: William Morrow, 1991), 68–70.
8. Also see Johnson, *A White House Diary*, 102–3.

the Kennedy appointees who were still in their places when he assumed the presidency. Of course, President Kennedy's brother was at the head of that list to whom he tried to extend loyalty.

Most of the Kennedy staff stayed on for at least some period of time: [Theodore] Sorensen and [Ken] O'Donnell...
And [Lawrence] O'Brien remained and was actually [postmaster general] in Lyndon's cabinet, a higher post than he was in the Kennedy times. And, of course, Dean Rusk and Bob McNamara and Orville Freeman were people that Lyndon had tremendous personal admiration and devotion to.[9] He liked Willard Wirtz fine.[10] I think they disagreed on things from time to time, but he liked him and his wife Jane fine.

Do you have any specific recollections about whether [RFK] might be President Johnson's running mate in 1964?
No, I don't, except that Lyndon would not have wanted that. He would have wanted a running mate that he had warmth for.

---

9. Dean Rusk was secretary of state; Robert McNamara was secretary of defense, and Orville Freeman was secretary of agriculture under Presidents Kennedy and Johnson.
10. Willard Wirtz was secretary of labor during the Kennedy and Johnson administrations.

19

The White House Years

Lady Bird Johnson transformed the institution of the first lady. Deciding early that her role as first lady would "emerge in deeds, not words," she developed a substantive agenda and established a professional staff in the East Wing to advance it. Bess Abell, Mrs. Johnson's experienced social secretary, now had reinforcements. Veteran journalist Liz Carpenter, who had served on the vice presidential staff, became the first lady's press secretary and staff director. Simone Poulain brought expertise with the mass media. Ashton Gonella, who had worked on LBJ's Senate staff, now functioned as Mrs. Johnson's secretary. White House staff member Cynthia Wilson coordinated correspondence and trips, while Sharon Francis, detailed from the Department of the Interior, focused on beautification and environmental issues.[1]

Mrs. Johnson documented her time in the White House extensively in her White House diary. Her recollections below, drawn largely from my two videotaped interviews to complement an LBJ Library exhibition, are often abridged versions of more elaborate discussions in her book A White House Diary. Although a comparison of the two validates her preference for recording recollections when they were "red-hot," the distilled version is also valuable. It underscores how significant Lady Bird Johnson's formative experiences were in shaping her tenure as first lady. The enchanting beauty of Caddo Lake in her youth, the journalism courses and social life at the University of Texas that had given her an understanding of the press, her work in the congressional office and her management of a radio station, her decades of social and intellectual interaction with significant men and women in public life, six political campaigns, extensive international travel during the vice presidential years, and life with a demanding perfectionist had had a profound influence on Lady Bird Johnson. She may have suddenly appeared onstage for a role she had not rehearsed, but she was certainly prepared for it.

---

1. Lewis Gould, "Lady Bird Johnson: First Lady Innovator," 7/16/07; Bess Abell Oral History Interview 2, 6/13/69, by T. Harrison Baker.

A WHITE HOUSE DIARY

How did you decide to keep a diary in the White House?

Very early on, after the assassination and after our return to the Elms that night—a beautiful, welcoming Elms against the contrast of all of the emotions we were going through—it began to dawn on me that I was going through an experience that was absolutely unique and I was the only person who would see it from my vantage point and that it was worth remembering, if for nothing else, for me to look back on in a quieter day and for perhaps future grandchildren.[2] I didn't have the vaguest idea what I was going to do with it. But about the same time, Liz Carpenter told me that she thought I ought to keep a diary and that her son [Scott Carpenter] knew how to work one of these little recording machines. I said bring it over, and I would see if I can do it. So I think I did begin with his. Later, at some point, I bought one. The White House, when I moved in on the seventh, had an ample supply. I probably used one of theirs, mostly. I am the least mechanically minded person in the world. Turning on and off a light switch is about the limit of my capability, and I had lots of amusing times trying to make that thing work.

Describe your daily routine of recording these diary entries.

Alas, it wasn't really daily. I tried to make it as nearly daily as I could, but I do think it was probably on an average of at least two days a week, maybe three. The place I did it was a place I'll always remember with love. In the White House, there is a little corner room right next to what was my bedroom that Mrs. Kennedy had used as a dressing room. And so I continued using it as a dressing room, moved in a small blue velvet sofa, which was my own, and a comfortable chair with a table and light, and a small desk. There was a corner fireplace and there were two wonderful windows. One looked right down onto the Rose Garden, and right across [from] it was Lyndon's office. The other looked out onto the southwest grounds and right down onto Andrew Jackson's giant magnolia, and through the limbs you could see the Washington Monument in the distance. I loved that setting, and I saw it in all seasons, sometimes with a fire going in this pretty little fireplace, sometimes with the crabapples down below coming out in their pink fantasy. It was one of my favorite spots in the White House.

I usually [recorded] in the evening because Lyndon was absolutely unpredictable about what time he would come home for dinner. He would come home when he got the work done or in a state where he thought he could afford to leave it. Therefore, that meant a lot of waiting, for me and for the kitchen. Thank heavens, they were mostly understanding. And I tried to make them know how much I appreciated their being understanding, because we

---

2. For a more elaborate discussion, see Johnson, *A White House Diary*, vii–ix.

were there for the work, not to keep precise hours and to sit down to a lovely, beautifully served meal on time. So I would go in there and turn on my little machine and begin to remember what had happened. After some length of time, I began to realize that if I referred to my date book and if, in the course of the day, I would put down the names of two or three of the most memorable people, events, feelings of that day, it would be helpful. So I would take a comfortable seat and turn it on. There was a wonderful little switch that you could stop it with. It was a slow process. Lyndon would come home for dinner eight o'clock, nine o'clock, sometimes at ten o'clock. If I had finished the duties of the day, that was my time. I had a little pillow embroidered on the outside [of the door]—gee, the children resented that little pillow—what did it say? "Busy, don't come in" or something.

Was President Johnson aware of your diary project while you were working on it?
Oh, yes. I told him about it. I can't say that it was of consummate interest to him. He was proud of it. He was glad I cared, but I wasn't exactly at the forefront of his thinking. There soon evolved a feeling within me that I wanted, one, to improve my intake, to absorb the events of the day and to remember them better. You remember them better if you make yourself record them, either by writing them down or by talking them into this machine. I also wanted to improve my skill in being able to describe something. If it weren't so hard, I'd like to be a writer. [*Laughter.*] But it is too hard.

Did the president read it?
Yes. He did. He read it, every word, he said, and I believe. As a matter of fact, he used to feel a little sad because I didn't read his more. But his was important, difficult, in some instances heart-rending, and always very demanding. My book was a relatively light book.

There was one traumatic moment before I had these [tapes] transcribed. We were sitting in the White House after March 31, 1968.[3] I thought to myself, I have never played back any of those tapes. What if they haven't recorded? What if some little wheel didn't get engaged? I better play back a random sampling of them. So I fished one out of the little cupboard that I had had built to slip them into and put it on and hooked it up. I was very un-mechanical-minded and I pressed the button, and it went round and round, and nothing happened. In fear I pressed another button. I made it go back. I tried again. For I guess about five minutes I was just scared to death that I had spent hours of my life doing nothing. Finally, it got properly in gear, and it begin to roll off, reciting events of this now long-past day which I couldn't possibly recall. So I relaxed. One of the virtues of doing this thing is that no matter how honest you tried to be, if you

---

3. At the conclusion of his nationally televised speech on March 31, 1968, LBJ announced that he would not seek or accept another term as president.

looked at it five years later and tried to say what happened, hindsight and the mists of time and the changes in your feelings toward people or events are going to color what you put down about that day. It is better to put it while it's red-hot. Everything I put in there was—I think the longest period was probably a week, at most two weeks. Of course, there was one month when I did nothing at all, and that was the month of October of '64, which was the campaign. And I would so love to have had some really accurate memories, but one worked from "can till can't" and fell into bed exhausted, so I didn't record in that month is my recollection.

THE ROLE OF FIRST LADY

How has the role of the first lady changed over the years?
I think it has changed with the role of women in general, because each one of these is an individual who comes there, elected by one man only, and from her own personal background, and almost certainly without ever having planned, anticipated, prepared. At least, that was the case with me. So it's a role that is bound to change with each individual, but it is bound to be affected by the general way that women behaved in the culture of the time that you're in. Of course, Mrs. Franklin D. Roosevelt was the trailblazer because she ventured out into all sorts of new fields, exploring and seeking out the message and carrying the message to people all over the country, beyond the field of being the hostess and the companion to her husband.

Did you yourself have a role model for your tenure as first lady?
No, I can't say that I did. I just wanted to live it up to the fullest, to do the best that I could in everything that I considered a duty, an obligation, an opportunity. It really is the most marvelous opportunity. Your first business is quite obviously to take care of your husband and provide him with a little island of serenity, a milieu to which he could return to rest and maybe laugh and be natural and comfortable and give him strength to return to that hard road. The second job is to tend to the children and try to make sure that they get as much out of it as they can and give as much to it and not suffer any of the quite possible bad effects. It's always a good thing to remember every day how temporary this is. I actually got into the habit of counting the days—X months and so many days, X years and months, days. It helps level you off and also reminds you of all of the things you want to clock into that time if you can.

Nothing had been contemplated or prepared for—just the most violent and awful beginning. I sensed something like I walked on stage for a role I had never rehearsed. At first, I had no idea what my role would be except to ease Mrs. Kennedy's burdens.

THE WHITE HOUSE

You once described the White House as having a triple purpose.
Yes, it's built-in and natural. First, it belongs to all the people of the United States and it's a national museum. It really records the way of furnishing and the memories of the lives of everybody who has lived there from John and Abigail Adams on—they were the first president and first lady to live there. About three-quarters of a million people, maybe eight hundred thousand, came through there each year during our time, every one of them feeling a sense of pride, curiosity, and part ownership. It used to be on my beat when Lyndon was in the Congress and in the Senate, and I would bring constituents through, first just to walk around the edges, because in the war years it was limited. Then through the public tours, or with your congressman or senator you can arrange a somewhat smaller tour about eight thirty in the morning.

The second aspect, it's a place where the head of this nation extends hospitality to visiting chiefs of state: kings, prime ministers. And as such, you want to be able to have a piece of America—the good foods, the good wines that belong to this country, the entertainment, the finest of American musicians, actors, ballet dancers—the whole scope of the entertainment—all in setting that speaks of America, of its history. So that is the place of hospitality for the current president.

Third, it's the home of a family, day in, day out. As such, it has its changing personality, depending on the age of the current president and his wife and whether their children are still at home, whether they're teenagers as ours were or really young folks like the Kennedys'. It's very interesting to follow the record of the lives there. It was on that aspect that in my time we put together a book called *The Living White House* with a little vignette of each one of those [families], beginning with Adams.[4]

There are certain things you do. I bless Mrs. Kennedy for moving a family dining room up on the second floor, because the psychological difference between the State Floor and the second floor, the family floor, is a world apart. You wanted to be ready to meet anybody when you were down on that first floor, and you might. You wanted to have your hair combed and your dress looking just right, and you felt a certain sense of responsibility. You put on a robe, so to speak, when you went down in that elevator and walked out. The minute you got back up to that second floor you could kick off your shoes and be as at home as you were in Stonewall, Texas, or wherever you came from. It has been used in many ways by different families. We loved to have the third floor for the children to have dates up there, and that charming round solarium.

---

4. Lonnelle Aikman, *The Living White House* (Washington, DC: White House Historical Association, 1966).

For that purpose, we had put in a little tiny kitchenette and television, comfortable chairs, and they could have dates and be totally natural and relaxed. I used to go out there on that third floor sometimes in a bathing suit—small alcove—and lie out in the sun and get a good sunbath when the angle was right.

Did you have a favorite room in the White House?
On the State Floor, I think it was the Green Room. It was charming and elegant, and above the fireplace in those days was Benjamin Franklin.[5] A good room to work in—not my taste generally, but a very good room to work in—was the Lincoln Cabinet Room, called the Treaty Room in our time. It was furnished in the very height of Victorian furniture, all done by Mrs. Kennedy and all superb, I thought. Not what I liked best, but it was all so good. You just had to respect something that's done just right of its time.

How did you respond to the pressure of raising your family in such a fishbowl environment?
Lynda and Luci could answer that better than I could. As for the end result on them, I very much hoped that they would live up to the responsibilities and the opportunities and also realize what a passing thing this was, how very temporary, and to both get and give everything that that place offered. You really have to be careful about a lot of things because the most casual word can be blown out of context. I remember Lyndon rather flippantly and casually one time describing Lynda as the smart one and Luci as the pretty one. Unfortunately those became known publicly, and the girls were just so tired of hearing about it, because it made Lynda doubt whether she was pretty and Luci think, "By gosh, do y'all think I'm dumb?" It's a place that you do certainly have to be careful in, but to me the opportunities to meet some of the most interesting and bright people in the world, a varied panorama that passes before your eyes. The advantages so far outweigh the difficulties. I hope they felt that way. You can't buffer them from the strain. If they've got ears, they're going to hear that shouting of objections to the war in Vietnam outside that window, and that is very painful, particularly in the last year, when each of them had a husband over there. But they also got to see this great country in a marvelous way in which they met a lot of people and had a lot of doors opened to them which wouldn't have been otherwise.

Did you devote a measure of private time to your family?
Yes, yes, yes. And that was the most fun time, to curl up on the bed and find out just how Luci's trip had gone and whether she thought she made any votes in Spearfish, South Dakota, or whether she had a good time at the college town

---

5. At the behest of Jacqueline Kennedy, Walter Annenberg donated David Martin's 1767 portrait of Benjamin Franklin to the White House.

where she had been to a dance. Or to listen to Lynda, who is a great history buff. One of the first things she did when she walked into the Lincoln Room and read the typed script below the Gettysburg Address where it says that he had freed the slaves in the [Emancipation Proclamation in 1863] was to tell the curator, Jim Ketchum, who later became one of our very favorite people, "That's not accurate. He freed the slaves only in those states that were in rebellion." That was historically true, because he didn't free the slaves in all the states until the end of the war. The curator just stood there with his mouth open. What? This teenaged youngster was disputing that text. They looked it up. She was correct.

The press was one of the main reasons that you lived in a fishbowl environment. What were your own personal guidelines in dealing with the press?
I wanted to accommodate them as much as I could. I felt like I saw more of them than nearly anybody. I knew a great many of them personally and liked them. And I think I got better than I deserved from the press in general. Just either say nothing or make sure what I was saying was accurate as far as it went was what I strove to do. And I tried to be available, and I tried to remember their duties. They had to get some kind of a story. Luci was much better than I was, though. If she couldn't tell them the story they wanted, she would tell them another which was almost as interesting, which seemed to work very well. In fact, I would say among the four of us, she did the best with the press.

DECORATING THE WHITE HOUSE

In February 1961, Jacqueline Kennedy organized a Fine Arts Committee for the White House to locate and raise money to purchase antique furniture for the building. The White House Historical Association, a nonprofit organization, was incorporated later that year; it offered the advantage of being able to raise money through the sale of White House publications. In January 1964 President Johnson issued an executive order formally establishing the office of White House curator and creating the Committee for the Preservation of the White House as an official successor to the more informal Fine Arts Committee. The preservation committee's statutory members included the curator and the chief usher of the White House, the secretary of the Smithsonian, the chair of the U.S. Commission of Fine Arts, the director of the National Gallery of Art, and the director of the National Park Service. Mrs. Kennedy agreed to serve as one of the public members but did not attend the meetings.[6]

James Ketchum, the White House curator during the 1960s, has emphasized that Mrs. Kennedy's decorating and acquisitions might not have lasted had it not been for Mrs. Johnson's "second generation" support. Moreover, although the foundation had been laid for a collection of paintings, Mrs. Johnson studied the gaps and ultimately acquired a who's

---

6. Johnson, *A White House Diary*, 60–61, 78–79; Clark Clifford, *Counsel to the President: A Memoir* (New York: Random House, 1991), 363–67.

who of American art for the White House. In her White House Diary, she conceded that
the committee should have been more aggressive in publicizing its acquisitions and its wish
list, admitting, however, that it "comes more easily to me to thank than to ask."[7]

I stepped into a White House beautifully done with taste and reverence and charm—the work of Mrs. Kennedy—and mostly all finished, except the collecting of American artists would never be finished. She had me over to tea, and she had prepared a handwritten memorandum on a yellow legal pad about things that she had done in regard to the White House. [It just showed] the quality of hours and work and knowledge and determination and love she had put into that house. I heard her friends say that she worked on it very hard. The way they would express it, there wasn't a Kleenex box that went into the room that she hadn't supervised to see that it was just right for the room. Indeed she was a worker, which I don't think was always quite recognized. No doubt she would have many other loves had she been there longer, but she really wanted me to safeguard that, continue that. Her words really fell on fertile ground, because I cared deeply about it, although from a different viewpoint, because I wasn't really knowledgeable about eighteenth-century furniture or anything like that.

The first meeting of the [Fine] Arts Committee, which we renamed the Committee for the Preservation of the White House, was one that I looked forward to with fear and trembling, because so many of these people were greatly knowledgeable, cultured, lived in elegant homes, and knew so much that I didn't know. So I studied and studied and tried and tried. Finally, the day came and I met them all. I enjoyed it and I think I may have made some friends. I believe they left feeling that their work was not going to be wrecked but going to be preserved, valued, and continued. Absolute tops in that committee was Mr. Harry du Pont, the patron saint of Winterthur, who was chairman. There were lots of people [on the committee] that I cared about; Jane Engelhard. I quickly added Mrs. George Brown.

We set about many things. One was to continue the work of Mrs. Kennedy in getting the beautiful gold damask drapes for the East Room. She'd done it all, but it took them forever to finish the work and be sent over from France, where one ancient man had been making the fringe. Then I knew we had to get drapes for the State Dining Room, and I took the wife of the chairman of the Appropriations Committee in there just to show her how the ones we had were absolutely shredding apart. It was going to be paid for mostly by the White House Historical Association. So we got those drapes, and we got china. [Designing] the Johnson china was a long, hard road, but I loved it. I spent a lot of time comparing all the early eagles and the borders on the Madison [china], the Monroe, and all the first presidents' [china]—down as far as Lincoln—and

---

7. James R. Ketchum Oral History Interview 1, 7/26/78, by Michael L. Gillette, 15–34; Johnson, *A White House Diary*, 752.

finally indulged myself in having a variety of wildflowers of the United States as a part of the motif, particularly the motif on the dessert plates.

My main aim was to acquire as many of the American artists and have them represented [in the White House]. After all, it is the showcase of the American people, and I wanted to have some of the best of us. The very first thing we got Mrs. George Brown brought, wrapped up in brown paper. I can remember her now, walking in the door, unwrapping the package with a smile and holding it up. It was *The Surf at Prout's Neck* by Winslow Homer. He loved the sea and painted it in all of its moods. Early on, we got a beautiful Mary Cassatt, predictably a mother and child; André Meyer gave it to us. Right across from it, there was a Thomas Sully of Fanny Kemble, so elegant. I can remember where every one of these hung in the White House of our day. Then Bill Benton gave us a pretty little gypsy girl by Robert Henri, one of the so-called Ashcan school. We got a lively and charming [Maurice] Prendergast; we hung it in the Queen's Bedroom. A [Thomas] Eakins was one of the last things we acquired. That came from Henry Hirshhorn, who had a storehouse of about thirty-two Eakinses, and it came in connection with our being able to acquire the Hirshhorn collection for the city of Washington.[8]

Some of them got away. All my whole time there I was looking for a George Caleb Bingham, who painted all these great riverboat pictures with the trappers and the river men and the canoe full of skins, or maybe these same folks were gathered around the saloon, lifting a drink on Election Day and talking about the candidates. These pieces of Americana I did want so much to add; found several but couldn't succeed in getting any. He eluded me. I never got him. I also wanted very much to get a better portrait of one of the earlier presidents, but I think I'll have to leave that story for another time. But in all, [we acquired] a good many pieces that I was proud to have, including a bronze sculpture by Frederic Remington of cowboys and horses.

STATE DINNERS

Is there a person in the State Department or the White House who briefs you on the protocol and the customary arrangements for various social functions?
Absolutely. First you have, hopefully, a good social secretary. In my opinion, I had just the best, Bess Abell. Then there is the wife of the chief of protocol. The one that we had was Robin Duke—wife of Angie Biddle Duke—who was President Kennedy's chief of protocol and stayed on for a year or so as ours and was very knowledgeable and skillful. It was her world. The State Department always furnished you with bios of every visiting chief of state and members of his family or party. Then I would get the National Geographic maps, a wonder-

---

8. The Hirshhorn Museum, a component of the Smithsonian Institution, is dedicated to contemporary art. See Johnson, *A White House Diary*, 275–76, 307–8.

ful set of maps given to Lyndon earlier, which I had hanging on the third floor of the White House. I remember the exact spot. I'd just go up and pull down that particular country and take a good long look at what its neighbors were, what it looked like, its placement in the world. The State Department always sent you briefings on its geographic, economic, social—its problems and what was going on there.

The conferences and the talks between the president and the head of state are quite important. The dinner is a matter of respect and hospitality and hope that you will meet diverse people not only from the government but from around the United States in the fields of interest to you. You'd bone up on learning about the country and the chief of state, and then you'd try to flock the guest list somewhat accordingly. The State Department sends you a bunch [of names], and you'd have your own personal friends. Lyndon always had a roster from the House and Senate and a lot of suggestions from people in his administration who he knew were interested. You'd frequently [invite] some kinsman of the visiting chief of state—for instance, let's say the King of Nepal's son was going to Harvard, or the ambassador who had been stationed in that country in years past and had become friendly with the president or monarch. You did your best to add whatever personal element. There was one king, the king of Thailand, who was particularly fond of jazz music, so we had that as entertainment.[9] Some were skillful aviators, whatever their role in life was.

I liked [the state dinners] just fine. I found them very frustrating to have only one language. I only speak English, and that was a big drawback. It is a very sizeable asset to be able to converse in two or three languages.

THE LADY BIRD SPECIAL

A month before the 1964 presidential election, Lady Bird Johnson embarked on an epic four-day, 1,700-mile campaign trip through the South by train. Joining her in the planning and the odyssey itself were a host of remarkably capable Southern women, including Lindy Boggs, Betty Talmadge, Carrie Davis, Virginia Russell, Bess Abell, and the indomitable Liz Carpenter.[10] Perhaps no chapter in Lady Bird Johnson's tenure as first lady underscored her southern identity as did the whistle-stop campaign trip. Although LBJ's passage of the 1964 Civil Rights Act only three months earlier had alienated many

---

9. Jazz musician Stan Getz was on hand to perform for King Bhumibol Adulyadej of Thailand when President and Mrs. Johnson visited in October 1966. Johnson, *A White House Diary*, 442.

10. The best secondary account of the Lady Bird Special is Russell, *Lady Bird*, 240–64. LBJ prevailed on former Tennessee governor Buford Ellington to locate a vintage train car with a large rear platform and an open interior layout for receiving guests. Bess Abell Oral History Interview 2, 6/13/69, by T. Harrison Baker, 8–14; Liz Carpenter, *Ruffles and Flourishes* (Garden City, NY: Doubleday, 1970), 143–71; and Lindy Boggs, *Washington through a Purple Veil: Memoirs of a Southern Woman* (New York: Harcourt Brace, 1994), 188–98.

southern whites, Mrs. Johnson insisted that the South not be ignored in the campaign. She hoped that bringing hundreds of northern reporters into the South would give them—and the nation—a more positive image of the region.

The Lady Bird Special was at once a nostalgic throwback to an earlier, rural America and, at the same time, a harbinger of decades to come. The trip marked the first time that a first lady would undertake an independent campaign schedule.

Her speeches beckoned southerners to look ahead to a time when racial antagonism would no longer stifle the region's progress. Less than six months later, the same formidable network of political wives assembled for the trip would be mobilized again to organize local Head Start programs throughout the South.

I have a strong sentimental, family, deep tie to the South, and I thought the South was getting a bad rap from the nation and indeed the world. It was painted as a bastion of ignorance and prejudice and all sorts of ugly things. It was my country, and although I knew I couldn't be all that persuasive to them, at least I could talk to them in language they would understand. Maybe together we could do something to help Lyndon and then perhaps to change the viewpoint of some of those newspaper people who were traveling with me. It was a marvelous, utterly exhausting adventure.

I never saw anything more courageous than Congressman Hale Boggs from Louisiana getting up and standing by Lyndon and espousing civil rights when all of his own constituents could just tar and feather him for doing it. But there were a lot of people in the South who did know that we were going down there and we must march with the times and put this behind us and free ourselves of the burden of prejudice, so we were just daring to take up something. It was uncomfortable. I do not think it was dangerous.

Did you develop the idea and then get the president's reading on going?
Lord knows; I don't remember. It just sort of germinated and grew. I do remember a good deal about the preparation. For instance, he did say to me, "Now you must let every governor and senator know that you're coming into their state, and tell them that you would be so pleased if they found it possible to join you on the train at any portion of the time as you went through their state." I myself, scared to death, did call every last one of them. I really got some very varied responses, some courageous responses, and some responses that were folks just having lots to do in other places. Everyone was thoroughly courteous.

BEAUTIFICATION

Shortly after the inauguration in January of '65, I knew I wanted to concentrate whatever I could do on whatever parts of Lyndon's program that made my heart sing, that came naturally, that belonged to me. And so I began to try to acquaint myself with all the facets of it. All my life, nature, scenery, the beauties of this country had been my joy, what fueled my spirit, made me happy. Lyndon made a speech at Ann Arbor, Michigan [in May 1964],[11] and a great deal of it was about the environment, about conservation. I decided that's for me. Stewart Udall, secretary of the interior, who was an expert salesman, came to see me hoping to interest me in the field of conservation for the National Parks, for whatever. We were both exploring. To me, it was the right choice.[12]

We were going to work right there in our home town, so we began to form the Committee for a More Beautiful National Capital. We put on it people who had spent their lives in environmental efforts, like Laurance Rockefeller, Mary Lasker, and the head of the Park Service, people who had a natural relation to that, and the head of the city planning commission. [Pierre] L'Enfant had laid out the city of Washington with all those circles and triangles, where there were [now] mostly just a dilapidated, a fallen down bench, and a few scraggly plants. The early concept was that if we began to plant those beautifully and make them centers for people to sit and rest on a spring or summer day and contemplate our beautiful capital, that it would have a ripple effect: not only pride of people in their capital city but also in their own hometown of Keokuk, Iowa, or Selma, Alabama, or wherever they might be. So we were just a bunch of pioneers.

The word "beautification" never really suited any of us. We struggled to find something else, but not successfully, so we stayed with the word. To me, it was always just part of the whole broad tapestry of environment—clean air, clean water, free rivers, the preservation of scenic areas. It had its niche in the whole broad field, which became a consuming interest to me in the next five years and will always be. I am hooked.

Was your role then to bring it onto a larger stage or a more national forum, magnifying the importance of beautification?
Yes, in a way we were both riding a wave and trying to make that wave surge forward. The time had come in our national consciousness to look at the environment and question what man was doing to harm it, how we could harness those harmful things; still let free enterprise and industry serve the country, but preserve the environment while we were doing it. We marched hand in hand with the thought, whose time was about to come. Whatever service we performed was to walk this onto the national stage, put it on the national agenda. Yes, beautification, prissy word though it may be, became the business of the politician, the businessman, the newspaper editor, and not just the ladies over a

---

11. Lyndon B. Johnson, Remarks at the University of Michigan, May 22, 1964. Since CTJ cited the time period of February 1965 as well as Ann Arbor, she may have been referring to LBJ's Special Message to Congress on Conservation and Restoration of Natural Beauty, February 8, 1965. Also see CTJ's reaction to LBJ's 1965 State of the Union Speech. Johnson, *A White House Diary*, 215.

12. For Udall's account of his initial conversation with Mrs. Johnson and their first trip, see Stewart Udall Oral History Interview I, 4/18/69, by Joe B. Frantz,14, and II, 519/69, by Joe B. Frantz, 7–8.

cup of tea. We broadened the scope of it, I hope, and made awareness of it. The more you read about it, the more concerned you became about the world you had known as a child and how rapidly it could slip through fingers, and the next generation would not inherit it as beautiful and clean and full of flowers and open spaces as you remembered. So, in whatever ways I could touch that problem, I tried.

You mentioned Stewart Udall, but were there any particular writings or other individuals that influenced your thinking on conservation and the environment?
People and events and memories. Early on, Laurance Rockefeller became one of those who influenced me, and I read about all the things his family had done on as wide a scope as Mesa Verde in the far west and in the Blue Ridge Mountains, huge areas there, and lots of land along the Hudson River; Mary Lasker and her determination to have a flag of brilliant color on Park Avenue in New York City, where she planted tulips and encouraged the owners of the property there to do the same. Yes, there was a spark that was struck in my heart, with a lot of people.

Then there were sights that I would never forget. For instance, one time Lyndon and I went out on a barge in Lake Erie.[13] We had as much press as we could load onto this barge. It looked like it was about to tilt over into the water. The subject was the pollution of our lakes and rivers. A huge bucket went over the edge, picked up a bucketful, swung it around onto this flat barge surface. We looked at it real close. It looked like sort of a mixture of ink and glue; all of that was waste that was being put into those waters. You could imagine that no fish could live in it, and no plant life either. We just had to do something about cleaning up our world, or else we couldn't inhabit it either.

I read that during your trips from Washington back home to Texas that the unsightly junkyards and billboards inspired your Highway Beautification legislation.
That's quite true. I'm a great lover of the beauties of this country, as I think people are likely to know. I hope they do. There were an awful lot of trips and campaigns, and a lot of them in cars. Those in cars I liked a lot better than those on planes, because I like to see and absorb the regional picturesqueness and the splendors of this country. That is when I began to say, golly, have we got to look at all those junkyards? Couldn't they be screened? It's a business. The whole country is built on business and depends on business, but is it too much to ask them to screen them with shrubbery or a fence? And all the billboards? That too is a business. Lord knows, I come from a long line of folks interested in making a profit. But taxpayers built the highways and besides being functional and safe,

---

13. See LBJ's "Remarks in Buffalo on Beginning a 3-Day Trip in New York and New England," in *Public Papers of the Presidents of the United States: Lyndon B. Johnson, 1963–1969*, vol. 3, *1966* (Washington, DC: Government Printing Office, 1967), 838.

can't we expect it to be a pleasure to see our country, too, and could we limit the extent of them? So we had to try.

How would you assess the accomplishments of the Johnson presidency in the field of beautification?
I would say principally in national awareness, creating a national awareness, and recognition that it was on the national agenda. Beautification is just one thread in the whole warp and weave of the tapestry. There's the whole mass of legislation that was passed during those five years relating to the environment: Clean Air, Clean Water, additions to the National Park Service, such as scenic rivers, national seashores like Padre Island, wilderness areas, new national parks. It was an explosion of legislation related to the environment. We just began to attack this vast national problem and made it a part of the nation's agenda for goodness knows the rest of time. Right up to the wire Lyndon was fighting for all these things, and the Redwoods Park didn't get added until October of '68.[14] Another thing in that [year] was the Land and Water Bill, which said that a part of the revenue from offshore drilling should go into a fund handled by the Department of the Interior to purchase land for open space use, park use, by—some of it would be available to states and smaller entities and a great deal of it to the National Park Service.[15]

Should the provisions regulating billboards have been tougher?
We did the best we could. It is a vested interest. People make their living out of that. I don't know. I hope we tempered the spread of them, perhaps confined them to an area more close to the cities.

Beautification, as it came about in our time in the White House, was based on pride in your hometown, whether it was Small Town, USA, or a great city, for it to be clean, with trees and flowers and places of refreshment for your spirit, and to get outdoors. For me, the wellspring was the joy that nature had been to me in childhood and growing-up years and pride in the beauties of this country and all the regions of it, the distinct character and difference. And I hoped that each would recognize his own and keep some of the best of his own, be it Vermont, Alabama, or Texas.

"SEE AMERICA FIRST"

[These] wonderful trips live in my memory like a string of jewels. The whole purpose of these trips was to promote a part of Lyndon's "See America First"

---

14. For a discussion of the Redwoods National Park legislation, see Stewart Udall Oral History Interview 5, 12/16/69, by Joe B. Frantz, 15–16, and Laurance S. Rockefeller Oral History Interview, 8/5/69, by Joe B. Frantz, 38–41.

15. On July 15, 1968, President Johnson signed legislation amending the 1964 Land and Water Conservation Fund to increase the fund through the allocation of oil and gas revenues for the purchase of wilderness and park land. Gould, *Lady Bird Johnson*, 233.

program, acquaint yourself with your own homeland—its historical sites, its beautiful scenery—and keep vacation money at home, because the balance of payments was beginning to worry us. Its mission was both economic and patriotism-producing. Also we tried to invite Europeans to come over to see us by having very low-priced excursion tickets worked out by bus companies. I remember the first couple who signed on for that bus trip across the United States for some small sum was invited to the White House. I loved getting to meet them.

We were accompanied [on the trips] by a lot of press everywhere we went. Perhaps it did make those who saw it on television want to go and see the Big Bend, Padre Island, or the theatre in the Midwest where we went with Muriel Humphrey [in September, 1967].[16] We went up the Hudson River, beginning at New York, going to the Sleepy Hollow restorations, to the home of Washington Irving. He spoke of it "as [full of angles and corners as] an old cocked hat"—past West Point, great baronial mansions up there along that river, no longer the sort of thing we could live in today. Jay Gould's home [Lyndhurst].[17] On the opposite side of the United States, we went down the Snake in a rubber raft and saw moose and elk and beaver dams and the majestic Tetons rising in the distance. One of my favorite trips was going to the Big Bend, a little-known national park in far west Texas. It could do with exposure to increase [visitation]. We took a trip down one of the three branches of the Rio Grande in a river raft. The Mariscal Canyon walls rose so high, and canyon wrens were singing, and just a little bit of cactus clinging to a cup full of soil in the cliff.[18]

Seeing the redwoods was one of the most profound experiences I'll ever have. Those cathedral-tall great trees were some of the oldest plant life on this planet. Their ancestors were here in the time of dinosaurs, and these very ones were probably little bitty saplings in the time of Christ. It just levels you, gives you a sense of man's place here on this planet. The majesty of it all!

What good did it do? I hope it stirred in the hearts of some of those people who saw it on television a little more love of their country, pride in their country, and the desire to go and see it.

HEAD START

How did you first become involved in the Head Start Program?
That too goes back to Lyndon's swearing in in 1965. I began to think what I could do to express his legislative agenda, his aspirations and dreams for this country. Stewart Udall was a good salesman for environmental issues, and so was Sarge

---

16. On September 20, as part of a four-day trip, CTJ, Muriel Humphrey, Orville Freeman, Robert Weaver, and Roger Stevens attended a performance of *The House of Atreus* at the Tyrone Guthrie Theater in Minneapolis. Roy Reed, "First Lady Hails Good Rural Life and Praises Minnesota Projects as 4-Day Tour Starts, *NewYork Times*, September 21, 1967.

17. See Johnson, *A White House Diary*, 672–76.

18. Johnson, *A White House Diary*, 376–83, 652–55.

Shriver, a top-notch believer and, therefore, salesman for the poverty program. He came to see me in [January] of '65, and talked about a number of the facets of the poverty program, Head Start being one that caught my interest. He asked me if I would be the honorary chairman. I don't much like being "honorary" something; I either like to know about it and work on it or just leave that to people who do know about it and work on it. So I said, "Let's give me a chance to learn." We had a session in the Red Room with the head of Health, Education, and Welfare, [Anthony J.] Celebrezze; some juvenile judges, I think; and some workers in health programs affecting the young.[19] It was a marvelous mixture of people, and, of course, Sarge Shriver himself, who talked about Head Start and how it could affect the lives of youngsters. It was thrilling and hopeful. Maybe this was a way to break the cycle of continuing poverty. Maybe you could make those four- and five-year-old children from their underprivileged backgrounds more ready to face the competition of school. The record of a whole lot of children in those homes was that they stayed in school until about the third grade and then they dropped out. If they could learn enough to be at home in school, capable of learning more, if they could stay in past the third grade, maybe they could make it on through. So I said, yes, I will.

I remember going to inner-city, highly urbanized areas like in Newark, New Jersey, and sitting around, talking to the teachers and the children in those Head Starts.[20] I was impressed by how the mothers of the family really did their best to dress them up and get them ready to come to these sessions. Then we were down in Appalachia, both in Lick Branch, Kentucky, and some place in [North Carolina], out from Asheville—it was called Canada Township—in one-room schoolhouses where we would see a version of Head Start.[21] All through those five years, it played a recurring role in my life in the White House. I would get reports on it. When I made a trip, at the foot of the airplane there would be a bunch of little Head Start children with one of their teachers and a banner that they had made with crayons themselves. It was an avenue of hope, the possible introduction to the competitive life of going to school that would make you do better.

I recounted [to Lyndon] with great pleasure my trips to see the education bills in action: Head Starts in big urban centers like Washington itself and New Jersey, Trenton, I think it was, and then in little bitty towns. Once there was a marvelous trip that I always remembered through Appalachia, through Tennessee and Kentucky. We saw the whole range of them: the Job Corps, the Teacher

---

19. Shriver met with Mrs. Johnson and Liz Carpenter on January 14, 1965. See Johnson, *A White House Diary*, 219. The meeting in the Red Room took place on February 3, 1965. Johnson, *A White House Diary*, 234–35.

20. Mrs. Johnson, Liz Carpenter, Sargent Shriver, and Governor Richard Hughes visited a Head Start project at Cleveland Elementary School in Newark on August 12, 1965. Johnson, *A White House Diary*, 308–10.

21. Johnson, *A White House Diary*, 493–99.

Corps, and Head Start, and then [Adult Basic] Education for returning to school when you're middle aged. And I'd stop and ask them, now, "What brought you back? What are you doing?" And this black person would say, "I never did learn to read. If I can learn to read and learn my figures, I can get a better job." Such a valid reason!

Was part of the task an effort to generate a spirit of volunteerism in staffing these Head Start programs?
Oh, yes. A lot of volunteer work and a lot of absolutely devoted work. Then there were some low-paid people who would likely be some of the mothers of the children, some of the neighbors and local folks that could relate to the children and help out with their very limited vocabularies. Of course, a major part of it was that medical examination. That was absolutely key: to have their eyes and teeth and vaccinations and all those basic medical things looked at and tended to.

So you saw it as a health program as well?
Oh, yes. Oh, yes, indeed, because if they're going to get into the school system, they've got to have the tools to work with and have the absolutely basic health problems either corrected or identified and an effort made to correct them.

Were there nutritional aspects as well?
Yes, in lots of the Head Starts there'd be one hot meal like maybe oatmeal and milk for breakfast.

THE MAN IN THE OVAL OFFICE

What was the most valuable asset that Lyndon Johnson brought to the presidency?
Without a doubt, it was experience. From his twelve years in the House and twelve years in the Senate, he knew the people who were going to be big factors in making any program happen and changing the course of the country in any way. It was not that he could manipulate or dominate; anybody that thinks that doesn't know those people. Lyndon used to quote in reference to the Senate—and he certainly believed—what Huey Long said, "Every man a king."[22] Those people who are elected by their constituency at home look to their constituency. They're not pawns of any president. But if you have shared their experiences, know their philosophy, have personal interchanges through the years, you can deal with them better. Maybe you can persuade them and appeal to them in the ways that they would be responsive to. So experience was a big factor. And I cannot say too much about Lyndon's admiration and liking for a great many of the

22. Huey Long's slogan referred to his economic plan to redistribute the nation's wealth. It was also the title of his autobiography.

senators with whom he had served. Oddly enough, a lot of them were southerners whom he had to test almost to the breaking point, and I'm afraid he lost some of them. But they went with him a long way. One of them, a businessman from Georgia who was close to the whole scene, said, "Lyndon, you've taken us about as far as we can go, and farther than we ever thought we would." Dick Russell was always the prince of them all. Lyndon had great interplay of friendship with some of the Republicans, too: Everett Dirksen[23] and a wonderful old gentleman from a far different part of the country, Senator [George] Aiken from Vermont. They had a lot in common on their agricultural—and indeed it came to be on the environmental—feelings. So experience was the first thing.

The second thing was an old-fashioned faith in this country and that it could do just about anything that it was determined to do. He tried to communicate that feeling to everybody he was around, to the Congress and Senate, the people in general. It's a large part in how far we did go with all of our social legislation. Also, he had a lot of respect for the business community and a secret hankering all his life to have been one of them. But public service was a stronger pull, and he felt that if we could keep the economy good, then we could do anything that we wanted to. That's why he struggled so hard to keep the budget balanced just as much as he could and [made] a huge effort to keep the balance of exports in tune with the balance of imports. We actually had a balanced budget in one of the latter years and not too much over in other years. He had a long-term vision; he could see over the hill pretty good. Sometimes the view only made him desperately sad, but he was a long-term man with an intuitive wisdom in many ways.

One of the attributes that you have written about in your diary is his capacity for hard work day in and day out. Was this an important asset as well?
Indeed it was—and it was certainly a major factor all his life, because he always was struggling to get everything done yesterday. He had a great sense of timing. He thought that when he was elected with that wonderful, overwhelming vote that he had a very limited time. He had seen it happen with Roosevelt's "honeymoon time," when you could get just a lot of legislation through and carry people with you. Then a tide set in that was harder and harder to buck. He had a sense of timing as when to push things and when it would only have been dueling with windmills. Very much to my dislike, he was a workaholic, because I thought it would wear him out. And it did, but whose life is it anyway? [*Laughter.*]

Describe President Johnson's daily routine in the White House.
That's hard to do because there were so many trips and so many crises, but he would wake up awfully early in the morning, five thirty or six. Someone would

23. Dirksen was the Republican leader in the Senate.

bring in a sheaf of five or six newspapers. He would turn on that three-faced television, only one of which had audio—they all had video—and then he would punch the button on the one he thought he needed most to hear. So he would consume the papers. He was a very fast reader. He was fast in everything he did. He had a digest of the happenings the day before in the Congress. He would look through that and drink innumerable cups of [coffee]—somewhere along the line he changed to hot tea. Then staff would come in and say, "Mr. Johnson, you remember that your program today is you see so-and-so and so-and-so and so-and-so." He would get some breakfast then. He was always on a diet. That was one of the things I was unable to control, because he either ate too much and became very much overweight, or else he was on such a rigid, self-imposed diet that he was eating what was not fun and what was so sparse. Then he'd get up, have a shower, and get dressed, talking to the staff meanwhile who would be at the door, and they'd be hollering in at each other, conversing back and forth. And then he would go to the office, I suppose, about nine. Stay there until lunchtime. Lunchtime was as variable as could possibly be, maybe at twelve thirty or one, maybe two, three, three thirty. He might bring home the same people that he worked with or some of the senators, some of the appointments. One day he even brought over former president Truman. I had planned hash for that day, because that was one of Lyndon's favorite meals. It was too late to change. He was walking in the door before I knew it. So we sat down and enjoyed hash together. I was delighted to see President Truman and cared about him very much.[24]

After lunch was over, Lyndon immediately went to bed for a nap. If lunch was terribly late, it had to be a short nap, but a nap of anywhere from thirty minutes to two hours. Then he got up, had another shower, got dressed, and went back to the office for what he thought of as his second day, which could begin four, five, five thirty, and stayed until a very late dinner hour if we were alone. Of course, there were very often receptions and dinners for the judiciary, the military, briefing sessions with Congress, visiting people, chiefs of state, or folk down the ladder a bit, where he absolutely must see them. A great many of these things, if he could, he asked me to do. There are many people who, if they can't see the president, will settle for his wife, or settle for his children, particularly if the children really did give great tours, and each one had her own special expertise. Then Lyndon would come home late for dinner. Once more, he might bring people with him. I finally tried to make a rule that if it got past nine thirty, I would send Zephyr home, and one person would just stay in the kitchen and heat up something and put it before him.

---

24. For a more elaborate and accurate description of President Truman's visit, see Johnson, *A White House Diary*, 123–24. After alerting CTJ that Truman would be coming for lunch, LBJ delayed their arrival for more than an hour while he held a press conference. Texas folklorist J. Frank Dobie was also present.

I remember one time only in the course of some crisis when he wasn't home by about eleven o'clock at night. He was in the Situation Room. I could always keep tabs on where he was through his staff or the Secret Service. I had never been in the Situation Room and wasn't about to be invited, but I was so bold as to think all those other women's husbands are down there hungry. Somebody might even faint if they didn't get a little nourishment. So I had a stack of sandwiches prepared and took them down there myself. I knocked on the door; got a frosty look. They let me put down the sandwiches and the thermoses of coffee, but I never did do that again. If their need was bad enough, they were grown men. They could find their way out.

There was something that I hated from the first moment. That was a package called "Night Reading," which was on his bed every night, which no matter how late he got to bed he would pick it up and read it. It concerned all those things that had happened that needed a decision that could not be made at a lower level. There was no good news in them, because he said if it was good news, they would have handled it down below. But the hard ones were always bucked upstairs. So I said, "In the morning when you're bright and fresh is a better time to do that, because that will keep you from sleeping." But he said, "In the morning there'll be just that many more problems, and I'll have to get to them." So that was a bad habit I never could conquer or help on.

Other presidents have reflected a siege mentality in the face of mounting dissent, press criticism, and congressional opposition. Did President Johnson feel beleaguered during his troubled times?

Yes. Frustrated, unable to explain or control, but you never cease trying. The frustrating times were mostly with the Vietnam War. One Christmas, I think 1967, we had peace missions by strong figures in former administrations, eminent ambassadors or secretaries of state, going out of the capitals of the world. I think there were about forty in number, including one going to the pope, to say, "Give us a constructive plan. What can you do? What can we offer to bring this to a halt?"

One of the things that he had the most hope for, but fell on deaf ears, was offered at a speech that he made at Johns Hopkins University in Baltimore.[25] It was a Marshall Plan for the Mekong Delta. Instead of all of us spending all this money, you on you all's tools of war and us on these, for the name of the Lord, let's just try to develop this area, so folks will be well-fed enough, have a way of making a living, and have a series of dams, if that is feasible, like there are on the TVA or rural electrification, whatever it takes. Let's spend this money

---

25. Address at Johns Hopkins University, "Peace without Consent," April 7, 1965. *Public Papers of the President of the United States: Lyndon B. Johnson, 1963–1969*, vol. 2, *1965* (Washington, DC: Government Printing Office, 1966), 394–99.

constructively instead of just blowing everybody to pieces. It didn't make much of a dent.

Was the president insulated from conflicting views?
What I just said a minute ago about when you wake up to the morning to five or six newspapers, *Time* and *Newsweek*, and all the other magazines, and when you have the *Congressional Record*, and when you have that three-faced television, there is no chance of you being insulated. In the Cabinet Room, he would go around the table and say, "All right, what's the other side of the coin? If I don't send more troops, if I don't do this or that, what can we look for?" He could always count on George Ball to express his views, which were frequently on the other side, in very knowledgeable, forceful, explicit fashion. Clark Clifford, in the latter days of '68, I do believe, did.[26] So, no, there's no way he could be insulated.

THE GREAT SOCIETY

Did the president tend to personalize such social issues, as poverty, health, education, and civil rights?
Yes, and from scenes in his lifetime. One little example about his early brush with civil rights is when he taught school for one year at Cotulla. And they divided the schools in those days. All the Mexicans went to one school and other children to another. He taught in the Mexican school. All those youngsters were very poor, and at recess time there was nothing really. The school grounds had no equipment, no games, and so he, out of his own money, had bought a basketball and one or two other things and asked the school teachers to go out on the school grounds during recess and supervise the children and maybe teach them something or at least keep them from fighting. [The teachers] were greatly incensed, because they wanted to stay inside and have their personal time. But he finally won them to doing it.

The Good Humor ice cream truck went by with the man ringing his bell and offering his nice big cones of ice cream. Lyndon loved ice cream all of his life. He would eat a cone, but he kept on seeing all of these sad little eyes looking up at him. About the third day, he couldn't stand it any longer. He said, "All right, y'all. I wish I could buy an ice cream cone for every one of you, but I can't. But I'm going to buy two ice cream cones, one for me, and this first day, I'm going to tell who is going to get the other one. It's going to be the littlest boy in the school, and there he is. And from now on out, y'all have got to choose who gets the other ice cream cone." So that worked. He learned a bit about discrimination and social put-down among races there. Also, he didn't know anything

---

26. George Ball was under secretary of state. Clark Clifford was appointed secretary of defense in early 1968.

about desperate poverty, but he met it there. It left a lingering impression on him. Years later when he signed the bill on elementary [and secondary] education, it gave him great pleasure to see these children now grown up and many of them in pretty good jobs—very much better than they ever expected. He invited all of them up to come and watch the ceremony.[27]

How about Medicare? Were there personal experiences that reinforced his desire for medical care for seniors?
Oh, goodness, yes. He had gone through an evolution on that because I don't know [how] he began. Socialized medicine was a big black devil in the early days when it was introduced. It took it twenty years or thereabouts to get through. President Truman tried to pass it. Lyndon had seen it take the life savings of families and keep old people in fear that they were going to be a millstone around the neck of their children. Old age, frightening enough, would be even more frightening if you thought you couldn't go to the doctor and be taken care of if you got sick. Yes, it was very personal thing and a very satisfying victory to him.

What was LBJ's most difficult accomplishment?
It was civil rights without a doubt because it was really the entrenched mores of the country. His position in the Southwest did not make him a deeply rooted typical southerner by any means. He wasn't. He was a southwesterner. But Texas was one of the Confederate states, and he strongly aligned with a lot of those senators and cared greatly for them. It was just a big change in the fabric of the country. He began this back in [1957] in the Senate, and that was an achievement that he was always proud of. Never satisfied the Negroes, Lord no, but it opened the door, got a foot in, made later progress possible. It's very interesting to remember and to see at the [LBJ] Library some of the vilifying mail. Wooo . . . [*Laughter.*] It would just fry you. Worse even than the Vietnam ones. Totally forgotten now, but what he was called and the dire results that were wished upon his head because of [his] leading the civil rights program were certainly as vituperative as anything that happened because of Vietnam in the last two years. I did feel an acute separation from a lot of my friends, particularly southern friends, because we were really flying right in their teeth with civil rights.

Lyndon was just as anxious to do it for the white man as for the black man, because he thought it left a burden on his shoulders, on his heart, that he just wanted to be rid of, wanted all people to be rid of. All ships rise on a rising tide.

Lyndon took a lot of satisfaction in [the civil rights legislation], and so do I. And he thought, if you get the vote, it can go a long way towards [African

27. See CTJ's description of the signing of the Elementary and Secondary Education Act on April 11, 1965, in *A White House Diary*, 258–60.

Americans] solving their own problems. If they have equal opportunities in education and jobs, that would go a long way. He was a person of vision. There are certain areas in the world that if he looked at them right now, he would take even more satisfaction in having gotten our civil rights laws and, indeed, a good deal of our customs in place and changed in the '60s. I remember distinctly something that the mayor of a great city, Mayor [Richard J.] Daley of Chicago, said to me. By this time Lyndon was dead, and I was going back to some ceremony there in Chicago, and he said something like this: "I hate to think how I would have run this city and held it together in the summer of '68 if we hadn't had those laws on the books and the pledge of our government." That was after the murders of Reverend King and Bobby Kennedy. So it's a bridge crossed. It's a good start.

If the president had had the benefit of hindsight, what would he have done differently?
I really don't know. What you would have done would have been to get out of Vietnam, if you could find that magic path. Not then, and not later, did he ever see the way. Of course, we finally struggled and gave and tried and tried and finally put together an exit that didn't last.

One of the things he might have done is to change his administration when he won the great victory in '64 and was inaugurated in '65. He might have kept those members of the cabinet that he had felt closest to and most in-tune with, like Dean Rusk, and gotten some new people, more committed to him. Was it really fair to him? Was it really fair to them, to keep on people who had given their allegiance and their caring to someone else? Certainly it was, in Lyndon's thinking, for the rest of that term, because the word "loyalty" was tattooed on his heart. He wanted to do everything he could for President Kennedy. Had he been in that position, he would have wanted his people to be kept on. But the end of the term was a natural point at which you could have shifted gears. The things against it were still, in part, this feeling of loyalty, and also in part the fact that Lyndon, from his background and from his education, had not met that wide expanse of people nationwide, a pool from whom to draw, that he could have if he had been educated at one of the top-notch schools in the country and had spent years aiming at the presidency, which he did not do.

A FIRST LADY'S INFLUENCE

I'm going to ask you to recount some of the substantive advice you gave the president on specific programs and issues.
It was more by osmosis. Lyndon knew where my heart was, in the environment, and that I was very interested in the arts too. He could see the elation in my voice and in my eyes and manner when something occurred like signing the bill creating the [National] Council on the Arts and the [National] Endowment for

the Arts.[28] It was a little bitty beginning. It was just $3 million; it was a foot in the door. I think my reaction to that bolstered his own feelings about the usefulness of it and about pushing it farther. As far as being an initiator, I cannot say that I was much on that. I had judgments and I gave them, but I didn't push them or demand them or say they were surefire.

One of the few times I was just darned positive what Lyndon ought to do was that he ought to run in August of 1964, and that he ought *not* to run four years later. That was a firm conviction from which I never did waver and which I wrote to him in those memos.[29] [In 1964, he was] approaching the convention time, and he had to definitely make up his mind whether he was a candidate or not. I remember exactly. Lynda and I walked around the White House grounds and sat under a great big tree. We were both thinking our own thoughts, but I think our thoughts were running completely in tandem. Lyndon was in bed and wouldn't talk to us. He wouldn't talk to anybody. He was wrestling with his own demons, I guess. I wrote him a letter saying that I thought he ought to be and all the reasons why. I also added, "And then when you finish, you will win, and at the end of that time, the juices of life will be sufficiently used up, and I think you should announce at a reasonable time that you will not be a candidate for reelection again." That is the way it actually did turn out, and I think that was the best way for it to turn out.

So he sought my judgment. I'm very proud that he did. I wasn't the most assured person around, by any means, and I certainly was not very pushy. But he especially sought my judgment on people, and sometimes I might have been helpful. Sometimes I might have made mistakes, but he was a bit inclined to go overboard on people. Either they had all the virtues in the world or sometimes he couldn't see some shortcomings or, on the other hand, some good points in people who were very different.

Did you ever disagree with the president?
Oh, sure. I disagreed with him when he talked in times of anger. Words out of your mouth have wings, and they've flown off, and you can't recall them. They're remembered, and the people who are hurt can hurt you back. Hurts wind up hurting the one who inflicted them. Lyndon was a very sensitive person and sometimes his worst enemy. He was also terribly sweet and caring and giving and so much more generous than I was or than most of the people I knew. But I would try to temper him and level him and keep him—say, "Feel that if you must. Go off and raise cane in your own room, or raise cane to me, and I won't let it hurt."

---

28. The National Council on the Arts was created in 1964. Broader legislation in 1965 established the National Foundation on the Arts and Humanities, consisting of the Federal Council on the Arts and the Humanities and two grant-making agencies, the National Endowment for the Arts and the National Endowment for the Humanities.

29. The text of CTJ's letter of August 25, 1964, appears in Johnson, *A White House Diary*, 192.

Can you recall occasions where you converted him to your point of view on an issue or situation?

There were many instances when I would hear opinions that I had delivered to him that I wondered, "Are you listening?" because he didn't say anything in response. Sometimes I didn't even know if he'd heard. Then maybe two or three days later, I'd hear him giving back the same thought like it was his own, and indeed, it was by process of osmosis. I'm sure I was useful. I am not a very creative, determined person and so my usefulness was in a milder vein.

Did you feel free to disagree with him privately?

Oh, certainly. Certainly, and then gently and, I hope persuasively, say why. But I was not always sure enough to say "Please, I hope you'll do that. If you don't do that, so-and-so and so-and-so is going to happen," because I didn't know it might not. The way ahead often looked murky to both of us, and I had the luxury of doing nothing, and he didn't have the luxury of doing nothing sometimes.

"BETTER TOGETHER THAN APART"

How would you sum up Lyndon Johnson?

Marvelous. Contradictory. Great natural intelligence. Showman sometimes; hurtful sometimes; very often tender and giving. He was many-faceted, a man of unlimited hopes and beliefs in this country. On the other hand, a little streak of leveling cynicism. His compassion was quite personal and genuine and carried right home; it wasn't just philosophy from a book. He was full of faults, too, and sometimes [made] misjudgments about people. He was an awfully good man to have around in a tight [situation]. He was one we always looked to when we didn't know the answers. He carried the heavy loads; I carried a whole lot of the exasperating day-to-day little loads. How would you sum him up? He was a man who was always built to be in some kind of public service, whether it would be in the political field or as a teacher or as a preacher. So I guess he found his best niche. It's sad that he found it at a time of such riven—in a time when there was a war he couldn't win and couldn't get out of and, to some extent in the last year or so, had to diminish his efforts on the war he cared about—the War on Poverty. It's delightful when the children come home and we sit around and old friends come in and everybody tells his own tale and we just find ourselves just laughing. We all got as mad as could be at him from time to time, and hurt. But we also remember how we always turned to him to help us in everything. He was an exciting person to live with, and I consider myself very lucky.

He did have an extraordinary sense of humor, didn't he?

Oh, funny as can be. He really could have done well on the stage. He loved to mimic, and he loved to tell tales, always tales founded on characters—real or sometimes rather blown up—from his childhood.

The phrase so often we hear associated with him is "larger than life." Was he larger than life?

Yes, in himself, and he also made other people stretch and strive and become more than they thought they could. He was a natural born Henry Higgins. He was always working on any of his secretaries, his wife, his daughters, the people he cared about. If he thought they had potential, he wanted them to use it to the utmost. I know he did with me. He believed in me too much. He praised me too much. He also used the weapon of sarcasm. I wish I had listened to him more. I would have probably have learned to dress better, and a few other not-too-important things. I did learn a lot from him on many important things.

What I wanted mostly was to give him an island of peace in which to operate and work and come home to and rest and be assured that he was in the midst of love and understanding and loyalty, and we could find there some fun and laughter, too. That's about it. I certainly was no great, vital dictator or even inspirer, because he was the creative one. But I think he valued my judgment, and I know we were better together than we were apart.

Afterword

Lady Bird Johnson's busy life after the White House years hardly qualified as a retirement. She published *A White House Diary* in 1970 and involved herself in launching the LBJ Library and the LBJ School of Public Affairs. In 1971 Governor Preston Smith appointed her to a six-year term on the Board of Regents of the University of Texas, a commitment comparable to a full-time job. She also gave President Johnson daily care and company until his death in January 1973.

She tempered the loneliness of widowhood with work, travel, and the company of family and friends. LBJ's legacy required much of her time as she often represented the late president at events in Washington, Texas, and elsewhere. She gave interviews to historians and journalists. Her office received as many as four thousand letters a month. She served on the LBJ Foundation's board of directors, welcomed audiences to major events at the LBJ Library, met with the students of the LBJ School of Public Affairs, and hosted related gatherings at the LBJ Ranch. She also participated in activities at LBJ's alma mater, Texas State University. Her appointment to the board of trustees of the National Geographic Society afforded new opportunities for foreign travel, as did her desire to take a trip with each of her grandchildren.[1] Her travels included such destinations as England, Portugal, Africa, China,[2] Venezuela, and the Greek islands.[3]

In Austin, her other favorite capital city, Lady Bird Johnson undertook new beautification efforts. She chaired Austin's Town Lake Beautification Project, creating a picturesque hiking and biking trail along the lower Colorado River where it flows through the city. During her walks among the flowering trees beside the lake that now bears her name, passing joggers frequently expressed their thanks to her for the creation of one of the region's most scenic exercise venues. She also established the Texas Highway Beautification Awards and presented a personal check to the winners for two decades.[4] Then in December 1982, she announced the creation of the National Wildflower Research Center as a clearinghouse of

---

1. Liz Carpenter, "The Ever-Gracious Lady Bird Johnson," *Flightime* 10 (October 1975), 26–29.
2. Excerpts from my interview with CTJ on her China trip appear in *Among Friends of LBJ*, September 25, 1981, 6–8.
3. Julie Gilbert, "Lady Bird: Living Life Her Way," *Magazine of the Houston Post*, May 5, 1985, 7–9.
4. Kathy Kiely, "Lady Bird Johnson Dies at 94," *USA Today*, July 11, 2007.

information on wildflowers.[5] The project became her principal focus during the remaining years of her life. The center, which was renamed the Lady Bird Johnson Wildflower Center in 1997, is now part of the University of Texas at Austin.

Mrs. Johnson also maintained an active involvement in the family business interests, which consisted of radio stations, television stations, cable companies, and banks. Although the Times-Mirror Corporation bought the television station in late 1972, she retained the use of the fifth-floor Austin apartment through the mid-1980s. She then bought and remodeled a home on Mount Larson near KTBC's transmission towers.[6] She continued to spend weekends at the LBJ Ranch, where she had life tenancy after donating it to the National Park Service in 1972.

The public read about a former first lady's life filled with significant civic activities as well as the recognition she received for her many contributions. The Women's National Press Club presented her with the Eleanor Roosevelt Golden Candlestick Award in 1968. When President Gerald Ford awarded her the Presidential Medal of Freedom in 1977, it was the first time a first lady received that prestigious honor. In 1988 the United States Congress commended her with the Congressional Gold Medal.[7] But perhaps only her Secret Service detail fully appreciated how much she also did privately during her last three and a half decades. She continued the pattern she had followed throughout her adult life of attending countless weddings, funerals, and other significant events in the lives of friends and family. She entertained old friends and employees at the LBJ Ranch; she spent precious time with her daughters and her grandchildren.

But, as Mrs. Johnson occasionally remarked, "The tooth of time has taken a bite out of me." Her eyesight began to fail in the early 1990s as a result of macular degeneration. She suffered a minor stroke in 1993, but a major one in 2002 impaired her speech and mobility. Her energy level declined. Although she was confined to a wheelchair in her last years, she continued to attend events at the LBJ Library, the Wildflower Center, and in the homes of friends. She died on July 11, 2007, and was buried at the LBJ Ranch beside her husband.[8] Tens of thousands of citizens lined the highways from Austin to Stonewall in silent tribute as the hearse bearing her casket passed by.

---

5. Anne Raver, "Spreading the Colors of a Great Society," *New York Times*, May 6, 1993.

6. Michele Chan Santos, "A House Fit for a Lady," *Austin American-Statesman*, August 2, 2009+.

7. These awards are reproduced in Harry Middleton, *Lady Bird Johnson: A Life Well Lived* (Austin, TX: Lyndon Baines Johnson Foundation, 1992), 179–83.

8. Obituary of Lady Bird Johnson, *New York Times*, July 11, 2007.

Appendix: Lady Bird Johnson's Oral History Interviews

All interviews are available as transcripts in the reading room of the Lyndon Baines Johnson Library (Austin, TX). Interviews 1–44 are also available on the library's website, http://www.lbjlib.utexas.edu/ johnson/archives.hom/oralhistory.hom/Johnson-C/johnson.asp. Interviews 1–35 are by Michael L. Gillette; interviews 36–44 are by Harry J. Middleton.

Interview 1, August 12, 1977 (ancestors, childhood)
Interview 2, August 13, 1977 (childhood)
Interview 3, August 14, 1977 (1926–1934)
Interview 4, February 4, 1978 (1934)
Interview 5, April 1, 1978 (1934)
Interview 6, August 6, 1978 (1934–1937)
Interview 7, October 9, 1978 (1937)
Interview 8, January 23, 1979 (1937)
Interview 9, January 24, 1979 (1938)
Interview 10, January 25–26, 1979 (1939)
Interview 11, January 27–28, 1979 (1940)
Interview 12, August 19, 1979 (1941)
Interview 13, September 2–3, 1979 (1941)
Interview 14, September 9, 1979 (1941)
Interview 15, January 4–5, 1980 (1941–1942)
Interview 16, January 29–February 3, 1980 (1942)
Interview 17, September 20, 1980 (1943)
Interview 18, September 26–27, 1980 (1943–1944)
Interview 19, February 6–7, 1981 (1945–1946)
Interview 20, February 20–21, 1981 (1946–1947)
Interview 21, August 10–11, 1981 (1947–1948)
Interview 22, August 23, 1981 (1948)
Interview 23, September 5, 1981 (1948–1949)
Interview 24, November 15, 1981 (1949)
Interview 25, January 2–3, 1982 (1949–1950)
Interview 26, January 9–10, 1982 (1950)
Interview 27, January 30, 1982 (1950–1951)
Interview 28, March 15, 1982 (1951–1952)
Interview 29, March 19–10, 1982 (1951–1952)
Interview 30, March 22, 1982 (1952)
Interview 31, March 29, 1982 (October–December 1952)
Interview 32, August 3–4, 1982, (January–March 1953)
Interview 33, September 4, 1983, (1953)
Interview 34, February 23, 1991, (1953)
Interview 35, March 8, 1991 (1954)
Interview 36, August 1994 (1955)
Interview 37, August 1994 (1956)

Interview 38, August 1994 (1957)
Interview 39, August 1994 (recording is blank)
Interview 40, August 1994 (1959)
Interview 41, August 1994 (1960)
Interview 42, November 5, 1994 (1960)
Interview 43, January 23, 1996 (1960)
Interview 44, January 26, 1996 (1960)
John F. Kennedy Library Interview, March 9, 1979, by Sheldon Stern (1960–1964)[1]
Interview, January 23, 1987, by Nancy Smith (1964–68)
Video interview, December 30, 1984, by Michael L. Gillette (1963–68)
Video interview, February 4, 1985, by Michael L. Gillette (1963–68)

---

1. Also available at the John F. Kennedy Presidential Library (Boston).

Bibliographical Note

The best biographies of Lady Bird Johnson are Lewis L. Gould, *Lady Bird Johnson and the Environment* (Lawrence: University of Kansas Press, 1988); Gould, *Lady Bird Johnson: Our Environmental First Lady* (Lawrence: University of Kansas Press, 1999); and Jan Jarboe Russell, *Lady Bird: A Biography of Mrs. Johnson* (New York: Scribner, 1996). Also noteworthy are Carl Sferrazza Anthony, *First Ladies: The Saga of the Presidents' Wives and their Power*, vol. 2, *1961–1990* (New York: William Morrow, 1991); Betty Boyd Caroli, *First Ladies* (New York: Oxford University Press, 1987); and Robert P. Watson, *The Presidents' Wives: Reassessing the Office of First Lady* (Boulder, CO: Lynn Rienner, 2000). Earlier biographies include Ruth Montgomery, *Mrs. LBJ* (New York: Holt, Rinehart & Winston, 1964), and Marie D. Smith, *The President's Lady: An Intimate Biography* (New York: Random House, 1964).

The biographies of Lyndon Johnson justifiably devote considerable attention to Mrs. Johnson. The volumes that I have relied on most often are Robert Dallek, *Lone Star Rising: Lyndon Johnson and His Times, 1908–1960* (New York: Oxford University Press, 1960); Dallek, *Flawed Giant: Lyndon Johnson and His Times, 1961–1973* (New York: Oxford University Press, 1998); Robert A. Caro, *The Years of Lyndon Johnson*, vol. 1, *The Path to Power* (New York: Alfred A. Knopf, 1982); vol. 2, *Means of Ascent* (New York: Alfred A. Knopf, 1990); vol. 3, *Master of the Senate* (New York: Alfred A. Knopf, 2002); vol. 4, *The Passage of Power* (New York: Alfred A. Knopf, 2012); and Randall B. Woods, *LBJ: Architect of American Ambition* (New York: Free Press, 2006). Also valuable are Doris Kearns, *Lyndon Johnson and the American Dream* (New York: Harper & Row, 1976), and Irving Bernstein, *Guns or Butter: The Presidency of Lyndon Johnson* (New York: Oxford University Press, 1996).

First among many memoirs reflecting on Mrs. Johnson's life is her own book *A White House Diary* (New York: Holt, Rinehart & Winston, 1970). This published version constitutes only a seventh of the complete recorded diary of her years in the White House. Also noteworthy for a discussion of her lifelong interest in beautification, is Lady Bird Johnson and Carleton B. Lees, *Wildflowers Across America* (New York: Abbeville, 1988). In Harry Middleton, *Lady Bird Johnson: A Life Well Lived* (Austin, TX: Lyndon Baines Johnson Foundation, 1992), there is a collection of insights about the former first lady from many of those who knew her best. Other exceptional memoirs are Liz Carpenter, *Ruffles and Flourishes* (Garden City, NY: Doubleday, 1970); Carpenter, *Getting Better All the Time* (New York: Simon & Schuster, 1987); Lindy Boggs, *Washington Through a Purple Veil: Memoirs of a Southern Woman* (New York: Harcourt Brace, 1994); Joseph A. Califano Jr., *The Triumph and Tragedy of Lyndon Johnson: The White House Years* (New York: Simon & Schuster, 1991); Califano, *Inside: A Public and Private Life* (New York: Public Affairs, 2004); Clark Clifford, *Counsel to the President* (New York: Random House, 1991); Eric F. Goldman, *The Tragedy of Lyndon Johnson* (New York: Alfred A. Knopf, 1969); Harry McPherson, *A Political Education* (New York: Little, Brown, 1972); Lyndon Baines Johnson, *The Vantage Point: Perspectives of the Presidency, 1963–1969* (New York: Holt, Rinehart & Winston, 1971); Lawrence F. O'Brien, *No Final Victories: A Life in Politics; From John F. Kennedy to Watergate* (Garden City, NY: Doubleday, 1974); and J. B. West, *Upstairs at the White House: My Life with the First Ladies* (New York: Coward, McCann & Geoghegan, 1973.

Several articles deserve mention: Jan Jarboe, "Lady Bird Looks Back," *Texas Monthly* 22 (December 1994), 112–35; "Lady Bird Johnson Remembers: An Interview by Barbara Klaw," *American Heritage*,

December 1980, 4–17; Kathleen A. Bergeron, "The Environmental First Lady," *Public Roads* 71 (March/April 2008), 16–23; Claudia Wilson Anderson, "With A Song in Her Heart" *Among Friends of LBJ*, September 1, 1999, 6–8; Claudia Wilson Anderson, "Lady Bird Johnson," in *Laura Bush: The Report to the First Lady*, ed. Robert P. Watson (Huntington, NY: Nova History, 2001), 131–35; Diana B. Carlin, "Lady Bird Johnson: The Making of a Public First Lady with Private Influence," in *Inventing a Voice: American First Ladies of the Twentieth Century*, ed. Molly Meijer (Lanham, MD: Rowman & Littlefield, 2004), 273–95; and Martin V. Melosi, "Lyndon Johnson and Environmental Policy," in *The Johnson Years*, ed. Robert A. Divine (Lawrence: University of Kansas Press, 1987), 2:113–49.

Many of the oral history interviews in the LBJ Library's collection deal with Lady Bird Johnson. Among those that focus on her early years are those with Ellen Taylor Cooper, Elaine Fischesser, Dorris Powell, Antonio Taylor, Winston Taylor, and Emma Boehringer Tooley. Lady Bird's years at the University of Texas and her courtship and marriage are described in interviews with the following: Malcolm G. Bardwell, Henry Hirshberg, Luther E. Jones Jr., Eugenia Boehringer Lasseter, Gene Latimer, Cecile Harrison Marshall, Nell Colgin Miller, Daniel Quill, and Emily Crow Selden. Others who discussed the Johnsons' lives and the political campaigns in the 1930s through the 1950s are Robert B. Anderson, Charles Boatner, Marietta Moody Brooks, R. Max Brooks, Paul Bolton, Russell Morton Brown, Cecil E. Burney, Horace W. Busby, Elizabeth Carpenter, John B. Connally, Donald C. Cook, Clifford and Virginia Durr, Virginia Wilke English, Arthur E. and Elizabeth Goldschmidt, Ashton Gonella, Betty Cason Hickman, Welly K. and Alice Hopkins, W. Ervin James, Walter Jenkins, Caroll Keach, Jesse Kellam, John E. Lyle Jr., Cameron and Lucille McElroy, Harry C. McPherson Jr., Dale and Virginia Miller, Robert H. Montgomery, Dorothy Nichols, James Cato Pattillo, Arthur Perry, Robert L. Phinney, J. J. Pickle, Mary Rather, George E. Reedy Jr., William Reynolds, Juanita Roberts, Elizabeth Rowe, James H. Rowe Jr., Willie Day Taylor, Donald Thomas, Mary Margaret Valenti, Margaret Mayer Ward, Terrell Maverick Webb, Harfield Weedin, J. Roy White, Eugene and Helen Williams, Isabel Brown Wilson, Wilton and Virginia Woods, Warren Woodward, Eugene Worley, and Zephyr Wright.

Many of the above interviews extend through the presidential years. The oral histories of Bess Abell, Lindy Boggs, Liz Carpenter, Nash Castro, Sharon Francis, James R. Ketchum, Mary Lasker, Laurance Rockefeller, Elizabeth Rowe, Stewart Udall are especially relevant to Mrs. Johnson's role as first lady. Also useful are Phyllis O. Bonanno, Gordon Bunshaft, Joseph A. Califano Jr., Marie Fehmer Chiarodo, Jane Engelhard, Melville B. Grosvenor, Harry McPherson, Vicky McCammon Murphy, Lawrence F. O'Brien, Jacqueline Kennedy Onassis, DeVier Pierson, Harold H. Saunders, and Jack Valenti. Two books that make extensive use of the oral histories and the authors' interviews are Merle Miller, *Lyndon: An Oral Biography* (New York: G. P. Putnam, 1980), and Mark K. Updegrove, *Indomitable Will: LBJ in the Presidency* (New York: Crown, 2012). Also significant is the documentary film *A Life: The Story of Lady Bird Johnson*, dir. Charles Guggenheim (Washington, DC: Guggenheim Productions, 1992), which draws from Charles Guggenheim's interviews with Mrs. Johnson and others.

The LBJ Library's recordings of LBJ's telephone conversations contain a wealth of insight to LBJ's political and legislative calculations. Most of his conversations with Mrs. Johnson deal with scheduling details, particularly her inquiries regarding his plans for dinner. There are, however, a number of very significant conversations between them. Her "B+" evaluation of his March 7, 1964, press conference (no. 2395) reveals her willingness to critique his performance and his willingness to listen to her judgment. Their March 10, 1964, conversation (no. 2446) features a candid discussion of the merits of her speaking in Mississippi and Alabama. Unfortunately, the sound quality of her report from the *Lady Bird Special* on October 10, 1964 (nos. 5842 and 5843), is of such poor quality that it is difficult to understand. The most dramatic conversation (no. 5895) occurred on October 15, 1964, in the wake of Walter Jenkins's arrest in the Washington, DC YMCA. This recording conveys her remarkable strength and their mutual respect at a very emotional and politically difficult moment.[1]

---

1. LBJ's secretary, Vicky McCammon Murphy, describes another, even more dramatic, conversation between President and Mrs. Johnson in the Oval Office shortly after LBJ learned of Jenkins's arrest. Victoria McCammon Murphy OHI 2, 6/8/75, by MLG, 30–38.

Lyndon and Lady Bird Johnson were rarely apart for lengthy periods of time. Consequently, they seldom communicated in writing in the pre-presidential years. Even as early as 1934 they employed the telephone. They did correspond, however, when LBJ conducted a long-distance courtship in the fall 1934, while he was away on active duty in 1942, and when Lady Bird was reorganizing KTBC in Austin in 1943. The LBJ Library has opened a few remarkable letters from these months.

Index